UNTIL THE FINAL GUN

By

Norma Rogers

*To Vince with admiration
and best wishes —*

Norma Rogers
6/19/09

ISBN: 0-7596-7486-8

This book is printed on acid free paper.

1stBooks - rev. 04/18/02

For Wesley and the 411th

true to their battalion motto

as they followed Patton

"Until the Final Gun"

Though weary, love is not tired;

Though pressed, it is not straitened;

Though alarmed, it is not confounded.

Love securely passes through all.

Thomas a' Kempis

CONTENTS

ACKNOWLEDGMENTS

Until the Final Gun, excerpted from the correspondence of Alfred Wesley Rogers, reveals in his own words an ordinary GI living in a world of duty and danger while writing humorously and poignantly of the world of the heart.

John Fawns of the 411th AAA Gun Battalion provided a copy of Edgar Busler's history of the unit (1979) containing eyewitness accounts by Leo L. Prue, Edward J. Umphred, Lloyd E. Marker, and Charles Vitt along with reports, now declassified, sent by the BC (Battalion Commander), Lt. Col. Irving D. Roth, to the Adjutant General's Office.

The European campaign record kept for Battery A by "Sarge," Stanley J. Gasi, and contemporary news items from Stars and Stripes and other publications circulated in the European Theater of Operations (ETO) furnished background and structure.

For tactics and revelation of personalities I am indebted to the memoirs of the generals: Dwight D. Eisenhower (Crusade in Europe, 1948), Omar N. Bradley (A Soldier's Story, 1951), and George S. Patton, Jr. (War As I Knew It, 1947). Patton's associate, Col. Robert S. Allen, used the Third Army's code name, "Lucky Forward," as the title of its history (1947).

Chester Wilmot, in The Struggle for Europe (1947), helped in understanding the British point of view often criticized and misunderstood by American colleagues.

Edwin P. Hoyt gave the dogface's slant in The G.I.'s War (1988).

For a long-range, over-all assessment I relied on The Mighty Endeavor (1969) by Charles Brown MacDonald, who during two decades interviewed the leading participants, wrote two of the U.S. Army's official histories, co-authored another, and supervised preparation of six more for the Army's Chief of Military History.

On a personal level one cannot express adequately the gratitude owed to Holly Rogers, Charles W.

Crawford, Colby H. Kullman, Coy Haraway, Patrick Plemons, and Chrys Dougherty for inspiration, encouragement and practical assistance. Joyce Tate, Sandy Muston, and Richey Grude turned a vision into reality.

Norma Rogers

Preface

Alfred Wesley Rogers "stepped out the door to work" one day for family, country, and God. The job took him from a dairy farm in Tennessee to the ovens of Dachau. Along the way he wore his young wife's picture upside-down on his dogtags so he could see her face and wrote her nearly a thousand letters.

In 1942, at a camp in Georgia, Rogers commented, "We have some of the darnedest arguments over the question: <u>That</u> <u>My</u> <u>Wife</u> <u>is</u> <u>the</u> <u>Most</u> <u>Darling</u> <u>Woman</u> <u>in</u> <u>the</u> <u>World</u>. Wouldn't that make a topic to write about? Why I could write pages and pages. It might even be a book."

This is his book.

TENNESSEE

Norma Rogers

1940

The first shot in his war landed in the mailbox. Somehow, like much else that followed, it came as a surprise. He knew that there might be a draft notice some day with his name on it, but wars were in the past or overseas. You learned about Europe in geography books. Travel didn't even mean flying in those days. You could take a fifteen-minute sightseeing jaunt over Memphis or go to Birmingham with a stop-off at Muscle Shoals, but just thirteen years after Lindbergh's flight to Paris planes were either for airmail or the Army for most folks. Even on a train you sat up all night with a pillow for your head unless you someway had a pass or could afford a Pullman.

Most went anywhere by car. Travel meant driving to Knoxville or Pontotoc to see relatives or crossing the Mississippi into Arkansas. If you found a second-hand car and took care of it, you were all set. If you were foolhardy enough to take out in it for California, though, the family held hands in a prayer circle before you left.

Farm life was too busy and hard to think about war anyhow. Cows to be milked morning and night, milk trucked to Memphis, vegetable garden planted and hoed, chickens to tend to, hogs made into sausage. As for cotton, at picking time you sat on top of a load at the gin until 1:30 A.M., then grabbed two hours sleep before heading out to round up enough pickers for the next day.

Even on the Lord's Day it was up at dawn to milk, preside over Sunday School, sing in the choir, then home for a big dinner and nap over the paper before back to church for Baptist Young Peoples Union and evening service. Your girl away at college did well to get a letter a week!

Her people, city folks, were newcomers to an area his people had lived in since 1837. Her father, expecting to meet grandparents coming for a visit, had found Daddaw in shock aboard the train, his wife dead of a heart attack just thirty miles outside of Memphis. His profound despair so alarmed them that they had brought him to the kind of rural peace he was used to in Kentucky. The small town welcomed them all whole-heartedly even if they were Republicans without a primary to vote in. Whoever won the Democratic run in August just coasted until ratified formally in November.

The plan to relieve the old gentleman's distress had unexpected repercussions. At a Christmas party his granddaughter, a junior home for the holidays, met a tall neighbor who had split his foot while chopping wood. She liked his shy smile and steady gaze. He noticed her firm handshake and angora earmuffs. In June he took her to an operetta. In August she made a big fuss over his birthday. In September they promised to write.

By the time she boarded the train for senior year up East, though, Adolf Hitler had seized Norway and Denmark and was blitzing his way across France. In response, Washington mobilized the National Guard and six weeks later instituted Selective Service. Yet the country as a whole, separated from all that foreign buzz by wide oceans, still did not comprehend the implications. The "free world" of America had new weapons on the drawing board and in wooden models, but its army on duty carried out-of-date Springfield rifles and worked with equipment left over from World War I. "Training" meant parades, usually for patriotic occasions, or drill, unless the weather was bad—nothing of use for a real war.

Even Dwight D. Eisenhower, serving as General Douglas MacArthur's aide in the Philippines, never suspected Japan, raising turmoil in China, as the first challenge. No one in Washington seemed to have heard of a suspiciously hospitable and overly-helpful "assistant postmaster" buttering up Americans with words of "national friendship," and "Hirohito" was far down the "in" list of household words.

As far as Europe was concerned, people thought the English Navy and French army would take care of those German and Italian dictators. Even if England collapsed, there'd soon be a million and a half men in service, the largest peacetime U.S. Army in history. Congress did release men over the age of 28, but extended the twelve-month period of service eventually, if only by one vote. And what did "arsenal of democracy" mean anyway?

In October, when the draft board fired its first salvo at the dairy farm, it seemed unreal. Guns suggested possum hunts or ROTC, and people who headed for London or Paris were probably rich debutantes in search of husbands with titles.

I went through what they call registering today. It didn't take me five minutes. Just answered eight or ten questions, signed my John Hancock, and I was ready to start carrying my twelve-gauge.

But seriously, I hope I'm left out for a while. I can't see any way of getting around being drafted some time or other, probably the sooner the better.

Have you seen anything of 1156? That's my draft number. They label us just like convicts. As well as I can make out, seven thousand two hundred and seventy-nine will be called in this district before I'm sent for. My number is so low down on the list I may not have to report until next spring, maybe not then.

By the time you get this either Willkie or Roosevelt will be elected.

Actually, his first sight of her, in a newspaper photo headlined "Sings for Royalty," had a Roosevelt connection. In the spring of 1939 the president's wife had invited some members of the Vassar choir to Hyde Park to present after-dinner music for the crown prince and princess of Norway.

Going into the big house empty-handed, as the Secret Service required, the singers noticed ramps for

5

the wheelchair the public never saw, so cleverly was Roosevelt's handicap concealed. The president, his eyes deeply circled, looked very weary. His mother sat stiffly erect on a couch while Elliot and John lounged in a doorway. When Eleanor Roosevelt requested "something American" for an encore to Mozart and Palestrina, the dairyman's girl suggested "Swing Low, Sweet Chariot," which they harmonized sweetly a cappella without rehearsal as it might have been sung in the Southern cottonfields long ago.

The only flaw in an otherwise perfect evening, beyond a tilted lampshade Mrs. R- should have seen to, was the curtsey one person dropped to the uniform and tiara. By informal agreement ahead of time the group had decided to acknowledge their personal introductions to royalty with respectful nods, American-style.

A few weeks later Hitler lined up his tanks.

1941

Today that <u>darn</u> (excuse me) questionnaire came in the mail. I feel so let down like. They can't do this to us, can they? It will take time to classify and examine me. Even the questionnaire may not be filled out correctly. By then I'll have gone to New York for your graduation and back by Washington. Who knows? I may have flat feet. It's certainly a pain in the neck, all right. When I answer all the questions they will know more than I do.

When you were here in the spring, do you remember the field next to the road? Well, we've turned the cows in now, and it surely is a picture. With green growth up to their stomachs and sun shining on them, it makes a fellow step back and take notice.

> 13 May 41
> NOTICE TO REGISTRANT TO APPEAR FOR PHYSICAL EXAMINATION
> THURS. MAY 15th, 9 A.M.
> (<u>Throw</u> <u>away</u> <u>if</u> <u>in</u> <u>bad</u> <u>humor</u>, <u>please</u>)

If there was anything wrong with me today they certainly found it. I was stripped of every rag and looked over by four different doctors. The first bully didn't encourage me in the least because he made some comment about me being a perfect specimen. If I pass the examination they will notify me in a week's time. Even after notification they give ten days before calling us up. By that time I'll be on my way to New York.

Every time I get my spirits up something comes in the very next mail. This draft problem has been on my mind, I imagine, the way your exams have been for you. Mine is different, though. Yours will pass, but my problem will be looking me in the face for a year or even more. I've made up my mind that I'll see your graduation. I don't think God will forget us and not let us spend those special days together.

Our board has asked for <u>only</u> <u>one</u> at most. I just couldn't be that one.

Today the names came out. It was a boy from Germantown. Whee! Jumpin' Jackrabbits! They missed old flatfoot floozie this time.

I got my classification today. Hardly know more than I did before. All it said was 1-B. One of the doctors said I had a slight hernia that might bother me some day. I tried to be passed up on account of farming and dairying, but the board didn't think I was a necessary help to my parents.

You seemed rather up in the air over Roosevelt's speech. The United States may just be inviting trouble. I hardly think we will be in war the next month, though. You spoke as if I were up on the news by listening to the radio and reading the paper. Honestly, I'm ashamed sometimes what I know about what is going on.

———

At the college outside New York City and just north of Washington she was surrounded by "War." Coming out of the postoffice with a note her dairyman had sent for a joke in a hollowed-out corncob, she passed posters of pro- and anti-war meetings and a petition about Lend-Lease, Roosevelt's mechanism for providing Britain with military aid. She and her roommates, one an Army brat, divided down the middle between intervention and isolationism in heated discussions. Even the visit of Norwegian royalty assumed new dimensions.

One Sunday afternoon, thanks to the college's support of scholars and artists fleeing the Nazis, she heard ailing emigre' Bela Bartok in recital in the chapel.

The physics department particularly supported the refugee effort, keeping in constant touch with Lise Meitner, Niels Bohr, and other scientists who might be in danger and need of rescue. "Radium" had been old hat since freshman year when she had seen a sample of it glowing in the dark. Of far greater import than she recognized at the time, though, was her trip to Columbia University where the physics professor had shown the class of three a long rickety-looking contraption stretched in a dark basement. The "cyclotron" was known to the public later as "atom-smasher."

Her parents and her pet correspondent not only saw her graduate, but celebrated at all the major showpieces of New York and Washington: the Statue of Liberty, the Rockettes, Eddie Cantor's radio show, "Citizen Kane," the Capitol and Washington Monument, the Lincoln Memorial by night, the Spirit of St. Louis at the Smithsonian, the Tomb of the Unknown Soldier, even a boat trip to Mount Vernon. America at its best.

That summer the Third Army was equally busy, with field maneuvers in Louisiana offering possibilities never before imagined. A viable air force had yet to be realized, but the military, discovering the usefulness of Cub planes as liaison and spotters, gained insights that led to a true ground-air partnership so valuable in the war to come. Washington had called Japan's bluff. The Germans were stopped at Leningrad and Moscow. Still time to correct defects and weed out any ineffective leaders or procedures if necessary. Everything was in good shape.

In September letters from Tennessee headed for Alabama where the new graduate had joined the faculty of a girls' school in Birmingham. Not trusting the farm for their future, her correspondent left the dairy for the railroad with guaranteed income and possibility of advancement through seniority. Uncle Sam still poked around. Distant guns still rumbled. Yet they thought "Army" rather than "War," as if strong enough arms could hold back a tide.

Then reality struck. Hard.

In Texas, at Fort Sam Houston, Eisenhower, weary after maneuvers there and looking forward to a two-week leave at West Point, retired leaving orders not to be disturbed.

In Alabama the Latin teacher, planning a holiday musical program for the school, realized that the symphony broadcast had been interrupted for an important announcement. Where in the world was "Pearl Harbor"?

Suddenly she recalled wavering broadcasts junior year with the sound of bombs and a deep quiet voice intoning, "This is London."

Next morning the headmistress gathered faculty, staff, and student body in the main hall to hear President Roosevelt's speech to the nation. The first graders, expecting something like regular chapel, judged the seriousness of the moment by the looks on their elders' faces. One teacher longed to hear from Tennessee.

———————

Yesterday was a day I never will forget. I came in after an unusually tiring day only to find we had gone to war. This morning I'm just wondering what steps to take next. This thing has come on us so quickly. I don't know how to take it.

Just think. I may have to go. War is the most terrible thing I know. So many lives just destroyed when there is no use. I hear all men from eighteen to thirty-five will be called for service.

"Will I see you Christmas?" has been ringing in my ears since yesterday afternoon when I came in the round house and found the United States had been attacked by Japan. Since it's come, let's take it with our heads up as we've done in other things. With an aching and trembling heart...

This war doesn't sound so good. I'd just like to go in there and whip the Japs so completely that they would never get over it. It seems to me it was all carelessness on the part of the United States not to be on their guard as they should have been.

Things are really happening fast up here. Memphis is in a complete blackout these nights. They have guards at the Harahan Bridge and allow no one to even drive by the airport. It may be sorta foolish for Memphis to be so strict because we are so far away who would bother us? We haven't got anything anyone would want anyway.

Don't get too worked up about my going to the Army. They don't want a 1-B cripple, so that lets me out, doesn't it? Sometimes I think if I have to go and fight I'd just as soon someone would shoot me before I leave and get me out of the misery.

1942

With Christmas joy muted by national pain he entered a realm of dithering between two vastly different worlds. The 1-B classification which seemed to have hurt his pride, but might have disqualified him once for active service, made not the slightest difference after Pearl Harbor.

The country, alive with rumors of enemy bombers and spies, loaded guns on flatcars and sidetracked patrons of deluxe Pullmans to move servicemen. Alaska became a special source of concern for the mainland as a possible base for enemy bombers if captured.

"Stop the Japs" was the current rallying-cry, but how long could Russia hold out against the Germans? A national revulsion against spying, which seemed sneaky and un-American somehow, had left U.S. Intelligence sadly lacking.

In Birmingham all one could do was equip the windows with blackout shades, sing patriotic music, and buy War Bonds.

I haven't heard a thing from the board. Everyone I talk to seems to have very little encouragement. Anyway, if every officer in the Army looks at my mail, I'll still write to you.

The Army doctors are in Memphis and want men to be examined from the group who didn't pass last time.

Now they're looking for 400. One of the boys here got a notice yesterday to come for a check-up. So did I.

We went down to the Shelby County Hospital at 6:30 this morning. A Greyhound bus picked us up there and carried us to the University Center for examination. We had to take off our shoes and socks as soon as we got on the third floor, keep them off all day, too. We kept our clothes off so long we felt natural without them. They had a doctor, sometimes two, for every part of your body. When a person comes through what we had today, he knows what's wrong or right with him.

I asked two of the doctors to pay special attention to what some of the others called hernia. Both paid such attention to it I felt they would cause some damage if I didn't already have some. On everything I passed as far as I could make out. I won't say positively I'm in, but can't help feeling I'm leaning that way. So few were turned down.

I'm not worrying so much about the Army. I'm eating and sleeping, so you know it hasn't affected me much. You see I haven't given up completely either. If things turn out I should go, I would like to be in the cavalry because I want to shoot the biggest men in Germany, the Japs, and anyone else that started this mess.

What expense they go to before a draftee even gets to the Army. They got my fingerprints, too. There were three sentences at the end of the questionnaire: qualified for military service, qualified for limited military service, and disqualified for military service. They drew a line through everything except qualified.

Know what I did today? I felt since I might have to help the U.S.A. out in its manpower, maybe I should help it out financially, too. I bought a defense bond which will be worth twenty-five dollars in ten years.

The price of cotton is up to almost $.25 a pound. See what I'll get for that one bale I kept back? I really ought to sell it before Congress puts its prices on everything on account of the present conflict.

I heard something on the radio this morning I may have to use. It's an insurance policy a boy can take out against his best girl. If he loses her while he's in service they have to pay to help him forget the loss.

Overlooking the fear and dread of things, there is always you.

I just looked around the library, where I'm writing you today, and there sits an old drunk that was examined the same day I was. He looks a little more sober today, God bless him.

If I do go to the Army things will move so fast I won't know from one time to another where I will be, but you can bet your life when I go you'll go tucked under my arm. I'll hang your picture some place, even if I have to live in a pup tent. Boy, will all the other boys gloat over my girl!

The time I seem to be spending now is so useless, indefinite, and unsettled. I'll try so hard if this life of mine ever gets its classification. It may be wonderful sometimes to have no idea of tomorrow when you come to think of your country, but if something doesn't show up this week, the gray hairs you'll see the next time you see me will be caused by life in general now.

I have so little to write you sometimes that I feel it's hardly worth the three cents. I've been sitting on pins and needles for days now, looking for anything from the draft. I've been through all kinds of hell the last two weeks, and today I got another classification, 1-A.

I have about decided to try for some part of the air corps, learning something about the instruments that detect when the enemy planes are coming. We may not get a chance to say what we'd like to do, but you'll probably have to ask for what you get. That may mean signing up for two or three years. We'll have to be in this army until it all finishes anyway, don't you think?

I wouldn't much care if my notice would come tomorrow. I am so fed up on living from day to day just sorta fearing and guessing.

I'm looking every day for a notice while helping out home with the milking, re-living the old life. Today I helped Dad on the building of his feed room. I can still drive a nail, believe it or not.

Do you think you can come home the weekend of the 14th? They seem to be sending off a number of boys that were examined the same day I was on the 17th. By the time you come I'll know if I'm leaving with that bunch. Maybe I'd better ask the girl to marry me before going off to the Army.

I didn't care who heard me talking to you tonight. Will you marry me? I'll see you this weekend! Whee! I'm glad you'll let me come to Birmingham and bring you home. Write me where I can find you. I can get away with murder since I'm going into the Army.

It won't be so bad leaving now because I'll have people all around that I know. One of my cousins and a few others around town leave the same day. Some say we go to Camp Forrest, others say to Fort Oglethorpe. Who knows? We may stop at Birmingham! I can't carry much, only enough for three days, but one thing's sure. I'll have you tucked beside me all the days I'm away. I can't be a good soldier otherwise, so don't let me and Uncle Sam down.

I'm sorta glad I had the time to be with my people before my notice came. I helped to paper two rooms and build the feed room since I've been "resting." Mother is so pleased. No matter what I ever do I can't pay her back for what she's done for me.

And if you like someone else, don't ever tell me because I'd just rather have you say "Maybe" or "No" when the preacher marries us.

I went into town today through a heavy rain and finished up the little business I had to do, to the round house and got my check, the big sum of sixteen dollars for two days in January, and paid my dues in the firemen's union.

I've just completed the rounds of goodbyes, even went by to say adios to your people. They made it so easy for me just a moment ago. This will be my last letter from Shady Circle Farm for a while. I'll try to find out in the morning where I'll go and drop you a card.

In the station all a-twitter. We are heading for Fort Oglethorpe. Will let you know when I get there.

He soon found out what being drafted meant - whistles, greasy food, picking up litter ("policing the area"), taking shots (and taking shots, and taking shots), lugging a heavy barracks bag wherever he moved, having either too much to do or nothing at all to do that took away thoughts of home, always bitching about everything - in short, learning to be a normal soldier. He had been to Mississippi and Arkansas and even to Chicago once, but the world now expanded exponentially. As for military training, many a soldier would have to use a broomstick to represent a rifle, mark a tree to stand for a gun emplacement, and throw tobacco sacks instead of hand grenades.

For now his world away would be the reality of marching and K.P., the other world a combination of a dairy farm and wherever-she-was.

I'm in the Army now. What a mess. Everywhere we go it's an order given by someone that's not even as old as I am. I'll get used to that, but is it going to be hard catching on the way the Army does things.

When we got in this evening around 8:30 I for one felt as though we were driving into a jail when we went through the front gate. We rode in those Army trucks from the station. You can guess how cold we got.

The first instruction was on how to make up a bed, then wash up and wait thirty minutes for supper. It tasted good. I was hungry even after a surprisingly

good lunch at Corinth on the way. We had to take a
shower and even wash our hair before going to bed.

I didn't know it was so far to Oglethorpe. The
train stopped at every pig path. If you can't make
sense out of this I won't be surprised because I'm
writing on my lap. Things are so unsettled I don't
know where I'll be tomorrow.

The second day was more of a topsy turvy than the
first. This morning I had only seven minutes to make
up this thing they call a bed. A friend from home
helped me, then I helped him. We rushed out, got in
line and ran to the mess hall for a huge breakfast.
Then we marched for nearly two miles down to the
hospital for three shots - smallpox, which will not ★
take if we have a scar, and two others for thyroid. (Sic)
One guy I grew up with came around. He's a sergeant
now in this "introduction" center and it was good to
see and talk with someone you know. They're working
night and day to get the men through. We may go to
Biloxi, who knows?

It's doubtful I'll get your mail, but do try and
write. I've grown so used to your letters. I'm not
homesick yet, but no sign I can't get that way. So
many seem to be taking it so hard that if it wasn't
for familiar faces your private would go down too. By
the way, if you write leave the Mister off my name and
put Alfred W. Rogers. They don't want that middle
name, so in case you ever come around, don't ask for
"Wesley."

It's such a noisy place in this barrack that I
can't even think, much less write. The cots are just
far enough apart so you can walk. The man next to me
may see everything I write. Who cares? It's about a
hundred men in this place, so you know how they smoke
and maybe even gossip like a bunch of women.

I just got the bestest letter a soldier ever got.
Just keep his spirits up and he'll even cut off some
enemy ears and bring them back stuffed.

My uniform fits very well except the trousers are a
bit too long. The coat and cap fit like they were

★ Typhoid

17

made for me. Our bag contains 1 pair shoes, 4 shirts, 2 shirts and shorts, overall pants and jumper, tin plate with knife, fork and spoon, 3 handkerchiefs, comb, razor, brush, canteen, one heavy overcoat, and a raincoat thrown in. I wish I had my slippers, though. Our feet get so tired and sore. I sent my other clothes home day before yesterday.

You've heard about peeling those spuds and such like. Well, the whole kitchen work is nothing to brag about. The Sergeant woke us up around 4:30 and until 8:30 it was just like the penal farm.

I slipped out to the canteen to call, but there was such a line in front of the phone I couldn't possibly make it in the hour I had. The first time I've been off this place we went to a show about a mile and a half from camp, only soldiers and draftees allowed. We certainly don't save the shoe leather either. We walk every place we go.

If you ever holler "Right about face!" don't think I can't do it. Have to stop now because the sergeant just hollered. When he says move, we must move.

With mail today after so long I feel the world turning around the same way once more. I'm the only one who can get two letters in one day from his girl. The sergeant thinks you must like me a little. Who cares if the Army knows? Maybe if we had a little more love in the world it wouldn't be in quite such a mess.

Yesterday I went to church with the sergeant from home, then got my first cookies and coffee for soldiers while playing ping pong at the Y.

K.P. is really all the things you've heard it called. I've had to work in the storage room, too, issuing shoes and uniforms. Everything is measured so accurately you can't help but get a good fit.

I leave tomorrow for a coast artillery camp in Virginia about 40 or 50 miles from Washington. The sergeant said we were very lucky to get this branch. We stay on the coast and never go across, that's something, but it's so far away from home I hate the whole set-up. I can't get any leaves until twelve weeks of training are over. You couldn't possibly come up for spring vacation, could you? I can't even get a weekend off since the war started.

No matter where I go, and it looks as though I'll go tomorrow, I'll come back some day rich or poor, lame or healthy, and ask you to be my wife. I hate to write it, hate to even think of all this, yet it's come to pass. Everything seems so blown up all of a sudden.

You'll have to help support my spirits.

The Allies faced problems at a higher level, the double quandary of enemies widely separated geographically and a command divided between two major world powers. Since Japan had to be stopped before Europe could be saved, fighting had to go on in one area while halfway around the globe a future war had to be organized. With oil a precious commodity for conflict, German U-boats had already sunk tankers by the score. Lines to India and Australia must be kept open, and the Japs and Germans could not be allowed to link forces through the Persian Gulf, the Red Sea or the Balkans.

Human potential needed attention as well. Diplomats of the period often qualified for strategic positions by being no more than personable men of wealth and proper manners. Intelligence officers, many without training in a G-2 school, had to rely on helpful Brits to accumulate and analyze whatever information turned up.

As the muddled global concept struggled to emerge, a draftee, as green as some of higher command and importance but equal inexperience, reported for his own basic training.

Norma Rogers

VIRGINIA

Norma Rogers

These are the first words to be written to you in Virginia. Just crossed the state line. We are on a Pullman train almost ready to go to bed. Gosh, I hate this trip going away. I didn't think I ever would get this far from home and all that matters.

It seems they have turned the tables on me. I'm so far away like you were at school. If I ever get back, will you marry me? I don't care when it is or where. The boys that married just before going to the Army seem unusually happy, and lots felt they would never be sorry for the time they spent with their wives.

We had a good train up, Pullman and all, but the direction never did suit me. I guess I'm so country I couldn't sleep much. The major told us coming up we were very fortunate to get in Coast Artillery. 'Course he said that to keep our spirits up.

This fort is about eighteen miles from Richmond, a fort I didn't know existed. As soon as we got here and had lunch they put us on K.P. again. I'm in a barrack full of Detroit boys. You know how they talk, draw their words out. Everyone is in the same boat, treated the same way. No one is given a better opportunity than others. All the boys are really friends and act as though they're just a big family working together.

We are having a blackout tonight. A plane has been flying over all night, the cause of the darkness. It's just practice for the boys on guard. We have some light stations in the camp, and with those on the coast, too, a plane has to be pretty slick to get through them. Did you know I'm in a very dangerous place? We have to sit around and take it all very calmly, can you picture that?

We were sent out this afternoon for drill for the first time. The men really put the pressure on you. 'Course some are nice. It doesn't take long to learn the different steps. They tell us to get our minds off everything back home, even our girls. Tonight they read us the laws and bylaws of the Army. They have a rule for everything, so it's no way of doing anything you might think they don't have laws to cover.

I'm going to stay alive in this war and come back a better man.

Today we went through the severest drill yet, this morning from 8 to 11:30, this afternoon 12:30 to 3:00. What a difference today is from yesterday. It's so much better. If it wasn't for one thing, being away, I'd fall completely head over heels in this thing. When you catch on to the drill work it's easy, and so much easier to get along with the instructors. All the tall men must line up on the right side all day. I like it, though. We'll get six weeks of drill and two weeks of work on the big guns. We do fire them, actually. You understand this is a replacement center. After eight weeks, that is if I make it, I'll be replaced. The things we need in this business are spirit, confidence and faith. With these three we can go places.

It's so many boys here that no matter how hard they try they never will make the grade. When they are so weak it goes hard with them. One of the boys in my barrack even came over last night for me to write a letter for him. Most of the men are so friendly and nice, and all seem to work together as a family. We must pull together to win. We will win, too. We have the guts and the training, so what else do we need?

If it wasn't for being so far away I would like this place. It's such a fine and ongoing group in my barrack we expect to go places. If it's a down and out one in the bunch, and you can bet all of us get that way, someone comes along and gives a cheerful word and sees your side of it.

We have eleven orders to learn for guard duty. Some can't read or write, so how will they learn? A number of the men have even taken it upon themselves to teach them the orders.

The wind and sun have given us all a tan that favors the ones in Florida. We have to keep well-shaven, shoes shined, clothes clean so we all look like good boys.

What would I give to sleep on that mattress of mine. Just to show how the marching and drilling are on our minds, someone the other night hollered "1–2" in his sleep. Some of the boys snore so loud they tear off part of the building when they breathe.

(Lights are out. I'll have to finish this in the shower.)

I was afraid when I came in the Army there wouldn't be a place to worship on Sunday, but you would be surprised at the chapel they have here. The benches are made of pine, floors varnished a dark color, there's a small organ, and the chaplain is the best. I enjoyed his message so much. The text was Multitudes and Multitudes of Decisions. Some of the boys that have been here eight weeks are leaving this coming week. When we began singing "God Be With You Till We Meet Again," so many couldn't hold back that lump that comes in the throat sometimes. You know how I enjoy church singing. This morning with nothing but male voices it sounded so full and good.

We slept late and ate breakfast around seven. They called it breakfast, but please always have in mind that I like my eggs well done. Lunch was really slambang, though. We had carrots, potatoes, pie, and coffee, and I even got half a chicken. Boy, it tasted good. Most of the privates, corporals and sergeants had Sunday off, so we had no drilling or marching. We have to put our beds out every morning, though. It keeps us from lying on and airs them out at the same time.

The church service didn't last but an hour, but we sang hymns everyone wanted to hear. I'm telling you these old Yankees really bear down on the singing.

We walked from one end of this place to the other this evening. If you come, let me know in advance or you might get lost. The barracks are about twenty-five feet apart, holding about 250 men. There are about five or six hundred in tents. Lucky we didn't get one of those.

The most perfect ending of a soldier's day is writing to his girl. He's bound to want to stand up and fight for a life he can live truly with her for always. I think that's what I'm wanting to fight for at least, if no other reason. To me it's the greatest, the free country life I always had with a home with wife and family to talk with, worship as we please, and live a lifetime together.

I get as much mail sometimes as all the battery put together. They called chow this morning after mail call, and I just kept on reading. I didn't care if I ever got anything to eat. Besides, it was rainy, and I didn't want to get wet in the long line anyhow.

We've been divided off into two sections, gunners and rangers. I'm one of the rangers. We get the correct position of the target or object, then pass it on to the gunners. We are shooting 155 MM guns 6 inches in diameter. Supposed to fire every 60 seconds. Also a number of lectures and work in operating and protecting ourselves in action.

This place is full from end to end. We had a quarantine because of spinal meningitis. It was lifted today, though, so you needn't be afraid of coming around. After eight weeks here no telling what place we'll be next. One of the boys wrote back that he was in New Orleans now, so you see how things are.

We have lights out at 8:30 your time, so I was half asleep and scared at the same time when your phone call came. I forgot to knock and remove my cap when I came in the office, thinking the commanding officer and top sergeant were gone. Both bellowed at me. In the meantime I was backing out the door. They left before the call came through, thank goodness, but there was still a corporal on duty to overhear. My knees still jump up and down a little when I know I'm going to actually talk to her.

My arm is so stiff I can't write the regular muscular movement. One of those sharp Army needles again today. I believe they tried to scratch the bone. We've had so many shots it's no fun any more, lockjaw, thyroid, malaria, and even vaccination again.

We need around ten men to fire, gunners and rangers, and I'm studying the levelization process. The instrument is on the side to lower or raise or even make it vary from side to side. I could be shifted from one place to the other from time to time.

We get our rifles issued tomorrow. They have our caps to put on the special border to give everyone here the emblem of the Coast Artillery. You'd be surprised at the way the higher officers are, just human beings like the rest of us. They really are the best we could get. The commanding officer gave us a little background of Fort Eustis this morning. It will be one year Thursday since they came and organized our battery. We have four, A, B, C, and D. Ours has always stood out very highly here and after leaving this post. They have culled down and out until by now we do have some of the best instructors there are. In all Fort Eustis has around 1600 men now.

We just had a blackout, and it makes a little shiver run over me.

My head's just so whirley whirley that I can't get sense out of anything. I guess it's your talking of coming up here, the best thing that can happen in my Army life. 'Course my name may come up for K.P. or guard duty, but with you staying in the guest house here on the post I can see you every day.

The more I think of your visiting me, the more I like the Army.

I passed the candy you sent around the barrack and told the boys it was from the bestest girl that ever lived. I did tell them that, on my soldier's honor. When you come around this post I'll have to get boxing gloves out because the boys have just taken to you.

We had our first practice with rifles today. No, didn't fire them, just learned how. We got <u>another shot</u>, too. I believe I'll be immune to everything by springtime.

27

Our days are so full that they use our nights for odds and ends around the barracks like taking up laundry and signing for our pay. During rifle practice we stood so long in one position that when we did move and walk it felt as though our feet were asleep.

You should see me in a gas mask. You wouldn't recognize me. It's so much to learn, and you can't be haphazard about it either. You can't ever be sure of yourself in this Army.

Did you know this fort is cut off from outsiders? It's just a place, it seems, that was dropped from a plane or something. They really are strict. We have very little to amuse ourselves with here. If you decide not to make the trip I guess I can make out until I don't know when.

I do want to ask you a most important question in person.

Here I am on duty in the barrack tonight. You didn't know I would rate so high so soon, did you? I was elected one of the twelve acting corporals of the three battalions that have been formed. Maybe you think I'm bragging, but that's the reason I'm on duty, to keep down disorder if any arises. I get special privileges that others don't have. If I work hard and don't get too big a head, I can keep the rating, but marks can be taken away, too. This goes down on my record and is sent to wherever we are transferred.

I got a special delivery and enjoyed it so much when the postman picked me out of the whole line to give it to me. I went on and took my shots without blinking an eye.

The 13th Battalion had its picture made Saturday. We can get as many copies as we like for a dollar apiece. Everyone is dressed alike, and we look as though there's no thought of war in our minds.

We get a going-over every morning out in the cool, fresh air, and I think we pull every muscle in our bodies. My arms are so sore I can't even raise them.

I never sleep on my tummy (quote you), but it looks like that or else tonight.

After some more shots, which took two hours in line to get, we had a movie on the use of our gas masks, to me the most important equipment a soldier has. We go in a room filled with tear gas to test them out sometime this week.

I just can't help but look for a letter now when that little short fellow comes around with the mail. I'm planning so much on your coming up here. I'm just on the end of every gun I'm so excited.

Falling out in different formations is getting us down. We came out first this morning with our caps, blouses, and rifles. Paraded around for nearly two hours doing different motions with the rifles. After that the darned things had to be cleaned.

Yep, I went to the range yesterday. Got three or four 4's on my practice shots, the rest 3's, not counting one miss. One bird shot at my target just before I shot, darn him, and they pulled it down on me. I did my best, but don't especially care for rifles. 'Course everyone has to go through the training no matter if he's going to Officers Candidate School.

We have inspection on Saturday, and this place has to be clean from one end to the other. The acting corporals had the advantage this evening. We get to order the others around, but it's almost as hard to get some of these Yankees to work as it is to do it yourself.

When the mailman handed our share out, the acting corporals hollered, "On the double! You privates get this place cleaned up!" We just sat back and read our letters from our best girl and saw it well done. Some really hate to move when I holler, but it's move or else.

Yesterday's retreat would have killed you. All of us got so tickled and couldn't laugh, just kept snickering to ourselves. We have to be at attention for the ceremony, but don't have a flag for our battery, just go through the formation while it's going on at the main flagpole in front of the office. About time everything was still and set, an old dog came trotting across the field with one puppy. She wandered around through the boys until the puppy got lost from her. As soon as the trumpet began to blow she comes up in front of it and barks the whole time. The pup was so scared he waddles and runs as fast as he can among the boys. Even the Lieutenant couldn't help smiling.

We went through all the forms of the front today, climbing 10-foot walls, under wire fences, over ditches and bridges. We really were put through the mill.

I can see you every day you are here. It's going to be the best spring vacation I've ever had, so you know it means a lot for you to come.

You can put in for a pass, then on Saturday noon it can be torn into bits because you have fallen down on something during inspection. About fourteen lost their weekend privileges yesterday because of a dirty rifle, bad bunk, or not knowing the officers of our battery. They have started really putting the pressure to us. Everything is in order on my end of the line. The first time I put in for a pass, though, something will turn up, watch and see.

There was a concert at the service club last night. A girl from New York sang, then another girl did a number of toe dances. She was really good. I almost felt sorry for her because we brutes kept calling her back for more until she was exhausted.

When you come to see this homesick private, maybe they will find me so I can take you down to the guest house, first kissing you in front of the whole post. I don't give a hoot who sees me either. I can't help showing the fellows I care, so I hope I don't embarrass you.

I'll try to break this gently if I can. When I went to the guesthouse tonight to make a reservation, the clerk took my name for two days only because of crowded conditions, then asked what relation you were to me. 'Course I'd never thought of that. I could have told him you were my wife, sister or something. I'll find out from the sergeant tomorrow about hotels in Newport News and say you're my sister so I can get a pass. I hate to tell a white lie about this, but if that's what it takes. All I want you to do is still come on. <u>I'll</u> <u>find</u> <u>a</u> <u>place</u>. Will you still come?

The stars are really close tonight. I know because I'm under them, corporal of the guard at the moment in Guard House #4. With five guards under me I'm able to sit in the office with the radio playing "Deep in the Heart of Texas," but mine is deep in the heart of Birmingham. I tried to call you tonight, but no luck. Got four hours rest, but can't sleep for wondering if you're coming.
Here comes the next shift.

Today is more on the up and up. I've been in a daze, but since I hung up the receiver this morning am a little eased. I do want us to be married. If it is at all possible to get our license in the time you are here, please let's make it now. The process in Virginia needs blood tests, which can be done on Friday so that we can be married Sunday, or even before.
There would be a place at the guest house then. You would be a relative of mine, you know. I want so much to make it this weekend. We have so little time. Why can't we spend it the way we would like it to be? It's just no fun any more this way.
Along with being your husband will come the making of a good soldier. I can be a better man when all is set. It will be the happiest moment in these twenty-three years.

Tonight has been a twist and a turn. I found we can be married in 24 hours. That includes the blood test. If I can't get to Newport News Friday I can Saturday evening, so maybe we can be married by Sunday night. My mind's made up. I can't let you go back

until you are my wife. If I don't get off, it'll just
have to be A.W.O.L.

————————

He had located a gentle lady who rented rooms in
her home on the highway to Williamsburg. Except for a
drug store where college students congregated, the
center of town had not changed much since Colonial
times. No powdered wigs, but no tourists either. The
marriage license had to be arranged for in the round
tower, a partly completed segment of Rockefeller's
restoration project. Perhaps a local minister would
perform the ceremony at home or allow his congregation
to be their witnesses after the Sunday morning
service.

With the seeming impossible accomplished in one
brief afternoon, her blood test satisfactory and the
marriage permit in hand, she waited joyously, then saw
his face. The lab attendant at the fort had dropped
the vial with his sample, and blood could not be taken
again and processed until Monday.

Disappointment became blessing, time to plan a
proper wedding in the chapel on the post. By Monday
night he had consulted the chaplain, invited his
barrack buddies, and met the organist, a talented
draftee delighted with the chance to play Franck and
Schubert once more. Next morning, on their way to the
fort, her hostess drove her by the local flower shop.

The men of his outfit, separated from their own
wives and loved ones, became family for the
festivities. After retreat they called the bride-to-
be to the flagpole to present their wedding gift, a
fatigue hat full of bills and coins - it was pay day.
Three hours later, scrubbed and polished, they
reverently filled the pews of the little chapel to
hear the old familiar vows.

When the surprised bride and groom came out the
door after thanking those who had officiated, they
walked down the steps through a saluting honor guard
who fell in behind them in double file and sang "She's
in the Army Now" while marching them to the Service

Club for refreshments. There they brought her the largest ice cream float on the menu, played her favorite love song eleven times on the jukebox, and tucked carnations from her corsage behind their ears to wear next morning in their fatigue pockets while digging latrines.

The guest house, as they sadly discovered, was off-limits to enlisted men. That night she hung her best dress on a long nail in an unpainted board wall and bruised her knee on a lonely metal cot. Back at the barrack he found his own cot short-sheeted and filled with corn flakes.

Made aware of the circumstances, a compassionate non-com produced a three-day emergency pass usually reserved for a crisis or death in the family. They could have dinner, then time together in her private room near Williamsburg until 2:30 A.M., when he had to wait on the highway for the last bus before reveille.

I'm so glad things have turned out the way they have. We had so little time, but it was the bestest vacation I've had because I was married. When I put the address on this letter it will be the first time I have ever written anything like it, a "Mrs." in front of the "Rogers."

Your pupils sound really excited about your surprise marriage. I had dreamed of a more full wedding and honeymoon, but times have changed, and March 31st will always be a shining spot in my mind and heart.

I had fired on the range Friday, so all I did this morning was coach and rig up the telephone on the firing line and target. It has been so much like summer here today we had to shed our red flannels. Some got so hot on the hike their feet were just dragging. I've been lucky. I get to go down in the truck every time.

Army Day we had the remembrance parade we'd planned for. Got in ranks around 2:00, but didn't start until way past 3:00. That old sun really did bear down on us poor children.

When we began to march it was just like a bunch of cattle running we raised so much dust. Think what 1000 men can do when they are walking. The dust came up like a fog. We had the rest of the evening off, didn't even have retreat. Had to clean our rifles, though.

The fellows ask me how is married life. I tell them like a man with lots of experience that it's the swellest and most wonderful life there could be. A wife is beautiful and sacred to me.

Just a week ago tonight the most wonderful thing that ever happened happened. I didn't show that I was nervous when we walked up on the platform together, but my knees were playing "Yankee Doodle."

I went to Easter service here on the post, a service out in the open. The platform was decorated with pine trees lit up with candles. The boys had gotten up such nice Easter music. Their voices blended in so well it sounded just like one, only a little more mellow and fine. Our general, lieutenant commander and a number of officers had their families there. Doggone it, who couldn't I have had mine?

A big fat letter came from your folks welcoming me into your family. Your mother wants me to call her "Mom." Would you send me your brother's Air Corps address? I want to get his consent, too. You do have the bestest people that ever could be. They really seemed glad to have another son.

Now that you have gone back to school and settled into your little groove again, how _is_ married life? That's all I'm hearing.

I'm wondering if you've hiked as far as I have today. You could have so much more fun with the girls than I could have with these old grouchy corporals.

First we went through that darned exercise for an hour. The lieutenant really puts us through. He starts at the head-bending muscles and goes down. I can touch my toes without bending my knees, but after all that was ready just to go back to bed.

The second thing was a hike with light packs including our tent, musket and canteen. We wavered along for nearly five miles, it seemed, then came to a sudden halt and pitched tents. You have to have two to make one tent because someone else has the other half. As soon as I got mine up I crawled in and rested until they hollered, "Down with the tents!" This evening we went back again, on the <u>same</u> <u>hike</u>, to set up the big guns on the James River. We practiced for nearly two hours. I thought we would fall in our tracks before they let us have a break. When it came time for us to stop, the lieutenant wanted us to stay on until everyone was through with chow. We don't get pay for over-time either, isn't that a shame?

It's the big gun first thing Friday morning, so I may holler in my sleep "<u>Home</u> <u>ram</u>!"

The boys got your thank-you note for our wedding present and reception today, and were tickled pink to hear from you. We have it pinned on the bulletin board. I think everyone has given it the once-over. You really did say just what could be said to a group we have here. That's all it takes to make us men happy.

We fire the big gun tomorrow, so look out in Birmingham! You may get hit. Lights are dimming now, so here I go. With lights out, 'night.

We were supposed to fire the 155 today, but unsettled weather put it off till tomorrow. It was already raining very hard when we left camp, but we still took a long hike, all for nothing. It was so misty we couldn't even see the lighthouse, but still were going to fire. All at once the major walks up, puts his foot down and says, "Take these men out of this mess," and at once our stations were closed. They don't seem to use their heads sometimes. That's what costs the government so much. Don't tell them I talk to you like I do, or I might get court martialed. They can do that, you know.

Don't you ever get tired of my just talking Army?

If I ever get out of this place I never will mention the word "Army" again.

There's just one problem now. We both want to stand on our own two feet, yet we want to walk in each other's shoes. How are we going to manage that? I never got such a kick out of a kiss as that jack-in-the-box you sent. It scared the <u>eleven</u> <u>general</u> <u>orders</u> completely out of me. I just knew it was a candy kiss, could just taste it. All of a sudden the thing hits me right in the face. What am I going to do when she socks me with my own mail? I had to show the trick around the barrack. The boys thought you were awful devilish. I do, too. I'm so happy now. The fellow's the happiest married man in Fort Eustis, not even starting a new paragraph during this whole letter.

Just think how old our married life is now. Yep, it's me again, your husband of two weeks. The school wants you back next year, but mark it down on your calendar. I need a housecleaning sometime next spring.

Do you realize you're actually the head of the family for now? I can't even think of the outside world the Army takes up so much of my time. I've been in charge of the barrack today, so my day has been full of outs and ins. You have to be on your toes so much of the time in this place, but if I didn't write, it would be just like not eating all day.

I've got to do a lot of things to make up for the time I'm in the Army. Finally got the lowdown on whether I go or stay. I'm going, I guess. I don't know when, but it'll be with the other boys in the barrack. I was just an acting corporal, but I'll be glad for a change, too. They say things will be better now that basic training is over.

This married fellow is putting on weight and looking younger every day. You won't know me when you see me coming up the walk in June or July on furlough.

Did I tell you about firing the big guns? You never in your life have seen such scared men. We stood around waiting for the firing command to come until we'd worked up enough lather to shave the whole post. The guns make so much noise they shake your ears and eyeballs and make every hair stand up. One of the gun pointer's hair raised up so straight that when it settled back down it fell over his eyes. He tried to get his aiming point, but kept hollering, "I can't see! I can't see!" When he came to his senses, it was nothing but his own hair.

This morning the battery commander, while praising us for such good shooting yesterday, joked about how one fellow got so scared his hair stood on end, so we gave the guy a shampoo with the soapy water I use to sponge the breech out with. After the first shot the firing was fun. Every major, colonel, commander, lieutenant, sergeant and corporal was down there to see us. We even talked to the colonel and major. We broke a record, too, the best that any battery has done at Fort Eustis <u>ever</u>.

The mail carrier and the fellows really like the funny envelopes you send. They always ask me while I'm reading your letters, "Does she still love you?" 'Course I turn it off with, "She's certainly fooling me if she doesn't." Married life is wonderful. Why didn't we try it before?

I have just finished washing my clothes and have them hanging over my head on a line. I had to use G.I. soap and now have dishwater hands. Washing is something I hate and put off till the last rag is dirty. I washed everything so I'd have it all clean when I leave here. Just when I don't know.

I'm on guard duty tonight at 6:00. Thought I'd get away from here before getting that duty again, but no such luck. We have to be especially watchful because tomorrow is Hitler's birthday. He might try something funny. I'm corporal, with eight posts to put men on and listen if anything goes wrong.

We've had a farewell party, but have just gotten an order to stay in barracks tonight. I think instead of Hitler's birthday they're keeping us available to leave at any time. Why can't we be treated more like humans than like a bunch of cattle being shipped? I can't think of one of my brothers coming into the Army. The youngest got his questionnaire last Monday. It seems they're rushing things up considerably now.

It's our weekaversary, but somehow our married life hasn't really started. Will you still care for me a teeny bit if I'm just a corporal? It's just so hard to keep a stiff chin. You do your best, writing and keeping me cheerful, but still the surroundings seem to drown those thoughts out sometimes.

Today has been such a push and a rush until my eyes, head and whole body ache. We've gotten a lot of "hearsays" about where we will go from here. The most reliable are Georgia, North Carolina or New Orleans. Any will put me closer to you and home. It's almost too good to be true. I'm with a group of Northern boys, but for some strange reason they'll be heading south, leaving around 7:00 in the morning.

My barrack bag is already packed in the baggage car. We take two lunches with us, so you see we don't go too far. Some aren't taking any food and are going Pullman. They really will scatter us to the four corners of the earth.

They have taken all our bedding except one comforter and the mattress. I don't expect any of us will get much sleep tonight.

As he boarded the train to God-knows-where, Allied High Command grappled with related uncertainty - where to send troops? what were Germany's intentions toward the Dutch East Indies? Syria? Turkey? Iraq?

And what about the command structure? Each nation had to have disciplinary rights over its own units, yet the need for mutual trust and efficiency also required a central control mechanism. Americans already on duty in England knew little of what their British counterparts were already planning with a somewhat doubtful, even scornful, mistrust in their revolutionary cousins' abilities. What could be depended on from a nation concerned with the imminent surrender of its troops on Bataan, the posting of guards at the vital shipping canal between two of its great lakes, and the shipment of 3000 rifles to Alaska? Could it have its mind on the military and political needs of Europe as well?

At least one of its draftees soon learned the answer to <u>his</u> primary question of the moment. His destination was Camp Stewart, Georgia.

Norma Rogers

GEORGIA

Norma Rogers

I really am down in the deep South. You couldn't guess in a million years where I've been placed. What would you think if I said, "Camp Stewart"? How do you like that? Now I can see you every weekend!

This camp is 43 miles from Savannah, Georgia. They wouldn't tell us a thing until we got on the train at Eustis. We had to dig it out of them then. When I learned I was coming here I really breathed a sigh of relief.

Just a few minutes after lunch Wednesday they called a bunch of our names out. We had twenty minutes to pack and get our bags on the coach. We thought all the while we were leaving right away, then didn't go until the next morning, getting here around 11 o'clock last night. The train was so fast and crowded, but the trip was much more pleasant than you might think. Three of the fellows I know are with me, two in my tent. Yep, I'm sleeping in a tent and like to have frozen this morning before I got my clothes. We are so close to the coast we can smell the water, feel the air and mosquitoes.

Eustis was so far from home, but I got to liking the place. When the breaking up came, so many of us fellows couldn't bear the parting, even wept like sissies. After you learn a bunch of fellows and like them so well, you can't just walk away and not have some emotion in your heart.

You would be surprised how the corporals and first sergeants rate the men at Eustis. When we arrived there it was a cursing to and fro, but something is different here in the officers. They treat us more like humans and seem to know what real Army life should be like.

When you come into a camp you naturally go under quarantine for seven days.

They tried to make me throw away my letters, but I have every one of yours, even kept a few handy and read them coming down. Honest, I had so much fun. I'd yell out "Mail call!" and the fellows would all look and wonder where I got mine.

What am I going to do with the girl? She even goes home to her folks and I don't know how I can get connected with no phones there. I called Birmingham knowing you'd be surprised that I was here, but since you picked up and left so suddenly something must be wrong. With no phones I've spent such a miserable day not knowing.

This camp is really a swell place. It's just like a resort down here, so much quieter and pleasant. We have four weeks of training on tractors, trucks, anti-aircraft guns and 90 M.M. guns. After that our furloughs should start. The sergeant tells us we will be here for nearly six months, and will not go across when we leave this place. Can we believe it? I can't say.

This regiment is just being formed. We have a wonderful opportunity of building up fast here. They really are short on men. I was so sorry to leave Eustis, but now that we have the opening we have here and I'm closer to you and home, life is better again. 'Course we see nothing but each other around here. When we suddenly see a pair of shapely legs we grow panicky!

Our weekaversary. Why isn't there a song about Tuesday night?

My time's so short here I couldn't even go more than halfway to Birmingham after all. Every sucker here is from up north, so it'll be hard to find out anything about Alabama or anything else.

You must be short of stationery. I just got the most wonderful wooden postcard today. It didn't have a sign of a knothole in it. The fellows thought it was a howl, and I have it tacked up by my bed in the tent.

You haven't ever been in a tent with four other people who talk, blow trumpets, and tell some of the dopiest jokes. The rain is cutting in on us, too. The tent is large enough for five, but after your remarks about my long legs, if you'd chop me down to your size, the privates wouldn't have to dig such a big foxhole for me.

Speaking of which, we went on our first maneuvers today. Boy, did we have a day. First we made

44

manholes and trenches. Then we divided off in sections and squads. My squad had only seven men in it, so we didn't hurt ourselves in defending the foxholes. It's a responsibility to lead these fellows, but they followed my signs very well. The heat makes it hard on us - 110° in the sun. Can you beat that for April?

So many talk about going over the hill just because their girls haven't written. Some have even married two or three weeks after the fellows went away to camp. How do you think a soldier's morale can stay up with things like that happening?

Anything from you, even a note on a plank, is welcome.

The first day we get off our week of quarantine what do they do but put me on K.P. I got so little at Fort Eustis I didn't know how to act. It didn't take long for me to learn. Here I sit nursing a sore thumb from peeling carrots. I never did like carrots so very much. Now I hate them worse. You failed to give me a remedy for such things when you were taking that First Aid course. Now how am I supposed to manage? Should I keep a hot water bottle on it? Really, though, K.P. here is just a hint of what it was at Eustis.

Went off base for the first time last night to see our local town. It's so small if you took one big step you'd be on the other side.

Oh, if I could just get out of this world of misery and be in the life I used to have. There's so much to put up with now.

I'm so happy there can be a date set for us to see each other. Who knows? Maybe by that time I can get three days off and come to Birmingham. Sometimes if you want to work all week on some special detail, you can get a pass from Friday noon to eleven o'clock Sunday night. If I get that chance, here's one volunteer.

The Guest House seems a bit nicer than the one at Eustis. You can at least engage a room for five days for the sum of 75 cents.

When we were at Eustis we were just on seacoast guns, only the 155's and nothing else. We had our minds pretty well up on them. What do they do but change us to something else that we don't know beans about. We have to start from the ground up again on 90's used only for anti-aircraft. They've switched me from the guns to the range section. Really, that's like the brains of the outfit because if we don't get the correct data the guns aren't worth two cents. Did you ever wonder how the shells burst and how the guns exactly work? We have to know every kind of plane, friendly and enemy included. It's so much to know and so little time to learn the set-up. "Want" will be the reward. Money can't ever pay us for what we are going through here.

I've just changed my insurance to a new beneficiary. I've got a <u>wife</u> now, and she comes first, so you'll have to be my main lookout, see? That's the sensible thing to do, always put your wife first.

I'm sleeping out under the stars and moon tonight. It's the most romantic night we've had here. They took the top off of our tent today, just leaving our beds in the open. Gosh, the air is so sweet and clear here. Every time you breathe you can just feel the freshness come into your lungs. This would really be the ideal place, but the same thing stands in the way always. You aren't here.

It's our wedding anniversary, five weeks tonight. Please miss me some.

At first I didn't know today whether I was receiving mail from a glamorous wife or a hillbilly girl. Your crazy letter sounded like you were still in college. I still have all those letters.

Let's try to say something every day even if it's just a hard luck story. In this army the most fun I get is at least the chance to tell you all the sillys.

Mother and my sis sent one of my favorite cakes, the only thing I've gotten here from home so far. It makes me want to see them all so badly. The fellows here are up to their ears in cake.

By the way, do you know my favorite dishes? I'll tell you some time when the Army isn't around. I'm so anxious to start housekeeping I'll even help with the dishes.

What burns me up, I'm not there to open any of the wedding presents you're getting. I'll get even somehow. It's impossible for you to be a winner. I can even beat you at tic-tac-toe by mail. I didn't keep track of that last game we had going, though I believe you fudged on me.

Please thank your pupils for that delicious candy mint and the whatever-it-was that got mashed. Now I'm ready to face Saturday morning inspection. There's so little to look nice for around here, but we have to just for some old pug-nosed officers, so here I go, shining my shoes and slicking my hair.

Just saw a scary movie, <u>The Man Who Wouldn't Die</u>. I still feel chills up the spine. It would have been more enjoyable, though, if one soldier had taken his Saturday night bath. Should I take along some clean socks next time, too, to give some of these heathens a hint?

We had a real Mother's Day here yesterday. Some Baptist church asked Camp Stewart to send sixty boys to their homes and church service. I went with a couple of young married people. They seemed so glad to have me, even invited me back some time.

I hear you can stay with your wife at the Guest House. Won't it be the longest time if I can keep you here all summer?

Everything is not altogether rosy here, but I've gotten so I take things as they come and believe just as little as possible.

47

I must think of you a great deal because the boys say I tell them all they want to know in my sleep. I sleep all right. Then the waking up has to spoil everything.

Saw Bob Hope in My Favorite Blonde and never felt better in the theater in my life. Then I come out and find I'm still in an Army camp, but have some of the best pals here, so friendly and all.

I can tell when you are dragging because your pen puts out much more ink as if you were sorta resting on it.

I wanted to be there for the father-daughter game you had at the school picnic. I would have helped the other men beat their daughters. You would have played with them, of course, and that would have marked up another score for me in beating you. We are still keeping score, aren't we?

This is the longest weekend I've spent in Georgia. We're getting Saturday evenings off now, but I didn't get to go to Savannah to check on a hotel for us. A certain group caused disturbance after a few drinks, and some went over the hill or did other things, so the whole battery is getting to suffer. Now lights will be out at 9:30, bed check at 10:45, where we did have lights on until eleven o'clock. It burns me up to have to bear the penalty of some nitwits.

Everyone was given a thorough going-over Thursday morning. We had an examination on drill, guns, range, first aid, hygiene, military courtesy, and guard duty. We were marched out on the parade field and questioned personally by the colonel and majors and some lieutenants. If you didn't know, O.K., but if as a whole the battery didn't know about these subjects and wasn't well-trained enough, we would have 4 weeks more of it. The commander was very well pleased with our response, but they say we'll have this kind of procedure from here on out.

Some say after the 15th of June we may be transferred to Maine, New York, California—or even to Birmingham?

They want everyone in this battery to have a driver's license, government-style. We are a semi-mobile outfit, travel by truck, so everyone has to take a driver's test. Two of us from the range section spent the whole week on the instructions. Here we are, fooling around and getting behind in our range division. One man even went and asked to be taken off the darn truck, but they said everyone needed a license, so...

My younger brother may even be in the Army before I get home. Mother and Dad will have so much to give up if all of us have to go.

You can't tell when furlough comes. I might walk in any time. They call your name out at a minute's notice. If you have the do-ray-me, you can go, but if you can't produce, it's out. One of the fellows in my tent left just thirty minutes ago. He didn't make it known, no noise about it. Just wait until I get mine. The whole place will know.

We are going on one of those super-hikes again tomorrow. We have one every week now. Sometimes I believe we are in the Infantry. The range sergeant says we would probably protect some large plant or factory in a city like New York or Detroit.

If you're as happy and looking forward to June 6th as I am, the kids will get an easy exam.

What a mess this place is in tonight. A strong wind and storm outside, so look for anything. Along with thunder and lightning a boy from Texas is singing his hillbilly song. It's raining on every bed but mine. Am I lucky! The other fellows are shifting from place to place to keep dry, and someone just came running in to say their tent has split in half. He looked more like a drowned rat than a soldier. Now it's "You Are My Sunshine" the guy is singing. What a night.

Sometimes I laugh out loud when I'm reading one of your frisky letters. The fellows say, "Look at him grin," and I just smile that much more. They get letters, too, of course, even read them out loud, but do you catch me reading mine that way? <u>NO</u>.

As for future plans, we'll probably go to that resort at St. Simon's. I asked the range sergeant about it, and his eyes flew open. He says it's really a great place only about 60 miles from here.

We got in all brands of new equipment for our range section and can really go to town now. We've had to use our imaginations to the fullest about the instruments. It was such a hardship on both the corporals and the men.

We are leaving tomorrow for a battery picnic as soon after twelve as possible, about fifty of us. Going down to the beach about eighty miles from here, taking our tents along and planning to camp out if we can't get a cabin free. You'd look cute in a puptent.

They'll have a big dance, I suppose. We'll come back Sunday afternoon worn to a frazzle, more so than on a hike, I believe. The only other news is that your husband has been washing pots and pans again today. K.P. comes around so often down here because the battery is so small. I'm learning fast for our household.

The so-called weekend outing turned out to be just a dance and a lot of drinking. Since I didn't learn to dance before we married, I had no enthusiasm for anyone else to teach me. About sixty girls came down from Waycross, the nicest that could be found. It was the corporal's job to keep us cutting in and being nice to the visitors for all the trouble they had gone to, so I introduced myself to one. I had guts enough to tell her I didn't dance and if she wanted to, just sitting and talking to would be easier on both of us. You see what a mess I was in. She had been sick for two days, she claimed, and really didn't much care one way or the other, so we just talked. Finally, there was a Paul Revere or Paul Jones, and I slipped out of the picture, then - darn it - had to entertain another one for about 30 minutes. She was about knee high to a puddle duck. Time passed more quickly than I expected, though, and coming back I was the only one without a big headache.

As for your falling for Bob Hope, I used to think he was very funny, but after you expressed such deep feeling for him, he's out of my movie going for keeps. I balk when my wife gets to thinking I don't fill the expectations she sees in another man, and so early in married life, too, does she tell me about it! I'll like you anyway, Bob Hope or no Bob Hope.

Will this letter make sense? No. Well, that's the way soldiers get when they are away for days at a time and without a shave.

<u>Eight weeks ago at this very second we were married</u>.

We are definitely going to the seashore when you come, and I want you to stay as long as possible. We'll spend the first weekend at the King and Prince in Savannah, then in that neat pleasant Guest House on the post. It's only fifty cents a day, a dollar for me. I think I can miss inspection and meet you at the Service Club. Can it be possible?

If you come in to be on K.P. with me, the fellows would all be looking and watching so they'd have full tummies even without chow.

The whole camp wanted to read the symbols and doodads on my letter today. They even wanted the corporal to read it out loud. He didn't. Good thing. I'd have broken his neck.

No one could be counting days off as fast as I am until June the 6th.

The service club director you wrote to about working here says they don't have anyone on staff under the age of 25. Brunswick is her home town, though, and St. Simon's only 7 miles away, so she dug up some books and maps for us. Bring your fishing pole and a pink bonnet.

No use asking if you enjoyed your hero, Bob Hope, last night. He even talked about Georgia. Lights went out at 9:30, and we listened to the boy's radio in the next tent. I couldn't help but think you were listening to the same program.

Your last letter is in the screen beside my bed.

Old Sol is really bearing down in Georgia. When we get up we have to slip into our clothes a little at a time to get used to the extra warmth. (Could I be giving out military information?)

I've just glanced out at a plane being followed by the floodlight and what do I see? A beautiful full moon all going to waste unless you are using it on the sly.

Of course, with my wife beginning to draw almost six times what I do, she'll begin to think she is better than me. I'll show her. There are corporal and sergeant ratings coming up.

If we could just be sitting in the family swing tonight.

I'm on guard at the motor pool gate. Can you imagine how it feels standing in one place just looking? A lot of things can go through your mind then. I went on at 7:00. Something just peeping over the trees is the loveliest full moon. I watch every inch it moves, wondering if June 6th is ever going to get here.

Can you make this scribbling out? I'm writing on my knee. You have the advantage of me with a lap, you know.

Off for 4 hours, then I go back at 1:00 A.M. What'll I think of then besides looking out for the <u>officer</u> <u>of</u> <u>the</u> <u>day</u>? Darn him, anyway.

Jumpin' swamp rabbits! This time next week it's no telling where we will be. This was an unusually hot day, miss. Better bring your fan.

I went to church today at one of the chapels on the post. They give me the most quiet and lovely feeling every time I walk by them, every time I go inside. They are all alike, you know, just like the one where we were married at Eustis. But now you're not here. Well, neither are some others.

We are on alert this weekend for fires, air raids and such like and will be all week. Can't even get out of the battery area.

GOSH! I'LL MEET HER AT A CHOO-CHOO TRAIN IN JUST FIVE DAYS!

We had to move our tent today so they could build barracks. We have no screens like we had at Eustis, so I expect the flies and mosquitoes to take us off. No telling what will happen if it rains tonight.

When you come I'd like to meet you at a train again. I haven't had that privilege in a long time. I've talked with the 1st sergeant, who gave me permission to talk to the battery commander about a three-day pass. The best he could do was a pass until Monday noon, so told the clerk to make it out. The colonel and major have to pass on it, too.

It's a drip drip here and a drip drip there until the next thing we know the whole tent may flop on us. This has really been a day full of those June showers that make August flowers in time for my birthday. I hear that down in Georgia they stop the mails and have sky-writing on August 7th.

Oh, stop fooling around, Alfred. I have papers to grade.

Yes ma'am, dear teacher. On my Camp Stewart honor the letter I got this afternoon was a howl. You have put such mischievous ideas in your pupils' heads. You mean they've guessed with our surprise marriage that I love you? Why teacher, teacher, they're learning worldly things.

Sure you can't get a faster train? You'll have to ride all night. It may be late. But what do we care? We'll Be Together.

We are without lights here, but Whee! Whee! The pass has been signed, and along with that I just came back from getting the dates at the Guest House.

I'll be there just straining my neck for a glimpse of you before you see me.

With windows open to combat the summer heat, her train ride was dusty as well as slow. Servicemen of every rank and branch, with no food available aboard, scrounged apple pies from a café at one stop, then sliced the loot with their bayonets and gave her two big pieces.

At Savannah he did see her first. The delayed honeymoon weekend and another week in the cool, quiet guest house on the base formed a real marriage at last, complete with a wedding-ring set with seven diamonds from a family heirloom.

Meanwhile, Eisenhower took passage for England to assume command of the European Theater of Operations (ETO).

One of the nicest habits you have gotten into is always leaving me with a letter to fill the emptiness till I get sorta used to it. I wondered all day if you got the bus and liked that ride better than the train.

It's a good thing you weren't coming back with me. I just got in front of my bus door, and the crowd pushed me in. Some even climbed through a window. Today was spent mostly just getting ourselves straightened out in this new area, a lot of cleaning up what the other battery left behind.

I got in such a pattern in a week's time that I even miss going down to the service club to see you.

I've packed all of my letters from you in the bottom of my locker so I can have them together when I start on furlough. Seventeen boys left this evening. My time will be about the middle of July.

I don't care about staying in this tent all by myself.

Remember the corporal that sat across from you at chow? Well, he gave me the bestest compliment on you.

Any time anyone says or asks about my wife I just glow all over.

I know you'll be put to work at home this summer in that small community, but listen. Writing to me is part of your defense work, too, so don't let me down. You aren't teaching school, but I want to know if you like that place without me. I haven't ever written to you when you were there at home while I was the one away.

We haven't any equipment now because we had to give it up to the other batteries or turn it in when we moved. All we're doing is drilling, hikes and doing details.

I go on guard tomorrow night. I'm wondering if the moon will be as beautiful as last time. I know you'll be having a lovely time at the bridal shower, so that's what really matters. People at home are simply wonderful to give all those wedding parties for us.

Can I really say "Us"?

I have the softest job tonight. For no reason I know I was sent over to be orderly in our headquarters battery. It's better than walking or standing guard.

It seems everything is backward in our marriage. The showers are coming last along with the selection of china and crystal patterns. Wish I could be around when you come in so I could see your face. "Surprise! Surprise!" everywhere you go. While I think of it, did we get a rolling pin? You sound so busy back home, and the whole town seems to have changed on me.

The furlough looks far off again, and I'm just sitting here in the heat with water running down my back.

Here I thought when she got out of school she'd have lots of time to just stroll around and get fat. That's what I get for having such a busy-bodied wife.

People have been too good about gifts for our household. You certainly mention a lot of beautiful things. I can't help but be a little envious. I'd like to write a few personal expressions of gratitude myself, but men are such poor hands at a flowery thanks.

We have almost boiled in this place. I believe Georgia is the hottest area outside of hell. What will we do for dry clothes for inspection shortly?

I don't suppose I'll be letting out military secrets if I tell you we're out on the firing range. We expect to fire at the target on the plane some time next week, usually a sign you won't be in this same camp very long. You must be warned in due time. They have stopped all furloughs for the time being. I'm so far down on the list I fear I will be unable to get one at this camp. We aren't well-trained enough to do much damage yet, so will be stationed at some other place when we move. They're forming a new set-up here, planning to fill the barracks with Negro troops.

You can't imagine how the attitude of the boys has changed since passes and furloughs are out. Lots had planned to be home for the Fourth of July, over the hill, or just anything to do better than this. In my branch you have to take your turn, and if it never comes, you just don't get one.

I had a short letter from your brother today. The air corps is about to station him elsewhere. We went in service about the same time and maybe will move along together.

Rushing our heads off seems to be running in the family. If my day could be any fuller, it would have to have twenty-five hours. On the go day and night on the range, tired as dogs at eleven, then up and going at six. I work on the director, twisting buttons and gadgets until my thumb and index fingers both feel blistery. We have to hike to and fro from work on top of all the other we do. Loads of trucks, but they seem to be saving on gas and tires.

I had a surprise in the mail today, though. Stars and supporters if my wife hadn't sent me a box full of kisses, and every one had "I love you" printed on the paper. I'm eating one right now.

Lots of fellows have given up on ratings, but I figure it's very important, this job, so I stick myself in there as much as possible. Someone is going to make it. Why not me?

Won't it be wonderful some day to be ourselves at home? We can go together here and there, down to Mother's and Daddy's, then to your folks and all around to our brothers and sisters. When I think of this and am bound hand and foot, I get fighting mad.

I sent home today for my big picture of you. Have to have something to look at actually.

You wrote such a good line for our situation here, "O say can you see by the dawn's early light?" Well, frankly, if it wasn't for the exercise each morning we wouldn't know if it was dawn or retreat. We'll be firing day and night for the next ten days and seldom get in before midnight. Didn't even have the weekend off we were so busy. I pulled guard duty out by our range equipment. Could you picture a person sleeping out in the open with just a net over him? At one point I found a shady tree and caught up with some writing. No, I didn't produce any poems like Sidney Lanier.

Did you know tomorrow is payday? We get our first fifty, I hope.

The place is flooded with money the fellows don't know what to do with. Most of them are shooting those little bones. I could have wrung someone's neck, though, till he choked. We hiked to the range (4 miles, mind you, 8 round trip), came in around 4:30, got our money, ate chow, and were feeling pretty peppy until "Stand by!" We <u>hiked</u> <u>back</u> <u>out</u> to the range, and as soon as we got the instruments set up, it was "Close stations!" We were so tired and sweaty and <u>so</u> disgusted. We just go in circles around here.

Like mother, like daughter, I say. Yep, the gal takes all the sugar rationing in her hands. You may be at work, but you can't make me believe you don't like talking to any longhorn signing up.

One of the sergeants is being married in a few days, but some are coming back from furlough with divorces. No matter how much you wanted to be free, I think I'd be too stubborn to give an inch.

Let me make this short again. So many things have occurred today that my mind just won't function. On top of everything else, we've just come off an alert call, standing by for an hour for who knows what. I had just picked up my writing kit when the blast went off. But please, don't you ever get writer's cramp.

They brought the mail out to the range today. I had my ears pricked up, and sure enough got out of the chow line to get the best thing in every day. You don't know how I feel when I read these little notes you sent from all our friends. Aren't they the best in the world?

What have you and our folks planned for the Fourth? We'll be out on the range here, firing Saturday and Sunday. No more time off, it seems. We thought once we'd have the holiday, but there's no such a thing any more. We are strictly Army forces now, so have to be on our toes.

Just you be sure to stick to the issuing of sugar...only to me, mind you. This is just a rattling of emptiness, but I get such a kick out of teasing you.

If I could just get down to those salt waters of St. Simons again, I'd even bathe in the sand. I had the best time I ever had there, and have talked enough about water now I'm beginning to feel cool, p u f f, p u f f.

Yesterday in the tent I thought about what I was doing a year ago. We had a big family reunion for the Fourth at home, but that night the best yet. You and I couldn't get very close to the grandstand at the Fairgrounds for the fireworks, so we pulled my car up to the fence of the baseball field to watch. All the show happened to be on my side, so I had a good excuse to ask if you'd like to lean over closer to watch better. Then we drove for a Coke, or maybe it was our first banana split.

Tonight some of us went bowling in the little town and had such fun for a change. We even went to a double feature afterwards. This morning I got up bright and early and went to church. The local people were really nice. It was a Methodist church, so don't tell any of the Baptists there or they might want their wedding gifts back.

It's a relief not to rush today. Two days last week we didn't get to pull our clothes off or even our shoes. We all looked like tramps when we came into camp last night, sweaty, whiskery, and oh boy, what a dismal smell. We slept on the good old innerspring ground with only a shelter half and blanket to lie on. Were we stiff and bit to pieces by the insects of downtown Georgia.

What would you say if the range section grew mustaches? We decided in a ten-minute break Saturday that we would be the Mustache Range Section of Camp Stewart. Some may go through with it, but mine is getting curled up already. It tickles and bothers me so I don't feel I can put up with it for more than two more days.

Just married and still have sense enough to be a little happy.

I read the mail until they holler "Chow!", then came back and finished the letters. I wouldn't let anything interfere with mail, but if I don't go when they holler, I won't get any, you know.

We have spent three nights and days on the range this week. Got through firing last night. Yep, we fire more at night than we do in the day. I guess it's to get us in shape for all conditions.

A certain sergeant gave me a range of ideas about when we plan to move. It's around the same age of your brother of this month. I just want you to know that the buzz is in the air, and since we have finished firing it's very likely. Remember, it's possible to go overseas when we go from here.

Is anything wrong at home? Mother isn't well sometimes and has never been so long in writing. Maybe just busy? Aches and fears have crept into my heart tonight until this has just been the worst yet.

You know what I think of most.

Could I be a little homesick? It does make me so peeved for fellows to be coming in off furlough and mine not in sight. Days mean nothing now like this.

The little kit and candy came just when I was the lowest. We had been out on the range all night and had gotten up very early this morning to hike back. You should have seen the glow on my face when I got two packages, from you and your mom. I didn't rush to see what your mother sent, though. Was that mean? I felt so good after mail call that I went with some of the fellows to Savannah as soon as we could eat, shave, and catch a bus to town. We took it all in stride, walked our toenails off. I'm really bench-legged today.

We went out to one of the parks with pool, ball park and everything I never knew Georgia had. Went in swimming for about three hours, even floated a few feet since I can't swim. Had the best bathing suit that fit me like a glove at first, but got baggy in the seat when the water hit it.

I'm like your brother. We haven't gotten any kind of rating so far. I try and work my head off in that direction and have stood it about as long as I can, so this week I'll ask if there'll be an opening in my work. I can't go on and just be a buck private always.

Happy weekaversary, though you are somewhere else this moment, I know not where. At least getting thoughts off my mind each day might make life a real day instead of a blank.

After we were told we were finished firing, it seems we are not. We've spent the last five days at it until our little trigger fingers wiggle in our sleep. It goes to show you can't make any plans in the Army. The colonel gave us quite a talk, and from what he says we'll have plenty to do for some time yet. Tomorrow night we spend on the range again. Why any place we can lie down now feels good.

We have some of the biggest arguments sometimes after we come to our tents and have our bull sessions. The one subject we always get on is our wives and sweethearts. You should hear the different opinions. Some come out so bold and brave and talk about their actions in civilian life. They have the idea you can't have faith in a lady. That's when I rise up. It just goes to show why the world is in the shape it's in. The man and wife just don't have it in them to make a home as they should. 'Course a lot of fellows have the right to think the way they do. The girl has found someone and married him, leaving the fellow out here without a thing to look to, you might say, when this is over.

You may not realize it, but I'm in one of the hardest branches of service beside the Air Corps. This director I work on is such a complicated instrument that you can work for a year and still learn something. In all the firing we have hit the sleeve target more times, showing more accurate shooting, than any other battery on the post. One grouchy old officer had to compliment our section for such smooth tracking and accurate data sent over to the guns. Some hotshots have made such fun of the range section that we just had to fall back and laugh.

Our sergeant told me I was going to make a measly P.F.C. Well, it's a start. It's so hard to make advance in this section. So many have been to school at other posts, then shipped in here, so we have to hustle to keep up with them. It's not hard to make corporal once you get P.F.C., though. It takes constant work, and it's so hot that all you feel like doing is just lying down, as high as 120° and 130° this weekend. My nose has blistered over and over again until it peels off terribly.

You won't see all this I'm writing until you're back from Kentucky. Without a doubt you were the most beautiful bridesmaid in the wedding. I met your

cousin's new husband once. When he was down visiting
your people they had a party for him, remember?
During one game he got to kiss you on the cheek. He
may be a lieutenant and a real relative now, but if he
does it again I'll knock his commissioned head off.
For that I won't salute him!

> Temperature-Over 100°
> Groom-Very happy
> Time-Passes slowly

I have a little dew on my upper lip.
In all our work and struggle we had some of the
biggest excitement since I've been working in the
Army. The other night during our alert in the range
we were out on the director practicing tracking on the
lights. Five of us just fooling around and thinking a
plane might come over from the air base at Savannah.
Sure enough one did appear. The lights got on him
right away, and we turned our instrument on him just
as soon as possible. We tracked along for about ten
minutes, then suddenly two men came bailing out, the
pilot banked, and he jumped, too. The plane crashed
about two miles from us. You should have seen the men
kicking in their chutes. The search lights stayed on
them until they hit the ground so we could see to
track them. What a glow of light the plane put up
when it hit. We were so flabbergasted we didn't know
whether to call the captain or what to do, but he had
seen it already.
These fellows had to be found, so we in A-Battery
formed a search party. We couldn't get close to the
plane, but they said it was literally torn to pieces.
The motors were about six feet in the ground. I
wanted a piece of it, but the M.P.'s kept us all away.
We got in around 1:00 or 1:30, having to sleep in our
usual nest on the ground. We were all rather stove up
the next morning. I actually got to feel one of the
chutes of the pilots, though.

In about thirty minutes we have to hike out to the
range and spend the night. Oh, what an evening it's

going to be, full of ants, ticklegrass and nightmares. When I get your letters I put them in my left pocket in my fatigue jacket. Then if I sleep in my tent, I slip them in my pillow. With time taken up day and night on the range I might not be able to see you even if you come.

Get your things ready for Stewart. It looks as though we will be pulling out most any time now, so you'll have to come here. I haven't actually been homesick until I couldn't get a pass through. I didn't want to eat a thing last night, but this time next week you'll be here. At least we can depend on that.

The outfit had the biggest blowout last night, the best dance I have witnessed, not because I had a finger in it, but everyone seemed to take part and have a good time. I was on the committee to decorate, clean up, and do odds and ends like sitting at the door of the Service Club checking off the fellows' names as they came in, girls, too. I thought it might be so boring, but the fellows seemed so surprised to find me there and kept telling me, "I'm going to tell your wife." So many from other battalions wanted to rush the door, but we had all the boys the visiting ladies could handle. I wouldn't have gone out that door for love nor money because they all wanted to eat us alive for not letting them in. About 10:30 I gave the job up and slipped out across the way.

Guess what I did then. Made reservations at the Guest House for a certain Mrs. Rogers starting next weekend. You know the Army. We can't stay here for always. Maybe we can paint Hinesville red. Saturday, come quickly.

Besides rushing all day on the range we had to get ready for a big inspection tomorrow. I've scrubbed, polished, and re-arranged stuff in my locker until I can't bear to wiggle. Still have to clean my eating equipment, shave and bathe. In the morning bright and early I go on duty as a Table Waiter, come off it after chow, then slip into clothes for inspection. What a day ahead.

Please make Saturday come with a leap.

The hospitable guest house again furnished space for a marriage - meals together, talking together, going to a movie together, falling asleep together, even doing some washing and ironing like a wife or fixing the clasp on a suitcase like a husband. Then back to the daily grind in Georgia and Alabama, but apart.

Bataan and Corregidor had finally surrendered. A plan to gain combat experience in Egypt had collapsed. Fast ships like the British <u>Queen</u> <u>Mary</u>, depending only on their speed for defense, rushed troops without heavy equipment toward a crisis looming in East India.

And what about the crucial oil supply? Would a pipe-line to Alaska or an international highway toward ports in South America be useful?

The need to settle the German question became ever more obvious if bases in England and Russia could survive. The attack some had hoped for in 1942 might come the next year, but no one had devised or realistically suggested feasible tactical plans or requirements.

Salisbury Plain in England provided a suitable training ground. Otherwise, nearly everything else needed for launching an invasion didn't even exist, particularly landing crafts not yet in blueprint stage or crews for those which did exist, the Navy not accepting draftees. Some forces were being trained in Northern Ireland (the south part remaining neutral), but how to fit two million American soldiers on an island already densely populated? And what about food for so many, natives and new arrivals alike? The arable portions of land added all together were not larger than the size of Colorado. And how to construct—in time, or at all - the ports, camps, airfields, and warehouses necessary?

"Ike" Eisenhower found his genius for compromise and reconciliation valuable at every turn. To many a Brit Americans raised on cowboy movies were a pain. Here they were, like sheriffs coming after cattle rustlers to save the ranch, in this case England. Britain had stood alone for over a year and considered itself the real savior of democracy. Obviously the new commander-in-chief had much to accomplish in adjusting personalities for future harmony.

After every little breathing space the whole mess started up again.

———

Back in the same Army rut. I got so used to rushing down to see you that I feel simply lost in this barrack tonight. If it weren't for your picture I'd probably go to the Service Club just in remembrance of the best days I've ever spent in the service, the actual married life I've wanted.

Wish you were coming instead of going.

If I'm drowsy, it's due to the unexpected alert on the range last night, the worst night we've had yet. It rained all night, the tents leaked, we couldn't sleep, the boys were cross. I couldn't even write you either, doggone it. Your picture is so real it makes me think you're just standing by watching everything that's going on here.

I always wonder what you did on the train back home. Could you send me just a pinch of Tennessee dirt to let me know what Memphis is like now? I want to be there so badly before you go back to teaching. I think I could run all the way from the station and still be happy and full of pep when I reached you and my people.

I got the shortest but nicest note from the lady of my house today. When they called out P.F.C. Wesley's name, I literally shouted, "Here! Whoopee!"

From the account you gave of your trip home the bus was simply a practice job from beginning to end. Did you have to eat off the mantle after the long ride? I just knew you were in that awful rainstorm. Sorry I didn't have that plane chartered as I'd planned.

The last two days have been some days of days. We'll be so used to guard duty we'll do it in our sleep. Some new secret equipment came in today, so secret that three times as many guards as usual were placed around it. Then after 4 hours sleep we were forced to go on the range this morning. Finally got off this evening around 2:30 after doing some of the jammedest firing that has been done on the range. Boy, are the range section good in our battery!

This place is really lonesome. Even the Guest House seems to be all gloomy when I look in that direction.

So many people have asked if you are still around. I wish I could tell them she's staying with me for the duration. This Service Club has a good atmosphere for writing, but somehow the walk was so much longer and hotter today when I knew <u>you</u> wouldn't be here. I just picked out a table, and among the fellows was a gentleman that out of a clear blue sky asked me if I was lonesome. I asked why he asked me, or did I just look that way, maybe because a certain person went home just a week ago. He saw us on the bus Saturday on the way to Savannah and remembered you were the only girl there.

This is such a wet place I don't know whether my mind can get the rust off to write. Here's what I'm up against.

Writing you out on the range, having to use a lead pencil instead of ink, a few boys in the next tent trying to sing the blues and can't find the tune, and nosy bachelors peeping over my shoulder. They do it for fun, and I joke about it, but they should know they're not wanted and click their spurs and jingle away.

You can almost mark it down that I will go to Camp Davis on cadre to help form a brand new outfit. Today all the men were interviewed to find out what we liked, what we did now and before coming into the Army. We will be dismissed from all duties of the battery and may leave Sunday for the new post. We get paid Monday, so why the rush?

Good as we should be after all the firing we have done, what we did this morning was the very worst, and this was supposed to be on the record, too. We always do poorly on Monday. I think some of the trackers even saw <u>two</u> planes this morning.

There's nothing to do but fiddle around in different classes the Davis cadre are attending. We go with some new men to the rifle range tomorrow and still have our hands full, but that will give us experience in handling men. We'll need it at Davis. We even drilled them this morning for practice.

There were so many letters in the outgoing box I couldn't get the ones I'd written in without cramming. That little squatty woman around the Guest House popped up and asked if they were so big to my wife that they wouldn't fit the slot. I just gave her one of her chewing gum grins and said, "No, madam, not yet."

Every Tuesday I think of the night we were married. Weren't we dummies to think we were happy then? It's so much clearer now.

So you think my brother's name in the service will be as strange as mine. So much for being called by our middle names at home. And that's a fine how-do-you-do. She consents to marry the man, then talks about his name. It <u>is</u> funny we have to change the moniker we're called by when we go into services. What a world.

We rushed in this afternoon around 3:00. Most of the fellows are being issued clothing and equipment they have lost, or other stuff. We go back to the range tonight for some night firing. I shouldn't have to go since I am cadre for a new outfit, but the man that takes my place here hasn't quite caught on yet, and this is record-firing. After your nice letter today, I just had to whisper hello real loudly.

I've been a bad boy, fallen far short on my end of the writing this week, but there's no time. Lights go out, and there's no other place. Even last night when we came in at 9:45 there wasn't even a place in the Rec Hall because the fellows were having their beer and singing their hymns. I just gave up until this morning.

We had another trip yesterday. There have been weekends good and bad, but this certainly was the worst. You'll soon see why. Another camping trip to a lake 80 miles from Stewart. I was asked to drive one of 17 truckloads of men. We were so sore, so dusty that no one felt like swimming or dancing if they had wanted to. We took over the camp kitchen and served meals as we do here. Eleven trucks went to Waycross for the girls. They enjoyed riding in an Army vehicle. Everyone was having the bestest time until twelve midnight.

Then the trouble started. All the time the fellows were getting tighter and tighter—never so much beer, liquor and wine. They can't even bring a few cases of Cokes so some won't have to choose between beer and water, the strongest thing I'd swallowed.

All of the men were feeling their oats. Some got so pert they jumped in a boat and paddled out to the middle of the lake and turned over. They were so drunk they couldn't swim, but all made it to safety but one lone Texan. Around 2:30 A.M. everyone was awakened to check on who was missing. He was nowhere to be found. The fellows had waited all this time to report it. Two hours had gone by before the rescue squad was called.

We got the trucks down and used their lights, but no sign of him. We got back in bed, no one really sleepy, around 4:30 A.M. Up at 8:00 Sunday morning, then all out to search for him again. The divers literally covered the bottom, but due to the blackness of the water no one could see his hand before him. Most of the fellows left at 1:30 for camp, but I had

to go with the truck taking the piano back to
Waycross. A detail of 20 men remained to look for the
body.

We stayed until 5:45, then started back. It rained
so hard, and we traveled so slowly it was 9:45 P.M.
before we got in. No message has come from the lake
this morning. If you can top that for a weekend,
don't ever tell me about it.

The battery has been put on alert, so all are jumpy
for fear they will move at any time. Our cadre group
leaves tonight for Davis. My new address from now on
will be:

A Battery, 411th Sep. C.A. Bn. (A.A.)

Time I find someone I can run around with and talk
over some troubles with, they switch us around. It
makes it so hard to have no certain one you can depend
on in camp.

So many of the fellows can't see how any one girl
can take up a person's mind so. That's the way it is.

1942 waned with patterns of future activity and
relationships falling into place. Airfields in Maine,
Newfoundland, Labrador, Greenland, Iceland, and
Scotland would ferry planes for the ground-air
coordination now considered an integral part of
strategy. Also Britain must get used to the idea of
being an armed camp of Americans, and Americans, used
to asking questions instead of just obeying orders,
must adjust as well.

Ike, to escape the various hassles in London, had
retired to a small cottage in the outskirts with only
four on staff - a naval aide, an orderly, and two
sergeants to maintain house and food supply. The
Prime Minister fought him on details, but remained a
friend throughout.

To encourage civilian morale and send an active
message to Russia during a period of seeming doldrums,
an assault would be made soon on North Africa,

supposedly neutral territory but actually run by Hitler's people. Success of the venture could forestall a naval blockade of Gibraltar if Spain decided to join forces with Hitler. The Mediterranean also needed clearing of enemy air bases and shipping. In command would be General George S. Patton, Jr., a shrewd battle leader with a dramatic persona, carefully calculated, and a loyal staff.

Part of Patton's future Third Army was already assembling at Camp Davis in North Carolina. They would be First Army for the invasion, then Patton's men for the rest of the war.

NORTH CAROLINA

Norma Rogers

You'll just click those spurs too frankly for words
when you see this place. I feel almost like the day I
came to Eustis. It's so large and so unfamiliar, and
no one around in the barracks except our fellows that
came in today. You can tell by the weeds, dust and
mosquitoes that no one has been here in quite some
time. We'll just have to start from scratch.

Old Stewart and even Eustis looked good to me, but
this place I don't know. It'll be some time before
we'll actually get settled down to work.

Some of the sergeants and lieutenants brought their
wives on up with them. One had the tiniest baby on
the train, and did he sound off this morning at
reveille. The whole battery on the coach came to
attention.

With the straight-back seats, drunks, stuffiness
and baby changing we didn't get much sleep on the way.
Know what I did when I got my bed made up, though?
Guess. I placed your little head up on the shelf over
my cot. Hey, I just looked up and honest, you are
still smiling, on my corn-fed honor. The main partner
now, my chief buddy, tells me he can't go to sleep
with such a lovely lady looking down on him.

I'm glad my brother is in the Air Corps. He might
learn a good trade and help in defense, too. Your
bud's fate is still uncertain, I hear. I just hope we
all see very little action.

We get a three-day pass this weekend for Labor Day.
Every member of A-Battery is on guard tonight. We
have only 24 men now, and yes, we do K.P. and guard
until they send our men to train. What a camp.
Everything seems so dead around here. We get up, take
our time, have the best meals we have had in the Army,
then do what little there is to do.

Just one thing. How in the world can a man call
his wife and let other people call her "the old lady"?
Some say it so innocently. A number have even spoken
of you that way, but I let them know somehow that I'll
never call my wife that. You are the best I have.

You should see our hair beginning to fall out. We got in a mob of rookies yesterday and last night. Here we had our minds made up for a good long rest, and in came more than we knew what to do with. I wonder if I could have been as green as some of these fellows looked and acted. We moved into a new area at the last minute Friday night, worked until ten o'clock, then last night it was 1:00 and 2:00 A.M. before we got to bed. Maybe when we get settled down it won't be such a headache.

I did take time out for a show, <u>Mrs. Miniver</u>. Some of the fellows don't especially like these pictures, but they run so true to life. They had one thing I won't put up with, though - two beds. That's simply a waste.

How would it feel to be in this terrible uncertainty and know I didn't have someone I wanted to live for? There would be so little use somehow to want freedom of speech or religion or the home I wish for. That's what makes me so fighting mad, the kind of folks that want to take away what people live for, just like me. I have that to look to now when all is well and safe again.

I talked to 10-15 men all day today, giving commands of right and left face, about face and dress right. They caught on rather well for the first day, but my mouth gets so dry I can hardly talk.

I have you only a foot over my head when I go to sleep.

I'm in the Service Club, away from all the corporals and sergeants and noisy and talkative people who take up time and say nothing. One fellow just talks the ruffles off my shorts and brags on himself so. You know how he rates with me.

You should see the group of men we are training. I never have seen a bunch of boys want to learn and try as hard as they do. Most are young, only a few older ones. Today we marched them down to the theater for a training film. The looey in charge went from front to back and then back to front. He whispered to one of the corporals we had the best so far. We drill them till all of us are blue in the face. The sergeant lost his voice yesterday, so who takes over but Corporal Rogers. I'm called that altogether now although the rating won't go through headquarters till next week by the 15th.

Now that you have started back to teaching we have two in our family instructing. You may not realize it, but we have that job, too, on the jump from 6:00 A.M. to 9:00 P.M. every day, more than we did at Stewart. These new fellows watch every move we make. Even in the P.X. they're watching us like hawks. You may have pets in school, but there's no such thing in my class.

This training to me is just the opposite, in fact, of what it should be. We get more out of it than the privates! Some day I hope you will be able to see how the third platoon out-marches everyone else.

It's no use wondering if the girls at school were glad to see you because when they say they wouldn't come back if it weren't for you, they mean it to the bottom of their little hearts. You can't be done without in this world, so don't try to wiggle out of your saddle.

The people at home certainly have been their best at giving us gifts, haven't they? When you told me today about having to put all our wedding presents away, I wanted to be there so you'd never have to.

No, I haven't had a quiet few by myself. I just thought with writing diagonally on the paper instead of straight I could seem to go as nutty as possible and get a discharge from the Army. If you put on an act well enough, they might think you were some kind of conscientious objector and give you a pardon in two shakes. If I go around like Dracula with both eyes crossed, they'll see they're really losing money by keeping me around. Wouldn't it be awful if you had to tear up your teaching contract and come home to nurse me back to saneness or would I have to go with the other veterans?

The days here are so near the same now that if I tell you what happens today that goes for tomorrow, too. Most of the time is taken up with the drilling of the men backward and forward, this way and that. Sometimes it gets tiresome, but again I do enjoy some of it because I know we got the best end of the bargain. We have heard from some of our battery, and their address is now New York, New York, just waiting for a boat, it seems.

Since there are but three of us that can drive a jeep, I'll have to help in guard duty tonight. We guard some areas by just driving around every 30 minutes. I have from midnight to 4:00 A.M.

On the go from 5:45 A.M. to 5:00 P.M. each day. The fellows simply went wild yesterday when we took them out on the 90mm guns thinking they'd be able to fire a few rounds before the day was over. They ran up rubbing their hands together as if to say, "Just let me get my fingers on it." Then the battery commander just lectured and instructed for an hour.

The other night in the barrack the sergeant and I were sitting in our room talking. All at once we heard something like a cat and dog fighting and a hog running. We sprang to our feet and opened the door to find one of the fellows doing the act he had put on one night on the Major Bowes Amateur Hour. He was so good we made him keep it up. In all my life in the Army these fellows, in our barrack especially, are the jolliest I have seen. We try our best, according to Army procedure, not to mingle with the privates, but catch ourselves doing it now and then anyway. To be informed on this and that, officers now wear one set of bars on the collar and the other on the left side of the cap. They claim these are less visible to the enemy, so in case you have seen them that way, please salute and cut away sharply - eyes, too.

I miss your joyous face and voice.

This day has been a <u>Jonah</u>. We still have inspection on Saturday as we had at Eustis, so much to watch, so much to do, mind going in whirls trying to keep everyone busy and doing what is to be done. We had lots of responsibility at Stewart, but you don't know the half of it here.

One thing I have to do day in and day out is put up with longwinded stories. With so much to accomplish I've become almost impolite, gazing out the window, sometimes just picking up my hind parts and walking away to break the pattern. Some folks never know, do they?

Let's always do something special on Saturday night, our date night, if it's nothing but make fudge. We can have so much fun together if we can just get around to it. Why does that word "if" always stand in the way?

We were rewarded for our work on the battery area for inspection. Sometimes an officer comes through like a fly on a straw that couldn't have seen anything if he'd had super eyesight. Yesterday it was altogether different. The battalion commander started with headquarters battery, then went to B, C, D, and then our own battery last. We stood around sweating and tense. Corporal Rogers was in charge of the upstairs, so when he poked his nose up, I hollered "Attention!" What do some of the fellows do but break out in a cold sweat and fall on their feet, Cpl. Rogers saluting at the same time. He gave us "At ease" and walked around like the inspector does when he inspects our barn for the Health Department back home. I walked through the other barracks, and I don't see how they passed. Maybe we stress little things too much, but we were taught it at Eustis, so we have it in our bones.

Mother asked if I want to sell my car. I sent back a big NO and told them to run it as much as possible until <u>we</u> get there. Someone else wants to buy my tires. He's a dunce if he thinks I'll sell. If the home place weren't so big they wouldn't feel our going away so much.   They seem to be having the best year with the crops and cows, just need help to harvest.

I've just had a dental inspection and a filling replaced.   A splendid job that isn't costing me a cent.   It's the Scot in me, see?

You don't know how high my feet are off the ground. This important G.I. is in charge of quarters tonight. Don't tell the general they're on the desk.

A new battery commander is coming in around the 1st or 15th of October, and we don't know what changes he might make on weekend passes.   Here's one person that's going to put up a cry, new or old B.C.   I haven't had a furlough at all and but one three-day pass since coming into the Army eight months ago, so I should get something.

You should have seen me down with the maps last night, bothering all the noncoms to get the quickest route to Charlotte for our weekend.   The ticket agent didn't know his face from first base, so we figured it out when I came back to my room.

Now that Uncle Sam has seen fit to have lots of mail in my pouch again things go off so happily.   In the last few days I've heard from everyone that has written while I've been in the Army, both our brothers, your mom and dad, and especially three from Super-person!

You've read and sung about the Carolina moon.   You should be here now when it's full and so clear, so golden and pure that it actually looks as though it's shining for just two people somewhere.   The idea of you in a church choir is the best yet.   When I get my furlough, I can come and hear you sing, but don't think I could sit by myself.

We just ate the last piece of that candy you sent. Oh, was it good.   The fellows enjoyed it so, too.

Feeling-Blue
Place-Service Club
Why-To avoid company

You busy? Put down the fingernail polish. I've read everything in the paper twice, so you'll just have to put up with my foolishness. If I say I'll buy you a coat or red flannels for the winter, will you meet me in a certain part of Carolina on the 16th? Well, I must say it doesn't take much to buy you.

Last night I went on guard, corporal only, and girlie, did it rain frogs and jack-rabbits. The fellows got soaking wet before we could get coats to them. It came down in sheets, then turned <u>so</u> <u>cold</u>. Most of us have been wearing jackets all day. There's a fire in the furnace at the Service Club, and does it feel <u>good</u>.

Something has been on my mind for some time. Since we came to Davis, everything has been the same course. I wondered about going to O.C.S. It seems we will stay here and just train men and send them out. I want to get higher, but everyone I talk to in O.C.S. says the school is living hell, and they're sending the officers overseas as fast as they graduate. Maybe I should forget the whole idea.

You should have been here this afternoon. I needed you to help in the singing. After we stood retreat, they gave out some Army song books in the battery. The fellows wanted some little ditty, so what does the sarge do but call out Corporal Rogers to lead the dopes. We tried "Dixie" but it wasn't too good, so next we did "Wild Irish Rose." Anyone can sing that, you know, and we all had fun and stretched our chow channels. What a time we have sometimes.

The little good luck clover came today. I've fastened it to my dog tags. The side of my room is covered with reminders of you. I may not pass inspection some day.

Since I couldn't have you as my date tonight, I helped get together a social for the fellows. About 50 were polishing themselves up to go when they realized I wasn't getting ready. Some never even knew I was married to such a special lady and seemed so surprised. They see the mail handed out, though, even get a little pert about it, but a letter from you is no joke.

It's so hard to keep warm now with the only cover we have. Sometimes I use raincoats, overcoats, anything with weight.

As we expected, two new officers came in, a captain and a 2nd looey. They both look very dignified and determined. We'll have to watch our step for a few days or the non-coms might be in the doghouse.

You may feel like twisting my nose and curling my head when I strain and try to hold back what I'm going to say next. I so looked forward to the 16th in Charlotte with you, but it looks as though I'll be in <u>Birmingham</u> two to three days ahead of that! My name is third on the furlough list, and they started on the 12th, so I should be among the first to go. It's the most wonderful news I've heard here and know for a fact. When I get those papers, straight to Birmingham will it be.

Just pray it all happens much sooner than we expected.

"What can you expect out of these Tennessee hillbillies?" these Yankees say when I have to stop and think what day it is.

I couldn't help but laugh today when I got my mail. The fellows were crowded around and saw your decorated envelope before the corporal could hand it to me. The giggly ones had the biggest laugh, even got brave enough to ask if it was from my wife. You just can't put on a thing, get a haircut or do anything without someone's noticing.

The boys don't know it, but I've slipped away from their scrubbing for a while. I closed the door as I came in the room so they think I'm busy cleaning up, too, I hope. I can hear them grumbling, and of course some others are telling jokes and singing. They do very well after getting started. They all got paid today and can't wait to play cards.

All the barracks but ours had put a stop to gambling, so we used what influence we had to stop it here. All the cooks are in our group. When we told the platoon to cut it out, they rose up real cursing mad and went to the captain, who gave the whole battery permission to play when they please and gamble as much as they please. What can two or three do with so many? So we have to put up with it. My pay seems to get less instead of more each month. Maybe I should try my luck. Insurance, laundry, dry cleaning and allotments make that $54.00 look like the $21.00 days.

You can't make money in the Army, I've found that out.

Without the main person here, we still had a celebration with that party kit you sent. When I pulled it out during chow Sunday, the jack-in-the-box trick scared the daylights out of some of our corporals and sergeants. They just flew up their hands and sat stiff with eyes wide open. Any package I get the boys want part of it, so I invited them up, and we stirred up a second Fourth or maybe the coming six-month anniversary of our marriage.

These days are so dreadfully long that at night this soldier wants to close all doors and not see a rookie until morning. Can you see how I may seem a little cross, even a little rough at times? What a handful all day. The sarge was out doing something with the height-finder, the other corporals were on guard, so it was me with all these soldiers. We worked with the rifle all morning, sighting and manual of arms. This afternoon we went on a hike, 10-12 miles. If you think that a school class is a job, you should have 30-35 grown men staring you in the face not knowing what to do until you tell them. When I see all I love on furlough for such a long time, fifteen days off post, I wonder if they won't have to draft me again. I've looked forward to it for eight months.

Today was the busy sort of day, like yours only in an Army way, the whole day on the range shooting 22-rifles. We have some real sharpshooters here. We spend the day coaching and giving them some extra pointers.

As for other news, <u>furlough</u> <u>papers</u> <u>are</u> <u>signed</u>. I leave <u>early</u> <u>Saturday</u>. You didn't <u>know</u> that?

His mother and father saw a son in uniform for the first time. The war had come home at last, but surrounded by family, farm, and loving friends, he found the furlough all he had hoped and more. He looked so handsome. She looked so happy. The little town glowed at the first sight of them as a married couple.

Even if there had been time to listen to a radio with all the social goings-on the news would not have mentioned a hush-hush operation called TORCH, the North African invasion still a closely guarded secret. The British being in disfavor with the French it had to be on surface an American operation to encourage either help for the cause or at least no resistance. British soldiers coming in later would wear American uniforms and drive American vehicles to preserve the fiction. A beach-head in unfamiliar rough terrain that had not seen a military campaign for centuries would be hard to hold at best, but the Germans simply could not be allowed to land in Spain as a future base.

Fortunately for the soldier in North Carolina his major problem after furlough had only been a battle with a clock.

Coming out of Birmingham on the bus the old moon was up and just shining in the windshield in my face. I watched you out of sight and almost waited for the 11:30 bus, but it's a good thing I didn't. The other men that left when I did got back on Monday night and thought I had gone over the hill. If I had taken that late bus I would have been A.W.O.L for the whole day. The first sergeant would have thought I was late if the clerk hadn't set him right about the date. As it is, all is well, and I'm a real corporal now.

We got into Wilmington at 9:30 P.M., and a fellow going to camp in his car was looking for riders. A bunch of us piled in at fifty cents each and got back at 10:30 before that midnight deadline. I was never so tired of just riding, couldn't sleep when I got to my bunk. You should have seen the fellows' eyes pop open this morning when they saw me. They even missed me.

Furlough was so much like life should be, don't you think? With both of us at home, at church, and out to dinner with other people, life was a dream, it seemed. Going home with you as my wife gave me the biggest head and chest around. I'm listening to Henry Aldrich and Baby Snooks just now, but try as hard as I may I can't get Birmingham on the radio. The closest is Atlanta. Radio is such a help these days.

I now have to catch up on guard and other duty, so I'm in charge of quarters tonight. A few minutes ago we had a fake blackout. Some dope heard the fire engine go down the street and ran out hollering, "Lights out!" We put them out for a few minutes. Then I called head-quarters to check and found it was just a mistake.

There's so little new here I only want to re-live furlough. The times I loved the most were those when we were with my folks. We haven't actually been with them as a married couple. It almost seemed, too, at church or the different homes we visited that we were married before I left for the Army. One of the nicest was the whole day we spent just to ourselves, shopping around and seeing a movie together.

I was getting my bedding together to take in the office last night to sleep there in case any telephone calls came in. Gathering up the blanket, I caught the radio aerial, and it fell six feet off the shelf to the floor. The cabinet is crushed, and Kate Smith is coming in with a loud squeak. I could have cried. I like a radio for the news, quiet music and good programs, but the ocean is so close it makes even ordinary reception bad.

You would have enjoyed looking at the water today. We went to the shore to clean our guns and practice on the equipment. The others had all been down while I was on furlough, so it was new to me. They had hiked down while I was gone, 14 miles in one day, stayed all night, and didn't get back until 9:30 P.M. Am I glad I didn't get in on that! You can catch all the crabs you want, so we'll have crab soup when you come. They are such filthy things, though. I don't see how anyone could eat them unless he held his nose.

I've been married to you thirty weeks now. Just remember, a man isn't worth shooting until he finds his mate. I'll always be a little selfish with you because so far other people have had you around more than me.

I've always heard that it takes around a month for a man to get back into the swing of things after his furlough. Well, you should see us fellows that come back. We catch ourselves with a gaze in our eyes sometimes, just dreaming of something far off.

Do you think we'll ever have a quarrel that will amount to anything?

Reveille is usually around 7:30 on Sundays, so we sleep late and get fat. We eat breakfast, then go back to bed. Today I put on my best suit and went to chapel, though, so you can't scold this Baptist.

We had the most sane Halloween here I've ever spent. At home I loved the parties. We could dress as tacky and silly as we wanted to. Once we boys put the Railway Express wagon on the post office porch. We even rolled a log up to the bank door one time so the manager couldn't open it without cussing a little. He was a Baptist, too. Will those days of fun and little care ever come again? I fear sometimes that they have gone forever.

I have pricked my finger so many times sewing these corporal's stripes on. You could do it without a waver. First I get the correct space, then pin them on where they should be, then go up and down just a-pushing and a-shoving with that thimble. I have one stripe on and another one started, but thought I should lay down my knitting and talk to you.

Summer life in Army camp seems to slip away somehow, but these cold nights with nothing to do get awful tiresome. I've always hated winter. This year I'll hate it worse. Days are so short and nights so long. Sometimes I think it's no use writing, but at least I can say I did talk with her tonight.

No one gets as many thoughtful gifts as I do. When a package came today, I thought it was something I'd left behind on furlough. Instead it was cakes I can make myself sick over, so many kinds, where to stop? I passed them around, of course, and the fellows think you are the sweetest wife in the 411th. No one has the backing at home that I have. The thoughtfulness counts as much as the gift. Just "Thanks" isn't good enough.

The days stay the same. We are going out to the range and catching the swift cool wind off that ocean. Boy, it'll cut anything from whiskers to toenails off you. My face becomes so windburned and dusty it seems it's on fire sometimes. All the fellows' are the same. We look like a <u>real</u> bunch of rednecks with dust in eyelids and hair. Some day we'll snap a shot of the gang on the director and send it to you. Want one?

The program is so rushed now. They want the fellows trained in so quickly. They say we are behind schedule now, but I feel our men know the instruments much better than any of the other batteries. They try hard, and that counts a lot, just knowing what to do.

Saturday the big Camp Davis football team got their pants literally ripped off, the first football game I'd seen in some time, and one of the lousiest. Two bands did their part along with the cheerleaders, but our men weren't in there to win. You should have seen how the bands spelled out "Camp Davis" during the half. Rather impressive. After the game I fiddled around with the gang a bit, but all back in camp by 11:00 P.M.

I want to see if I can ride back and forth with the sergeant during the time you are here. He leaves around retreat every evening, stays with his wife, and reports back around reveille each morning.

It does make my step lighter to think of you.

In the guard house again, M.P. for the first time, which calls for us to be more on the jump than ever. The guards have charge of the most important buildings and plants, so naturally have to keep all eyes open for fires, thieves and sabotage.

One corporal and three privates have to help take down the flag at retreat, so we had that experience of handling Old Glory with kid gloves. I have seen pictures, but never quite knew how it was done. I'd like to have a picture made here some day for old time's sake.

So your brother's finally headed overseas. He'll be all right, though. The men in our family are coming out of this thing bigger and better men for it. Don't worry.

Her brother, turned down by the Navy when he tried to enlist at seventeen right after Pearl Harbor, served in the Eighth Air Force scheduled to prepare the French coast for invasion by low-level bombing. As attack plans heated up, Americans would take the day shift required for precision work, and the gallant RAF, which had held off the Luftwaffe all alone for a year, would work at night.

Currently activity in the air centered about Gibraltar as American troops pulled their onslaught at Casablanca. Troops aboard the invasion boats were almost as surprised to be there as North Africans were to look out and see them coming. Trained in Scotland in miserable weather and delivered by boat crews assembled at the last minute, they got their first instruction in use of the bazooka, a primary weapon, from an officer aboard ship who had at least read the instructions.

Eisenhower, supposedly in Washington, awaited news of the attack in a cold, damp underground room at Gibraltar. As he remarked later, it was a world of feeble light bulbs and drip-drip. Above ground every foot of the airfield sported a gas can or part of a plane.

The troops, never before committed to battle, were to land as seekers of friendship, not as occupying forces but cooperating with locals to clear out the Germans. Obviously the Arabs they met on landing hadn't received the news. Reaction ranged from apathy to outright hostility.

Back in the states their service buddies planned to celebrate the ending of World War I.

––––––

It's our Tuesday night in the barrack, and the rug's rolled back for our all-time favorite, Bob Hope. But that's not all. Tomorrow should do Armistice Day up brown for Camp Davis. Different battalions will compete in sports, games and work with guns. First of all, a parade will take up the entire morning.

Today I got a letter from Mother that Dad must have carried in his pocket all day on the tractor. It was so dirty, but that didn't affect the contents. My sister's having to move to Memphis for her job—gas rationing, I guess. Getting back and forth every day impossible, I imagine. Won't that big house be empty now?

It's the coldest day here since this soldier has been in these swamps. For the parade we had orders to wear only our shirts and trousers, no jacket. We've been frozen all day. My hands are still stiff. Can't even make a fire in barracks—some part is missing. We tried to throw out our chests and pull in our chins, but were so cold we couldn't look our best. Still all joined in the contests and had a boyish time. The games were really rough, strictly he-man such as Man-of-War, piggyback, football and drop-the-handkerchief.

At 11:00 o'clock all were called to attention for the moment of silence, and all stood in the direction of the flag. Your church bulletin said Birmingham would do the same. It was sort of funny, though. We even kept our ears strained toward the radio in case someone had a second armistice overseas.

You might know there'd be some sort of beer party to celebrate. They've already bought 17 cases of it and no telling what else, so look out. Some of us may bring a strange blonde back to the barrack. I'll hang around for a while, then Sarge and I will slip off to a show.

Just keep on thinking of me.

Weekends are so dismal. Your suggestion may be the cure. Last Sunday I attended the 10:45 service for 514th men and a different chaplain for a change. Got there early as all Rogers are accustomed to and what does the new man do but let me help select the songs and put the numbers on the register board. I felt so important. A good boost in the right direction.

Yesterday morning we grabbed our packs full of blankets and anything else that would keep us warm and went on one of the longest hikes ever. Worked until noon, stopping only for ten minutes out of each hour for rest. Around 15 miles we walked, ate our lunch, then put our guns in place just as if we were setting

up to defend some position. The place was so swampy
and wet that we had the awfullest time getting the
guns in. They would just go down in the wet soil.
'Course the truck <u>would</u> stick and have to be pulled
out. We had just pitched our tent for the night and
bedded down after spending all afternoon getting in
position. Then just after dark what do they do but
give orders that everything had to be pulled out.
These guns weigh 17,300 pounds, so you see how they
mire down in such soft ground. People who map these
positions out never have to fool with guns, so they
never know what we run into. It was after midnight
before we got the last one out. We were so cold and
wet we had to stand by the fire to dry.

We rose early around 5:00 o'clock, had chow,
cleaned up the area and got ready to move out for
camp. I have no blisters, but it's hard to get
limbered up again. Some of the older men were afraid
to lie down on the wet ground for fear they wouldn't
be able to get up the next morning. All is quiet here
for the lack-of-sleep, footsore and weary. We hiked
19 miles today, so naturally most of us will turn in
early. What looked good to us in the cadre was that
the men gave their best and stayed in there and walked
the whole way, although they had blisters and pain.
We do have the smartest and jolliest fellows I have
seen in an outfit. The humor we keep up is what
brings us through. When we can laugh and tell our
different experiences time seems to pass off some way
faster.

What do you think we men think when we have to stay
out like we did last night? So many of us say
sometimes how we would love to be starting for home
tonight. We live because we have someone who loves
us. A man does want to know that you love and miss
him. Tonight I went back and read all the letters you
sent me this week, read them all over again.

I have to tell you all these things. No one else
would care to listen.

We've just finished the last cookies you sent.
They stayed so fresh for such a long time. I'd like

to have the formula when our Uncle gets through with me. Since I can stay in the squad room, only the fellows that come in to visit us get any hand-out. 'Course we have <u>lots</u> of <u>friends</u>.

Clean as a spanked baby, that's me just now. You didn't know I had started to school again, did you?

I'm attending the Chemical Warfare school this week to get some information for myself and, too, to bring back to the outfit. It's important that all should know about this stuff. Some day they may start using it, and what damage they will do if we're not prepared.

No mail for nearly a week. Sometimes I wish my ration card wasn't so short of you.

With me looking so downcast at mail call yesterday I certainly hit the jackpot today. I've gotten so I can pick your blue letters out of all the stack even at a glance. If I don't see one, I walk away and let the mail boy bring up the rest.

With us being so advanced in firing they want us to get more training in setting the guns, director and height-finder more quickly. That's the real reason for all the hikes, I suppose. We have a 25-miler (one way) set for tomorrow, but since I'm in a school and have to be in class, another fellow and I will stay here and hold down the fort. Gosh, I'm glad. The school lasts only a week, so we will have to attend every class.

Now you need not have lockjaw or an attack of growing pains. I just got notice that I'm chief of section and a <u>Sergeant</u>. This went into effect the 15th, but notice didn't reach the battery until today.

We also heard from a man we left at Stewart. Everything sounds the same, but they have twice the number of men as we had there. He has the best eyes for our instrument of anyone we know. We're trying to get him up here with us.

But it's <u>you</u> for <u>me</u>.

Just think. We'll be celebrating your birthday and our weekly anniversary Tuesday night. What I want most is this time next year to be there for all the celebrations.

Here my thumb has just healed from all the corporal needle-pricks, and what comes but another lovely stripe. I had everything sewn on but my blouse. Now there'll be another week of stitching.

Have the bestest birthday and Thanksgiving for both of us. Eat lots of all that good Rogers food. It'll do you good. I just don't want you looking at any sailors on the way, see?

With things stacked up in our minds to do when we get our own home, it'll take to the end of time to finish them all.

Most Mondays may be blue to some people, but as long as a person can get mail, "White Christmas" is my theme song.

Today has been successful, I suppose, leaving out a few odds and ends. We went out this morning and finished camouflaging certain gun emplacements. This afternoon the guns and other equipment were taken out to the beach and put in firing position for target practice.

We just came back from a meeting of the officers and non-coms. Now after every hike and field problem all the officers and the chief of section discuss the problems and faults of the project. It really helps to point out the mistakes to avoid next time. Now we've had more experience in setting up position than we had the whole time at Stewart.

Something happened to my surprise today. When we came out as usual to stand retreat at 5:15, there was no one to take charge of our platoon, so I took position. Then the sarge came out and stood beside the other men. When the bugle had stopped, the B.C. bellowed out, "Corporal Rogers!" I did a right face, Lord knows how, and came in front of him. I was a little shaky, too. Imagine! Yes, 3 other fellows had promotions and came up, too. The men acted like your kids, calling me "Corporal," then in a stammering way, "I mean Sergeant Rogers." Funny.

She says she loves me. I begin to believe that she does.

It's the biggest day of the week and year, too, I betcha. Happy Birthday, and if I can say it in the same breath, "Happy Anniversary," too. We have to make the best of this one because it may be years before we can have these two important dates on the same day, see?

Some think such things are so unimportant, though. Like one man here. When I spoke this morning of its being your birthday, he said, "Just when is my wife's?" as if he didn't really remember, and he's only 7 or 8 years older, too. It's such an important date to me because if there were no you, it wouldn't matter whether it was night or day. If thinking waves could pick up brain waves, you'd know I'm thinking of you so hard.

Just remember where we were last year at Thanksgiving. Sometimes we think we are catching it hard, but think of the things we have that others do not, our health, being able to see you and my folks, that Christian home all us kids were brought up in, the blessing of not being overseas yet. God knows and has His ways about us, doesn't He? Whenever we think back to a year ago, we couldn't have planned to save our lives what has happened to us. Last year I didn't have a special wife to be thankful for.

Thanksgiving for the men in the armed forces was the best it could possibly be, I do believe. We spent the day until 2:00 P.M. on the range doing just as little as possible. We saved our dinner for the afternoon meal and had soup for lunch. Got in camp around 2:30, dressed up in our blouses and went to see Camp Davis and North Carolina play here on the post, then came back for supper at 5 o'clock. Even had tablecloths on the tables, and not only turkey to eat, but lots of English peas, dressing, sweet spuds, beer, coffee, candy, all kinds of pies and cakes. Some ate so much they were in misery afterward. Everything was well-cooked and good, but we think wouldn't it have been nice to have had that dinner at home. When I saw other soldiers with their wife or best girl, I did get jealous.

With milk prices as they are folks at home should be comfortable for a while. Something that scared me was the bull getting Dad down. Did he get bruised or crippled in any way? Tell me how things looked.

I've already used the little surprise you sent. That sewing kit comes in handy. I've been sewing up every hole I see and sewn the stripes on some of my shirts and jackets. It has a world's supply of thread that should last until 6 months after the duration. You've made me a real sew-and-sew.

Some day life will be at rest, won't it? Close to all I hold dear.

I want to just live, I want to just have the feeling of life for once instead of just imagination. I want to just stop all this. If it calls for another year, life just won't be the same.

When you finished the pages of hometown gossip, I let out a little sigh. I enjoy hearing it from home. You even tickled me about being good on the way when I can't be sitting with you on trips.

We just can't see anyone else, can we?

Yesterday I came in and found you lying on your face. You had been that way so long I wondered if you hadn't got a crick in your neck. Honest, it's such a comfort to have you here looking on with the smile that would make me smile no matter how low I could be.

While I was on furlough, a number of the boys came in the room and began asking questions about the picture I had of you. Some had seen it, and you know how news travels in the Army. Well, when I came back, a few of the nosy old maids asked about that wife I'd visited. "How did you catch <u>her</u>?" or "What did she see in <u>you</u>?' Yes, they did say it jokingly, or they would have gotten <u>gigged</u>.   Men are so funny about their girls and wives. They take so much pride and love to gloat.

I've thought a number of times of the long pencil I pecked you with on one of your red fingernails.   What happens today but it's coming through the mail tied with a tag on a cotton string.   Some postman must have gotten peeved and broke it in handling.   When things like this come in the mail, what a kick we get out of it.   I sharpened the longest piece and tried to write this in pencil, but was afraid the writing would get so cold you couldn't read it.

Yesterday I was so absorbed in what you were saying the men went out of the barracks, loaded the tools on the truck and were ready to pull out to Topsail (the range) without me.   I went out the door so fast with pack in one hand and gas mask in the other you would have thought I was Dagwood catching his morning ride.

As for Christmas, you're smart to ship your luggage ahead up here.   Traveling then will be so crowded and tiresome you will do well if you keep up with the places to get off and on.   Some of the boys came back off furlough as tired as dogs having to stand in aisles for miles.   Promise me one thing, if you have one of these fresh soldier boys to sit with, you'll stay awake and not rest your head on his shoulder.

Will the 18th just rush and get here?

You mustn't let things worry you when I fail to write.   If you want to box my jaws in a few weeks they may be flabby enough to stand it.   We do the same things most every day, and what we have done I have told you already, so I think she knows what I do.   And if I get sick, my hands won't be tied.   I'll either write or have the nurse write, see?

We're practicing tracking targets so we will have full cooperation when we do actual fire.   I was on guard yesterday when they fired 76 rounds and tore the sleeve into bits.   After ripping the thing up, they shot it right down.   The B.C. and lieutenant jumped off the ground in glee when it happened. I just wish I had been there. In the Thanksgiving ceremony the colonel and major gave us all the bighead by saying A-Battery's the best in the whole battalion. It's just that we have been lucky.

Next week will be a boner, "harden troops" they call it, a whole week of encampment. I hope to get in in time to meet you.

Never let me let you go.

I'm looking for a place still. If I can't find one by tomorrow night, I'm going straight to the Baptist minister and see if he can't help. I can't stand the suspense any longer. The Travelers Aid people are supposed to get soldiers' wives a place to stay, but you aren't actually here. Just hold tight.

It's now after nine, and I've just gotten rid of a talker that doesn't know his elbow from first base. I'm on C.Q. (charge of quarters), and the office has been full of conversation tonight about a dance with lots of Waves and what we call <u>Wacks</u> there.

Do they lose all the being feminine when they join this Army? They look like bright intelligent girls, but what are they really like? If they didn't have a very high place in life, they will sure go down after being in the armed forces for a while. Yes, I know they think they are doing such a splendid job if they join up for service to the country. Some are well and good, but to my mind the place for them is in the offices, factories, schools and homes.

If the days will only rush by...

Never in my life have I been so helpless. I've plowed through mud, rain, and I believe it even snowed a little, looking and calling for places. Finally found a room for a week only. Not what I wanted, not the best, not nearly as chummy as our other places have been, but I hope you realize what it takes in such a crowded city. At least it's near the bus line, and the others were 3 or 4 miles out of town.

Just think. On Saturday you'll be here. This time I'll be there to see your little foot step out on North Carolina soil.

Just six more days.

Nothing must stop you now.

The Government will be really cheated this week. Who can have his mind on his work when his lady will be here in <u>hours</u>? The train will be so crowded and the ticket office so <u>full</u>. Get there early so you won't miss the train. The men that go on furlough say they had the hardest time making connections. Just put something in your seat before you leave it. If a sailor or soldier could help you, I might consent for them to be nearby.

I've written to your brother to see if he could come the 26th. Christmas, even in the Air Corps, will be lonesome for him, I'm sure. We can make room for him somehow. It's hard to be in service at this time without your folks.

Since I've been old enough to go to church I've gone to our little church at home for Christmas service. I don't think folks in the city know what they miss when they don't have what we did.

Your husband may look like Santa Claus some night when he comes home to you. You may not recognize me with the big bag on my back, but the way things have started coming in the mail, we will have lots to open either Christmas Eve or the next morning.

With the days growing slower and slower, will Saturday ever get here?

———————

He was right. The train <u>was</u> crowded. A mother rested gratefully while a Marine walked her small, fussy baby down the aisle, cradling the little stranger as gently as if it were his own. People old and young sat on their suitcases beside seats meant for two holding three wedged tightly together.

As for staying awake and not resting her head on some soldier's shoulder, it was a sailor's instead. Jerked suddenly awake by the train's lurching, she raised up, stammering, "Oh, I'm sorry!" The Navy man just smiled and whispered, "Hope you had a good nap, ma'am," then closed his own tired eyes again.

Christmas came to Wilmington. He <u>was</u> there to see her put her foot on Carolina soil.

The first tree of their marriage, in a dark rented room, was a bushy foot-long twig left on the lot where a vendor had closed out his stock of holiday greens. A harried clerk in the dime store provided scraps of cellophane from torn packaging and a damaged Christmas corsage with red berries and blue foil leaves. The movie theater lobby had popcorn to string.

The elfin tree with its white roping, shiny red bows, and tacky "ornament" at the top was just right. The Movado watch she gave him disappeared somewhere in Europe. The Benrus, his gift to her, kept perfect time through the rest of the century with only two cleanings.

1943

The pattern for the 411th was now complete. Another cadre had gone out, their spots being filled by replacements from New York and New England. What they practiced in North Carolina and in what teamwork as they fired for Officers Candidate School and the AA Officers Training School became second nature for the rest of the war.

Although there was nothing to look forward to here as I had last week and the week before, I simply ached for this place after the week on bivouac, couldn't wait for Saturday to come. We left camp Tuesday morning by truck, thank goodness, and went about 35 miles from here. Arriving at the position close to 1:00 o'clock, we started digging in our emplacement and didn't stop to eat until three. No noon chow, mind you. We pitched our tents after dark, most of them in a swamp or hole. Then, too, we were so conscious of an alert we got very little sleep.

Wednesday morning it was raining and continued throughout the whole encampment. Never have I been so sleepy and couldn't sleep but about three hours that night. Next day we continued to work on the emplacement in a drizzle.

We were given the regular field rations used in combat, six cans to be our food for one day. One contained pork and beans, 1 stew, 1 hash, and 3 hardtack biscuits with a package of coffee we were supposed to make on our own, but after the first cup I used pure H$_2$O.

Thursday night we moved in blackout to a new position the chief of section and gun sergeant had looked over that afternoon. Got there about 9:45 P.M., but didn't have the gun ready to fire until 11:45.

That night so few of us got sleep we couldn't do anything but drag the next day. Our clothes, bedding and feet stayed wet throughout. Since the weather had set in so bad, they decided to call everything off Friday afternoon and come to camp. We were ready and packed at 2:30, but no trucks were available, so we just sat around a fire until 12:45 A.M. and pulled in this morning at 3:30 A.M., tired as hounds.

I washed my hands only once and didn't touch my face with water the whole time. You would probably have disowned me if you had seen me this week. I can just lie down and sleep for a month. I was so dirty it took me thirty minutes to shower. It's over now, and how glad we all are. It's just that we hear the sad news that we may take one of these each month.

It was such a glad and glorious feeling to hear all about your trip this morning and the way you arrived safely. The little pattern I crept into of getting away from camp each evening was so nice. So many little things amount to big things in our life.

How happy being married to you has made me.

Most of Sunday has been one of just resting and getting over that bivouac. I was actually sore from sleeping in a bed this morning. Don't tell anyone, but this Rogers stayed in his bunk until close to eleven o'clock. I was so worn and tired I felt it was no use to get up. The clipping in the paper about our encampment said we stayed in a drizzling rain 72 hours, which was quite a <u>miss</u> in the reporting.

I was called in the office Saturday morning to let them know who I thought would be best to go on a cadre off my section. I saw right away I wasn't on the list, so told the commanding officer I'd like to go. He seemed rather shocked. I told him it looked to me that the 411th was ready for sea duty and, since I am a married man, wasn't especially ready for that yet if I could be of service on this side for a while yet. He saw my point, but said we will be here for months now attached to Battery Headquarters training men for outfits that don't have their quota for overseas. I also found that the cadre may go to California and has none of the key men here on it. If I can stay here with the 411th gang, I'm satisfied.

The higher-ups seem very proud of the way the bivouac turned out. We had some flaws, but we'll straighten them out next time. The colonel seemed rather proud of us, or maybe he was shooting us a line to make us feel good. In most outfits, though, you have A.W.O.L's, but do you know the 411th hasn't had one court martial since we started? It seems the men must be satisfied, doesn't it?

You spoke of a Valentine's Day date Feb. 12-14. I had already been thinking the same thing. We can have that much pleasure and fun in these troubled times, can't we? If you can meet me in Charlotte as we planned once before, that will be all I will ask until spring break.

I do want to encourage you to throw things to the wind and stay with me. We've put up with it as long as it looked like I'd be shipped around. Now I want you here.

In all my thinking about how you might join my battery I came on one today. So many of the outfits have secretaries. Why couldn't our battalion have one, too? They're the best thing that ever came into the Army. Would you like to be mine? Wouldn't it be funny for some rookie to come in for a three-day pass and find the sergeant's secretary on his knee? Just something to think about in case you ever get tired of teaching.

Now I can even get away without standing reveille, but as soon as it's over here's one chowhound that hits the sand-covered floor. Not that they have so much these mornings, but something to hold me to noon.

Speaking of chow, remember that sergeant that talked so lengthily to you (doggone it) Christmas Day? He'll be our chief cook and mess sergeant from here on out and has become very strict, watches every plate that comes out. Chow is one of the chief topics in this Army. I didn't know I was going to get off on

<u>this</u> subject when I started, but we can't help but talk about it here.

We have such a big guard room now that it's a man-sized job to keep everything smoothly. We have 32 privates and 6 corporals to be responsible for along with the area they guard. Just think how much property that is!

Here I am writing you before we stand retreat. Have I ever done that before? The real reason is an overnight bivouac at 7:00 P.M. The chiefs went out this afternoon to look over the spot. It's not as bad as we have had before. Can I count on you never to ask me to sleep on the ground once I get out of this Army? If we had bedbugs and froze all over in our bungalow, I'd sleep there if you would.

You make me sing "Deep in the Heart of Carolina" when we speak sorta thoughtfully of coming to see me in February.

> In a cubbyhole
> With a blonde
> (Baby Snooks on radio)

When your bottle-sized package arrived the boys just knew it was a <u>quart</u> of some kind. I thought it might be rubbing alcohol for my aching feet, but it was a pecan roll so sweet that we almost ate it all at first cutting.

The way we work now is very hard, so much more than I've been called upon before. Since we are school troops, we work for the men who are officer candidates, firing the guns and doing all the work beforehand. Instead of just having one crew I have to have enough trained men to operate 3 crews on the director and 3 on the height-finder. It's quite a task.

You may not realize it, but I was a houseboy at home until I was 14-15, then was promoted to barn work for good. What a promotion. Here it's clean-up for Saturday inspection. That household experience is of real value now when I have to see that the men mop and wash windows.

At home, when I could eat and then walk out with the other men without having to do the dishes, I was a real he-man. Funny, when you have such a large family such tales you have to tell. Wouldn't it have been nice if you had lived next door then instead of later? I had your picture on the shelf, but moved it down beside me so I could see you just as I turn off the light and as soon as I open my eyes.

I couldn't dream of seeing anyone else on Feb. 12-14.

What I get afraid of sometimes, when I hear on the radio of the shortage of teachers, is that they'll freeze you in your job. Then we'd be in a pickle. So many are quitting jobs to go into defense work. Let's pray they won't until after June. If you see that they are going to do that, I'd urge you to slip out immediately. If you plan and wish to be with me, I'm for that 100%.

The inspection today was the toughest we have had since I've been at Davis. The regular sergeant in charge of the barrack was in the hospital, and as I was next in rank I had to take over. We are required to display our field equipment, which called for cleaning. If you can get things placed uniformly on the bunks, everything is o.k., but some you slip up on. Three lieutenants in our battery and the colonels and major came through, with little me, shaking in my shoes, leading the way in front of the bunks. If a man was on duty elsewhere, I had to know where he was and give the inspector an account of him. The men get so shaky, too, when the officers ask questions. They don't respond although they know the answers very well. I'd tried to impress upon their minds yesterday afternoon what to expect. They did have the place clean, including the equipment. I was surprised when the officers <u>thanked</u> me for showing them the barrack.

Went to church today in Wilmington and couldn't help but wish that I was sitting in the same pew we last sat in together. The people are the friendliest. Before I could get out the pastor's wife invited me to dinner. You know me. I took her up. Before I could get to the door another cute lady asked if I could eat with them today, and while I was waiting outside, a young lady with a little boy about eight came up and said he wanted me to go to dinner with him. I did lean toward the little fellow's asking, but couldn't back out on the first invitation. Hey, why didn't I think of saying, "I'll be glad to be around <u>next</u> Sunday?"

The couple were as nice as they could be. The pastor had five years in the last war, and we got in the groove before long. It was the first home-cooked meal I've had since furlough. Everything was so good and cheerful.

I'm sorry to hear your brother's headed overseas. He's probably like the rest of us, though. We get darn tired of this cops-and-robbers stuff. If we couldn't travel from place to place we'd get awful tired of this mess. I've made up my mind when it's time to go, it's our time, so it's not as hard now thinking about it as it was when I first came into the service.

Maybe you won't have to go back after our February weekend.

Lately I've been learning what goes on in the office every day. The reports can drive you nuts. I hold reveille each morning, get out the sick report and get the morning report in shape by the time the top kick gets in. I think if I could be just a staff sergeant that would suit me better. If anything else comes up, I'm inclined to say "No."

There's a new regiment forming just below here, and so many new men are coming in the whole place looks

greenish.   They   were   discussing   the   whys   and
wherefores of this place compared with all the others
they have seen, and of course they have seen <u>so</u> <u>many</u>.

With all the force of one's backbone this chowhound came out of bed today for a scrumptious Sunday
breakfast.   I put on only enough clothes to pass the
mess sergeant's inspection, figuring I'd fall back on
the nicest bunk in the barrack as soon as I swallowed
the last flake of cereal, but I couldn't go back to
sleep.   The cutest face kept smiling at me.   The
fellows laugh at the way I carry on over your picture.
Before turning out the light I act sometimes as if you
were there and talk so silly.

I hope to meet you when you arrive in Charlotte.
It just wouldn't do for a lady to get off in a strange
city with strange men and women.   Too many strange
things at once.

Only two more little weeks.

Will they ever let me come out of all this a better
man for it?   I want to so because there's one person I
want to have the best there is in life.

Another long weary day of this man's army.   We go
out to the 90mm gun range and observe what's going on
so we'll know how to carry on when our battery takes
over the school firing in about 3 weeks.   Only a relay
man and a gunner from each gun crew and 5 men,
including myself, in the range section.   This business
of firing for Officers Candidate School will become
very boring, I'm afraid.   I don't see how some of them
get by the first weeks with the foolish questions they
ask.   I believe any of our men in the battery might do
as well as most.   One thing, though, we do have good
hours, 8:00 to 4:00 or 4:30.   That still means getting
up at 5:45.

You would have strutted yourself last night at a
barn dance at the new Service Club.   Hayseeds were
flying.   None knew beans from rice about it, and they
had only a small amount of music.   The little hostess
tried so hard, but the violin player even slipped out

A.W.O.L. So many of us old country boys, like your hubby, just tickled under their feet to get their dogs in the straw.

Postal Telegraph   5 Feb 43   9:43 PM

Afraid plans be upset. Must use streamliner and risk next weekend. If no transportation to Charlotte Feb 6-8, wire your plans.

She switched her tickets. The weekend came and went like a dream. "Hello" on Friday and "Goodbye" on Sunday. Too short a time. Too long apart.

In case you worried about my coming in late, there wasn't a word said when I walked in. The 1st Sergeant spoke as if I had been there all the while. My bus ride was as long as yours and more. I stayed on the thing from 12:45 A.M. until 9:30 this morning. What a tired man.

I hate to say goodbyes.

If we never go back to Charlotte again, this past weekend will be with me for a long time. It surprised me that it all came true so quickly. Life is beautiful.

If you worried about me getting into the brig, you can take a ten-minute break. Come to think of it, though, it might be fun to have a day off and be on K.P. once more. Anybody could straighten things out once we got to peeling potatoes together.

Did you know you could tell a person is pretty nice by just looking at the face and eyes?

After seeing you I have to start all over again getting along the same old way. I suppose they count this as having the ox in the ditch.

We worked so late last night, then the 1st Sergeant asked if I would take charge of some 25 men coming off a troop train. You should have seen those rookies frightened stiff. The train was late, as usual, so we were very late getting them all to bed. It's so much to go through with before new men can come into an outfit, such as getting name, serial number, a physical check, and whether they are classed to be in this outfit. Poor fellows hadn't had but three sandwiches since morning and were nearly starved. We had to get the cooks up to feed the chowhounds. You see, we ship out a bunch, then others come in to take their places. It's a constant job of training them to be ready when called for. I couldn't be harsh although I got rather peeved at the way some acted, because I still remember when I stepped off that first troop train.

We had lots of fun tonight, though. A program had been posted on the bulletin board before I left for Charlotte, 1½ hours long from start to finish with so many laughs and some swinging music.

We're all enjoying that huge package of sweet, crisp, fattening cookies you sent, but there's no need of a further "Thank you." You were the biggest thanks for the weekend that I'll ever need.

Your big Valentine pin arrived early, too, so I slipped it on and wore it to chow. The fellows just whistled when they saw it. Then I even wore it to the show tonight. It's love from your little heart out.

Whoever invented Valentine's Day must have been in love with a beautiful lady. It's such a special day of doing and giving little things that wouldn't be thought of otherwise. So few men here seem to value the greetings as much as I do.

Think how it could be possible we were together so suddenly. I no more than got over getting there until I was sorta shocked to say "So long." I'll just have to look at your picture today until the heart fills and runs over.

It was down to 18° this morning. Oh what a frosty nose I had! With the weekend over you probably had a lovely Valentine date with a defense worker in Memphis. In case you want to know, I can cut off the allotment any time.

I hope you get to see my folks. My wife has become quite a tourist these days, here one week, there the next.

I'm dead for sleep. Only two pages to you in the last two days. Well, the intentions are good. Nothing matters but saying "Hello."

You should be here. Then I wouldn't have to waste all this paper the government needs so badly. I've wanted you to come ever since Christmas. We're taking up where another battalion left off, firing for OCS. They stayed 9-10 months working for the school troops, and we have only begun. So nothing is in the way of your coming and staying with me. I've been in an Army barrack for a year now.

Last night we did the first night firing I've been involved in with this group of men. We knocked the target right out of the sky. The officers were so surprised and gave us so many pats on the back. The fellows did such a splendid job of tracking and observing, then the few corrections I put in on each course made the shell bursts pretty and in line. We just fired away and the old sleeve had to come down. It was a good show to demonstrate to the OCS men how effective 90s are and how we operate at night. Some even got shell happy over it.

Tomorrow we have a huge celebration and parade for the retirement of a general here on the post. He has been in command for a number of years, so we'll march, fire guns and do double time for him. It'll be the biggest thing at Camp Davis until you come.

Love is even larger than that big heart you sent me.

I had just reached up for the writing paper when suddenly the lights went out. I thought of the night you turned out the lights because we didn't have a blackout curtain. Then a fuse blew, and I got the real effect.

Here we expected to fall out of the barracks, but just stayed put until I located the little flashlight you sent and found our shoes where we had thrown them. When we put out the lights ourselves it's one thing, but we had so many of these alerts at Stewart we get uneasy. It's easy to pull off shoes after a hard day and just give them a sling, though.

I talked to a sergeant-major at headquarters today and found we were slated to go overseas before this outfit was formed. They even shipped part of the equipment to the port of embarkation so it would be there when we got the men trained. Somehow orders were changed, and the equipment we are now getting (and there's lots coming in) is coming from the embarkation station!

You couldn't be as anxious to have you here as I am.

There may be millions of germs on this paper. Maybe you should put on rubber gloves. There's something going around this outfit that makes people speckled as a guinea egg - measles, of all things! A few cases now and then have been popping up in different batteries. They were restricted to camp, but of course wandered all over the place here. Now we have to stay in our little cubbyholes. So many have been taken to the hospital that the place is beginning to run over with the blasted things. I hope the quarantine will be lifted and all will be well before you come up spring vacation.

I think about you having to travel on that old slow filthy train. One thing I want to warn you about is not to forget and buy a round-trip ticket this time. I know the girls will go straight up in the air the minute they find you won't be back. Here's one thing I promise. No matter how hard it turns out with you leaving, here's one who'll spend hours making up for the ones you left behind.

If you think back this morning and believe my phone call was just a dream, I'll let you know now that everything seems in super order about your coming and staying with me.

I'm so built up about it I'll forget to even give the order to fire on target.

The coming four days will be full and whiz by, I hope, very fast. The 1st Sgt. is on a 3-day pass, so I'm in charge. Just think. I may help inspect tomorrow instead of being inspected. Whee!

But what's life with no you around?

Nothing can talk me out of having you with me even if they give me K.P. You know the penalty for A.W.O.L., so don't be absent. If they don't give you permission to leave, stick in there. You can have my black cap to look mean in. I'll even slip out and defend you with my bayonet if it comes to that. Oh, I have lots of ways to help.

You'll soon be with me each time I enter a room, every time I walk out. Only 13 short days.

Sometimes there's no end of questions here. No one has learned to just sit tight and let the Army be your mind. It's so human for folks to be curious about things, I guess. With the top kick away it did give me a chance to learn the ropes and the way to handle things, though.

No matter how you plan, it only matters how and when you get here.

It's light for nearly two hours now after we eat chow. We had the best tonight, lots of rationed meats, sweets, coffee and even ice cream to top it off. Lots of times we get a good old volleyball game or softball started. It's so much fun to play with the fellows, but oh we nearly come to blows sometimes in our disputes.

You never know what may pop up, though. Furloughs have been changed making me one of the next to go on the 24th or 25th. I hope we can spend my furlough and our anniversary together. This may call for our waiting a few days longer, but 13 days at home will be our reward. Then you can come back with me.

Wait till I wire you.

Don't send your clothes here.

You could meet me in Memphis.

A week alone in Birmingham or with my folks?

Please don't call because I can't tell you anything definite yet. The time between us hurts to the heart.

You can't know what it does to a soldier's life when furlough is mentioned. He can't see anything but that. Can't sleep, eat, think, know what to wish for until he has the papers in his hand and takes off. I had my first chance this week as first sergeant to give out four. It brings such a light to a man's eyes that you can't help but pick at him a bit about it.

It'll keep us apart 6 more days. I hate that. Just remember. He wants to come with you and show the world he thinks he has the best wife on earth.

It just looks as if everything will turn up before we get together. I had a feeling the school had another offer in mind. You have already done two months' work in one by staging the operetta in addition to teaching. We have a choice to make since you have a contract, either leave with an honorable discharge or without.

You still, I see, feel responsibility and want to have the personal satisfaction of fulfilling your original agreement, but we had this settled way back.

Such a mess. Life shouldn't be this way. I've been worrying that the furlough will be cancelled, and now this.

You've done so much there and must be feeling real pressure now, but tell them I'm coming and you would like to come back with me. That isn't selfish these days, is it?

Today took the cake. We left early for a march which carried us cross country. Never in my life have I walked so far and through so much undergrowth. If the jungles are any worse than this bunch of swamps we went through today, God help the men over there. By using a compass we managed very well. Oh boy, will this bunk take a beating tonight.

There's even more confusion on the home front, too. Just as I'm coming home, Mother is scheduled to attend a Woman's Missionary Union convention. When a chance for furlough comes up, you're afraid to put it off for fear either you won't be here long, you'll be shipped around or you won't get one at all. It's so useless to plan in the Army.

As for your staying an extra two weeks, to prepare the girls for that final exam or whatever now seems so important, you'll be doing just the opposite of what we had planned. We won't spend the furlough or our anniversary together, but maybe we can make up for everything when all is settled and smooth again.

It's awful. It can't go on like this.

Just think. A week from tonight I will be on my way. I can't wait to get started for home.

Can't you read between the lines? Just come back with me. That's all I ever ask of you. Do this one thing. Come back with me after furlough.

She came. She stayed.

After one day as a substitute in a large public high school so different from the sheltered atmosphere she had left, she found her niche at the local radio station reading the news and writing commercial copy to convince a doubting public that regardless of the missing cream line on the bottle, the cream was still there in the new homogenized milk. At the turntables she ran 33 1/3s (transcribed spots and The Lone Ranger) and 78s (the Big Band music of Glenn Miller, Benny Goodman, Harry James, Count Basie et al).

Miller was a special favorite. Informed of plans for their junior prom in 1940, she and some of her classmates had asked in genuine puzzlement, "Who is

Glenn Miller?" By fall, his reputation having hit the stratosphere, the new seniors could quietly, even smugly, say, "We had Glenn Miller." She had even danced again, at a West Point hop, to his arrangements of "String of Pearls," "In the Mood," and "Tuxedo Junction" loaned as a patriotic gesture to the cadet orchestra.

"Let's Dance," her morning record show with theme by Goodman, could not accept requests in war time, possibly cues to initiate some subversive activity or convey a message to a spy. With an Army base at Davis, a Marine base at Camp LeJeune, and a shipyard turning out vessels vital to the war effort, consciousness of "the enemy" pervaded the area. Bathers at the beach sometimes saw oil on the sand, perhaps from a tanker sunk offshore, and rumor had it that a rubber boat had been found among the dunes, a craft for infiltrators brought to the coast by German submarine? Each night, in the large room he rented in a beach house facing the sea, they could hear "Lights out!" when the Shore Patrol discovered negligence about blackout curtains. No one could walk on the beach after dark without official permission of some sort.

If he couldn't make it to the station, she'd find a note from a sleeping partner or a letter from a bivouacking soldier.

———————

Awaken if found asleep. Fell into dreamland somewhere around 10:00, or 11:00, or 12:00. What a date!

Maple Hills on bivouac

Hello, familiar voice,

I happen to be listening on the radio from one of the many stations around Wilmington and somewhere, some place it seems I have heard your voice. When you said "Goodnight, everybody," it seems you were pointing straight at someone. Have you been running long there, or do you take ten-minute breaks one after another when I don't hear you announcing? One would think you'd have the best sort of people to work with, do you?

It's funny my wanting to write you, but I always liked unknown pen pals. You just can't tell what's on the other end of the air, can you?

All I want to tell you is that you should visit from station to station and let all the men in service hear your soft cool voice. Can I call you by your first name? It sounds so close and a bit more homey. We soldiers do like to feel welcome in these swamps although sometimes only dive-bombers (mosquitoes) are at the door.

This is to let you know the people of my section enjoy your programs so much. Just wish we could run into each other when we have a weekend off.

Luck to you now, and toodledoo.

A <u>Listener</u>

Somewhere in Skunk Hollow on bivouac
With the gnats and everything related to them eating me I have to grab a snap at you between times. We got off to a late start this morning, but arrived here much too soon as it was. Oh, what a lovely spot we picked, just out in the wide open spaces and so hot we all are cooked.

Did you get wet in the rain last night? I got soaked going up to the U.S.O., but it was so cool I didn't mind.

Be good until Thursday nite.

Happy anniversary of the week on bivouac

That lovely song keeps coming up this morning, "You'll never know just how much I love you." That's such a good one, one of the best ever written. Remember how the men played it for us at the Service Club after our wedding?

I've just stuck my head out, struck my tent and am waiting for chow. We had a fine night, no gnats or mosquitoes for a change, but the ground was a bit knotty. We aren't so far from town, just out 23rd St. But it's just far enough that I can't see you. I can spot the radio tower from here, but the red lights don't shine in the daytime. We are guarding the world-famous Wilmington airport and radio center of communication. (That last is my make believe.)

Wait at the Cape Fear Hotel Thursday night, will you? We might take in a Western.

On bivouac

You would have been tickled topsy turvy a few minutes ago if you could have seen us taking a bath. You wouldn't think about our having running water on bivouac, but we do. It's not the clearest I ever saw, but gets the dirt and sweat off. We felt so good after the dip we're tempted to stay there all day. It's a stream from a spring, so it's cold as ice, but as refreshing as a kiss from my wife.

Another very hot day, but all turned out well. The inspecting officers seemed rather pleased with the positions we built. One night more, tomorrow somewhere around camp, noon chow in camp Thursday and Whee! I'll be home.

At least we're having a pretty moonlight. You could put your slippers under my pup tent any time.

On bivouac

Can I come across country and give you a big kiss on our weekaversary in front of the whole staff? I've done it before all the water and fish in the ocean.

We had lots of officers out today. They seemed to like the position, but not as well as last week's. We don't want to get too good at it, or it'll be overseas for sure. Tomorrow morning brass coming around again— about 30 officers here about 8:15. Whoever heard of a colonel getting up before that time? Lots don't turn over the first time by then. We have to change the camouflage late so it'll be fresh and pretty for them.

We have had chow (supper) and very good for a change, but I'm on a really lumpy mattress. Hope I can be in town Thursday night.

Coming home on the bus one Saturday afternoon they saw a beach house ablaze at Station One. Later, at a jewelry store to have his birthday watchband engraved, she overheard an elegant lady arranging for repair of a silver teapot that had been damaged in a fire. The family would be leaving town shortly, so the clerk promised to get on it right away. Almost immediately the officer who had rented the burned house disappeared from the base to surface in England as part of the invasion staff there. Not that a chance remark overheard in North Carolina could affect the outcome of the war, but "Even the Walls Have Ears" assumed new relevance for anyone possessing vital information.

During the busy summer announcers at the radio station learned how to pronounce "Pantelleria," the stepping-stone to Sicily and Italy, and Hollywood came to camp. The feature they filmed, "There's Something About a Soldier," starred Tom Neal as an OCS candidate.

General Patton, commander of the Seventh Army in the Mediterranean area, starred in a less appealing role. On a visit to wounded men in a field hospital he had slapped a soldier and berated him for cowardice. The swashbuckling leader could shed his own tears in private, but the public façade had always to be one of strength and courage. Whether he genuinely did not understand "combat fatigue" or was using shock treatment to restore pride and backbone, the general victorious in Sicily was grounded there fearing his career ended as his army was being melded into the invasion force he might have led in Normandy. Many a soldier would have slapped or even shot him on sight, yet knew and respected his military genius.

With bivouacs over, activity in North Carolina slowed down as well. In September the 411th had

115

celebrated its first birthday with a parade and presentation of colors. The battalion commander declared a holiday. The dinner dance for GIs and their guests was interrupted by sirens sounding a black-out, but true to the spirit of the outfit, even in the darkness, the band played on.

On September 16, 1943, the soldier from Tennessee was promoted to Staff Sergeant of Battery A. For the duration he had the rating he wanted, the outfit he admired and loved, the work he did well, the girl he cared for. Everything in place.

On November 5th the 411th was alerted for overseas duty, their refresher training and target firing completed, final field exercises rated "Satisfactory" and "Highly Satisfactory," and a large black TATS encircled in red painted on their equipment. Furloughs also signaled a big change ahead. Italy? England? The Pacific? West coast duty? As usual men in the ranks could only guess and wait for orders.

In late December the radio announcer received a call from a friend with connections to the railroad. Something interesting happening tomorrow. She recognized what was hinted, but knew not to ask questions. Next morning at 5:30, she took the earliest bus to camp only to see soldiers already lined up in ranks to board a troop train. Clutching his Christmas presents and dashing frantically along the track, she shouted "411th! 411th!" until someone yelled back, "Tomorrow!"

The sympathetic hostess at the Service Club immediately put in a call to A-Battery headquarters and supplied a key to a room for a holiday celebration that might be the last. No decorations, no curtains or rugs, only a large bare space with cold metal folding chairs lining the walls and in the center a Ping-Pong table. Still, a "home" where no one would disturb. Then they could have dinner together and listen a while to the post orchestra, with a special wrench at hearing "White Christmas."

In an eerie repetition of their wedding night he returned to his barrack, wondering if he would ever see her again, and she spent the night alone in a room painfully reminiscent of that spare cubicle at Fort Eustis.

But now, as then, came an unexpected blessing. In view of the circumstances the office issued a temporary pass for him to escort her back to Wilmington, the only real home they had ever shared. They had moved from the beach for the winter to a lovely old white house across the street from the local showplace, the Governor Dudley mansion. There he knew she would be safe with a family who had a serviceman in the Far East. They could say goodbye just as if he were leaving for his work every day.

When he turned around down the block for one last look, he saw her smiling and waving from the front porch steps. By this time they were too far apart to see each other's tears.

On December 23rd, after sixteen months in "Swamp Davis," the outfit formed there on September 1, 1942, left for war with a commanding general's deep appreciation for their service and dedication while on his post. They had learned their equipment, run check problems, maintained the vehicles of a mobile unit, readied guns to fire, and passed final inspection by a representative of the Inspector General's Office. They were ready now, even for Patton.

Their present destination? Camp Shanks, New York, to prepare for embarkation.

Norma Rogers

NEW YORK

Norma Rogers

You are probably hanging up your stocking for old Santa tonight. Would you just hang one up for me and mail whatever he brings me by airmail? Some folks would say I'd get only ashes and switches, but he was good to me before I left.

I've wondered if you'll go ahead and work tonight since it's Christmas Eve, or did you go to work at all? It's one of those times now when we don't have Christmas together. When I got your picture out, someone from Davis had stuck a Christmas card inside. 'Course I had to destroy it so as not to give our outfit away. All the fellows seemed so surprised that you had received our A.P.O. number already. Rogers always first, you know.

What do you think of this classy Army paper? I had thrown all my old away, so had to go to the P.X. and buy a bit. Everything up here is much cheaper, 3 to 4 cents off on some things. That mounts up sooner or later.

The place is a madhouse tonight. I'd like to tell you all the things I want to say, but will wait till I get more to myself.

You couldn't have been sweeter than the night I kissed you goodbye.

You know, old Santa came and went, and I haven't got the Christmas spirit yet. I don't believe anyone could have it the shape we are in the last few days. Uncle Sammie kept his promise in giving us plenty to eat today. Yes, turkey, dressing, peas, cranberries, potatoes and candy. This place makes me feel I'm just coming into the Army the first day. Most of the fellows are looking forward to a pass, but no one is allowed out of the area.

We talked of having our letters censored. It's hard not to write certain things, so I know you'll understand when I don't tell what we did for days and what our plans are for the future. It's constantly being driven into us not to write certain things, and after all the caution one man got a message from home today, but to me he's not at fault 'cause you had my A.P.O. before I left and could very easily have wired me. I often wondered what is the effect of a censor looking over my shoulder. I know the feeling a bit now.

I thought of you so many times this special day. It's many years since you spent a Christmas as you did this one. May the Lord make this the last one. Don't be surprised if I don't let you out of my sight when I come back.

This little picture of you is the brightest thing in the room.

What a gladness I had this afternoon when I got the letter you wrote after I left. It seems everyone was looking at me when I got down to the bus station. My eyes were so red they probably thought I'd had too many beers.

I have so much of your Christmas around, the watch and band, the I.D. bracelet from last year and now the warm gloves, the scarf that comes in handy as a windbreak and pillow, and the billfold with all the pictures.

I got two letters today, one from you and the other from the Presbyterian preacher and his wife back home. They mean so much. You know how much, I believe, because your morale gets low, too, now, doesn't it? I'm going to try my best to keep the 4-F and civilian spirit up.

Today has been very sane and quiet, but not like I want Sundays to really be. You can't keep up with the days hardly unless you watch the calendar closely. One day is so near the routine of the other you forget time.

We were wishing for Wrightsville Beach tonight in the Mess Hall. A number of fellows had letters returned by the censor because of things they said. I hope mine got through. You need not worry about a censor reading your mail to me because they just pick a letter here and there and don't check each separately.

It meant so much to let me see you wave and smile when I went away.

We wanted so many times in Wilmington to grab a good hot dog some place. Well, that's what I just got through munching, an American-style hotdog with all the trimmings. They try to please the servicemen here, it seems, in P.X.'s and service shows. They fry you hot dogs, shake you a milk shake and even put milk in cartons so we can bring it to our barracks. Honest, I might gain weight if I stay here long enough.

There's a terrible mix-up in the mails. I failed to write last night because it was the first time we had to get away from the area. A bunch of us went to a movie, Kay Kyser in some dopey film, then lights out at 9:00, so I didn't have much chance. The mail stays in the box for days, though. No one has censored it yet, so don't get uneasy if you don't hear regularly.

Tonight lots have gone on pass, the first we've gotten. The place we spent two days in after coming down from your graduation in 1941. I may go tomorrow night, and you know I'd like to be there New Year's Eve.

Life won't be life until loved ones can be together for always. That's what we are all fighting for. The strongest thoughts of you on our week-anniversary.

I've been fortunate enough to be the one to give out the mail in our barrack since we have been here. When I got two letters today, the fellows thought I had two gals on the line instead of just one. I was so excited about getting the first A.P.O. mail I nearly about threw theirs down to run to a private corner.

A letter from Mother was full of Christmas, but my oldest brother's chest trouble cut no ice with the draft board. He may be called the first of the year. My younger bud has bought a bike and is riding all over the place until his status is settled.

Your letters are like a short visit. I know that Christmas there alone was bad. Surely none could be worse. I'm glad good friends invited you for dinner. That did help.

Can you please come into one of my dreams?

When I called the mail out, I couldn't stop laying mine aside. You were such a nice dope to send all those familiar postcards with the little comments.

Something happened that your V-mail got here after the Christmas mail. I gather you think I'm not in the U.S.A. The people at the station must be lots of comfort just now. Stay as long as you like there, but I do think you'd be happier at home.

No matter where we go, how long we stay away, you are the girl in my life.

When we hit this place, who would have guessed we'd have stayed this long? Tonight makes a week since we arrived. You'll never know when I leave, but you were right about the neighbor who left early. He lived in the house with the red walls we saw that afternoon with all the people gathered around. You saw his wife later in a shop downtown.

Our hopes fell the other afternoon when we came off a hike and all passes were cancelled. Now we are spending a lovely New Year's Eve shooting craps and playing cards. You'd think the games would get old after a while, but they play continuously. We got paid today, the first time on the last of the month since I've been in the Army. I got the measly sum of $14.00.

Old Santa came today with lots of useful things. So many surprises this year. Folks have been so good to me. Your mom sent me a foxhole pillow, a horseshoe shape that fits one's head perfectly. I can sit on it, put it in my helmet, use it to sleep on trains, even wash it without harming it.

But nothing will be as sweet as when we can be together in a house after a good day of work. I'll come back to you.

---

2 January 1944   Left P.O.E. 1200 hours (Camp Shanks, New York).

Their last vision of America was the New York skyline and the Statue of Liberty, whose crown he had gazed from in 1941. The <u>Queen Elizabeth</u>, traveling without escort, zigzagged across the tossing wintry sea with the largest troop shipment so far, a load of soldiers eating fatty pork chops, sleeping in shifts in cabins or on deck, getting sick, and shooting craps all the way to Glasgow.

I know for sure lots of the letters I wrote in the States failed to reach you. The censor didn't pick them up, and they're here on the boat with us now. You'll probably receive them some time in June. The last few days in camp I had no word from you, but two days after we left I got a handful of mail. It must have come by carrier turkey. I couldn't read them all at once, so spread them all out through the trip. Never have letters meant so much. I'm safe <u>so</u> faaaaaar. Lots of good rumors, but nothing definite. Your guess was better than mine as to where we are going.

You should have seen this outfit about 2 days ago. I lost all color, all care of eating (you <u>know</u> that was something), and even thought I had the last thing ever in my tummy. I used my helmet as my chief output. I'd have run all day if I'd tried to make the latrine.

You spoke lots of times about a cruise after the war. Well, you'll have to take yours with some other dope 'cause this will be my next to last one. The next will be back to the States.

You sound just as mischievous as ever. You've been the bravest wife any man ever had.

'Bye for now.

The Third Army staff followed almost in their wake. Tired of playing cowboys and Indians and ready for the real thing, they had celebrated New Year's Eve at

125

headquarters, then traveled to Camp Shanks to head for Scotland aboard the Ile de France. Their general had not conducted a final meeting, but his luggage was in place. No one suspected that as they crossed the ocean, a literal sea-change was also taking place.

Headquarters in the states received within the week a letter addressed by Mrs. George S. Patton, Jr., to her husband as Commanding General, Third U.S. Army, APO 403, New York, N.Y. The secret had been so well kept that Patton's presence at the Firth of Clyde appeared to be a welcoming gesture only until he straightway announced that as their new commander he was glad to see them, hoped they felt the same, and expected them on the train for his headquarters within the hour. Before debarking the senior officers had learned that all but one would be replaced by the general's old comrades from the campaigns in Italy and Sicily. Their enlisted subordinates would join a staff made up primarily of ordinary GIs and cavalrymen, the only group in the ETO to wear riding breeches with boots and every officer a tie.

Both Eisenhower and Omar Bradley knew there might be headaches in the arrangement. Patton had been General Bradley's superior officer in Sicily and still had to learn to tame his theatrics, but he was so relieved just to get back in the fray that he paid the proper attention, did his best to conform, and maintained the role of friendly collaborator for the duration of the war. His spit and polish eventually reached the 411th.

As for the Brits, who would become their hosts and comrades-at-arms, few had seen any beyond some officers visiting the states. Strolling on the streets in shorts and knee-high socks might be suitable in India or the tropics, but in North Carolina it had raised eyebrows, especially among the males, no matter how steamy the summer got.

ENGLAND

Norma Rogers

1944

9 January 1944   Arrived at P.O.D. 1900 hours.
10 January 1944   Left P.O.D. 0940.
11 January 1944   Arrived at destination 1000 hours (Fairford).

A train brought the outfit south from Scotland to a town in Gloucestershire well-known for its church with remarkable stained glass, possibly the work of the master craftsman of King's College, Cambridge. A conscientious GI, with little or no liberty for tourism but much concern for preserving secrecy, at first spoke only of her and him and memories.

That was the famous Red Cross paper I used on the boat. I'm just too far away now. It's England, and nothing like I supposed. We had to run the cows out of the meadow before I started making my straw mattress.

I'm going to write every day when I can. Don't worry and lose too much weight. I like you just the way you are.

You don't know how good it feels to take a shave. I've just had one of the best with the lotion and powder you gave me for Christmas. I hear these are pretty scarce over here. The gals just flock to you for a box of Lux, they say. But you sit beside me as I write, still smiling away.

By the time you get this you may be back in Memphis. Just tell any man who tries to bother you on the trip that he's a coward, 4-F sneaking snake in the grass, and even a yellow rascal. That should hold him until I get back. I do wish you'd make this your last month in North Carolina. To me Memphis is much safer. I may be away a long time, but there'll never be anyone but you.

It's now 10 o'clock here. You've just had lunch and gone back to the station.

You tickled me yesterday about the mouse. It must have been the same one who got into the package of cakes when I was there. Look him in the eye and he'll run like I do when you get devilish.

So few letters come into the battery that I'm almost forced to let the fellows in on some of mine. Letters are what keep us going. You've given me a head start on the rest.

Tonight's Saturday night, just another one going away, but that means it's one closer to home. It's 8:15 our time which is 5 hours ahead of you, a lovely Saturday afternoon your time.

Last summer on the beach was the best. If I live to be fifty, we'll have to go back there and spend a spring vacation. I'm so glad we have all these little happenings to look back on and live over again.

You'd brighten any beach.

What would one do if he didn't have the fellows he knows with him? We have our ups and downs in this place. If it wasn't for our humor things would get awful. Someone has a tale going of what he did back in the States, and a boy from Memphis is telling jokes. We've laughed until we couldn't go to sleep if we wanted to.

We may not have the chance later, so I let the fellows talk and do lots we weren't allowed to in camp back home. We have lights out at 10 o'clock. Plenty of sleep these long nights, and very little time in the sun. You see lots of white faces running around, especially after the boat trip. I lost weight, but am gaining it back with such good chow.

The English money is a problem to us at first, but I'll catch up to it. Just don't _you_ change, will you? I can't be gone _that_ long.

So many men have yet to pick that one they can cherish as I do, but my only idea of going out over here is just to pass the time away and mainly to see

130

and tell you what the country is like. Otherwise I'll do just as I did before I met you while we're apart.

Mom finally sent your brother's address. Maybe I can locate him if I get a 24-hour pass. Things are about as crowded here as they are in Wilmington, and they do funny things. Different fellows come back with such tales.

Did you see who's going to be in charge of the invasion? <u>Our</u> <u>buddy</u>. The news looks good to us over here. I'll start writing to your Memphis address about the middle of next week.

<u>One</u> thing's right and will be forever—my wife.

Eisenhower, seen as the soldier's soldier in the European Theater of Operations (ETO), forsook London to house his Supreme Headquarters Allied Expeditionary Force (SHAEF) in the English countryside. Each staff officer - air, navy, or ground chief - would help to develop the over-all plan, then command his own portion of its execution. All three would report directly to Ike.

Patton, warned to avoid the press and any unauthorized public statements, had late-night discussions with friend Ike, then almost immediately raised hackles again. Asked for a few informal remarks at a private function, he at first demurred, then made the mistake, being what he thought gracious, of referring to Britain and America as rulers of the postwar world. So much for Russia and the pressing need for unification. In the ensuing hullabaloo he offered to resign, but it was not, in theory at least, a "public" speech. Besides, Ike needed him. Badly.

You have had word by now, I hope, that I have gone, and any hope of seeing me in New York has fallen. I hated that I didn't take my first chance for a pass to the big city. I might have been able to call and talk to you one more time.

We had some new experiences when we went to town here on pass. We ate in a place with what they call "high music." They even served the food in courses. It was fun, new and different.

I tried to find your brother in the neighborhood, even sent a letter to the Air Corps field director to try to locate him, but the office was closed by the time we got there. Guess I'll just have to write him.

I'd like to write you airmail, but no stamps or envelopes. These people want to charge a shilling for one, so you'll just have to rush me some. I can't talk to you on V-mail.

It would do me so much good to let you in on all the military rumors, where I am, how far I am from different places and what we are doing, but what would you get but a blank page of all the sentences cut out. This soldier is well and has his hands full. I used to be able to tell you all I'd done during the day and even the prospects of a few weeks ahead, but overseas it's different. As long as I write and you know my health is good, you need not worry, if you do, about anything else.

One thing that keeps reminding me so of Wilmington is a clock that chimes every quarter-hour, so we keep up with the time.

Now it was official among those in the know - D-Day in May, a full summer ahead for campaigning before bad weather set in. The problem continued to be landing craft since General Montgomery advocated a wider assault front than previously visualized. The U.S. Navy balked at losing any from the Pacific theater. Also Eisenhower had scheduled a landing at Anzio to relieve the stalemate in Italy. And what about ANVIL, the projected attack in southern France which the Brits thought merely a diversion - like Anzio?

General Bradley, behind blackout curtains in a fashionable flat in West London, had a 24-hour guard posted at a room full of maps marked "Top Secret" where sergeants typed troop lists, revised daily. When a bomb crashed the roof and landed on the office floor, volunteers came rushing in from the street to fight the blaze set off among the records. On another occasion papers blew out an open window, leaving the staff on edge until all were recovered. Still, security held. Each night agents searched through desks, rattled doors, checked on safes. The general also advised Ike to send home a friend of West Point days whose carelessness about secrecy made him too great a risk.

What one reporter described as "a trickle of khaki" became a stream of young men loaded down with duffel bags, their baggage including such practicalities as dental floss. Planes rode the air as if on a highway. London became a big office complex, one cafeteria so closely resembling a Detroit assembly line that its patrons nicknamed it "Willow Run." With the millions of extra tonnage of men and materiel the old joke surfaced that the only thing holding the island up was its barrage balloons.

Yet as Ike tamed Patton and Bradley kept the calm, back in the states cities were experiencing shortages, race riots, strikes, even attacks by juveniles on Navy men to the degree that Los Angeles was declared off-limits to service personnel for a time. At the other extreme, many a window bore a Gold Star as the reality of war hit home to grieving families whose warriors would not be coming home.

Among those still at risk the dominant emotions included anger.

You'll never know how Hitler and his gang are hated in this outfit. It's his fault we have to be away from our dear ones. I've promised God that if he'll let me return to you and the States, I'll work and do more and be all He expects. We come so close to Him while we are here. Every night when all is quiet and all the lights are out in the barracks, I thank Him for the care of the day, asking Him to watch over you and all my loved ones. Never have I felt so close to God as I have since I arrived on the boat.

We had a good chapel service today. I thought of you on the way and would have gone back tonight, but the weather is really bad. Church is helping so, though, in our sort of life.

I have your picture pinned up on the wall so I can see your smiling face the first and last of every day. It's the best thing in the room. So many walk through and comment on it.

The letters are all scattered by the days now, but are so grand to receive. I still keep getting some a whole month later where you didn't know I have gone.

Keep your beautiful sense of humor. We can't lose it here so don't <u>you</u>. I was glad to know straight from you that you will be going back home the first. It will give you a change, new things to do, people around you who really care.

We haven't had over a week of sun since our arrival. They keep us busy, and I may not get to write for a few days. We plan to take a visit to another part of this land, so it may be some time before we get settled. As for the food, it's like they say - not too much around. We get plenty, though, thanks to the good old U.S.A.

---

25 January 1944   Left APO 645, 1000 hours by motor convoy and arrived at APO 115, 1730 hours.

You'd be surprised at the kind of quarters we have tonight. Two of us have a room only about as large as our bath at home. It's not bad here, but we realize the blessings of the good old U.S. We have hot and cold water in our room, so the place we've moved to is no better, but no worse either.

Some fellows don't care enough about their wives or girls to carry pictures, and some say it makes them miss them so much more, so they don't have one as I have on the wall. You are very popular, as always. Pictures are so scarce with no magazines, no pin-up gals. They all think you are like Judy Garland. I let them think that, but let them know, too, you're a whole world better.

Do you suppose the postman would let you be a stowaway in his pocket? You know, when the time came for me to leave, I'd drawn such a picture of leaving in the morning just like I was going to work, but it didn't happen that way.

All I pray for is for the will of God to let the war be over this year.

Letters are the only thing that bring home to me. You could even put in a good rumor if you happen to hear one G.I. talking to another. And it does a man so much good to know his best girl misses him. It keeps him fighting for the life he once lived. I used to think we'd have to be going somewhere or doing something special to have a good time and enjoy the day, but we just spent quiet Sundays, and the days on the beach last summer were the happiest days of my life.

Here it is Saturday night, and my date's on the loose over there. We haven't had passes yet at this place, and things are getting dull. We are planning to take a convoy to church tomorrow. So few men go ordinarily, but when we can't get passes, you should see the Sunday crowd swell. The truck is full.

It's your last day on your job. I'm just wondering who'll take that heavy bag of yours to the railroad station. I pray every night you're being taken care of.

She had loved her work, but wanting to set his mind at ease she packed for Tennessee where he could think of her as protected and sheltered. He had not imagined that "home" for her now was Wilmington, the only home they had shared together as a married couple. At the radio station, with her finger on the pulse of the war, she felt closer to him than at any other place.

———————

I have decided that I don't care what the censor thinks any more. He knows already I think the world of you by now. I wonder sometimes if they do pay attention to what our letters say anyway. No one has censored your letters to me yet, so they don't know what's getting into this man's army. For that you get promoted to T/5, so shine your brass. I can't talk anything but our uncle's language any more.

Have you heard this poem, naughty boy that I am?

> Mary had a little lamb
> Whose love she much preferred,
> But couldn't wait
> And so she wed
> A wolf who'd been deferred.

You know, you have the corniest hubby in the army. The fellows all say I am, so I'm beginning to take their word for it.

We went to an Anglican church today. It was all Greek to a Baptist and a new experience learning more about the people. It was a beautiful church, and they even wanted to hear us sing, then picked songs we never had heard of.

The country is really pretty here. I'm wondering how it could look any better in spring and summer. You'd just enjoy getting out and walking across the green pasture with sheep and lambs running from place to place. We got thirsty strolling across the hill today just for exercise and fresh air, so we walked up to an old farmhouse built in 1865 and asked for water. Instead they asked if we didn't want tea. We went in and had a long talk with the man and his wife and two daughters. It's lots they think about America that isn't so. I learned a lot just being with them such a short time. They are very kind and generous to us here, but there's something lacking without you.

Another day without any postman. What a lost battalion. Our Uncle Sammie can't find us.

The last day of the first month, one month closer to being home. That's what I think of every hour, day, week and month. Would you be my Valentine every day of this coming month? And all the rest? Miss Memphis, I have polished your face and you are just beaming all behind the ears tonight.

It's our anniversary, I mean weekaversary, one of the best days in any week. Then too, it's Groundhog Day, which I don't think they count in England. If signs mean anything, though, we'll have 40 days of lovely weather. Back home I always looked for some kind of little pig to run out when Mother and Dad talked so much about it. That got me believing it really meant something. If it takes this day to change the weather, let's hope so. Maybe it'll help the invasion that we are wishing for so much.

You should see this room. Everything from long handles to hankies hanging up. My laundry may turn out white, but oh how it makes me have dishpan hands. We can't move around much, but I can still see your face. I have it pinned close to my head.

I think we have more visitors than anyone else in the battery. The walls smell when we breathe sometimes the bull sessions are so strong. I'd as soon leave off one of my meals, though, as not be able to write you. The next day is all wrong when I can't.

Your trip home reminds me of the days when I was a civilian and wore white shirts. Tonight I suppose you have arrived at, or are pretty near Memphis. I try to follow you from place to place even if it's 15 or 16 days before I find out if my guess was accurate.

I long for that day when I can get that furlough that'll never end. You give me such lovely thoughts when you tell me your boss's idea that this job may make me stay away another year. Well, maybe my famous radio star does have something there, so let's get it out to the public and not have another public relations scrape like General Patton's.

Some of the fellows can't understand how I deserve such long letters, and I wonder sometimes myself. It's a lovely moon tonight, the clearest we've had since North Carolina, and I'm more determined than ever to see one with you at this time next year at least.

When I came back from chow tonight, there was a fellow whose wife had just had their baby, so he had to tell the world about it. It was a boy, so with the others just having girls, he thinks he's hot stuff as a father. We're always around for the sad and glad cases, aren't we? Like one man's wife who hasn't received any mail from him at all, but said you had received some from me. They must be the ones from (censored).

The last two weeks in North Carolina they kept your little feet to the fire (the English wouldn't know what to think if I said that here). You really liked the work there, didn't you?

The newspapers you sent from Tennessee looked so good to me, especially the Sunday funnies. They'll be worn out in the barracks. They're from home, and anything connected with that we just gobble up.

Send $20.00 to the church for me, please.

All the beautiful songs on the radio today really hit hard. I can't even sing in the shower loud enough, though, for you to hear my voice. At least they tide me over until those newsy letters bring back real life. You should have seen the load we got today, even a special truck to pick it up. In all I got 16 letters, 6 from your folks, one from Mother, one from the preacher, and the rest from guess who.

I never realized the paper from Camp Davis would look so good. We've about worn it out and still daydream of the days we spent there. No one has even bitched about North Carolina. I think they'd go back tonight if they had the chance.

As for the income tax, wait till I come home and we'll straighten it out then. Boys over here have too much on their minds and shouldn't be bothered with that just now anyhow.

By the time I get home I'll be so far behind I won't make sense for ages.

Those dopes in N.C. couldn't locate you on the 28h and sent one of my letters back, and on top of that one of your letters was postmarked three days from now! What has happened? Have they lifted the A.B.C. liquor rations in N.C. and got the whole postal service tight?

Things went about the same today as in the States, only a bit more serious. It reminds us of when the cadre was formed. The hikes are really long, but nice here.

Time out for a pep-up. I don't think they have Pepsi-Cola in Berlin "cause I haven't even seen one in these parts. The best pick-up I could have would be a word from you.

Hey! Your cablegram just came in this very minute. I was so surprised, but didn't get jumpy until I had read it all through, including the nice name at the bottom. Nothing means as much as a word from the one I'd do anything for.

If we went on a date in these parts I'd have to make it a spot of tea. That's the English chief refreshment. I just had one I brought from the Mess Hall. The chow is usually fair, about the same as the States, but sometimes, wellll... (the censor won't co-operate). I would like to have some pure Tennessee milk on my cereal for a change and some real hen eggs.

Some of your letters have such weak postmarks. They must have some 4-F that hasn't the strength to hit the letters a strong blow. We got packs of mail again today, though. Over a month late old Santa was still coming to lots of fellows.

You wanted to know if I saw Oxford University. You bet, and it's just like the pictures. We couldn't miss that while we were here. I took a pass to see what I could because after this war I may not have the chance to come back. We didn't get to much of the town. The day's so short, and blackouts come early. Now we've moved to a place that would take longer to get to than passes allow. I sometimes think of the animals like the whiteface our neighbor at home trades for. This may be a little over your knowledge, but ask Dad about it.

No one here seems to know about an air raid except the fellows who were caught on pass in London before we moved. Our brothers in the Air Corps must know by now. It's a shame I can't contact them. We are so close and yet so far.

Got a Christmas package today from one of our relatives, a present for our home sent on from Davis. I'll have to wrap it back up in the presence of the censor, then hope it gets back by banana boat.

The "whiteface" he referred to were Hereford cattle. He had come upon a system which kept the censor happy, evaded enemy detection if any, yet kept her informed of his location for the rest of the war. Whenever she came across a strange or unusually emphatic statement or a truly awkward turn of phrase she knew to look for something behind the lines.

Your trip home sounded rough. I wonder if the Army has done the right thing in taking over the trains. It was hard enough when both of us traveled together, but we kept up each other's morale by our silly humor so fanny fatigue didn't bother us much. Things must be getting tough if you had to go that long without something to eat.

The way you made your "berth" up opposite that strange man reminded me of our trip to Camp (censored). They had every seat on the coach laying flat, and we all stretched out. 'Course I was a little cramped, being tall. When you spoke of your dress's being mussed, I remember a lieutenant said to us, "Your clothes look like you'd slept in them."

It's nothing to go without a bath here. You may have to make me take one every Saturday night when this is over, and I hope you won't have to take but one more trip, to meet me some place.

When I fell for you, I fell so hard I haven't gotten over it yet.

You asked today about certain ones who came with us. All the fellows that left camp with us. No one was turned down. Anyone with a little warmth in him could pass their physical. All they did was pop us with needles and shoot us through as nude as we were born. Just a formality, it seems, that they had to go through. Your guess as to how we traveled varied a bit, but you came pretty close. Also, remember that neighbor of ours you observed at the jeweler's after something hot as hell destroyed their home? He arrived on the scene here just as we did. I'm telling you something.

After a long search we finally found a Baptist church today. For the last two Sundays we have been to the Episcopalian, so much formality I couldn't make heads or tails of it, and the talk was very confusing. The service this morning was interesting, though. They had a missionary from Africa who was so glad to see a few Americans in the crowd. He said they have so little to work with in their mission station, only the Bible and Pilgrim's Progress.

Tomorrow is the day few people think about here, but since I met you, Valentine's Day means more than it ever did. I've placed one of your letters in each pocket I have - coat, blouse, jacket, two shirts, fatigue jacket, and yes, even one in one of my gas mask carrier pockets.

If things worked out as I asked at home, I hope you like the flowers I'm sending. I'll think of you every hour of the day. And as for the food my mother used to cook, yours will be a thousand times better than the slop we eat now, so don't worry about <u>that</u>. Please let me help in the kitchen, and if the Army comes along again, we'll both be conscientious objectors.

Some of your letters come with hearts written on the envelopes. What I want to know is that a friendly or enemy plane on the airmail stamps? And did you know that when I'm walking back and forth during the day, the letters in my pockets give off little puffs of your perfume?

I've often thought it would be good to have one special pal in the Army, but there are so many friends in this outfit. I seem to get along fine with the fellows and can go out with a number of them and feel close.

From the time I set foot on the boat I've thanked God at the close of every day for what He has done for us. I prayed each day on the boat for our safety. I never prayed this way before and feel so close to Him each night after lights are out. That's when I ask Him for you to be comforted, for our safe return, for the care of the battalion. Our preacher at home sent me the Sunday School lessons for Jan., Feb., and March including the daily Bible readings. Each night I read my testament before going to sleep. May God keep us as we are to return real soon to each other.

Know what I plan to do with that special Valentine you sent? That sweetheart hankie is going inside the pocket closest to my heart and will go with me everywhere I go, no matter where I happen to be. I have your picture by my head and all the Valentines you sent. It's the most attractive corner in the building. The folder is open and tacked up, too, so I can put in some snapshots as well.

My room-mate said I gave away some of our secrets last night, talking in my sleep. Funny, I can't remember a thing. I do get so happy when I read your letters that I laugh out loud sometimes and get the gang curious. You know just how to amuse me with jokes and cartoons.

When I read that item about the Japs, though, it made my blood boil for them to treat our men like that. Some day we'll pay them off for good.

I'm so glad to know you are home. Those soldiers must have been pleased to ride in the same car, but we fellows have made an agreement in the Army not to cut one another's throat if we see the gal is married. Just keep the civilian morale as high as possible.

You had my mouth watering so badly I thought I'd strangle when you told of that good home dinner. I never thought I'd eat just plain bread and enjoy it before going to bed. Carnation milk tastes wonderful mixed with water.

Americans have too big appetites anyway. They say the English will have to go back to their way of eating gradually after the war because they have gone so long like this that their stomachs won't stand the richness.

He was right about the servicemen's code. One Saturday afternoon on the main street in Wilmington she was surrounded by a tipsy quartet out for a romp. They danced around her singing "Ring around the rosie," then saw her staff sergeant's pin with the ETO ribbon. Backing off and saluting with "Sorry, ma'am," they looked for another target. It worked every time, both parties respecting loyalty as a way of life.

On the same street, on the way to church on Sunday, she saw used condoms. Some men had just come from hell in the Pacific, others were headed for it in the other direction, and in the distance, what?

The way I stutter along sometimes you might think I've visited one of these old-fashioned pubs and tried this English beer, but none for me. You speak of living a sane life over there. I see the effects of

strong drink here, and we're headed for battle. If
anyone could lead a saner life, it would be me. If I
go to a show or fiddle around on Saturdays and once
during the week, I've done wonders and made the
fellows faint then. They say this beer is much
stronger than American.

Yesterday came the letter full of the station's
offer and wanting you to stay. I knew the boss valued
your faithfulness, and they have given you a fine
chance. Wilmington will always be a very dear spot in
my heart, and you're right. I didn't want you to go
home like it was the only course, but I believe if you
can find similar work in Memphis, you'd be much
happier. You know the place better, and there's more
to let you be comfortable and easy with. If you don't
find what you want to do there, I sincerely approve of
your going back to North Carolina this summer. I
won't worry. I just trust Memphis to make things more
convenient for you. You are always in my thoughts.

He still could not imagine that just as he wanted
her to be exactly as he had left her, she wanted to be
exactly <u>where</u> he had left her, following his every
step, his wife with a career that kept her at the
forefront of earth-shaking news. She had lived apart
from family anyway since leaving for college at
sixteen, then teaching in Alabama. The new notion of
"extended family" which he had realized with his Army
buddies somehow did not include for him her own new
family - her lovely young landlady with a small
daughter, a husband on Air Force duty in the
Himalayas, and "Pops," the father and grandfather
figure for them all.

Some people think I'm not human, but I have someone
waiting and loving me as I love her, so I'm perfectly
happy and satisfied with just my wife. Nothing can

make me change unless you fail to tell me you love me now and then.

Yesterday I forgot to mention the two-year anniversary of my being in our Uncle's service. I hope before this time next year he'll say "Greetings, soldier. You are now a civilian." I don't think they'll have to blindfold me to get me on the train this time. As for the two lieutenants who censor, they do have a tiresome job. I bet sometimes they get so fed up with letters they just say, "Oh, what's the use?" and let the information go on through. The Valentine letter with all the hearts and flowers literally stood out in the postman's hand last night. It kept pulling toward me, and he couldn't imagine what was wrong. He looked to me like a civilian, but he had chevrons and G.I. shoes on his 4-F feet.

You must know by now that thinking of you is hard to get away from.

Down in rural Herefordshire he may have heard the sound of bombers taking off to launch their pre-invasion campaign. In mid-February a thousand planes flying in close formation for mutual protection headed for twelve vital factories in the Reich. Five days later, after weather cleared again, a "Big Week" of 6000 sorties set out to decimate other major targets.

In the process both sides lost around 500 planes each, but the number of German pilots lost did not compare with the thousands of airmen sacrificed to the effort by the Allies. A bad bargain indeed since the Germans, anticipating such activity, had dispersed industrial centers so cleverly that they could take up production again without missing a beat.

Far from the aerial combat, a soldier listened to a voice from North Carolina. Before leaving for Memphis, her parents' new home thanks to gas rationing and her father's wartime responsibilities, she had recorded a Valentine greeting for him.

I had been wondering if you had been out to the country to see Mother and Daddy by now. They do enjoy having you with them just as we'll always like to visit them some day. It's grand to know you like my people as I do yours. Wouldn't it be terrible if we happened not to have that sort of marriage? Once my people like a person they'll cling like a grapevine unless the person melts away or does something unforgivable.

The other part of my Valentine came today. You have my curiosity so aroused. I'm so anxious to get to some Red Cross or U.S.O. to hear that sweet voice of yours on the records and hear what you have to tell me. Just think, I can play them over and over. They'll never wear out. The largest one was cracked, but with a bit of tape I may be able to fix it so I can hear you talking.

That head of yours really thinks of unusual things.

All by my lonesome in England

There used to be a big Friday afternoon when we at school would plan for that Valentine box. We'd all put ours in for days ahead and watch the sides bulge out, just wondering how many each of us had. When that afternoon came and all were given out, I never, as far back as I can remember, got as many as I did this year, so many I have pinned them all around the wall. I've gotten six already, and that doesn't include the voice you sent me yesterday. I'm so anxious now to go on pass and find one of the music boxes in the Red Cross or Recreation Building. If I don't find a Victrola, here's one that will go to every farm house in this country until I find someone who has one.

I get all the soap, blades, clothes and eats I need. The rations are really better than we had in the States now. I haven't weighed lately, but think I may have gained a bit. With the stamps you sent in the box I have enough to supply the King and Queen when they write to Mrs. Roosevelt.

The other night I was in a convoy with a guy, and when we came in, he burst into my room, plastered a bit, and proceeded to read me two of his wife's letters. I undressed, crawled down into this wonderful straw sack and was almost asleep when he slammed the bed with his hand and said, "I love my wife, and if this war doesn't get over soon, I'll go mad." I think he partly means it. I love you, but I haven't asked to let it be broadcast on the air yet. Would you let me?

Thinking of you

There are some questions that came up today I would like my personal P.F.C., one who is constantly bucking for promotion, to know. First, I'd like to inform the interested parties that under recommendation of Ike and his Wolf-pack (me?), you have been upped in rank to Cpl. Temporary. You know, all are made that way now. You do surprise me the way you remember so much of this Army set-up. You know what kind of rifle we carry, what T.C. means, the grades of all the men now (I hope) and the names of our officers.

We place our mail in the box to be censored before it is sealed. I imagine the censors have to keep a pan of water handy to close the envelopes. I don't see how any person would have that much moisture in him, do you?

You must know by now each time we move our A.P.O. number changes. When we moved this time, it was in the opposite direction and not as close to London as we were. I read in today's paper that London was bombed Sunday night. The wireless we have is so helpful, but oh what music they play! Some of it, put on especially for American troops, takes us back to when you and I were young, McGee.

I just don't know what to do with my arms now.

What does the tax man do but find me here? Just think of a man receiving his tax blank in a foxhole some place in Japan. There ought to be a law against it. What figuring I did the night it came made me satisfied we won't have to pay anything, or at least

147

not much. The fellows here see I don't go out much, so I'm hit for money a great deal. 'Course we may be here and gone tomorrow. I'd just rather send it home.

You mentioned about the English Broadcast. Yep, we do have a large radio and get more news over it. Lots of times it's Germans giving the Americans the devil and trying to stir up hatred among the British and American people. You have to listen closely to one of them because he sounds so British you think he's giving you the straight dope. The British newscasters are very good indeed and are to me a bit superior to ours, giving the exact positions and happenings in a fight without personal thoughts. The music is 3 to 5 years old, though. I hear <u>Three</u> <u>Little</u> <u>Piggies</u> and a few other popular songs that were on our Hit Parade in 1938 or '40.

7:30 A.M. Here's one who hasn't got the sleep out of his eyes, although we've had chow and are waiting to go out and limber up with good old exercise. I wonder sometimes how a drinking man gets going for that.

I heard your voice, so much like you, last night. I was going on pass for a few hours, so carried the small record along. It was so good it made me think of you on the radio and feel like North Carolina again. It's a long story about how I found the Victrola. Just wanted to say "Good Morning" while I have your voice still ringing in my ears.

I've changed my mind and wouldn't give you a divorce now on any ground, even cruel and inhuman treatment. If the dishes came flying at me, I'd just juggle them on my nose, forehead and bony knees. I like you. <u>Honest</u>.

You never will get the picture of the 411th mail call. Your blue envelopes fairly shine. I not only pick them out before the mailman gets down to them, but the other fellows see them, too, and holler back to tell me if I happen to be too far back to see.

Last night on pass a couple of us went to a movie, then I went into every cubbyhole asking if anyone had a phonograph. I almost never made the ladies at the

Y.M.C.A. understand what I wanted. When I finally did, they said theirs was out for repairs. 'Course they were interested in how we talked, and we told them we were from Tennessee. They know nothing but New York, it seems. We also went to two servicemen's halls, but they didn't have one either.

Finally, just walking down the street, I recognized a man I had seen in church in one of the shops, so went in and asked if he had a machine. First he said, "No," then stuttered around and at last invited me in upstairs where he lived over his business. He had a nice place and a good player, just like American. So we nervously placed the record on and listened with all ears. It was so clear and like you that I'll play it lots of times, whenever I have the chance.

We talked with the man and his wife some 30 minutes, and he invited me back to play the large one some Sunday afternoon or any time. Yep, they even wanted us to have tea. They were such nice people, and it did give me a lift a bit to find and sorta know someone a little bit like I think about church and all it means. I'm so anxious to play the other one now.

Every day with you will always be surprises.

When I see pictures of beaches I at once picture us during those quiet lovely months. The real joy of each day was having you see me off to work each morning. I'd give my left leg now to get up, no matter how early, as long as you were fixing my cereal, grapefruit, toast and eggs.

Since chow I've been batting the breeze, reading the papers, and grafting a piece on to the big record you sent. I got some strong Scotch tape, more glue, and have it almost like new. We'll get in town tomorrow night and hear what you have to sing, say, or even shout. Maybe it's "Murder!" I fairly wiggled in my skin when I heard you the other day. This is such a super idea.

Your last three letters from good old N.C. came today. Wilmington is our life, it seems. I can't picture you or us together anywhere else now, but so many places there. If I had only gotten the two letters that came today, I would not have put so many ifs or buts in about your going back. There's no doubt in my mind now that you really will be happy there until I come back. Just to be where we were and where we started our real life together.

If I had only known you wanted to stay where I left you, I'd have encouraged you, but I honestly thought you'd like home better. Why not just rest and take it easy, then go back during the summer months? I'll want you as close as possible anyway when I start home.

Their Tennessee families were loving and supportive, and she made half-hearted attempts at a radio audition and scriptwriting for the Red Cross, but, with his approval, returned to North Carolina shortly to work and wait for him there.

Someone dreamed of a white Christmas last night, and what did they find this morning when we poked our noses out but the ground all covered with snow, and still falling. They told us when we arrived that spring was just around the corner, but we've been around the corner and found only a draft. You've hit the nail as to where I am now. I knew you would figure it out and am glad you can keep track of us.

I was full to my short lip when I came from mail call. How useful those sandals are. When I'm up on my bunk, I pull off my shoes, letting my poor feet rest, but had to stop and slip them back on every time I went out of the room. The sweater will be nice and soft, too, under this wooly shirt that scratches like I have the crabs. When you send such things, my thanks make such a poor showing.

I was surprised to know my neighbor is stationed in the Far East. What a strange lonesome spot he's in. I can't picture myself getting mail only once a month and not being able to write every day or so. That <u>would</u> be the last straw.

You're not the only one with a new hairdo. I thought I should keep in step a bit and cut mine short, too. It's very hard to keep clean and combed here, so I had it cut about two inches all over, a nice feeling. It sticks thickly up, but is smooth and feels so much better. All the fellows comment and want one like it. While the barber was working, a number stood around wanting him to use the clippers and just give me a complete shave all over, including my face. The barber in our battery is very gentle. Another outfit had a hair-cutter they said was gentle as an <u>ape</u>.

Today four of the fellows asked me for money. 'Course I let them have it because it was payday pretty soon, but I'd sooner get it off my hands as to risk some of my debtors.

We'll never have our little talks finished, will we? There'll always be something to say.

When I wake up tomorrow morning I'll say "Rabbit Rabbit" for good luck all month long. Last month you gave me all the luck there could have been that way.

I'd really love to taste that new lipstick you wrote about. Who but you will know what it tastes like? I might let your granddad try it to tell me, but no one younger.

One of the fellows found a farmer around here with real honest-to-goodness eggs and with much persuasion managed to get a dozen out of him. I looked to see powder roll out of the shells when I broke them, but they turned out to have yolks! We have a small stove in our room, so we got a skillet with a little piece of meat for grease, and I take over as cook. They all think I'll make you a good chef who can flop the cackleberries over without missing the pan. We have eggs every morning, but powdered ones lack the flavor of real. That's the good part of knowing some of these farmers. If they have something, they'll sell it even if they take a chance of doing 6 months for it.

They seldom have the latest movies here, but do have some good ones. We saw "Stage Door Canteen" a few weeks ago and Betty Grable in the Rosie O'Grady picture. Maybe if I'm here long enough they'll get some new ones, but honest, I hope I'm not.

When the big record came cracked, I was so afraid I'd never get to hear what you had to say, never giving it a thought you might sing and play. I went back to those nice people, who were so happy to be in on something like that, though I'd hoped for some privacy with you. It was the best thing you could have done while I'm away. I carried both records along and played them to my heart's content. There'll be lots of times I'll want to refresh my memory like that.

Since there is moving in our bones, you may miss a few letters. We couldn't be going too far because you said "Rabbit Rabbit" over there, too. Wonder where that saying came from. I hope it works again.

I can still hear you singing and talking.

---

2 March 1944   Left Foxley, Herefordshire, APO 115, 0830 en route to Nettlebed, APO 230. Arrived 1730 hours.

The 411th had arrived at the area in Oxfordshire which, save for a gunnery excursion to the north and a brief mission to the south, would be their home until the invasion. Since the Third Army they would join eventually would have no formal troop assignments until activated in Normandy, they would hit the beach with Bradley's First.

General Patton, their future commander, had been denied promotion for yet another faux pas. Valuable as he was to the cause, his next mistake would be his last. General Bradley also instructed censors not to pass on any direct quotation from any commander without his personal perusal and approval.

By this time the British countryside and its people were so familiar to the 411th that a move hardly rattled their routine - training during the week and soccer on Saturday afternoon. They also made friends along the way. In spite of differing accents and customs, all shared a common goal - beat Hitler!

That night in the little shop was a strange one. After I got to play the records, we went to the next room and talked for maybe an hour. No, there wasn't a daughter, not even a small baby to attract my eyes. I did find out, which they admitted, they would have starved if it hadn't been for Lend Lease and American help. The other thing that impressed me, they are talking about driving on the right side of the road over here after the war. We Americans do have influence. I mentioned not getting much fruit to eat, and when I was leaving, the man's wife went back and brought out an orange. I knew they were rationed and hated like the dickens to take it, but they insisted.

Can you picture a cloud of smoke in our theaters? Here all during the movie they smoke continually, the women more so than the men. One of the fellows in the battery asked me to give him my week's ration of cigarettes for his lady friend since I don't smoke.
There's wonderful peace that I know some day will come true.

I promise you any American nurse or Red Cross girl, or even Marine will beat the daylights out of these girls overseas. It might be from so many years of worry in war, food problems, and maybe a little too much cycling on their bikes. I have no basis for thinking it, but I imagine they know the U.S.A is a bit ahead of them. 'Course we are a little newer as a country.
Any day now we may get a new A.P.O. In fact, I know it now, but can't tell, and when we get a new one, you can draw your own conclusions. Places around

153

here are worse than Wilmington about military movements. You see how spies can work, so we don't dare let things out.

You think of so many ways to outsmart the mail clerks. I got a good laugh out of the "cigars and cigarettes" you want to send. I know you need a request from me to get a package mailed, and I look forward to seeing what will be in that one.

The moon's all going to waste here. You'll get so moon-burned when I get back. I've had enough of this stuff of being tied down and not doing what we want to ourselves.

Just from the sound of things the boys are starting out early tonight to give old Hitler all the hell he deserves. The air is full of those special birds. One can awaken and hear them all through the night.

Their current station, near Oxford, probably furnished protective cover for the airbase in the area. Assaults on the Reich may not have halted production for long, but Hitler faced another serious problem, a shortage of trained pilots. Having curtailed their indoctrination to preserve precious oil, the Luftwaffe could only strike back on occasion. The difficulty would make a huge difference down the line.

Meanwhile resistance stiffened in France. The French had suffered long in silence while the Germans looted their supplies for the army of occupation. Even the communists were offended by the invasion of Russia. In London nationalist Maquis and units of similar bent were drawing up codes and unifying plans of sabotage to be set in motion by broadcasting over the BBC such innocent-sounding sentences as "The tomatoes must be picked."

As their day of destiny approached, persons of every rank and nationality felt an almost sacred responsibility for keeping the terrible secret.

Yep, time you locate me at the exact spot on the map, river and all, we up and jump all over the place. We may be closer to your brother now. Mine, too. You remember how far I used to travel each day a few months ago to see you? Well, it's about that and a few miles more to where the guard is changed and has been for many years. We got used to the other place so much, but will be the same way here when we've settled in. I don't have the privacy I had, though. Now I'm with <u>all</u> the fellows, and there's a lot more talking and griping giving you and me competition.

No letter of yours has been censored yet, so why not write on back and front so I'll have twice as much?

People can whistle at you all they please and ask unimportant questions to stop you on the street and make your acquaintance, but the minute they ask for a return salute, I'll go to the chaplain right away. I'm a jealous man when it comes to wolf-y 4-F's and may have to appoint a special Wac to watch you. Of course, as soon as you get your next promotion from me for faithful service and ability and get those extra stripes on, you can give any upstart sailors a few orders and put them in the kitchen to clean the grease trap or peel spuds.

This straw felt so good this Sunday morning I couldn't resist going back to it after the powdered eggs (again) and dried milk (likewise). I can't get to bed before ten or eleven, and 5:30 comes awful early these mornings. After we moved this week, we've been busy. I got to looking at the ads today, though, and found one of the best mattresses I want when this war is over. I intend to try it out before we bring it home.

We get to talking here in the hut about how good certain foods would be, how sheets will feel again (even <u>one</u>) and most of all, be on furlough forever with our wives. So many things come up that we need to have that never really mattered at the time, but

155

are life to us when we get home. You remember those cold showers we used to have at the beach? At this new place I took one of those blasted things that made my teeth chatter for minutes. The former experience didn't help a bit.

My brother hoped to meet me in London on the 5th, but I had to cancel, and he didn't get my letter until he'd tried in vain to make the connection, then went back to camp. Every time I put some place I can meet him they cut it out anyway, so he doesn't have any idea where I am now, and you can imagine how hard reading would be as being so important in both countries. We'll figure this out some way, if <u>you</u> can. Remember, we used to do a lot of it on a lazy Sunday afternoon.

I fairly memorize the letters. You are always in my thoughts.

Once again an awkward sentence and finger-pointing clue helped her to locate his new position - Reading. To avoid calling attention to place names he even left out capitals.

I've been on blind dates and had the usual horrible time most people have, but never have I gotten a don't-know-who-wrote-it letter. One came in an envelope covered with stamps for S/Sgt. Rogers <u>Jr.</u> They had marked it "Not in this outfit" and at another place "No place to be found" and just got tired of looking for Junior, so sent it on to me. It must have traveled by carrier pigeon.

A girl attending school at Columbia University had written to a boy in the infantry who had just gone overseas. It had been turned down so much it couldn't seem to go any further, so we saw no reason for me to keep it or send it on. After I destroyed it, though, I thought later I should have tried one more time. Maybe it was the only letter, silly as it was, that the soldier would ever get from her even though it didn't seem important to us.

The rules and regulations around here do, have, and always will get on one's nerves. There are so many that people are bound to disobey, some through just plain not knowing them all. It's about as bad as Army regulations. I try to keep legal, though, and every time I go to town keep up my spirits by stopping at the bakery for extra eats. Clothes I don't need because I'm already loaded to the gills when we move.

If you write on backs, upside down, catty wampus or any way, just so I hear from you.

So far, with us moving, the months go by pretty quickly. It must be, as they say, a bit harder on the loved ones back home than it sometimes is on the man overseas. I can thank God for having you to look forward to. I'm so lucky to have you in my heart to keep me happy and jolly. If anyone can, you can.

> You know where
> It begins with an E

You know me. If I can't spend Sunday with you, I'm just satisfied to do bunk fatigue, read and write even if this bunk I'm sitting on is made of straw and slats. It sleeps rather well when you're tired.

I didn't wake up until 7:15, had 2 sunny side eggs, cereal with powdered milk and stump water coffee, then tried for a warm shower. I turned off all the cut-offs and threatened a man's life if he used any water first. Then when I came to my hut for clean clothes, I hollered there was hot water. No one had a shower this week, so they all came storming out of their bunks behind me. Thinking I had all we'd need, we turned it on full force. Lo and behold it began to run cold before we even got started. They wanted to string me up. We laughed while the chill bumps rose. It was so cold, but felt oh so good after I came back and crawled in the covers. I have 4 blankets now, sleep on one and put the others on top, even adding my overcoat and shelter half sometimes.

After a full week we went to see the town and catch a movie. If you want to know the people of England, see "Lassie Come Home." It's just the way they are, the country, town, talk and love for animals.

8 o'clock B.B.C. time

As soon as I saw the envelopes in the stack, I had a feeling you had a letter for me. I can tell them at a glance, and they're not so big that I can't slip them in my field jacket and let you ride along with me.

All the words are beautiful.

We'll have a busy day tomorrow going to (censored), then back here again. You'd think I was going to Nashville, it happens to be that far. We will see the country, and when we go rocking along on these narrow trails, you'll go along with me on my back. I have you packed in my field bag. Do you feel comfy or sort of squished? 3:30 A.M. will be here before I turn over.

---

22 March 1944	Left Nettlebed, Oxfordshire, APO 230, by motor convoy at 0630 hours enroute to Whitby, Yorkshire. *Bivouacked Staging Area. Traveled approximately 145 miles. *Staging Area (Doncaster)
23 March 1944	Left Doncaster Staging Area by motor convoy at 0830 hrs enroute to Whitby, Yorkshire. Arrived at 1730. Traveled approximately 105½ miles. Temporary changes of stations.

"Nettlebed," as later on the continent, identified the lesser-known village or small town at which the unit was based outside a large town or city.

Whitby, their destination, had ancient claims to fame. Surviving ruins of the old abbey recall the seventh-century synod which settled the future course of the English church at a time when Caedmon the cowherd was becoming "the father of English sacred music." A millennium later Captain James Cook, a local resident, had ships constructed there and sailed from that harbor for his journey to the other side of the world.

For men of the 411th the chief interest, beyond the search for hospitality to break military monotony, was firing at targets over the North Sea. Bad weather would hamper their efforts, but a man from Leeds was much impressed by their skill. By shooting down the practice sleeve before noon one day, they gave their British counterparts the only afternoon off since their disastrous combat experience in France. Now both outfits prepared to fight side by side to bring Hitler's monstrous campaign to an end.

9:10 P.M. - COLD

I have such a poor place to write that I can't keep steady. You'd be surprised to know where we are now. You'd like this place on vacation. No heat here, so I'm sitting with coat and scarf on and would put on my gloves if I thought I could write in them. We pulled in late this afternoon, and after much fiddling around found a place assigned to us as quarters, which could be worse.

Even when moving I ask God to shorten the days.

The mailing system is so bad for us here in the northern part of England. When they hollered "Mail call," I rushed down the steps with my buddy so fast I left him so far behind that I'd have all of his before he finished the first lap. We were pretty much delighted when the mail truck pulled in loaded to the sidewalls.

I'm staring at this new picture of you that came today. I look at you all over the room, making remarks to the fellows how she's watching me as I move from place to place. You know how some pictures look as though the head is turning or the eyes following you.

The seashore here reminds me of Wrightsville Beach. This is a similar resort, and when one looks out over the sea, one can think back on the beautiful hours we used to have there.

You might think I'd leave you behind on our trips, but you know you wouldn't be left alone with the wolves in that barrack. Besides, they sometimes tell some off-color jokes you shouldn't hear. So you always travel in my field pack. Think of yourself as being a little papoose.

The first thing I spoke this morning was a word to my special wife, who seems to smile every time I look her way.

Today has been rather foggy, so I thought about taking my jack knife out and cutting a hole in the reveille bugle so the tooter couldn't tootle his toot. This weather must be cool the year round. We have to wear our wools and won't be issued any cottons.

I must be beginning to favor the British in my looks. One sergeant said I should like this country because I look as Rome looked. And should I consider this a compliment or knock him for a row of lulus?

The missing hurts sometimes, but then I think how wonderful it is to have someone to miss.

Mail call before chow tonight, and lots did without to read theirs, but I'd have gotten pretty hungry before bedtime. I was pretty excited, though, when I saw blue envelopes in the stack. My sergeant was smart. He went through the batch and brought out all five from you, then had the nerve to say, "How could anyone fall for a guy from Tennessee?" They don't make them any better for first sergeant. All the fellows at headquarters think he's about the best in the battalion.

This country is so funny. One part is cold and foggy, raining every day, then another part has the sun shining. Today on the range the sun came out, then before we came in it's sleeting and cold as the devil. North Carolina, I'll come back to you any day. No fires are allowed except in the orderly room, so I'm writing there close to the fireplace. We have to wear steel helmets all the time, and I get a rub properly from mine, so even my scalp gets exercise. It gets sore, though. My hair seem to be growing faster in this English air.

As I came in from firing this afternoon, you followed me all the way across the room. I feel good for looking at you.

I'm humming, "She is always in my heart, Even though we're far apart," or sometimes it's "My bonnie lies over the ocean," which is old, but that's where she is. Some days one couldn't get up a whistle to save his life, but then he gets to feeling thankful he's alive, and the music comes out, especially the night before our anniversary.

A story in the paper today is so true about England. The streets are so narrow, mostly of brick, with houses just as close to the street as possible. Usually there is only about 2 feet of sidewalk with a pub every 10 to 20 feet. They do like their beer, not cold like the Americans. One thing you won't find is a drinking fountain. They must drink beer instead. Even when you go on pass you die for a drink of water. The girls don't have that fair skin they claim the English have either. This weather is especially hard on skin, and their cheeks are red as lipstick, one could say.

I can't stay up late and get up so early. Ain't my life a mess? I need you here to straighten it out.

March 31st Our Anniversary Night

So many times today has the sweet scene of us on our wedding day come back to me, how wonderful it was when the boys flocked around and gave us a big send-off with a hat full of money and the party. In my bitterest times I know you'll be there with me to take me through all of it. I might not think of you at the time, but you'll be there somehow, with me some way. No matter how far I go, how long we are apart, where I go you go, and where you go I go.

I hope you got my roses and cable today. Wish I could be there, too.

When I was going to school, so many took advantage of All Fools' Day and really pulled some boners. We were so busy here that no one thought of it until this morning. Someone called "Chow!" and after we came out and lined up, there wasn't any! We had to wait a while (April Fool!).

Up here on the range we are on the same level as Limeys, so we get the same chow they do. You'd think the American pirates had captured a tea boat or even a Chinese rice field. It's all in what you're used to, I've found. The bugle blows so early these mornings, and we have to stir around to be ready by 7:30, then stay out in the cold until 6 at night. We can't fuss. We've been lucky so far. Some have it worse.

The Germans had already discovered what "worse" meant. Their troops, top-scale at first, now consisted principally of men either untrained or burned out in the eastern campaign against Russia or newly formed outfits without experience or full equipment. Instead of an army of racially pure Teutonic stock they were forced to field so-called "racial Germans" from their borderlands and unwilling "volunteers" from the countries they conquered. Their Luftwaffe was down to a couple of hundred planes, not all operable at the same time. Furthermore, they couldn't divine the Allies' strategy. Why the landing at Anzio? Would there be other unexpected commitments elsewhere that would need defending?

By contrast, except for the weather, matters for the 411th went very well indeed. On suitable days they

162

had racked up an impressive firing record even in the eyes of the Brits. The accomplishment loomed larger since they had to march each day through narrow, curving streets and climb nearly 200 steps toward the ruins of Whitby Abbey to set up the guns. If a man had visited too many pubs the night before, his nerves and stomach could really be rattled by a beer hangover.

Some also developed a fancy for the other national drink.

———————

The people in this country do like their tea and push it at you every chance they get. Once we thought in the States that all the sugar was going overseas, but none can be found here either. Around ten o'clock each day the Limeys have tea and cookies. Once you do it a few times you get to liking it and miss the cakes if you don't have them, so we take a few minutes off for tea and cookies, 10 A.M. each morning. 'Course it's a bit of "queueing" in line for an hour, but we've waited in lines three-fourths of our time in the Army anyway.

So you liked the roses. I'm glad.

It's another cold, rainy day. Since the time was advanced one full hour, we won't be able to catch up on our shut-eye. It's 9:45 P.M. now and still light outside. We had a good movie, though. I never used to go to movies on Sunday at home, but this was fun on a day that hampered firing practice anyway.

And since I came back in, you're watching to see if I wink at you. <u>There</u>. I <u>did</u>. <u>Honest</u>. You see I still like to flirt.

Just found out that the oldest Rogers boy is going to be a sailor. One in the Army, one in the Air Force, and now one in the Navy. I never believed he would have to go. We talked once about his changing jobs. My guess is he might find a new opportunity there, and in so many cases that's not true in the

Army. He spoke of leaving his wife and child. I know that cute little boy will make it difficult. I had hoped they'd had enough with two of us in service already.

You know me. I'm crazy about my auto and was mighty glad to know it had been taken care of before he leaves. You must feel like getting into it when you go out home to visit, but don't take out any of those 4-F's. Besides, the tires are off, and they have chains on it so it can be pulled out of the shed quickly in case of fire. It'll be ready when we swing out in it for a ride some day.

His future general, now on resplendent good behavior, was touring England and giving inspirational speeches to foster a cooperative fighting spirit. Veterans of North Africa, preparing up in Belfast for action, thought Patton a first-class con man in many ways, but thoroughly respected his capabilities. His supposed First U.S. Army Group (FUSAG), alluded to in conspiratorial fashion at some of his appearances, so convinced even Stars and Stripes of its existence that one headline read "PATTON IN UK TO LEAD INVASION FORCE."

As April began, with furloughs and passes canceled, the southern coast bore the brunt of the coming onslaught. To their everlasting credit the British people, with barely a complaint, saw beloved gardens and lawns trampled and run over, stood in long lines for everything, waited for trains that arrived late or not all, interrupted their meager ration supply to enhance troop movements, and suffered all with the patience the French for the most part would show in coming months as well. Calm acceptance was the last gift they could offer to men who risked their very lives. Unhappy necessity.

For some, "necessity" meant "bath."

This coming Sunday will be Easter. Could I have a special date with you that day always? If I get back, you'll have the biggest and best corsage the florist has in his shop. I had planned to be with one of our brothers near London if possible. We will be back at our other place by then.

Just a few minutes ago I got extravagant and used more than my ration for a bath. The air was off the water, and it was lukewarm for a change. They need a lesson in American plumbing over here. The rumor is since the Yankees made their invasion of England, they haven't had a day of rest. Some of the kids have even gotten so bold as to ask for gum, sweets and what-have-you for their big sister. What is the younger generation coming to? Here's one brother who won't wait to see. Can I come home now?

He wrote lightheartedly, but a chill unrelated to the weather began to be felt in the bones ("_If_ I get back," for the first time). A small trembling of the heart as activity intensified.

BODYGUARD, the Allied deception plan of "Army Group Patton," continued to fool the logical German mind with dummy landing craft in the Thames estuary and huge false tent encampments near Dover. Though the invasion was expected at Pas de Calais, Hitler had doubts, even suspected Normandy. His generals, Rommel and von Rundstedt, knew a landing would happen but where? One advocated a strong stand at the beach, the other a mobile strategy behind the front. Rommel's assessment paralleled Hitler's, but the other commander managed the panzers.

As for troops, those who should have been receiving further training in combat had been put to work installing water obstacles, digging entrapment ditches, and laying mines. Hungary had relieved the need for fighting men there by accepting occupation, but a 200-mile advance by the Russians required divisions meant for invasion defense, plus panzers and assault guns, to be sent east.

Eisenhower and Bradley stressed "confidence" as the key word for OVERLORD. They had a back-up plan ready in case the invasion failed, but staff members were not to hint by attitude, word or deed that it would ever be needed. No grim faces.

The 411th prepared for another move.

———————

Today's mail call was blown, and here's one who's there before the echo has died out of these hills. If I even take a ten-minute break, you come into my thoughts, but I'm not sorry one bit. As long as you do, I won't be afraid.

In a few days now we'll be going back to our camp closer to London than your father is old. It's typical Easter weather here, cold, raining and unsettled. I've tried to let you know just how we move about, but am afraid if I'm telling too much. This place would be a fine vacation spot in America, but here in wartime, of course, it's a flop. The hotels we live in are not what you'd expect of the word. They shouldn't even say "hotels" now because they have no fires, no hot water, no mail service, and no elevators. If we climb the six flights of steps once, we climb them a dozen times a day. Some even try the banisters to get down quick when they holler chow, but no other time. One corporal has found my name is Wesley in the middle, and for about a month now he's been trying to make me mad by calling me Sgt. Wesley. The joke's on him. My name was Wesley long before I even knew him.

I was pretty keyed up with the beautiful wedding ring you sent me for our anniversary. I notice it over and over and remember each time all that it means. You judged my finger so well, too. It's just a bit large, but so I won't lose it until I get to a jeweler somewhere, I may wear it on my middle finger. One of your letters was looked into way back, but not one since. Just think what an unusual airmail that letter with the wedding band would have been for any censor to open. Someone was with it all the way, and it must have been your wish with God's answer. It did come on a Tuesday, too, so though late, it was almost on our anniversary that way.

For keeping her man in the best of spirits I again think she deserves a promotion. As far as I can see our T.O. calls for another Sergeant. That's you. You can fill in so beautifully and work along with me. All the time, too. 'Course you'll have to remember to deduct $2.00 for your stripes from our income tax next year. That's what we are allowed.

This business of lending money out didn't work so well last month. At the last 15-20 fellows hit me, and I haven't collected it all back yet. This month I'm putting my neck out and my foot down.

In our move tomorrow we stop at a place that's no good for camping. It's an old fair grounds area. We stopped there on the way up and rested our tired bones on some hard floor in a tent. I met an old man who was keeping the fires going in the kitchen for the Limeys. I asked him for the paper, and what does he do but go and get out of a barrel a paper from 1941 - honest. He said, "You can see how the war was then." Sure enough, they were catching it in London then so badly.

| 6 April 1944 | Left Whitby, Yorkshire by motor convoy at 0730 enroute to Nettlebed, Oxfordshire. Bivouacked at Lutterworth Staging Area. Traveled approximately 160 miles. |
| 7 April 1944 | Left Lutterworth Staging Area by motor convoy at 0800 hours enroute to Nettlebed, Oxfordshire. Arrived at 1430 hours. Traveled approximately 75 miles. |

They headed back south where GIs flooded the pubs with American dollars at triple the buying power of their British counterparts. The local ladies were well aware of the difference.

In London, to the east, planners laid out on the floor of St. Paul's School a relief map of the Normandy peninsula the width of a city street. Eisenhower and Bradley would witness the first of two invasion rehearsals, and King George himself would be present for the second, on the Devon coast near the Dartmouth Naval Base.

As the role of air forces escalated, Eisenhower assumed over-all command. British General Montgomery had given grudging approval to an air drop near Utah Beach (Varreville), but others predicted a casualty rate of 80% for such an operation and 50% for the airborne landing in gliders. Risk 17,000 men, particularly those who had already made such landings in North Africa and Sicily and might have used up their odds? Though the Air Force chief himself objected outright, Eisenhower needed their experience, but was also troubled by a figure of 80,000 civilians suggested as possible victims.

The Normandy invasion, unlike that in Sicily, would begin at dawn after the RAF had laid down a heavy bombardment during the night. As troops began to land beginning at thirty minutes after daylight and ending no more than an hour and a half later, the U.S. Air Force and Navy would continue gunfire.

The 411th, having completed their own practice at Whitby, had only to waterproof their equipment and go through the motions they would need for a genuine invasion under real fire.

You know by now that what I say goes "twice" and "double," too. Maybe that means the same thing in the States, but it's different in "the Isles."

We've come down from our long visit. When we started this morning, we thought we'd have chow on the road, but made such good time that we came on in camp and had what <u>they'd</u> call chow. What was so good was all the mail the orderly had for me.

Thinking of you.

When I get so many nice blue envelopes, the boys all perk up their eyes and ears to know what we talk about. We do arouse their curiosity. I get so absorbed in the letters that if they hollered "Fire!" I'd sit there and let the shack burn down and just keep on with you.

The Easter Bunny is ahead of time. The package is here on the shelf, and I've gotten rather curious to know what you sent. I wanted to open it at first glance, then noticed the note <u>Not To Be Opened Until Easter.</u> It's only a few hours now. Couldn't you just let me peep a little? I'd like to stay up till one minute after twelve, but don't think I can make it. Maybe it won't spoil. Never does there come a red letter day that you don't remember.

After chow tomorrow morning I'll be with you to sing "Happy Easter," then dress in my best new Easter <u>issue</u> and go to church. It's been ages since I've had the chance, and although we may have to walk miles in getting there, a bunch of us plan to go together. I've always looked forward to Easter and going with someone special to church on that day.

I'm surprised to hear about your brother, but he's had such real action in the air for so long that would bring a case of nerves to any man. They at home are so proud of him, and whose mother and father wouldn't be under those circumstances? Personally, we will never send a son away because we'll end it all <u>this</u> time.

Her young brother, turret gunner in bombing raids over the French coast, had been hidden by the Free French after landing behind German lines, then spirited by night in a car with drawn blinds to some conveyance to safety in Ireland. On another occasion, in a plane so badly shot up it was losing altitude over the English Channel, he and his crew had recited the Lord's Prayer together; their wounded bird settled

169

in with nose just clearing the white cliffs and tail trailing in the water.

While they waited for their turn in combat, the 411th enjoyed springtime.

You have one more month before going back to Wilmington. It'll be a good time to enjoy the beach and have fun with the girls sailing, swimming, and just taking in that good old fresh beach air.

I wish you could send me some of the cookies you sent to Davis. They were so good and fresh. If you can't find them now, I'll settle for Hostess cupcakes.

It's the most beautiful Easter day, one to remember in England. It was rainy and dull until 8:30, then cleared so nicely for us to go walking in the countryside.

I ate chow before I came back to open my Easter package, then had the fellows come around to see what the Bunny had brought me. You should have heard the roar. They like you for being so helpful and cheerful, keeping me in good spirits. The bunny has been so cute all day, and I'm munching on the candy eggs right now. Then in the noon mail call I got the nice sayings in your letter and Easter card. The snapshot you enclosed was extra. I don't give a darn for the dog, but take the biggest interest since you were holding him. And what a hailstorm you had! It looks like eggs all over the ground. The one pictured beside the orange is the biggest I've ever heard of in Tennessee.

When I looked at the bulletin board yesterday, what did I find but a surprise from a friend in Memphis. The board was so crowded I couldn't get up close. The fellows were all laughing and thought you were so clever to promise to send them what you did, just what they are interested in. Even the first sergeant thought it was a good April Fool joke on the company. And what a discussion we had about all those ten new cars that would be coming over for us and all the extra ration cards you were supposed to be sending. We couldn't figure who would get to use them first, especially the cars before the tires wore down. 'Course most of them knew I was from Tennessee, but they didn't know exactly who had that much humor.

You might have guessed by now the place we visited up north. Since we have already left, you can know it was Whitby, just along the coast. You can keep up <u>after</u> I have left a place, but I can't tell you too much until I've been there and gone.

We had class in the mansion of the Duchess of Yorkshire and even some in the stable. It's a rather historic place, took years to build, and was a national landmark. One thing I remember most was some steps we climbed each morning, 199 of them, to reach the firing range. We counted. Oh did it get to those pancakes so early in the day. For many who were out late the night before and had the big head (hangover) it really was hard. It seemed strange, too, for us to be marching through the narrow streets. The people just stand and gaze, and the kids go between our ranks and ask for American chewing gum. Some are so cute, but some are filthy dirty.

8:30 B.B.C. Time in England

At last it came our time for the Range Section to have the radio, and we are enjoying good old American music. It's been months since I've heard Bing Crosby, and it was news to me that he and Frank Sinatra were supposed to be having a feud. It hit all of us to the quick when Bing got in the groove. We went back to those days when we used to be with "that girl" or "my wife," or even just "a friend." You spoke of Frances Langford the other day as being the one all us fellows in the service like best. We do think she goes as far as she can to keep one's chin up. You need not be jealous a bit, but she is one in a million of the stars. Dorothy Lamour does her part in bonds, of course, but we all lean toward Bob and Frances.

You are thoughtful about donating blood. When a person gets that blood of yours, he'll snap out of it, whatever he's got, and feel so frisky and devilish for an hour afterward. In all you do over there for the winning of this struggle, one thing is keeping a man happy. I got three of your letters in only nine days from your hands. Isn't that great?

When you write and tell me of the place where I am, it's more than I can even find out here. You'd never know they have a biscuit factory you mentioned when they are so short of bread in these parts. I didn't even know about General Patton, either. The Yank news came late. I may repeat some things, too, to be sure you get them if letters are lost or cut out, sure as the devil, by a censor for some reason.

The Easter cards are so cute that they'll be on the wall around you for a long time. Your picture looks so alive as though you're about to speak.

In pup-tent. Bow-wow

One would like this place for a camping trip, but it's no fun at all without you along. It's been a real weary day, full of that "heavy fog" we call "rain." My tent partner and I have a fairly good shelter. Still, a fellow six-one has his troubles when old Jack Frost gets to nibbling on his toes early in the morning.

I was so tickled with the comic books you sent, but some of these dopes had the nerve to ask for Superman next time. So far I've kept your street address away from these other wolves, but since you included me in that group, I want to be one with you, too.

They have an all-service program on B.B.C. 'Course the programs are transcribed, but they do bring us some interesting shows, those we might miss back home. We've heard Fibber McGee and Molly, Sinatra, even Jack Benny coming on in the morning. What I want you to do back in Wilmington is get on a short-wave program we can hear over here.

Please send me the biggest box of chocolate candy you can find. I'm getting choosy a bit.

You may think you have been in most every kind of shower, but tonight I've had one up on you. I thought the cold ones we had at the beach were the last straw. 'Course you know me. You know I'll keep clean if it kills me. There was a mobile shower truck down the road about a mile, so we climb in a truck and take off. We marched in with the biggest smiles like some tow-head getting a new pair of shoes, thinking, "Oh, isn't this going to feel good!" Sure enough, it's the best shower I've had in ages. They just had to run us out the water felt so good. Lots of suds, water, and a good soaking was what we needed, and we felt we were really splurging when we found this.

No mail this rainy day, so no greetings from you when I walk into my puptent and bark. One of the jeep drivers just pulled his jeep up in front of the tent, so I'm having competition with corny humor and loud records. I console myself, saying they couldn't have come from America, but maybe they are Lend Lease, too.

Most of the fellows have gone on pass tonight, but I took that great bath instead. It's such a bother to clean up under such difficulties as we have here. I was sound asleep when I heard a noise and thought it was time to get up again. Grabbed my "torch" and found it was just some blokes who'd had too many. It was only midnight!

You'll have to re-locate me on the map again. It looks like we'll be close to where we were before. As soon as we get settled, we get moving in our bones and pull up stakes. I can break away rather easily, though, not like some who've found something they don't want to leave.

You're nice every day and twice on anniversary Tuesdays.

Yesterday was Sunday, but we wouldn't have known it if we hadn't just taken off for an hour to go to church. We just left what we were doing and went in fatigues, leggings, helmets and what we had on our faces. I once thought you couldn't really come to God so closely by just forming a church out in the open. Now when we take time out to sing songs and have a moment in prayer, we seem so small when we think how large God's wonders can be. Never do I feel so humble as I do now when I go to Him in prayer. The chaplain used to be at Davis. All the fellows liked him there.

I was glad to hear you are leaving for Wilmington where you'll be so close to the news again. The job you like along with the days at the beach will keep you more satisfied while I'm away. I still want you to watch out for wolves and 4-F's from the shipyard.

Got a letter from my brother before he left for the Navy. He did seem a bit blue about leaving the little one. Who wouldn't? Missing the growing-up time. When I've talked with Navy men, though, I'm so pleased that one Rogers took to the water. He'll be a good sailor, you know that.

19-30 April 1944   ALERTED FOR DEPARTURE

Everyone in the outfit knew that meant "Any time now." Yet all she heard back in the states was comic books, candy, and the hope she was getting his letters. Without comprehending the impact, she unfortunately threw him a last-minute zinger. A high-ranking officer in the reserves, a veteran pilot of World War I, knew of an opening for limited service in England and offered to use his influence in her behalf. The opportunity combined self-interest with service to the country. It was not the W.A.C. they had discussed in the past together, but her soldier readying for D-Day panicked, thinking that was her intention.

It was so late last night when we came in I couldn't write. On top of that a dimming of the lights came early for reasons you can guess. The question you asked me about wants the quickest possible answer. I couldn't get the connection, having read the long explanatory cable before I read the letter. I've often thought of what would happen if you suddenly decided to join some of these military auxiliaries. You seem to have forgotten all the danger, all the worries, and the things unsettled in my work, and most of all you and where you want to be when and at all times, especially after the war. I'm certain I want someone to look to meeting me at home and not trailing six months to a year later. One day I'm here and the next might be across the channel or in some other seaport. Try as I may, for four months now I haven't been able to see our brothers as much as I've longed to and tried my darnedest to work out. If I could get passes to see you, certainly I could see them now and then.

We may have our last weekend here. Our time of doing as we did in Wilmington is over. Someone must have given you the wrong idea of this life and the way things are in this country. Where I want you to be is in the states, not over here where all the hell and turmoil are being raised. Stay on the other side for my sake and your safety always. I like the idea of your wanting to help in this war effort, but not overseas duty.

Somehow I feel capable of taking care of myself and going back home safely, but if you don't stay put, you'll worry me plenty.

The first lengthy letter with full details was, of course, the last to arrive two weeks later. At the very least the untimely mix-up revealed how resolute his spirit was as his big crisis approached, and he at least forgot the Channel for a bit. Within weeks she was safely back at the microphone in North Carolina, and he could once again concentrate on Hitler.

Along with that candy, the best I've ever tasted, what does she send me but the key to our big city. The mail clerk and the fellows got such a laugh. Yep, even the censor got a smirk by cutting out the most important part, the name. I, of course, passed the candy around the hut, but had the whole bottom layer to myself afterward. We all pass our packages around and enjoy it so when others get one.

You may never figure out how flatly I refused your going to the Wacs or even one similar to it. You'd fall into something you'd be surprised at having done because things don't work out in these services as they do on paper. I don't doubt your judgment one bit, but I do know what you can expect and not expect in these unsettled times. Even if you were to take only five weeks of training there, I'd be surprised if I remain in the same situation as I am now. You must realize we have our hands pretty full and will have until I can come back to you forever and ever.

Just remember, we both want to bear each other's problems no matter what we go through.

I always enjoy the magazines and cartoons you send, especially the comments you add. Sometimes I start an article and if you've written No Good, I think it not worth reading and go on to the next.

You and I seem so small when it comes to that big mail they're taking to Berlin tonight. It's about the biggest they will receive. It's quite a feeling to be here with so much noise all about you. You speak of the planes around home. You have just the view from the sideline. I don't see how those Jerries can stand up under the strain much longer.

I hope my cable has helped you to decide about joining the service. If you did join, heaven forbid, you might never reach England anyway. It would be the greatest disappointment you've ever received if you planned for us to be together even a little. Thinking about that makes me want to change my mind, but I can't let my heart guide me. I'm still hoping they won't draft women, and as long as they are still as far from it as they are now, won't you go ahead as planned?

What you should be is an officer anyway. What I see happening to girls over here and what they have to put up with, I think you'd become so disgusted with it all, and we couldn't see each other either. You want to help, and that being so, be just as you are.

I have a big Private Property sign over all the pictures and little things that remind me of you. Lots of the fellows remember you at Davis and comment the picture doesn't do you justice. I let them know it's nice to have a symbol of you, but it's not the real self anyway.

My brother's APO has changed so he must have moved again. He told me the place we could meet, the only one possible, and as usual the censor cut it out, so we are still no closer.

I bet you can't guess what army your soldier could be in. You say I'm first in your heart, and it turned out we are first in all armies, the First Army. We have our patches, and I wish you were here to sew them on. You can look up the insignia to see what they look like. This paragraph may be cut, maybe not.

Hey, did you see this morning's paper? They seem to be keeping all the people in Britain now. They don't expect anyone to leave until no one knows when. So much is going on over our heads no one can tell what could be happening. When we went out for chow, they were still coming back from the raids. I always think of your brother when I see them.

Sunday night in town I saw James Stewart in Destry Rides Again. I can't remember seeing one of his films before. He's been in the Army so long. Didn't the gals take over him once like they did Frank Sinatra?

Never will I let you out of my sight when I get back. That's a threat and a promise.

We talk a lot about our minds working in the same channel. It never occurred to me that you'd think of us Southern boys as you did. We had been talking about sending for some watermelon seeds and never thought you could read between the lines somehow. All the fellows roared when I showed them the envelope of Ferry's Best. We'd not only have to put up a scarecrow to keep the Limeys out, but would have to post a guard detail. You remember how they liked

watermelon when they visited Davis. Then, too, we
don't stay in one place long enough for the crop to
sprout.

A funny thing happened the other day in (censored).
One man complained he was short three pairs of socks.
That night we forced him to take a shower, and what do
you think? He found his socks all right, but we all
looked for clothespins for our noses.

I'm having to set up a ration system all my own.
Packages don't come every day, so I pass the stuff
around to the fellows, but remind them it's rationed
to make it last as long as possible.

I am almost afraid to open a letter now for fear
you had already joined a service before hearing from
me. Always I want to have you to come home to, just
thinking what you look like and what you're doing each
day. Life will be so changed if I can't picture you
this way. Please always just remain yourself.

Yep, tomorrow is the usual inspection day, which
will be far different from what we had in the states.
More brass keeps popping up from some place and
keeping us on the ball. It's got so there's no room
behind the eight ball. They have to get behind the
seventh.

Always looking toward you and home.

———————

In final preparation for the big job ahead the 411th
journeyed to a coastal assault training center near
Plymouth to waterproof and "wade" their vehicles. The
English Channel became a reality. The Tennessee farm
boy had paddled in the stock pond back home, the
draftee had floated a few feet in a pool in Georgia,
but the combat soldier in England preparing for
invasion didn't know how to swim. His greatest fear
on going ashore was not of being bombed or shot at,
but of drowning before he even hit the beach.

Men in the upper echelons fought a war of nerves as
well. Though news of Patton's fake army had been duly
leaked to the enemy, everything else was designed to

cast doubt. Montgomery's headquarters at Portsmouth sent out signals to Kent to be re-transmitted as if originating there. Convoys, playing up the notion that Devon and Cornwall were the deception instead of the real thing, began running with their lights on as if begging to be noticed. The Luftwaffe suspected a build-up around the Isle of Wight, but no more at Dover.

Unfortunately the rehearsal turned into disaster. German U-boats infiltrated the fleet, sinking two LSTs with a loss of over 700 men, a number not exceeded on D-Day itself. Another ship also suffered a hit. Not having been briefed on details of the invasion landing, troops if captured could not have revealed information of import, but high-ranking officials did not breathe easily until every man, dead or alive, was accounted for. General Bradley himself, while witnessing the actual event, did not know full details until four years after the war was over. GIs stationed at the scene, though, had the story. Bodies washing up on shore day after day made reality all too evident and the need for secrecy even more apparent.

These months are certainly slipping away. We've done lots and been places I don't see how we could have traveled to in such a short time. We never want time to drag while we're over here. There's only one aim in the next day, doing as much as we can to fix ourselves to get this thing over and go home to the best in life. My weakness is you.

We got paid yesterday afternoon. After that, four of us went boating on the Thames, and to think I was so brave in all that deep water. We paddled all over the place and got one of the first English blisters from staying in their sun too long. It was the most fun we'd had in some time, just relaxing and doing what we pleased for a change. Then we saw a movie I remember hearing on Lux Radio Theater.

Yesterday we went on convoy to another Church of England service which proves so difficult for me to follow. You know how many churches of different kinds I've been to since I came in the Army. When I was at home, I never thought I'd attend anything but Baptist. Now it does me good to go to different ones from time to time.

On payday yesterday instead of taking the money and being burdened with it during whatever comes, when the clerk asked if I wanted to send any home, I handed him twenty pounds back. He almost fainted and smiled all over as though he was a firm that was paying off and getting the money back again.

It's our little life. What we do is for both of us, sharing all our thoughts.

As you've already seen, the letters you'd think would get here first come last, like the one you sent with the first notion about the W.A.C. You can count on the mail you're really wanting to get here to come on the tugboat instead. I hope everything is settled by now and that you are happy with it all.

I think so many times how lucky I am to have everything I ever want to seek and never have the worry of some fellows I know, even if we are away for years.

I never realized, though, how you knew I wanted to plant a Victory garden over here. By the time I plant all the seeds you've already sent I won't have room for the tea seeds.

It's time for lights out. Guess who's in my deepest thoughts.

I was thinking last night how I enjoyed the one letter I get from you each day. Then today I got three.

About your question, yes, the whales did pipe up and down on the way over.

There haven't been any eggs falling in these parts, but you can never tell when they'll be shipped over with all the trimmings. What gets me is that the generals never tell me these things. I'm going to see my lawyer.

I'm so proud of my wife for giving all that special blood to the Navy. Why can't the Army get on the ball down there and have a place for donors? I can just see the devilish look in the eye of the person who gets yours.

It makes me so proud when you say "Your Wife."
                    Your Haywire Hubby

We never get used to this climate. It's spring, I guess, but it's blackberry winter every other day. I got so warm last Sunday I shed my longies, then about two days later felt the breeze around my ankles blowing so strongly I reached back in the duffel bag and got them out again. I can't stand this wooly blanket without them anyway. You know Frances Langford wore them to keep <u>her</u> warm on an overseas tour and even borrowed those from some G.I.

Some of your letters lately are coming out the end from such a long trip. Send them anyway.

It's one of those beautiful nights, full moon and all, but what does it do? Just a good night for bombing.
                    Sweet dreams.

When we went to Henley for that beautiful afternoon of canoeing, I thought how you'd enjoy this lovely stream. We fellows do have a good time together, but have so many different opinions we spend too much time hemming and hawing on what we want to do. Somehow you and I start some place and end up both so pleased, just a natural understanding about what we'd both like. I love to live that way.

Today was the nicest. No, not because we weren't busy. Usually we are now. Just because of two real letters and a heavy, delicious package. I was so hungry for something sweet. You know how you can get that way sometimes. We might get our rations from the P.X., but I eat my two candy bars up before I get back to the hut. Thanks a million for sending some just now. The boys think I have the sweetest wife.

Another thing that was so amazing and surprising is the way my wife can set me back on my heels and dress me down. I know you had a good idea if they start drafting women, and your idea of being in such service is super if you'd just not plan to come overseas. I'll always like you to stay on the other side. It's gratifying the attitude you have toward helping to win the war. I just wish a few more could have the same feeling in Washington. In fact, it makes me feel so good that I want to do an about face and let you burn the letters I sent from Whitby. They'll ruin the whole flock.

There's always so much to talk about, so much to tell you. Think how it'll be when we can dress, eat, sleep, play, work and worry together. We may have disagreements, but I don't plan for them to be more than a fizzle.

You'll be interested to know about my helmet situation. I now have it padded, but somehow the hair still wants to stand to the left. Hair cuts have become a sore spot in the battalion. Now all are required to have short cuts. That's all we've heard for days. Vaseline and Fitch are all I need to keep the scalp in shape, but don't know what controls the gray. Will your hair be darker or lighter when I return?

Yesterday I knew you were on you way back to Wilmington and would be tired when you got there. If only I could get a long distance call through, but it's so hopeless.

You've sent just what I've been wanting for a long while, Chapstick for my lips, face and hands that have been so sore and rough. The only trouble I have now is my feet. They still itch, and I'm afraid of an infection that's going the rounds. I was wishing for some powder that you sent today. How do you read between the lines so? Or do you just know me so well? And another surprise, after all this time, more Easter candy still fresh and good in the middle of May. With the shampoo fixing me up, I also have enough soap, stamps and blades to last me for heap big days now. You should have seen the crowd around that postcard you sent of our pin-up, too. You would have thought it was mail call for everybody.

Thought I'd get a few clothes washed and a few letters written, but what do I do? Start reading the paper that came today and fall asleep before I could find out the price of cotton on the Memphis market, and here I have bales set aside back home to sell.

We used to come in pretty well fagged out Saturday afternoons at Davis. Somehow it's worse here, so it's a real privilege to have one such afternoon off to yourself. I even got the beach fever so badly that I've slipped on the brown sloppy-joe shirt you gave me.

The Memphis in Pictures book caused quite a stir in my hut last night. Some discussion when one of the fellows wanted to see what our fair city was like. You know by now any man in the Army will hold up his town even if he thinks it falls short in some things. This man couldn't have much to say because he's from Ohio. He found the picture of the historic Peabody Hotel with the 1918 car running by it and spoke up, "Why these people are twenty years behind!" I was about ready for bed, but that tipped the lid for a big discussion for almost an hour. They all had to finally admit that they'd like to visit there some day. One man was through Memphis on furlough one time and found two pretty girls to date, so he likes the place.

You wondered what I do with the magazines you send. By the time and sometimes even before the time I get them read someone puts his name in. I have a hard time keeping them in the hut. As long as they stay in here with the section, it's o.k., but some slip them out without asking.

A few weeks ago I got those cartoons the sergeant at Davis drew of us. He's a good artist, all right, but oh how he butchered our faces. With mine so long and you with eyes closed laughing we both look like morons. I get a big kick out of them and just showed them to some of the fellows. Did they get a laugh. I was re-arranging our pictures on the wall and remembered I had packed them away.

Now I have both of your faces cleaned and polished. Yep, the ankles are attractive, too.

In addition to their work as an antiaircraft outfit the 411th now trained for possible use as field artillery in case of emergency. The effort proved well worth while before the year was out.

As for the Brits, Churchill knew they wanted one of their own with battlefield experience in command, but Ike was in charge. The fact that his deputies for land, sea, and air were all British enabled some, at least, to feel that the American was only a figurehead while Britain would really run the war.

I have some new V-mail ink. How is it to your eyes? Better? Did you know you can see yourself in another person's eyes if you get just the right distance? One Sunday afternoon I saw myself in your eyes so plainly, me there inside your eyes. Just so this new ink doesn't clog my anniversary pen.

I often wonder about my favorite suit at home. It's one of the best I ever had, and I certainly wouldn't want the moths to destroy it. 'Course it'll be out of style and all, but I'd still like to keep it unless this thing lasts too long. Every time I put it on it made me feel all dressed up, especially when I'm going out with the best-lookin' girl in the country.

Things seem to change from day to day until one never knows what the next order might be. It keeps us guessing as well as you people about the big question. You know what I have on my sleeve? Well, it'll be changed. You might add two and have the one we'll have. You know all the things you used to sew things on. Well, to our surprise they didn't think we would need them any more.

I wonder while I'm up and about over here if you're asleep and dreaming of me over there.

Wearing the insignia of the First Army for the invasion, the 411th now knew they would be activated as Third Army eventually in France. They also learned a modicum of French, at least enough to ask a farmer for fresh eggs or an introduction to his daughter.

Last night we went to another movie. As usual there was so little to do. Most of the time it's a double-feature I've already seen, but this time a British picture, and they've never heard of a comic film apparently.

I liked the cartoon you sent of the censor going nuts and cutting out paper dolls in a string. The horoscope in that same magazine said you were my best medicine and that I'd make a trip to the west.

I was so pleased that you let me know the exact time you were leaving for North Carolina. Somehow I could feel you all the way there. I did think of your trip all the way through, did you know that?

You'd be very impressed with the place we have found to get away from the G.I. atmosphere and into home life. There's a lady down the road who takes it on herself to form a sort of club of her own, a little U.S.O., we call it. She does a pretty good job, too. Years ago she attended college in the states, so thinks she knows Americans about as well as any of the English might. She tries her best to get every state represented in the book she keeps. I happen to be the fourth from the good old state of Tennessee. While her husband is away in service, a major in finance near London, she wants to help the Americans pass time more easily. On top of that and all else she does for

185

us she serves cakes with a cup of tea around ten o'clock. This is my first visit, but the fellows kept after me to go. The radio is going full blast from Boston, yes, good old U.S.A. She really must be a smarty to handle all the crowd that's here tonight.

Your guess was exactly to the point as to the whys and wherefores of our APO and will be as good as mine as to what will take place now. What you hear over there about what might happen seems to be coming to just that. When I was in high school the talk was that everyone should be required to take a foreign language. It probably would help me some time in the near future.

It always seems like the Italians in this outfit pick the stuff up so easily that it leaves us Southerners and ridge-runners in the shade. I'm just hoping I will stay here till pay day. Oh the rumors I could tell you, then have to censor them myself.

No matter where we may go, there'll always be a time when I'll miss you more than whatever I am doing. When I miss you, I feel good. It may seem funny to say that, but as long as I know that you're with me these unknown days the missing doesn't go away.

When I climbed up on this make-believe bunk, I'd forgotten my watch in my field jacket, so to make time pass and make it seem one minute shorter, I got up and slipped it on again. One minute closer seems so much now where it didn't mean much before.

No blue envelopes Sunday or Monday. There seems to be a slowup, why we can't figure out unless it could be D-Day ahead. Then today three with news about Mother's Day at home. I'm glad you and my Navy brother could have the understanding of what the service is like. With you eating two big meals, heaping up and so mouth-watering, too, I'm expecting to hear you've gained a few "stones." If you enjoy a good meal any better than I do, you'll have to get up before sunrise. Our icebox will never go lacking in anything. I can see you grabbing a Pepsi, or would you rather have Orange Crush?

You'll be surprised, as I was, too, but when the chance came yesterday after mail call to go to London, off I went.   I wouldn't have much time there, but would rather go than not even be in the place at all. Two of us got there at (censored) and were lost before we could get out of the station.   You know how it was in New York.   Well, it wasn't <u>that</u> bad, but almost. The only thing I knew was to grab a cab.   The driver took us around to where we were going to stay, at the Red Cross, that night.   We saw lots in such a little time, looked over Buckingham Palace, failed to see the guard changed, saw Big Ben, the big circus run by Piccadilly.   Oh what a mob. Lots of statues, museums, beautiful parks.   The city is crowded to capacity, trains loaded to the brim, but they all seem to take it in their stride and look happy.

I was so glad to sleep, eat and get away from this place for a change.   The big city hasn't been raided for some time, so I thought it surely would be the night for it that night.   We could see, of course, where the blitz had been and was cleaned up rather well.   I was so tickled to sleep <u>between</u> <u>two</u> <u>sheets</u> again.   I thought I would sleep sound as a log, but rolled and tumbled and thought of everything on the other side of the ocean.   What may have caused it, I was so happy to find real <u>Cokes</u>.   It was a grand pass, but I kept thinking, "Wouldn't she enjoy this?" and wasn't satisfied until I got a cable off to you.

I have been literally floored with all the packages you sent today so full of the goodies I've asked about.   You had them wrapped so well my fingers were all thumbs trying to get at them.   I was expecting cakes some time, but not this many and so many kinds. The boys wanted me to open my own P.X., but I told them plainly we'd ration them out slowly each night. The box of chocolates went fast, but they said the candy was so good.   They now believe me when I say I have the best wife on the home front.   Since there may be a little floating around in the future, these will come in handy, so I'll just pack them away to munch later.

Two men are now out of the outfit, the mess sergeant from Davis with a cold that went into pneumonia and another transferred because of vein trouble in his legs. We miss fellows like that who have been with us so long. The range officers are still here, though, still with us.

I didn't see much of London, I thought, but really saw a lot, too. So many thought I'd come in tired and worn out as they seem to, but I was feeling so good they couldn't imagine what happened. You know the reputation of the London square where some think lower than others. I kept looking straight ahead, never wanting to settle for so little when I have the best. It's you walking with me all the way.

We just came back from a real feed, and from American girls, too. For some time it's been posted on the bulletin board that the Red Cross truck would be around tonight, so we all grabbed our canteen cups and went out to the parade grounds for coffee and doughnuts. They were so good and crisp. The girls said they had spent all day making them. They certainly made lots because they were feeding men from two different outfits and still going strong at the end of an hour. They made a little speech saying they had been over longer than we, but always looked forward to serving American fellows. You don't have to look at a girl twice to know she's American. There's just something about them, it makes you know without their even speaking. Their skin, their actions and figures. It makes you proud of the American girl.

I must be lonesomer than I thought. The newsy letter telling me about the house in Wilmington hit me pretty hard actually realizing for the first time that you were back exactly where happy hours were spent. I have so many plans for the days ahead when all that comes again.

I'm thinking you'll enjoy being with those good radio people. If not, write me before you're classified 1-A! Speaking of stripes, you never turned yours in so you must feel you're doing the Army justice. That and not feeling you're qualified for your work are the only acceptable reasons, and then it's expected. In my estimation you're still the same as when you were promoted last time, so consider yourself as an ideal soldier and one to look up to always. At least I will look up to you. Then, too, if they took the stripes away, you'd probably do the same work as you've always done anyway. So I want to award you extra wings and extra polish because to my mind you are the best wolverine in the line of duty.

Your husband is really proud of your new position and work at that radio spot. The hours sound good, too. Just think. If I could be there now, I could come in every night, stay in every weekend with the best wife on the beach, and have the best time kicking up our heels together. What a dream.

It's the faintest hint tonight that I can write only two pages. I want to write so many more, but the censors, knowing you like they do, would give me competition.

My dreams surround you. Just remember that.

You would be surprised at the way your letters come to me now, always as though you had just sealed them, just shooting out hearts from all corners. I collect so many after staying one place and was finally forced to dispose of them. You know it's not best to have any trace of the address of what our outfit is, so I'm keeping the anniversary letter and a few others that seem very special to me with no other identification. I wish I had a very special letter for D-Day.

There's something about us here that's almost the same as we were when we first left. We know things, but can't know what's really ahead of us even a few days. I just want to give you some peeps that our talks may be cut off right in the middle of a week.

While munching on the candy, cakes and gum I sometimes think, "Do I make her believe I appreciate these as much as I do?" The candy is so fresh still that I grab a bar each time I'm hungry and eat cookies when coming in late from a pass or work. I wish often for a fresh glass of milk with them. We enjoy them so, and I've packed some away for later. In the future they'll come in handy because most of the time in travel you do get hungry.

There's no use of you sending the camera now. The corporal in headquarters mailed some film to be developed about two months ago, so there's no use if it takes that long. Besides, we may not be able to have a camera where we plan to be.

One request - will you please find me a big hunting knife? I'd like it for my birthday, one of the long ones that can be carried on my belt. You could have your name engraved on the holster if you like.

Just don't ever lose me.

The news ticker alerted her to possibilities every day, but his letters with broad hints, held for a month to prevent any leakage of information and delayed by wartime shipping, did not arrive until well after the day for which he was obviously bracing.

At the end of May about a quarter of a million ground troops, some already up the gangways in the far west, were primed and ready to take to the Channel as soon as weather allowed. Beginning on May 21st air attacks targeted positions north of the Seine, thereby reinforcing the Germans' expectations that the invasion would center on Pas de Calais.

If the Reich's complacency seems naive from hindsight, credit should go to their self-defeating logic along with clever notions planted by Allied intelligence agents. Since Eisenhower had not attacked in perfect weather in May, would there be any attack at all? Over a hundred different reports flooding foreign capitals further concealed the facts. At the time of the invasion the enemy would find their communications jammed as well.

Eisenhower's Air Marshal again approached his general about the risks of airborne landings in difficult territory. If a thousand men were lost, Utah Beach might be lost and possibly the whole Allied cause, a stupid waste. Ike, alone in his tent, concluded that without the port of Cherbourg, an intended goal of the operation, the cause would be lost anyway.

As if momentous military problems were not enough of a challenge, new political questions surfaced as well. Charles de Gaulle wished to be recognized as ruler of France, a move Franklin Roosevelt opposed unless the French people themselves demanded him as leader. In any event he would be allowed to broadcast along with the Supreme Commander on D-Day to obtain underground support among his people and quell any native uprisings that might occur, for whatever reason.

Churches joined in prayer for "our boys." Stalin, who had hoped for a cross-channel attack in May, needed one in June to reinforce the morale of his own beleaguered and battered troops. Had the railroads and airfields near the French coast been bombed enough? Would the prediction of 80,000 French casualties and homeless civilians come about? All depended on the success of D-Day.

Questions. Mounting tensions.

To have one person close is the most important thing in the world now, to live and breathe with all the joy anyone could have. I want that so much and will go through lots to have that in years ahead. We will have many years.

Again I'm back at the little lady's canteen. She makes this quiet place very comfortable for us, but some take advantage. The other night a band started practicing, just walked in without asking permission or howdy-do either.

The weather has been unusually warm. The English can't seem to tan much, but we get dark as the dickens. They have such fair skin, like redheads.

One thing I didn't tell you about was the famous burlesque show we saw in London. You might think it was the bare to the bone kind, but to our surprise they did the acts in a special refined way with flowers, drapes and such like to keep the crowd peeping and guessing. Still on the up and up, though, the main actor talking in verses all the time while the strip was going on. You couldn't help but wonder what would happen next. You'd have enjoyed it, too, because we never liked the kind of performance that made us feel really dirty in vaudeville shows. One thing I will bring next time is a set of opera glasses. We had good seats, and they had such good stunts, tricks and the best dancing I've seen. 'Course I admit I haven't been to any place to compare this with, so I'll just let this go as being good.

I never dream any more, just sound sleep. It's good in one way, but I really want to dream tonight.

———————

Only days before OVERLORD German intelligence actually learned of the invasion plans via an agent in the British embassy in Ankara. The cue for launching would be broadcast by the BBC - a line by the 19th century French poet Verlaine. Airing of the second line sometime later would mean "Within 48 hours." The German high command rejected the idea as ridiculous. Spread such an earth-shaking secret by radio? In such a silly fashion? Absurd!

Yet on the first of June a lieutenant colonel in Pas de Calais picked up "Les sanglots longs des violons d'automne," the first line of Verlaine's "Chanson d'Automne." Just that. Nothing more.

———————

June first. This morning you said, "Rabbit rabbit" again to bring good luck all month. Can I say it for the luck we must have? All I ask God is to keep us close, and I'll never be afraid of anything. You know, if ever something happens to anyone, he pulls out of it if he has determination and something to live for. I do have so much built on our future.

You were so right in your guess as to what may come about some of these days. Some get pretty low, and here's one who tries not to, but does even though he has the constant mail from those he loves. Some don't even have that to keep them going, so I consider myself a little better off than other men.

Something you will get a laugh out of, maybe even saw Ike about it. A few days ago they said, "No more helmets." We were to go bareheaded all the time except on pass. You know how we liked this. The short cuts are so convenient, and those with a baldy look like peeled onions. It seems funny not to be out with something on your head, but they change the rules so often, whatever the reason.

You mustn't worry if the mail is shut off sudden-like. You know the action as well as I do now. There'll be a cable on the way every now and then to let you know I'm all right if other mail isn't home to you.

Your latest picture is the best yet. That camera is doing a super job for me. I'll hold on to this one for dear life. You look fresh as a daisy seated on that bench with flowers in your hair. I've even had to re-arrange my Private Property section around it.

I do feel good about your being in Wilmington, and it amazed me that you've joined the church there and will help out in the choir. I'm pretty pleased with the way things are with you now at our home. I do see a difference in your being where you are.

Around 8 o'clock Britain way

We get to talking among ourselves and before I know it we have ourselves on the way home. With the news like it is now we all feel pretty good about how it's all coming along, but know there's still a long pull to victory yet. What I feel good about is the way the Japs are being taken care of and things are not just at a standstill over there. You'd like to know our prophecies, and I'd like to tell you, but maybe we might be rushing things.

You no doubt have heard about the <u>Stars</u> <u>and</u> <u>Stripes</u> that is available in the E.T.O. It comes in every day with the <u>Yank</u> thrown in once a week for two shillings. It's such a good bargain one can't refuse because it gives first-hand information as to what's going on here as well as at home in our capital and other things of interest. It even had some moron jokes today about a sad sack who strolled up to an M.P. and asked if he'd ever pinched a Wac, and another who saw a Wac driver sitting in a jeep with Prestone 1943 on the radiator and thought that was her phone number. And there's the one about the censor who asked the G.I. why he always double-spaced his letters which made them over-weight and was told, "That, sir, is to allow for reading between the lines."

I'm still unable to cable you from the battery. They seem to be becoming more careful and cautious on the thought that information might leak out. I know you wonder, and this outfit does, too, how many more A.P.O.s we'll have in this darn place not to make a move either. Out of a clear sky they drew these numbers, so you might just use the one on this envelope on a few letters.

I remember how I could reach around your wrist with two fingers.

On June 3rd a negligent typist's mistake could have blown secrecy. On June 5th a German hearing another line of Verlaine's poem ("Blessent mon coeur d'une langueur monotone") notified his commander at once. Alerting the unit, the officer returned to his card game without contacting either von Rundstedt, preparing for an inspection tour next day, or Rommel, stopping at his home in Ulm to deliver his wife's birthday present before reporting to Hitler. In such bad weather what commander of common sense would dream of invading? With winds of gale force hitting the Channel, the German navy wasn't worried, and the Luftwaffe was busy transferring fighter squadrons to airfields from which they could defend the homeland more efficiently.

In England Eisenhower met with his meteorology expert twice daily, at 9:30 P.M. and 4 A.M., to check on conditions.

---

4 June 1944   Left Camp at 1344.   Traveled by
                motor convoy 62 miles.   Arrived at
                ... 1930 hours.   Morale excellent.

Departing from the camp at Nettlebed in Oxfordshire, their English home for three months, the 411th drove south into an area of "assembly points" at Southampton on the coast.

In oval-shaped barbed-wire enclosures called "sausages" near the "hards," concrete ramps for loading for the cross-channel journey, they would find themselves completely cut off from the outside world, British soldiers patrolling the perimeters. No military personnel were allowed in or out without a special pass - and no civilians whatsoever. Two thousand counter-intelligence agents saw to it that nothing intervened in the cordoned-off areas. At briefings, when officers and men learned what would be demanded of them, security guards at the closed doors witnessed neither joy nor complaint, merely quiet acceptance.

So excellent was the camouflage, so clever the dispersal of traffic that enemy aircraft never attacked a port seething with activity, some of it bawdy. Like knights of old who wore a lady's sleeve on a helmet as a token of her affection, a number of vehicle drivers flew more intimate items of feminine apparel.

I have failed to write for the last two days. In the rush we sometimes get in it's almost impossible to write although I pray at night she's well and thinking of me.

Getting a letter to you is working against the odds with the set-up we have here. I know you can read between the lines as well as anyone, so you must know it's something like it was when the last week rolled around us. We didn't actually know it was the last, so stayed happy, but tensed.

Did you get the news about Rome? It came to us second-hand, and not till we got Stars and Stripes did we know for sure.

No matter what happens, I'll remember you always in my subconscious mind. To go through all this with you along, then to come back to you is all I ask.

———————

As the Allies entered Rome on June 5th the Germans canceled a practice alert because of bad weather. Beaches driven by the raging surf were obviously invasion-proof. The midnight party for a commander leaving at dawn for war games in Brittany could go on as planned.

Thanks to renewed mastery of the Atlantic, however. Eisenhower had access to weather stations in Nova Scotia and Greenland, the base the Nazis had used with such success in their U-boat attacks. He could postpone the landing for only three days. Half-tide for Utah Beach, a late-rising moon for the airborne, and a sunrise timed suitably for ground troops would not coincide favorably again until June 19th.

Meteorologists advised that the wind and cloud cover of the 5th would dissipate enough by the morning of the 6th to allow bombers and naval guns to prepare the beaches. Conditions would not deteriorate until later in the day after a primary beach-head had been established.

Narrowness of the predicted time slot caused differences between the Air Marshall and General Montgomery at the 4 A.M. conference on the 5th. The invasion long planned for that day had been postponed, one fleet already at sea having to regain port and refuel. A German convoy scheduled to travel from Cherbourg to Brest also changed plans. But troops had been penned up, some for a week, and what about continued secrecy? How to disengage, then re-engage a quarter of a million men?

The one ray of hope in a basically negative report, plus the impossibility of dealing with the complications of another postponement, called for the Supreme Commander to rely on instinct, desperation, and what became known later as "the Eisenhower luck." Over the qualms of several who heartily disagreed, he made the lonely decision ("O.K. We'll go"), then wrote a note absolving all others of responsibility. He carried it in his pocket until he was sure the invasion had succeeded.

While waiting for "Go," one man did a last laundry, hanging a line between two tanks. Others used a loading ramp as a diving board. Veterans of Africa and Sicily, hair cut short to avoid lice, sharpened their knives, packed explosive charges and toilet paper in their heavy assault jackets, and rolled their I.D.s plus ten dollars in francs into waterproof condoms. One soldier awaking with a fierce hangover found some joker had stuck the barrel of a carbine in his mouth.

Bradley's final words rang in their ears - no retreat or surrender unless wounded or out of ammo. They also knew "Take no prisoners in the first 36 hours" conveyed more than a mere inability to care for them nicely. Some wrote letters, others shook hands and blackened their faces.

Deception continued to work in the Allies' favor. In London one prominent official made a point of hitting the night spots and sending false messages, knowing the spy network about him would relay all to Berlin. The fake tank tracks of Patton's supposed army still fooled everyone but Hitler and Rommel, but Hitler slept under sedation at Berchtesgaden, his staff ordered not to wake him and grateful to avoid his tantrums. In bad weather planes which could have seen Southampton from a height of 10,000 feet were grounded, hence ignorant of the latest goings-on. And on the crowded coast the packed "sausages" and windowless bunkers were managed so quietly and carefully that many a small English town nearby was unaware of unusual activity until people found themselves waving at gliders overhead and realized the time for which all had waited so long had finally arrived.

Churchill, whose bomb-proof shelter prepared for Ike had never been used, yearned for the chance to view the invasion from shipboard, but the general could not expose such an important international figure to possible danger. He promised his friend to be at the German border by Christmas, but the Prime Minister would be satisfied with Paris by then. Their staffs struggled still with fear of some ghastly secret weapon. Atomic? Bacterial? The sooner across the Channel the better.

In the marshaling area near Southampton dock men of the 411th AAA Gun Battalion heard the faithful bombers through the night, over 1300 RAF planes ranging in the dark from the Seine to Cherbourg to prepare the way for the landings. The air shone with sparks and streaks of fire.

At 1:30 A.M. paratroopers began bailing out near Utah Beach. Some missed their drop zones by as far as 35 miles. Others drowned or hung up by their shrouds in trees to become target practice for the enemy. Yet within two hours the Allies dropped around 16,000 men through the darkness to communicate with each other with metal toy crickets - you snapped once and if someone else snapped back twice, you knew not to shoot. To rattle the unsuspecting enemy further some of the falling bodies were dummies loaded with delayed-action fire-crackers to simulate the paper-tearing sound of small arms fire.

Local defense centers, unable to comprehend the meaning or pattern of the activity, vacillated between "Major attack?' and "Just another raid like Dieppe?" Paris interpreted blips on its screens as interference in bad weather. Some searched from 1 A.M. to 4 A.M. for a "ghost stream" of bombers, but never sent the Luftwaffe up to investigate or challenge. Even the great armada on the Channel was not detected until 2 A.M, then by the very volume of its sound rather than by radar.

As C-47s and gliders took on their loads, ships eased out of the ports at Plymouth, Dartmouth, Torquay, Exmouth, Portsmouth, Portland, and Southampton. Gathering at the Isle of Wight, they turned south toward five landing spots along fifty miles of French coast.

On board the Augusta, in the same room Franklin D. Roosevelt had occupied during the Atlantic Charter Conference off Newfoundland in 1941, General Bradley, not even removing his shoes, had fallen asleep surrounded by a Michelin map of France, diagrams of enemy troop positions, and a sailor's Petty girl pin-up. At 3:35 A.M., roused by a clang to battle stations, he reached for his Mae West life jacket.

On the Channel men were putting final touches to their own battle gear and on slippery decks in tossing seas shook hands, prayed, and listened to the throb of motors and creaking metal.

At Utah Beach around 5:30 A.M. German soldiers mustered out to handle any minor problem climbed up to a church steeple to assess the situation. Relieved to see no Allied troops on their ground, they stared through the mist toward the sea. The entire Channel from Caen to Ste. Mére Église was covered with ships all the way to the horizon. You could almost walk from one deck to the next.

Before the defenders could recover from shock, naval guns began the bombardment covering the landing of 30,000 chilled and seasick soldiers and their 3500 vehicles. Not expecting such an amphibious attack at low tide, the Germans fired wildly as the invaders dashed across 500 yards of sand to the safety of the dunes.

Compared to the struggle against crack Nazi troops at Omaha Beach, the assault at Utah was described at first as "a piece of cake." With holes blown in sea-walls and minefields swept, the beach was cleared in about an hour. Before the enemy could re-group, turning the area into the "hot spot" referred to later, the 411th's advance team chose the location of their base of operations. Swept farther along the coast than previously planned, they found Germans where gun emplacements would have been established. New and perhaps better sites were designated instead. Like the entire operation, American ingenuity and resourcefulness emerged. If the weather held and the beach-head was firm, their outfit would leave port next day for the main crossing.

Back at the staging area in England their buddies, alerted to their own prospects and responsibilities, heard the news that would shape the future. The sergeant from Tennessee wrote one more letter.

Today of all days I want to be with you. You know as well as I we'll never know what's ahead of us until we feel free to do what we plan and think together. The outlook here is that it shouldn't take too long, but even one day will be too long to be away from all that I love. One can't get away from the issue before us no matter how hard he may try. He must face what's ahead of him. I for one find that if one can just keep the confidence in himself and all the loved ones back home, and with God's help, we can't fail to come through this with a more beautiful faith. This may take weeks to get to you, but still I know all during that time you'll be praying for my safety. Never have I been so close with the Lord as I am now.

You above all have given me so much to look forward to. Life would be miserable, especially now, not to have that. Some wives have already failed to make their husbands believe in a future, have stopped writing soon after we reached this side. If they only knew how it helps to keep in sight a loving home and the land to come back to.

You know there's lots to say, but one's mind just goes around in whirls in the position we're in. All I want you to know is I'll return some day, and I know you'll be waiting.

In England church bells pealed, voices raised a triumphant "God Save the King" and at noon, to a crowded House of Commons, the Prime Minister announced landings in force with more to follow. King George himself took to the airwaves to read a psalm for strength and peace.

The tidings reached the east coast of the United States at 3:33 A.M., newspapermen springing to action to cover the biggest story most would ever publish in their lifetimes.

In Wilmington a local newscaster woke to the sound of "Extra! Extra!" as a newsboy ran along the street beneath her window. At noon the church in which she stopped each day to read his letters and have a little prayer was packed with townspeople, many kneeling or standing in the aisles to seek divine protection for their loved ones and all who headed into battle that day.

Back at the radio station the news ticker bell rang constantly with flashes and bulletins. The time for thumbtacks on a map had arrived.

Eisenhower, anxious for any news at all, waited frantically while a snafu at Montgomery's headquarters delayed decoders for twelve hours. If Omaha were a failure, as already rumored, would there be a second chance elsewhere? And Utah had not been heard from since paratroopers scrambled communications there to protect their operations.

By the time the Supreme Commander had caught up with progress, received reassurance, and vented his frustration to Bradley all was well. Wounded at Omaha huddled in foxholes and scrounged canteens and bandages from the dead around them. The Graves Registration team was doing grim duty at Utah, and Hitler thought the whole affair would be drowned in the Channel within a week. But there were footholds ashore, an Allied presence even if it were only clinging by its very toenails.

Not until after the war was it revealed that at a chateau near LeMans that evening German leaders had

201

searched the map of France trying to discover the enemy's intentions, then settled back again on the familiar old assumption, "Calais." The experts, the professionals, the military veterans who might have known better continued to watch for "Army Group Patton" for six more weeks until a whole German army under their supervision had been destroyed.

With troops above the Omaha cliffs and headed inland by nightfall and units scouring the causeways from Utah Beach to the main road leading to the port of Cherbourg, Eisenhower could breathe a sigh of relief and discard the note he had carried all day for fear of having to assume blame for failure.

Delayed for 24 hours either by the weather or the traffic jam developing along the French coast - or both - the 411th, originally scheduled to load the day after the landing, assembled the morning of June 8th at the faithful LSTs which would take them into combat.

Her soldier knew she was safe and cared for. He knew he was good at what was required of him. He trusted his comrades and their training. He had committed their efforts to God's protection. He was ready.

Back home she had surrounded him with prayer from every imaginable source, even the nuns at a convent near her college up east. She naively promised God never to complain again if her soldier were spared.

---

8 June 1944   Left..0630 hours by motor convoy. Arrived at Southampton Dock at 0800 hours. Embarked LST 239 at 0903. Began journey on LST 1015 hours.

FRANCE

Norma Rogers

9 June 1944   Arrived at UTAH BEACH, FRANCE 0800 hours.   Disembarked 1830 hours. Convoyed by motor to assembly area. Arrived 2348 hours.

One of the first heavy gun outfits ashore, A-Battery landed at Ravonouville north of the Vire estuary, over forty hours en route. Since Southampton they had spent a day and night on the Channel, another day waiting to disembark and five more hours reaching their final destination. Nerve-wracked and lacking sleep, they committed a major error, failing to dig in. The Allied air forces controlled the skies, theoretically, but this was combat. Their colonel's reprimand served well. Enemy bombs fell the very next day.

10 June 1944   Left assembly area by motor convoy 0945.   Arrived at combat position at 1138 hours.
11 June 1944   Standing by for action.

With other units delayed or separated, some by chance even diverted to Omaha Beach, A-Battery had come ashore intact on June 9th to assume combat position near Ste. Mére Église, noted for the image of a paratrooper helplessly dangling from a church steeple. Andy Rooney, arriving the next day to serve as reporter for Stars and Stripes, headquartered there, saw what they may have seen already - dead soldiers laid out in endless rows where sand met grass, five still hanging from barbed wire off shore, three draining blood on the beach. He noticed that all dead bodies float head down and that GI boots sticking out from under olive-drab blankets all look alike.

Along with other grim reminders - wrecked gliders, parachutes (red, white, green, camouflage) used for dropping men and supplies - was the ever-present stench of death. Soldiers peeping through a hedge into an area marked "Off Limits" and guarded by MPs saw a mass grave of bodies being buried without coffins, just as they fell. The road to town was lined with dead Germans laid head to toe, so many that the picking-up job became commonplace. A man might hold up a corpse, grab a snack, and reach for the next while still chewing on his food. Hardened veterans already.

By June 14-15th the whole 411th battalion was at full strength, the enemy only six miles away.

Conditions were looking up in Rooney's arena as well. The first reporters hit the beach with crates of carrier pigeons as back-up if radio failed only to find their stories disappearing in the skies toward Germany when the befuddled birds were released. Now they had an office and links to the outside world.

The prisoner march began. Long lines of Germans and others forcibly recruited into their ranks passed Allied troops coming in while they, dirty and beaten, headed for safety in internment camps in the states. To compound the irony, the GIs on the ground found their foes had lived quite well on shore duty. Tunnels in their concrete blockhouses, with sturdy walls several feet thick, led to mess-hall, barracks, showers, and toilets steam-heated in winter and air-cooled in the summer. In an area where water was considered poison, they had a generous supply of cider and wine, much of it left booby-trapped.

Usually there has been a let-up for us to talk each day, but how hard it may be for us now. The system is set up so that it's almost impossible. You no doubt heard all about D-Day before I did, but you couldn't have much sooner, or did that station you operate really get the inside dope before the rest of the world?

The last time I wrote, a week ago, I was completely on edge and will stay that way so much now. Already you may see the change in the way I will talk. Days now all mean for keeps and one more day closer to home and all I love. It's lots you'd be interested in, but I can't let you in on them. They'd just cut it out.

Just remember I'll pray each night we'll be together soon.

No one but the ones with us could have had the feeling we had when we first found out where we were going. You know our nerves were on edge from then on. I was glad to know for once what we were going in for and not like we usually do, sorta stumble into our movement blindly, just by orders. They gave us the whole story and how many days we would be there after the big D-Day.

We were welcomed here in some cases, but again I do believe it might have hurt others. The country is almost the same as the one we left, only it's not so well-kept and clean. Never have I seen the country more beautiful than England when we left. We were there long enough to see the change of seasons a bit.

As long as I can let you know I am well and living, others will have to wait until I can find the time. Just remember, I always want to keep you as easy as possible. I never want my dear one to worry about me. Just keep faith, and you'll always hear from me.

Now I want us to be together and let all other worries go out of my mind.

You should have heard the roar when Capt. Turitto came in with a sand bag full of mail. I do believe if they had listened closely they might have heard the roar at the fighting front. Mail seems all the Yank soldier cares about except a few dried eggs now and then to keep his fanny and tummy apart. We seem sorta cut off now. No papers, no magazines like Yank and Stars and Stripes that we became used to while in England, but here's one who was glad to hear from home and will be even more now than when I was in England.

After so many weeks you sounded more like yourself. One could have felt like working night and day because behind it are people and loved ones back home who love us a lot for what we are trying to do. We have a full program and have to just pick our times even to shave and eat. I'll talk to you at every possible moment. I

207

won't be able to let much out on how and what happened coming into France. After 14 days I can give you more of how we did. Now we are unable to leave the surroundings, you know that. So far I've found only a few hours to myself taken up in sleep, washing up, writing <u>you</u> and eating. We do burn things at both ends and expect nothing more. I'm for getting as much done as possible and getting home all the sooner.

I rationed things so I had some cookies, candy and gum from your last box when I got here. Ready for some juicy steaks and pork chops.

Midnight

This is almost like working night shift on the railroad. I didn't like sleeping in the daytime then, either.

Someone keeps writing me all these letters I live for. You looked like college days in the raincoat picture you sent. Each expression I keep tucked away in my heart.

---

20 June 1944 IN ACTION

The outfit remained "in action" for the rest of the month, guarding the vital causeways and Route Internationale 13, supply link between the main continent and the peninsular port of Cherbourg, a prime goal of the invasion. St. Mére Église, at a major intersection, had been taken by dawn on D-Day, the enemy completely surprised to find men dropping from the skies into apple orchards and cow pastures. As the experienced Brits suspected, American pilots given only sand-table briefings a few days previously and new to the sounds and vibrations of combat bungled considerably at some landing sites. Yet the unplanned dispersal disconcerted the Germans as well as the paratroopers, unexpectedly adding benefit to the confusion. If you hadn't hung up in a tree or drowned in a marsh, you clicked your metal cricket, looked for the red light on an equipment pack landing nearby, and somehow got together with friends in your outfit or not.

From the very beginning GIs made some surprising discoveries, one of the most useful being that the potent local Calvados worked quite well in a Zippo lighter. Also, since German soldiers wore their medals actually attached to their uniforms, you could put them to shame by stripping their decorations off without allowing the foe to surrender them honorably.

Exotic personnel showed up in the area as well. A company of Japanese imported to instruct the Nazis in camouflage techniques were captured near Omaha along with numerous Hungarians and Mongolians. Two entire Russian battalions riding Cossack-style on black horses and clad in cream-colored coats, red-lined capes, shiny black boots, and black Persian lamb hats with swastikas were also taken captive.

Thanks to the French partisans and Allied bombers, German troops deprived of rail transportation had to use French buses and bicycles or arrived on foot, their equipment moved in horse-drawn conveyances. When one battalion fled, Americans fell heir to over a hundred bicycles and motor bikes left behind.

The Tennessee sergeant, in a blacked-out anti-aircraft trailer, drank coffee and wrote letters to keep awake until radar signaled, "Aim the guns." While dreaming of the familiar world at home, he lived in a world where bombs fell and flares lit the night so brightly you could read your mail by them, working mainly in the dark hours and sleeping as best he could during the day. Even with all the night training he had somehow not suspected that most of his duty would be done after dusk and before dawn, sending instructions to the guns and eventually traveling lickety-split at all hours for old Blood and Guts. The few months of night work at the railroad already seemed like a dream, so for a life-long dairyman raised on "Early to bed, early to rise" the contrast in his new world was striking.

As schedules changed with the times, his writing style changed as well. He now spoke of "the states" instead of "the States" as if a mere local reference had replaced a large national or governmental idea. "The U.S.A.," however, often preceded by "the good old," showed in its firm, strong capitals his devoted patriotism. More tellingly, the comrades with whom he now served in combat had been "boys" in his draftee letters and "the fellows" in training and in England. Once they set foot on the battlefield in France they increasingly appeared as "the men," as if a new bond of maturity and brotherhood had been formed.

In Frenchy NO-SUN country

Two of your letters the other day came with corners spoiled with oil or maybe partly burned. Anyway the insides were still fresh regardless of what happened to them on the way.

Just had my first chance since we came in over a week ago to cat-lick really good all over. What a mess it can be when you don't have anything to do with. I have plenty of soap and clothes, but very little water and such a small pan to bathe in, all six feet of me. I could stand the itchy feeling no longer, so went to the kitchen and boldly got about half a gallon of water and washed head, shoulders and all. One thing we have to watch is camouflage, so with so many white things to handle, I was in a ditch covered over with trees and brush, a real outdoor bath house.

One thing American scheming has given us. These puptents don't give much protection, so we decided to dig in about 3 feet just the shape of the tent. Yes, we do sleep soundly when we get the chance. With sandbags all around one does feel he has something, even the soil, to be thankful for in France. One likes to call something his own, too. The first thing installed was the picture of my special wife. That made everything complete.

So far, as you have probably guessed, there hasn't been much more than K-rations for us since we left England. No one especially likes them. You can't gain on them, certainly, but don't let anyone tell you that you can't lose because I have. As soon as the beach is well formed class-A rations will be supplied.

No one should grumble about this place, though. The way I look at it there are other branches who really have to hit their stride to keep alive, like the infantry. As long as we get along as well as we have so far, morale should be high. Even if it does mean burning the stick at both ends we are doing so much more than we did sitting back in England. It can't last forever.

1:00 NITE and morning

"I love coffee" and now "I love tea" since I came from the Limey country, and I even love the gal that loves me, to finish the song in a different way. What has happened to my hometown paper? The man on the banana boat must be using it for building fires. You'll have to keep me posted on the home-front and still be the best production manager in radio.

No more ten-minute breaks in France, so I've learned to say a lot in five. Oh how I wish for a good old Tennessee barbecue. Even tomatoes and butterbeans would be super.

Sunny France they call it - what a snow job. Somehow I can't figure out how you know so much about the invasion. You may not know it still that this soldier had a small part in the big history-making event. Just think, when children study their history, you and I can both say we had a part in it. You did, too, you know.

I still can't let you know but very little about myself or what we do. The first of next month, though, I can tell you almost anything or even give you some good rumors to pass on. Mostly we just do our job and very little else, and when we've done that, we only

211

have a small amount of time left for sleeping or anything else. I will let you know how this <u>ports</u> always. I don't want to worry you a bit.

The special time I used to write you is almost the only time now that I wouldn't be able to, so if you're wondering about the change, I can tell you in a few weeks.

Even in a foxhole I have the nicest thoughts of you.

The "ports" reference, underlined and so awkward and incomprehensible in the sentence structure, hinted at their location and responsibility to protect landing sites as well as other avenues of supply and communication.

Just as she had not comprehended much of his activity abroad, he could not imagine her position at the center of world-wide communication even encompassing his own activities. While he knew only the most rudimentary facts (the next command and "Do it!") she had gained access to large movements and interrelated patterns on a major scale day by day, minute to minute, that he had never witnessed while she was at the mike. When he had come to the station at night to take her home after the evening shift, network carried foreign news. Now that was often her venue as well, with pronunciation hints to guide through the unfamiliarity of foreign place names. He often commented how she would give him information men on the scene didn't even know, but obviously not secret since cleared by Washington for broadcast. Two other different worlds, but the unique double vision of both combined cemented the sense that they were in the campaign, on the trail <u>together</u>.

For three weeks after D-Day there was nothing in the postoffice mail box. She could not imagine where he was. Still in England? Waiting to come in? On defense on the English coast? Until more than two dozen letters arrived all at once she only knew no telegram or representative from the Army had shown up with a grim message. During those weeks the 411th, stalemated 18 miles from Omaha Beach, about 200 miles from Paris, and nearly 400 miles from the Siegfried line, had brought down planes, heard terrible stories about dead badies stacked like cordwood or still in ditches, and listened to mortars fired in the night. At whom? By whom?

After days of desperate effort supported by the French underground, Americans had pushed past the marshy causeway area into the "bocage," 10,000 little fields outlined by five-foot hedges from which they fired like Revolutionaries at Concord. Farmers having long since left the country-side, their dead cattle lying bloated, all four feet in the air, every road, house, or church steeple threatened danger from snipers or booby-traps.

German forces, aware of the obvious thrust toward Cherbourg, moved troops by night, half stationed toward the port, the other half forming a line at the neck of the Cotentin peninsula. They had captured the invasion plans from a boat left in the Channel and a dead body on shore, but too late for evasive action. General Montgomery even fretted about a release of casualty numbers that might reveal Allied strength though the lower-than-expected totals reassured folks at home. Bradley believed there was nothing the enemy didn't know about that anyway.

While the Nazis remained uncertain about the location of a major assault, the Allies' fears of a secret weapon escalated with news of the first V-1 flying bomb over London. Launched from hidden ramps in the Pas de Calais sector, the small pilotless planes putt-putted along, each loaded with a ton of TNT and trailing orange exhaust behind. The few that reached England had detonated with terrible force outside the city, giving the Brits new reason to fear while still rejoicing over the success of the invasion. Two days later, however, a fleet of V-1s landed within 24 hours on the civilian population of the metropolis. And what else was Hitler plotting to drive the hated "Anglo-Saxons" into the sea?

Der Fuehrer, meeting with staff in a 1940 bunker built for his invasion of Britain which never happened, sat on a high stool ordering his armies, even if entrapped, to fight on and keep Allied forces pinned down. The hold-at-all-costs policy had worked successfully throughout a Moscow winter, but now he had new reason of his own to fear. The "ghost army" he still expected at Calais was Patton's Third, a <u>real</u> army code-named "Lucky" and prepared to land <u>real</u> troops in Normandy early in July. Their leader had already challenged his officers to make glorious history in the future or not be around to offer alibis for failure. Awaiting them were the men of the 411th AAA Gun Battalion, already veterans under fire and slated to serve from time to time as his close follow-up, sturdy defenders, or personal bodyguard. As soon as Cherbourg was taken and the seam between the forces at Utah and Omaha securely stitched, something brand new would happen.

The 411th knew as little of this as Hitler. Just do the job at hand and wait for orders.

———

Some may think I want to give out information to the enemy, but they couldn't do much with just this weather and love between the lines on a warm day. I'm sitting out under one of the largest apple trees in this orchard, but of course I've promised never to sit under one with anyone else but you, like the song you may be playing on the air this very minute.

If one closes his mind to all the sounds overhead in the far distance and all around, he takes this as one perfect day, but what else do you find there? Lots of things that would make your eyes pop out at more than just a beautiful day. I think about our days in the land of sunshine and plenty. So little will I ask God for when I come back. If I can have a comfortable home, my wife to myself for two or three years, and a family some day, life will be perfect.

On the railroad I usually slept till noon, then did the few things that should be done, then back to work

again. Here, usually in the morning, I find some time
to scribble off don't-make-sense V-mails. Maybe if
regular mail won't get through, V-mail will still tide
my better half over.

I hope you'll keep our tithe going to the
Wilmington church, and we do want a part in the
building and buying of new property for the church at
home for God, who is so near and close now.

Just rambling along like this has been the most
pleasure one could ask.

Today has been just another day closer to home than
you'd realize. Lovely in every way and respect except
for the word war on both sides of us. Not yet will I
be able to let you know all about us, but until then
you must not draw too big an imagination. We'll just
slide along to try to see what's ahead.

Yesterday we were out looking around and found some
French wooden shoes that would be super for the
shower. I'll stash them in my duffel bag, and if the
war doesn't last too long, they'll come home with me.
They look like the ones in Holland, never been used,
perfectly new and never broken in a bit.

Before coming overseas, if you'll remember, I
always had a little drawback when I went to see a war
picture. Now if we happen on one you'll expect me not
to see it through. I saw so many things that I'll
never want to be reminded about. Sure as anything the
picture companies will want to reach out and do some
certain scenes up brown. I've seen enough of this and
will not want to bring it back. 'Course you'll hear
the humorous side of the picture and the good things,
and lots comes up that you'll be interested to know
about, but these will come when we're quiet together
with no interruptions.

We love those Army comic books you sent. I'll read
at night in the trailer when the radar doesn't alert
that old Hitler is flying around. We have been giving
those smarties a bit of trouble since we arrived.
Don't think for once they haven't made us know they

mean business, too. You just keep pulling for us like a football team, and we'll shoot the fire out of them.

All of a sudden I've become bathing-suit conscious. One thing, I hope yours won't be as scarce as they claim. From a G.I. observation, some say there'll be only two pieces and nothin' in between. Of course some optimists hope that the painted stocking fad will be extended even further. Now don't you start getting too far ahead in fashion.

Have they stopped the mail coming out of Wilmington for lack of trains?

I always like to stay away from the present set-up because we live in it so much we'd like you to think about other things.

Even when I hit the embarkation port I couldn't fully believe that we would be in on the invasion. After staying there for a few days, getting fed the best we had in ages, we came to realize what was happening, what was shaping up. In preparation one morning someone said D-Day had started. Well, that's the way I knew we'd hear it, and I'm guessing peace will be the same way. Anyhoo, we knew something was cooking because the planes just flooded the air and kept a constant hum both day and night. What news we got was mainly good. Still, some didn't seem to be going so well. We came off the ship on (censored) on the beach into France just as scared as you'd expect. I do admit I was a bit nervous, but the tiredness didn't let it show, and we did mighty well, I think. So far the call for the use of French hasn't come up, but when it does I'll have to use my hands lots. I do know a little French, but couldn't order a decent meal if my life depended on it. I sorta hinted we were having French lessons, but who would have known for sure when and where we were going?

You know, of course, what we are doing. What could an A.A. outfit be doing but letting Hitler have it with both barrels if we possibly could? The most I want to think and talk about, though, is when this is over what we plan and intend to do for the rest of our lives. That's what each man's hope is in this fight now, soon seeing the home, the wife, the family, the place he loves in his heart the most always. You think of America as always being the best. Oh how I can love the very smallest grain of sand that forms that land.

Somehow when I landed here I didn't have the deep fear I expected to have. Since I've heard from you about the community prayer service and know what was going on all the while, I realize who was protecting us. Never has the force of prayer come upon me as it has in these trying and uncertain days. When I read that you sent your little prayer each day in the church after picking up the mail at the postoffice, I was full of thankfulness. No matter where, even the smallest closet can be a place with God.

Now as it stands we're still working a good part of the night and have given some planes some trouble. Can't say how much, but you know how good we think we are. <u>Ha</u>, that <u>is</u> a laugh.

Since I got here, though, it makes one more homesick than ever. I've been that way ever since I arrived.

———

With the big push stalled, commanders now sought ways of raising morale. Ike, weary of weeks of inactivity in England, left SHAEF headquarters for the field, only to be razzed for trying to get a good night's sleep away from the buzz-bombs. His German foe, unable to reach his men at the front, had Iron Crosses dropped by air to deserving recipients. Career officers on both sides, some quite young, kept things going, moving units around like pawns on a chessboard.

For the Allies Problem Number One from the very beginning was <u>supply</u>. One of the "Mulberries," artificial harbors installed off the coast at a cost of $100,000,000, crashed into uselessness in a violent storm. Forces with only enough food, water, gas and equipment ashore to last for three days had to ration ammo in one sector to 25 bullets per day per man. Were they settling into trench warfare á la 1918?

Cherbourg finally fell on June 26th after weeks of siege and naval gunfire. The Germans had been encouraged to surrender by leaflets reminding them of starvation and painful death ("and don't forget your messkits"). Strauss waltzes played by a sound truck each evening carried thoughts of homeland. In the end, surprised at 3:00 A.M. by a demand to give in the following morning or be annihilated by bombs, some came running out in camouflage shouting, "We're Americans!" only to be betrayed by the long neckline cut of their German helmets. Other defenders, having fired some rounds to satisfy their honor, marched out with bags already packed.

Then it was house-to-house searching until July 2nd, the French spitting and throwing rocks at the Nazi captives just as they had done to Americans marched as captives through the town only days before. The port, its ships scuttled and installations dynamited and left in ruins as ordered by Hitler, could not be put to use for three weeks, but Allied troops were now free to cross the peninsula to the west, then head south for the big drive across France.

30 June 1944 Standing by for action.

The fellows think all you do is write me (which is wrong, you hustler). When all the airmail letters came through, what howls it did cause. You make me feel so important. We have just about cut out all ten-minute breaks since we landed in France, but tonight I'm pulling the graveyard shift again, so we can be alone even while on duty, which is all the time.

Most of it seems like, well, you know, cops and robbers over there. It changes every step you take here, though. I'll never forget how we pulled out at

New Year's and knew then it'd be so long before the future would be clear in one's mind.

She's right by me so plainly just as she'll be when I return.

Some articles say you get prepared to die before going into battle. I was so calm and at rest as we were first coming in. Afterwards I became a little nervous and wondering what the future would be for us. The greatest help was the way your letters kept coming, so steady at just the right time. With our faith how can God keep us apart too long?

———————

By the end of June eight battalions of long-rifled 90mm guns had come ashore to serve either as ground or air artillery as needed.

The 411th AAA at Ste. Mére Église, having already engaged 77 planes in combat, were still jammed up in a narrow strip of marshland between the Channel and roads parallel to the beach. All about them every day were reminders of the invasion. Ruined farm-houses had been torched by the Germans needing light for better shots at paratroopers. Strewn among dead cows were remnants of the gliders launched for only one flight to end in wreckage among the obstacle "asparagus" poles set ten feet apart in the fields. Church steeples suspected of harboring snipers had been removed by tank fire.

Hitler, correctly assessing the threat of mobile warfare, continued to insist on confining the battle to the bridgehead - lay more mines, send up more flak, defend aggressively whatever the circumstances. His generals, summoned all the way to Berchtesgaden, then left to cool their heels for six hours after the long motor trip, variously suggested suing for peace, or slowly withdrawing to the Seine, or making a stand at lines that had worked during World War I. Their Fuehrer would have none of it, forcing them again to hear only "Calais."

An opposition power-grab code-named "Walkyrie" developed - a plan for moving troops into the cities, seizing installations, killing Hitler, and delivering command to the army. General Rommel, judging the Normandy front about to collapse, listened favorably to conspirators wanting new leadership. If they wished him to become head of state, they would have to act as soon as possible.

Though not in mortal danger, other commanders suffered certain disrespect from subordinates as well. General Montgomery's staff, for example, sometimes rankled at forever supporting _him_ or _his_ plans as "advisers" while actually doing all the work. Even Eisenhower, while smiling and accommodating soldiers' needs, talked mostly to officers, sought publicity more than some thought necessary, and had a "driver-secretary" posing a security risk and possibly, herself, being a British agent.

General Bradley alone escaped relatively unscathed. A calm, shrewd father figure, he mingled among both rank and file, explained plans ahead of time so that one knew what to expect and why, switched arrangements almost miraculously to serve necessity, and stressed the personal pride that boosted morale.

Both Eisenhower and Bradley had to deal with Patton's inimitable ways, a vital part of his personal style arousing either loyalty or disgust according to circumstances. The genius at mechanized warfare often came down hard with professional discipline on an army of amateurs. Thanks to both his associates, however, he persevered as to duty and eventually circumvented to his own satisfaction, more or less, what he saw as a foot-dragging Monty in the Third's dash for glory.

Stalled in place for the time being, men slept in dugouts under logs, or tents piled around with sandbags or boxes of dirt, or whatever shelter they could improvise, and fought trench foot weather. Spirits were high, though, and at least one GI who wanted to share his thoughts had the opportunity for the time being.

Drizzly France

Before you opened this you probably wondered if he thought of "Rabbit rabbit" the way we always said it on the first of every month for luck. We did have good luck this month. In fact, we always have the superest kind because we're such a good team.

The sun must be bearing down on that North Carolina beach about now. I often think what a joke it would be to make a landing from an LST at Wrightsville Beach and come marching down Market Street instead of New York's Fifth Avenue. What a war bond drive that would be. What a beach-head.

About voting, I'm for Roosevelt in leading us out of this and will be perfectly willing for him to serve the full term of the war, which he may. Still, I feel as soon as all things seem cleared up, he'll call it a job well done and hang up his fiddle. Dewey would be my next choice. From what _Stars_ _and_ _Stripes_ says he still could carry on just the way the war program is going. He couldn't very well do an about face on many things.

We expect to be home for Christmas, so if you cast your vote with a big wish for me, that's all we'll do in time for me to come home to decorate the tree. The news keeps sounding good, at least in _Stars_ _and_ _Stripes_ it does. I wish you could get these. You'd get more of a part than you do out of the home paper.

There hasn't been much doing around this area so far this morning and afternoon. When we have to grab sleep the way we do, we feel like just getting the most of it when we can. So much of our actual work is done in the wee hours of the night. Sleep has to come from the time I used to get up in Wilmington to go to camp until around 2 in the afternoon.

We are somewhere around the lucky number from the place they have cleared. You couldn't guess how close the front lines were ahead when we first came in, but now it's a bit of a distance.

You're constantly in my dreams and prayers.

As one goes up and down the busy roads here one can see that all could be worse in this branch. Thanks to God we have been kept safe so far. Often I've just taken a ride because the truck was going that way and to get away from this spot. You see them coming in, clean equipment, rifles in the air just the way we did when we came in. We laugh and think, "Well, it's some new recruits." We got the same laugh when the others saw us on our first day. Always have we been told that they'd welcome the A.A. and be tickled pink when it rolled in as the beach-head was secured. That night the boys all along the road were all smiles and cheers, even holding up the familiar two fingers like the English victory sign to cheer us on. We did feel chills run up the spine and the tension grow stronger at meeting these sights.

Do you see any change in my writing? Sometimes, trying my best, I seem to just scribble. What causes it I can't say, but I can't seem to spell the way I want the pen to go.

Luckily I did get to London for I'm hoping I won't be able to go back that way home. The shortest route will be all I'll want. I have lost some of the 182 pounds I had in England and will have to become accustomed to the food, home life, even the way America drives.

I wonder what your Fourth will be like tomorrow. If they can celebrate here by pounding the daylights out of that army that knows no feeling and seems never to run out of men, that will be the best we can ask for on this side. Sometimes it sounds in the distance that it <u>is</u> a big celebration with every gun going full blast.

When we left England, I weighed the most I've weighed in some time, but K-rations don't have the food value others do. I can almost feel myself losing. All the rest are the same way. One thing I have found is a French lady to do my laundry. The fatigues and O.D.'s I can't manage very well, so she does them for almost nothing. Sometimes I can't make her understand me very well. We take the soap, and she does a very good job.

But I hurt inside without you.

———

At noon on July 4th an Army custom required firing 48 guns in a national salute. General Bradley suggested that on this occasion every gun in the Army should aim directly at the enemy a Time-on-Target display in which 1100 shells would explode together precisely at twelve o'clock. The fleeing Germans were suitably impressed.

The beach-head at Utah, except for an area twenty miles in around Cherbourg, was still not more than five miles deep in some places, with troops still able to hear waves breaking on the shore. Montgomery and the British seemed to have stalled as well, not even gaining enough space for supplies and an airfield, but apparently satisfied with their effort so far.

At least no poison or mustard gas had surfaced, and American equipment the Europeans valued most highly - amphibious ducks, jeeps, bull-dozers, C-47s, and the ubiquitous 2½-ton trucks - slugged away to get more men and supplies in place for the break-out, if it ever should happen.

The Allies' primary goals were to block the enemy on the east coast of the peninsula, thrust through to the west, and use air support to disrupt, sea forces to supply, and a combination of both to maintain communication as they prepared to head south.

On July 5th elements of the Third Army had sailed from Southampton. Patton himself was now in France with three corps waiting to be formally activated on August 1st. While they were still on the shore, enemy bombers attacked, exploding ammunition dumps, but fortunately missing the soldiers hiding in hedgerows and apple orchards about 15 miles south of Cherbourg. Flying in under tight security, the general had marveled at the mass of shipping near the port, the impressive defenses, and the appalling destruction. He would bivouac on the Contentin until a week after

Bradley's First Army went on the move. The new arrival, older and brasher and not Bradley's first choice, nevertheless stayed the course throughout with admirable loyalty and his usual skill. Whatever his failure or fault in other venues, in this one he just had to be pointed in the right direction and let go.

You know just what an A.A. outfit is called upon to do. The first weeks are the hardest, getting settled and all. Although we might keep on edge a bit from just not knowing the future, we are fortunate in being in a branch that has advantages to outweigh the disadvantages. Take, for instance, the war in the Pacific. Pretty rough all the way through, not only to keep alive from the enemy, but with surroundings being so bad. Catch anything from lice to lockjaw, and in between there are a few of the most horrible diseases. I thank God for His guidance and the care He has given this outfit so far in their training and action. Sometimes you feel the protection.

One of my favorite wants is a clean body if at all possible. Well, with a little American ingenuity the sarge has made a new 1945 model water heater that gives you hot or cold water in either hose. Some of the higher officers are carried away with it and come down for a shower now and then. We have a heater that can be placed in water to your liking. On some of the pick-ups he found this large tank. Place the heater in, and inside of an hour you have all the hot water you could want. It really is a diddy.

If the Germans find out about this little playhouse we've made, they may start keeping clean themselves. You'd be surprised at the fixtures the English had. There seems to be a need for their plumbers to go to school again. Maybe that's one reason they sent us there first to sorta get into this situation gradually. You'd walk all around the place in that country and never find any water fountain. I'd perish for a drink of water. They had the pubs, so mostly had beer with bean sandwiches, or some other sandwich that would choke a mule.

Starting the rest of our lives when this is over, I'm leaning more to the dairy farm each day because of the fear of a depression after a few years.

Where D-Day started

Although the mail is handled with a steam shovel now it's so battered, the words inside never change. I was the most popular guy in the bivouac area yesterday at mail call. They all want to split fifty-fifty with me from now on. No can do, though.

Even if I can't find a place to write and scrawl up and down all over the place, I'm hoping you can make my words out. The knee is just so big, and sometimes the paper will jiggle something terrible.

Half of the game in A.A. is wait, wait. You wait and have to be ready on the spur of the moment. By the time something comes in sight, if you aren't ready and waiting it's gone before you have a chance to even get off a round with your pea shooter. This branch is really some sport when you think about it, but I think what a busy time we would have if we were on the receiving line. We'd probably burn all the barrels to a crisp and still be reaching for ammo.

What do they have in this country? I'll tell you. Mostly pillboxes and the same old K-rations. What a force of the latter seems headed this way.

You know, even in places like this a lovely moon shining down would be worth more to us than even to some of these bombers. One can think back on some of the times that now seem like riches, not in money, though. Some fellows don't want to think back on what they used to do. I'm crazy enough to like our good times.

All the time I'm away it's one hope of mine to give you just about the location of our group. So far in England you had it pretty well pictured. Now you'll just have to leave me most any place you'd think it was important for us to be. You know more about this section than I. When I think back on history and

225

geography, I can't recall anything pertaining to this particular countryside. I'll have to confess you found out what was at Reading before I did, at least what they made there.

We have so far gone as planned, only came in a few days late, so you see how early we could have been. Being trained as long as we were, they tell us, we were especially picked for this job. Who knows? They might have been watching us since we were with the OCS. You will believe that we get up around the top compared with other units. Not to be bragging a bit, but you'll have to let me once in a while.

The cable that arrived in London June 5th came with all the other mail that was held up and got here July 4th. Quick service. An airmail got here before it did, but it let me be happy because you thought of me at that time in your special way. I will never have a doubt in my feeble mind that you hold me close in your thoughts.

When I come home I can start from the very day we left Wilmington and give you a full picture of the whole affair. It won't take just a night, a day, but a full lifetime.

When we knew we were headed out for here, there were so many things I've picked up that would make it hard to travel. We have to use every available space for equipment, clothes and such like. I'd saved all your letters, couldn't throw them away without a little ya-ya to myself, so I picked out some of the best and tucked them away in my shirts, fatigues and, yep, I still have one in the gas mask. I didn't know how long it would be before I'd hear from you, so I couldn't go across the Channel empty-handed. I'll always have the anniversary letter along.

The large record was cracked on arriving here, and the more I handled it the more trouble I had with it. So much to my sorrow I did away with that, but kept the small one and can play it on another fellow's victrola. It's a comfort to remember your voice.

Although we could have come in somewhere along here, it wasn't at this spot. At least it was in trucks and not on foot as I saw so many we passed on the roads. Some looked so tired I just wanted to stop and let them ride a while.

All the while I was in the states and would see newsreels of fellows overseas seeing a U.S.O. show, I wondered if I ever would look forward to one as hard as the articles and pictures seemed to say they do. A notice came out on the bulletin board about a show here. Of course, we had the biggest outlook for days. It wasn't one of those fizzles that last only 30 minutes or so, but one of the best that could have been put before the man in the field. Whoever says the American girl will ever be run over by other women anywhere is crazy. I'll take the American girl for our country any day. As usual in a G.I. show the sound system wouldn't work, but they went on with the performance anyway.

There were three naughty, but nice for the morale, girls with lovely dresses, nice legs and some of our favorite songs. Lots of the jokes the M.C. told were so clever and funny that we all lay on the ground half the time. It was "Broadway Bandwagon" with a director from New York. A-Battery was host to the whole battalion, so all the gang was here. It was the colonel's birthday, so the girls floored him with attention. Naturally I invited them back to celebrate my birthday on August 7th, but I'd be scared stiff if they came. Two of them sang and danced. The other one was a slight-of-hand gal who thought she was pretty good. They all put heart and soul in the show and gave us a real build-up. They came in dressed in fatigues and looked like hogs then, but the dresses and hair looked so good to us later.

———————

Wedding Day in Virginia

Base Chapel

Bunk Fatigue in Georgia

Furlough on the Family Farm in Tennessee

and in Memphis with In-Laws
Whose Son was With the 8th Air Force in England

A Fine English Afternoon for Boating at Henley-on-Thames

Buddies Ready For a Shower Before D-Day

Together Until the Final Gun

Pillboxes on Utah Beach

A Blasted German Tank at the Seine Shoot-Out

Morale Builder From the Home Front

A Smile for a Soldier

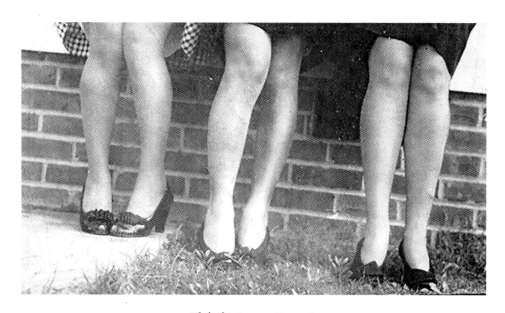

Which Legs Hers?

Weary at Chalons After Non-Stop Dash Across France

Then Rested While Fuel Supply Caught Up

Pass to Paris Before the Bulge

Hitler's Balcony and Car at Berchtesgaden

Bronze Star at Home and Victory Parade 50 Years Later

9 July 1944   1/25000 Montebourg

After a month in place since the landing the 411th went on special mission a few miles north of Ste. Mére Église near what had once been the town of Montebourg, now completely leveled. Frenchmen there, having lost everything, were obviously more sullen than grateful. To add to discomfiture, the dead place had also become a temporary cemetery for both Allied and enemy corpses. Actually, many so-called bodies were merely remnants of human beings - the usual arms and legs, intestines scraped out of burning tanks, even a charred scrap that at first looked like a tree stump. Normandy reeked with the odors of clean fresh-mown hay and decaying humanity.

Hedge-rows, sometimes ten feet deep among hills and woods, surrounded orchards of sour apples that produced the equally sour-looking Calvados, to GIs "lightning in barbed wire." At divine services among the trees on a damp, raw day Patton's army and the 411th which would join them heard artillery bursts to the east and saw hundreds of bombers flying south. By this time soldiers could judge the direction of a shell or bullet by the sound.

The whole northern peninsula contained many a launching site for V-1s aimed at England. Americans had learned to identify them by small concrete roads leading to slabs with holes down the center where a temporary ramp could be installed and dismantled after firing under cover of night. One item, never identified, was a huge block structure - wedge-shaped excavations filled with enough concrete to construct a pyramid. Thousands of slave laborers had worked on it for two years, to what purpose?

Within hedge-rows and marshes were more than a million troops with enough supplies to load a freight train a hundred miles long. The plan was to head for Coutances, then south to Brittany, on receipt of a clear day's bombing and a certain code-word. To prevent bloody man-to-man slaughter by the yard, the key for Patton was the kind of mobile tactics that had proved so successful in North Africa. General von

Rundstedt, seeing the writing on the wall, again proposed peace feelers only to be replaced politely, with reference to his age and health, by a Hitler favorite pledged to obey any order, no matter how stupid it seemed at the time. Rommel knew then that he would be the next to go.

The common soldier on both sides, cut off from all contact except the job ahead, could only wait, guess, and hope for the best.

You may think the news you send is late and that I already know what has happened. Not by a long shot. If you find the time, keep sending the world news round-up section from the news ticker. I read it and pass it on to the men of my section. We pick up a lot we didn't know about.

It's the hardest month we have had, but the months and years ahead will be the best thing to count on. Nothing can harm us, I know. In all my days life wasn't happy and steady until I was married to you. Just suppose we had waited until all this is over. I don't imagine what would be going on in our minds and hearts just now. I'm so thankful it's all settled between us.

Even when you are so busy that you don't take time to get enough sleep, you go to the effort of cutting out these cartoons and clippings you know I'll enjoy. I like your funny little comments, too. That way I can laugh along with you as I used to at home. I don't dare let them out of my sight before I read them, and even censor them a bit! We can't let other people have all our thoughts. You couldn't have sent them at a better time. I don't intend to spend an evening with an English girl any time soon, but you know you can't ever tell about these Frenchies.

No one could enjoy so much just doing what I'm doing now. It's the deepest pleasure I get and will be until I come home where there'll be no leaving again. Bless you.

P.S.   Please send one of the largest boxes of my
favorite cigars, stuffing in a can of Spam, peanut
butter and a box of crackers.   Most any kind of
cookies would go so good now.

Your Staff Sgt.

Time is flying, and do we feel good when we can
look back on what has occurred and what we went
through without a hitch.   You'd think by now I could
give you some idea of where we could be, but it's
pretty important yet.

You spoke of the way the Channel looked when the
big day came.   I haven't been around boats much, but
they were so thick when we went in that you could
holler over to the next and almost get the message.
'Course on some of the dry runs we'd experienced some
of the happenings so all did not seem strange to us.
When we moved in, the large Navy guns were still
pounding away.   We couldn't picture going in then, but
we did.   When we came off the boat, I didn't know what
was next, and no one else seemed to.   I thought surely
we were going up on the front line.   I knew it
couldn't be far away.   We just kept going the way the
M.P.'s directed us.   I asked the truck driver if he
had a map or anything, but no, he had the same dope I
had and followed the directions of the M.P.'s.   What a
good job they did, too.   I take back all I ever said
about combat M.P.'s.   They did a swell job and knew
just how to do it.

After a while we looked around at what the enemy
had.   Never have I seen such pillboxes.   If they had
had them completed, it would have been certainly hard
to come in.   They had enough supplies, food and
ammunition in the ones here to last for days.   No way
in the world to knock these 3-4 foot walls in without
a direct hit.   They have some good equipment, it's no
doubt about that, but with our determination nothing
could stop that infantry of ours.   What struck me was
the tired paratroopers so thrilled to see these guns
of ours come rolling in so soon.   They knew then all
was going well, and they were making some headway.

You know, if one has an ounce of brain he's done a little thinking about what he would do if ever that day of invasion came and he was in it. Somehow it didn't seem like what I expected, and I didn't get nearly as excited as I thought I'd be. You were with me all the way in your thoughts and prayers. Surely God did have a hand in leading us through all the trying hours.

Deception which had worked so well before the invasion continued to be a factor in the campaign. General Montgomery, for example, though publicly heading the main Allied effort, actually had primary responsibility for diverting and pinning down enemy troops to the east, a ruse not even newspapermen were privy to. Criticism of his strategy and apparent inactivity at some points, no matter how hard he pressed to fulfill his personal commission, rankled so that even the British endurance gave way to long-lasting resentment. A reminder of the "ghost army" haunting D-Day also re-surfaced in a "rubber division" of inflatable tanks equipped to simulate radio traffic on a threatened flank.

Mutual support between ground and air escalated as well. Men in the sky became an armored airforce observing, advising, and directing men in tanks and jeeps below.

Patton was now on the field, Eisenhower in new personal headquarters in France, and Bradley installed with maps and charts in a tent with a wooden floor. All the cause needed was a success. With weather too bad for bombing, Cherbourg harbor not yet ready for business, the Germans able to re-enforce during the delay, and folks back home getting restless, the need to pierce through a narrow path and burst out of Normandy seemed imperative for all concerned.

The 411th, having returned from the back-up mission at Montebourg, now headed south to defend two advance landing strips.

12 July 1944   1:50000 La Haye Du Puits

Crossing the peninsula toward the west coast they had temporary duty at the northernmost point of a line of attack which would proceed south to Countances, continue to Avranches, cut off Brittany, then wheel toward Paris. Although weeks behind in the schedule proposed on D-Day, they and their comrades had no reason to apologize. The beach-heads were linked, the peninsula divided north and south, the major port captured, and attack started afresh in weather so bad planes couldn't take off to support them and tanks were unable to blitz through the muck. For news of progress they only got what they read in the papers. Even Bradley had to depend on the BBC to learn of Russian advances.

Stars and Stripes boosted anti-aircraft pride with the report that 100 Nazi planes had been downed since D-Day, and Ernie Pyle commented in his popular column that guns boomed and planes droned all night overhead. The same issue also contained the story of a Nazi trick to avoid. British soldiers, rationed to one egg per month, almost picked up some lying temptingly by a roadside. Sure enough. Booby-trapped. The staff sergeant sending the paper home to his wife in North Carolina marked an item on the man who wrote 25 pages a day and twice that much on Sundays ("He sure beats me!").

———

So many times now I'll want to talk and laugh with you but can't make room no matter how hard I try. Never did I think I'd depend solely on writing to keep and make life come true. There has been a little change in where we were. That's the real reason I missed you the last few days. I can't even find out for sure what day this is, but finally have located the date on one of the messages we received from outside.

You remember my old outfit at Stewart. They came into France a few days ago and moved in right across the road from us. Never in my life have I had so many to come up and around that tickled me so as it did that night we got together for a long bull session. I never realized there'd be so many I knew, but as I walked down the road, every few feet someone would pass that I knew. We had chow together. About 35 of the fellows were there telling us about their stay in Iceland. Oh did it sound cold. Some of the stories were so good we actually rolled. I've wanted to have something break me loose like that for so long, so long since I've laughed that hard. What made me feel good, too, was that a number asked about you. They remember you eating with me in the mess hall. Yep, even the fellow who teased accusing you of slipping hamburgers in that large purse of yours, remember?

Having returned from temporary duty at La Haye du Puits to their home base near Ste. Mére Église, the 411th learned of the death of Colonel Teddy Roosevelt, scion of the all-American family. After service in Sicily and Corsica, he had offered to swim into France if necessary to participate in the great undertaking there. Landing at Utah Beach, inspiring courage in his men by joking under fire, and notified of a new command under way, he had died quietly in his tent of an unexpected heart attack.

In Germany death just missed Hitler. In 1943 a time-bomb placed aboard his plane had turned out to be a dud. Recently, two more attempts failed when Himmler and Goering, the other targets, did not show up at meetings. With the secret police alerted and ready to arrest a ring-leader, the crucial last try occurred on July 20th.

Plotters thought advancing Allies would look with favor and more leniency on those who would rid the Reich of Nazis. On exchange of a code-word they would seize key installations in major cities, kill Hitler, and empower the army to form a new government to deal with peace-making. A young colonel would plant a time-bomb in a briefcase, then excuse himself. The plan had been under way since February when Rommel had agreed to help.

Though Goering and Himmler were again absent from a conference, the bomb duly arrived at Hitler's headquarters with a veteran whose arm had been maimed in Tunisia. He had to draw the fuse-pin with his teeth. The meeting, in a small wooden hut instead of the reinforced bunker, took place around an oak table under which the assassin placed his loaded briefcase just six feet away from Hitler's chair. Excusing himself "to make a phone call," the delegate headed for his car, driving off as soon as he heard the explosion. Surely Hitler was dead. He immediately sent out a message that seizure of the government could proceed.

Unhappily for him only the Fuehrer's left trouser leg was blown away. Two hours later Hitler greeted Mussolini, arriving to review Italian troops being trained for the Russian front. Before nightfall arrests had begun, signaling a blood-bath which included filming of conspirators dying slowly and painfully while hanging from meat hooks. Rommel, recovering at home from injuries received when a strafing attack had crashed his car by killing the driver, was given the choice of honorable suicide or the disgrace of public execution. He opted for cyanide. Officials attributed his death to war injuries and gave him a glorious state funeral with eulogy by his old comrade-at-arms, von Rundstedt.

In Normandy the break-out, as with all other noteworthy Allied excursions of the period, was foiled again by the weather.

Hot Spot on D-Day

All we can do is keep alive and not think too much. As far as being safe no one will be until we reach the homeland, but no outfit like A.A. could be as we are, sorta in the background. We should stay about the same from the main work. You mustn't worry too much.

For the last few weeks we have been getting in A-rations, which are good, if not better than we sometimes had in England. Now the belt does seem a bit tighter when we finish. Sometimes we've thought we were starving. The rations are issued free. Every week each man gets cigarettes, matches, candy, gum, tooth paste (no good) and a <u>small</u> bar of soap. It's more than we could draw with <u>our</u> shillings in the P.X. in the British Isles.

Since news travels fast these days, I'm sure you've heard about the lovely weather we've had the last few days. It becomes unpleasant when you touch your tent and the water comes flowing in like it used to drain out of that fast tub in Wilmington. The longer it continues the more of a break the Jerries have. That's what makes me mad. Still, who'll ever complain again about a little barnyard mud after living in this stuff? Once I get home the rain won't get a whimper out of me.

'Morning, miss. I think of all the voices I'd like to hear now it'd be the one I used to hear on that radio station even if I couldn't get in to see you sometimes. There may be lots of high business men to attend to, sponsors and all, but don't ever get too busy and think I won't care, 'cause I will. Even if our housing situation in the future calls for shelter halves, plaster walls or even <u>ice</u> <u>cubes</u> like Eskimos, I'll be willing.

What a surprise to hear your brother's news! Just think, a whole month there. I want my next furlough to be everlasting, though. The war shouldn't last over two more months. It makes one feel so super to learn of the news and how we soon may be seeing each other.

I'm just wondering what kind of weather these folks have in winter. 'Course we all plan to be moving out of this country by that time and home almost in time to trim a tree or two. Even now the rumors do fly, and some sound so good we want to believe them. Honest, did Stalin and Mr. Roosevelt have a meeting, or was it Wallace?

Sometimes we get so absorbed in the mail when it has come through that all could break loose and we'd be at loose ends reading our letters. Wouldn't the enemy like to know when the postman arrives?

It surprised me to hear that you had visited your brother on R. and R. in Atlantic City. Travel is such a headache now. You were so empty without food. The trains must be pretty rotten now. They'll have to spruce up a few things, else the war may come to an end suddenly and they'll find customers on strike.

I have at last received the invasion news from home. They did use especially large type about it. The article by Ernie Pyle partly reminded me of our 90's outfit, but again it may have been 40's. You should have a pretty good idea of what a gun battery is like. Can I have the privilege of telling you my side of it when the war is over?

In today's mail came some water soaked envelopes and paper someone must have hit the beach with. It's especially hard to keep envelopes from sealing and sticking from all the dampness we have in the tent, and I have all but no stamps. Help!

Somewhere in France 5:00 A.M.

I bet none of your big shots writing you at the station ever get up this early to do it. I've been up since 2:30, so don't get too high with all this soldierly attention. It's time for the alarm to go off to catch that bus to camp. Wouldn't I like to jump at the chance of that again? Well, even in the wee hours of a French morning I'm thinking a strong wink.

Since that V-mail I wrote this morning very early, and half asleep, too, here's one fellow who did some awful hard sleeping. I don't exactly like to sleep too hard because if anything happens I like to be awake and not found crawling out after it's all over. The hours are so confusing that one has to be able to crawl up and sleep any place and any time. Just think what pleasure I used to get out of sleeping in a good bed at home, and it really wasn't too good a bed at that. Now it seems like an innerspring.

Afternoon

You remember the mattress covers some people used out on the beach? Well, I got my hand on one, a new one, went out and cut some nice clean grass, let it cure, then stuffed the thing full. Sleeping on it makes all the difference in the world. When I move I can take the 3 blankets, make my bed, then wrap my shelter half around, rolling it up in a roll and carrying it everywhere we go. I wouldn't part with it for the world. It's almost as good as the ones we had back in England. In fact, mine is just as good. You might think the straw would stick and scratch, but after one blanket down and two to cover, I feel pretty snug. If we were infantry we would act differently, but since we aren't we spend time keeping ourselves as comfortable as possible.

Now with the shower we keep as clean as we ever did. I like this one, in fact, better than those in England. They were always cold. Now we can get a hot shower one and two times a week. The kids around take our clothes back to their mammies and get them washed. We have to furnish the soap, but they boil the fatigues and jackets. I do my own socks, shorts and shirts which pile up on me sometimes. To lighten up on the clothing our blouse, overcoat, cap, gloves and a few other things were turned in. 'Course we will draw them back, I suppose, when we start home. At first we wore our O.D. issue as a combat uniform at the time. Now we wear fatigues, which are much cooler and more comfortable. No ties any more till we start home. We wear leggings and this super derby of a headgear. No, that "without a helmet" routine didn't last very long for a <u>very</u> <u>good</u> <u>reason</u>.

Some of the news that's coming in from inside Germany does sound a bit encouraging. Whether it's a lot of hooey or not no one knows, but if they start their own revolts, that will help end it all the

sooner. Don't think they don't put up a good fight.
It's that or else. They can't last for long, though,
when the bombing, communications, supplies are being
cut off. Some day it'll all end so suddenly. At
least we hope so.

I'm hungry these late nights. Send me cakes,
canned meats, any kind of candy bars, and if juices
are not rationed, you could send a few cans just for
me.

Thank you, pin-up.

Staff

Mid-month he thought they would "sorta stay in the
background," but hadn't cleared it with "Blood and
Guts." While Churchill merely regretted that the
assassin's attack on Hitler had "missed the old
buzzard," Patton feared that revolution in Germany
might end the war before he could redeem disgrace with
some spectacular success. Along with service to his
country and personal fulfillment, his professional
legacy was at stake. He was <u>ready</u> for break-out.

General Bradley called newsmen in to brief them on
the upcoming operation, advising them as always to
maintain secrecy. Even the French in the affected
area would not be warned for fear of losing the
advantage of surprise. To launch the offensive,
planes would use a road as guide-line to avoid harming
friendly troops in the pattern of carpet-bombing
needing split-second timing.

An unexpected benefit had surfaced with invention
by a sergeant of a pronged attachment made of scrap
metal to ease tanks through the thick hedge-rows.
Welding equipment sent from England and ordnance
companies on 24-hour duty could have half the tanks
fitted within a week. Sadly, the 29-year-old inventor
lost a leg and was sent home with a Legion of Merit to
console and honor him for his nick-of-time
contribution to victory.

Unfortunately, Mother Nature failed to cooperate. While flying across the Channel in the only plane able to take off that day, Ike moaned that his own burial service should take place in a storm some day since weather would surely be the death of him.

The Germans, their poorly camouflaged airfields and railroad facilities severely bombed, now relied on ferries, pontoon bridges, and convoys traveling twenty miles a night while their foes on the beach-head were overloaded with supplies. Still thinking the Allies had 42 more divisions waiting in England in addition to the multitudes already landed, they continued to immobilize nineteen of their own divisions a hundred miles away from the scene of coming crisis. The biggest hoax of the war went on.

Somewhere in France 4:20 A.M.

You'll get a six o'clock class today on what I do, think and even fall short of, that is if no censor interferes. Yesterday's mail delivery was the largest and best since I came to England or this dam(p) country some call Sunny France. Twelve letter hits and two V-mails. Pretty good for a day's wooing. I'll even give the reader of this (the censor) a tip that a wife is the best morale builder on earth. Take your hat off here for the tribute.

Lots is still secret and will be till this is over, but I can tell you a few things now. I'm in charge of 32 men in this section, not because I'm any smarter, maybe just a bit more experienced than some in handling men. There's lots to take up before firing. I don't have too much to do with the guns, but with rank I'm just a bit higher than the four gun commanders. Since I'm Chief of Section of the range section, it's my duty to see that the men turn in clothing, shoes, get their rations, shave, sleep, and even wash themselves now and then. 'Course a number of Sgt. T/4's, a Staff and privates, if it came down to that, would take orders from me and the range officer.

My position is in a trailer which has lights available and windows blacked out. It's responsibility, but I'm not one to brag when others are doing so much more.

Time to get set for the night.

The other day I was completely surprised when a dentist showed up wanting to look over all our teeth. 'Course I thought it would be just something for his records and he'd never get around to filling the many cavities he'd find after we'd spent a month on K-rations. I guess they knew our mouths would be in such a state, so if they didn't take care of us now, we'd be gumming it out in a few months. After the check-up he came back in a few days to fix the bad ones. He had the latest equipment a field dentist could have, a drill pedaled by foot. It sorta looks like a hokey-pokey dance when he gets started, but runs smooth and does the job.

I wondered what your Fourth would be like. In war time I'm supposing they were all pretty calm over there. What I always want will be the biggest barbecue we can find with all the families and our close friends. The Fourth meant a lot to me. Now after the peace we will have a real celebration.

There could be a lot of guesses you could have made, but you hit me all around, never coming close. At least I can let the fellows know you are Hot Stuff, and I do mean vibrating. 'Course on the isles of mere I had found you on the set side that you could probably figure out to the O in the glass. Some would think this cognac is the best drink in the world, but I haven't had a drop. You have always read between the lines with me.

––––––––––––

The rambling, disjointed sentence pointed to his location near Ste. Mére Église, known widely for the fierce fighting there and at nearby St. Lo, both "hot" spots. The set (Ste.) side, isles of mere, and O (Lo) as water (eau) in a glass (sounds like "Église") formed clues in a clever, sophisticated code message he knew she would use all her wits to decipher. Fortunately, for a man whose French barely sufficed to order food and manage laundry, other challenges of the sort proved less formidable.

>   28 July 1944   Engaged hostile aircraft 2330 hours
>   27 July 1944.   Fired 15 rounds.
>   Engaged   hostile   aircraft   0230
>   hours.   Fired 21 rounds.   Result
>   undetermined   for   the   two   above
>   engagements.

The break-out began in a scene of horrifying confusion and miscommunication. Airmen, changing the alignment Bradley had laid out for the carpet-bombing over a 5-square-mile area, had accidentally killed or wounded over a hundred men, including General Lesley McNair by a direct hit on his foxhole. McNair's deceptive role as supposed chief of an army group made his death a matter of comfort to the enemy if disclosed. Burial days later had to be secret, attended only by his personal aide, the Tactical Air Command chief, and Generals Bradley, Patton and Hodges.

Zooming in low in formation a hundred at a time and assisted by tiny spotter planes, bombers had left behind dust, clothes-shaking concussion, wrecked German tanks, decaying flesh covered with green flies, and two old ladies with broken legs. By noon, after one of the largest air raids in history, the countryside resembled a moonscape, craters touching and everything in between pulverized. A strong wind blowing astray the smoky guide-line had sent cheering Allied soldiers and war correspondent Ernie Pyle diving for cover in foxholes, along hedge-rows, toward farm-house basements, under heavy wagons - anything to escape the unexpected terror from the skies.

The very fate of the whole operation now seemed in doubt just as Hitler, apparently preserved for his people by some miracle, gained in attention and power. All must now give the Nazi salute, fear of Russia inspiring an almost mission-like aura to the cause.

Shut up in his bunker and issuing only recorded messages, the dictator assumed an eerie sort of godhood undergirded by oaths of loyalty to the death, though all whose fates were linked to his already knew what the outcome would be.

At Utah Beach the front stretched for fifteen miles, but one slice was only one mile deep.

A while back there seemed to be something about me that caused me to be a little jittery. That was when I couldn't write the same familiar scratch. Now the bunch of nerves has settled down a bit, and I find it's my own self again and can make sense and even spell for a change. I did make some slip-ups I thought I never would when I was writing them. It was either all the coffee I was drinking to stay awake during the night work or else getting adjusted to this D-Day stuff.

I've wondered what your brother's plans are after his furlough is over. When one has put up enough for that many missions, surely he won't have to go back overseas. I know your trip to Atlantic City was a long-awaited reunion for you both. He's seen so much of what I saw in England though we do see things with different eyes in our branches. I kept track of you all the way there and back and could just see you peeping out at every pig path and waving at all the lonesome sailors. Did you sit up on the edge of your seat? Do I have any tall competition? I hope not.

You did sound pretty sunburned. You just needed me there to tell you when you'd had enough sun. Those blisters will hurt, I know, I molted for days when I got my burn last summer at the beach.

Already my birthday messages for August 7th are coming through, but no can open until that day comes a little closer. You taught me how special birthdays are that very first summer. Ever since they mean lots to us both. I've already begun thinking of yours in November. What I'd like to do is be on my way home about that time.

Frenchy Way

I've cut a small piece of rubber from a gas mask hose to hold the glass over your picture I've placed on my dogtags. The glass protects your face. I've already caught myself looking down at you. Do you mind if you have to be bottom-side upwards? That makes it so you can look up at me. If you feel hot-headed, you know I'm carrying you upside down to see you smiling.

Somewhere in France 8:00 A.M.

You can bet your life the wolf about this time of morning begins to howl. I've finally smartened up a bit on the whys and wherefores of the way girls wear bows in their hair. I saw yours on the right side which, according to the article I read, means she's deeply in love. I hope so. I'd hate to find you with one at the back of your head. No interest in a man at all. How sad.

———————

Less than twelve hours later her soldier and his buddies of the 411th could begin to say with pride, "I'm with Patton." The Third Army, though still theoretically part of Bradley's First, was designated verbally as "operational" with the leader listed as "Deputy Commander" until formal recognition took place on August 1st. Appointment merely by word of mouth, however, had unleashed a torrent of activity.

Patton believed that armored divisions, preceded by air-bursts from heavy artillery and followed closely by infantry, could cut down the west coast of Normandy without needing a blitz from the air. Such tactical sense, according to documents captured later, revealed why both German and Russian generals rated Patton as the most modern, most dangerous, even <u>only</u> master of offensive warfare. Where others stalled and allowed the enemy to re-group, he alone - bold and unpredictable - improvised, altered, devised, circled, penetrated.

Beyond his inability to discern between battle shock and cowardice, the general received respect from GIs whose interests and welfare he constantly sought to promote. If somewhat aloof and reserved to cover his true feelings for them, he was the only senior officer to thank people formally for their service, write letters of commendation for his troops, and when decorated, consistently give the credit to his staff, his subordinates, and the men who did the fighting. Most importantly for all their sakes, he never lost a battle.

Eisenhower, recovering from the bombing debacle of July 25th, was ready to try again. The problem he faced with Patton's strategy included traffic jams while moving troops through a narrow slot. He also lacked a city suitable enough for SHAEF headquarters in the area and a solution as to what to do with General Montgomery, whose status remained a constant source of friction. Until SHAEF moved across the Channel Ike could not diplomatically assume over-all command of the war.

The 82nd and 101st airborne units, who had turned into infantry in the hour of need, quietly departed elsewhere to rest and re-train, leaving behind ditches filled with dead Germans and "mustard pot" mines that killed you if you ducked into a ditch for cover. Germans who had survived, many in a state of shell-shock, required feeding and guarding in large numbers. The French Resistance also called for help, but the OSS unit dropped in to relieve pressure lost a quarter of its men within days. As for the corpses, you could tell whether one was an American or German by the smell of his uniform as he decomposed. One death brought a genuine smile, though, when a sergeant, scrounging for food and hearing no response to his challenge of a rattling noise, fired away only to discover that his slain enemy was a juicy 250-pound pig.

As Patton himself might have said, it was time to just _do_ it. Not settling for some high-sounding code-word like "Eagle" or "Mighty" he named the command post for his "Lucky" Third Army "Lucky Forward," what else? He never believed in retreating. When a gap opened, the troops he had trained among the hedge-rows thrust right through under cover of Thunderbolts on patrol in half-hour shifts. Tank columns identified from the air by fluorescent panels were also connected with pilots by radio, every means of progress seen to.

By noon of July 27th the Third had crashed through the enemy crust with Patton himself right behind to clear up any confusion. Crucifixes at road intersections strangely blessed the effort by providing signal corpsmen with bases on which to install supplementary telephone wires for all-important communication, whether terrestrial or celestial. As one man declared ironically, what a lot of lethal words those sacred structures carried.

Across to the west coast, then directly south behind Old Blood and Guts came the 411th. With only slight delays they would not stop running until they reached the German border. The shoulder patch they now wore - a white A on a blue background circled by a red border - had been a symbol of the Army of Occupation after World War I. They would see action in a primary sector of that war, an area in which Patton himself had served a quarter of a century earlier.

1 Aug 1944   Left Ste. Mére Église 3 Mi SE T3193 Nor D'Guerre by motor convoy at 1845 hours. Arrived at Lendin, 3 Mi W T2365 Nor D'Guerre. Traveled 25 Mi.

2 Aug 1944   Left Lendin, 3 Mi W T2365 Nor D'Guerre by motor convoy at 1030 hours. Arrived at 3 Mi W Coutances T2057 Nor D'Guerre at 1740 hours. Traveled 8 Mi.

There couldn't have been a more pleasant happening today than the mails to come through. Your soldier was lucky in getting lots, which pleases me very much. The picture of the beach looks pretty much like it was the day we came in only there weren't quite so many boats near shore.

Lots has happened in the past few days. You know if I miss talking to you it's because I couldn't possibly reach my pen. It was that way yesterday on another of our goings from place to place. I'm pretty fagged out tonight, so this will be one of those feeble attempts of letting you know how much I think of you.

———————

At Coutances, in a camouflaged tent on the grounds of a fine estate, 12th Army Group maintained contact with Montgomery ("Lion"), Hodges ("Master"), Patton ("Lucky"), the 9th Air Force ("Conquer"), and Eisenhower's SHAEF ("Shellburst"), the code names revealing a great deal about the outfits which chose them.

With the Germans in the north now entrapped, the 411th's responsibility, then as later, was that of guarding major transportation areas through which men, supplies, and equipment moved. The enemy was sending all available forces and tanks to block off the narrow exit from Normandy and cut off the Allies from the rear. Thousands of Free French armed with weapons dropped by the RAF added to the muddle. The planning and control needed in such a mix amounted to miraculous.

If Patton's do-or-die attitude seemed heartless at times, it nevertheless precisely reflected the desire of his men just to get the whole damned thing over with. By risking, even losing some lives, you sent a lot more men home still breathing. An ounce of sweat, as the general believed, really was worth a gallon of blood.

As the headlong dash proceeded, Old Blood and Guts ("our blood, his guts") had several brushes with death himself - a soldier, almost cut in half by a bulldozer, to whom he gave morphine before the medics got there; a German corpse dug up, to the shame and disgrace of the American military, by his dog Willie; and (a sight he had never before seen even in World War I) a half-sitting, half-lying Nazi in full uniform, with helmet on and chin-strap neatly fastened, whose body had turned entirely black. Unforgettable.

In the now dim long ago Patton and his wife had spent a night in Pontorson while visiting Mont St. Michel. When the Germans realized too late that Normandy was the main thrust after all, not Calais, they pushed toward Avranches to seal off the peninsula, destroy the bridge which supported the Third Army as lifeline, and bomb the dam at Ducey nearby. Rushing down to protect this vital area, the 411th fanned out, sending A-Battery to cover the western flank at Pontorson, no longer a vacation spot.

4 Aug 1944 Left Coutances, 3 Mi W T2057 Nor D'Guerre by motor convoy at 1000 hours. Arrived at 2.5 Mi NE Pontorson, T1904 Nor D'Guerre at 1900 hours. Traveled 48 Miles.

I think it's the 4th or 5th, maybe Friday

One tries his best to keep up with the time, but it marches on so quickly that in running at the speed we do I can't keep up. I'm trying my best so my birthday on the 7th won't slip past me. All the greetings are locked away in my locker. Things have changed so in the last week that no one knows whether he's coming or went. At first we moved in and set up for a while. Now it's every place. You couldn't ever guess what this country is like now. In a mild way, it's a H—of a mess. Since our General Patton has come up, we too have been more on the move.

We jump at the chance of bringing out our pictures. I can tell if the person is actually interested or just being polite. One of the fellows you met on the boardwalk last summer has never forgotten that night when you seemed a little flirty and wanted to make a choice of either him or me. You put your hand on his shoulder and then on mine, saying as you did that you'd take me. We still get a laugh out of it, but it made me feel good then, and it still does. All the fellows remember any little kindness you ever did for them. All these make the gang a little better here.

With the turmoil going on inside Germany and the way the advances are going like mad, the news makes us feel good. Some say they've issued the Yanks motorcycles to keep up with the blokes. Others have a good rumor that they have to catch up with them in trucks. Wonder if anyone knows who should be where? There should be lots of new flashes at that radio station for you to announce.

Any little nothing coming from you means the world to me.

Now we've moved about so the mail orderly can't ever keep up with our postoffice. We keep on his head until he has to do something. You'd have a hard time shaking this ball and chain. I never knew what a beach was like, a quiet life, no one bothering others, just rest, take in the sun, and get fat with a person you care for. I wish so often for just one of those ice cream sodas we sometimes waited for at the beach shop. All those moments must come back. I know they'll be waiting for us both.

————————

6 Aug 1944   Engaged hostile aircraft. Fired 95 rounds.
Result undetermined.

For the 411th this experience was one of the four major challenges of the war. On the night of their arrival at Pontorson, swarms of Luftwaffe, planes from the entire bomber force of Air Flot III, came over all night long dropping flares and releasing bombs at ground level. The pattern continued, night and day.

With one hand on the range-finder instrument to aim the 90s and the other hand on a pen, the sergeant, now able to sleep under any circumstances if tired enough, stayed awake in his trailer by writing of his birthday between attacks.

On the Brittany peninsula

This as you have guessed hasn't been the best day of my life, but it has been as far as you and I are concerned. Last night before going to sleep around three I kept going over and over again just what she had in that birthday envelope. I couldn't imagine anything so small unless it was a specially made pair of dogtags with a new picture of you instead of the number.

You know already that I've saved every greeting you've sent so far ahead so I would have the nearest to a birthday celebration possible. Around twelve I reached into my personal locker and brought out the best gift a woman could send to her husband so far away, your heart in that little silver pin. Even if we don't wear our best O.D.'s all the time now, I'll have it pinned under my left pocket flap to match the one you'll be wearing over there. We'll both be close always.

There couldn't be a party, of course, so I took down the boundary a bit and went out with the fellows. They wanted to have a big celebration with French champagne. We wished for the years to be many ahead, and I wished that I could be with you very soon.

The "celebration," probably a gathering around some bottles liberated among the ruins, didn't last very

long.   The rest of the birthday featured two solid
hours of bombing.

7 Aug 1944	Engaged hostile aircraft. Fired 96 rounds.
	Result undetermined
8 Aug 1944	Engaged hostile aircraft. Fired 32 rounds.
	Result undetermined
9 Aug 1944	Engaged hostile aircraft. Fired 96 rounds.
	Result undetermined.

Hitler's officers, having to obey orders issued far
from the scene of action, had hoped desperately to
confine Allied mobility, trap soldiers in the hedge-
rows, cut off re-supply, even bag some extra gas and
ammo for their own troops.   Instead, they lost an army
and with that, in the opinion of many, the Battle of
France.

Patton meanwhile had left a minimum force in
Brittany, wheeled east, and was already at Laval
pointing toward the Seine and Paris.   At the Avranches
corner, thanks to the valiant efforts of the 411th and
other outfits, the dam at Ducey had not been touched,
his men held a narrow gap, and the vital roads,
undisturbed, allowed bumper to bumper traffic to flow
south 24 hours a day to provide supplies.   Destroyed
German vehicles were pushed aside by bulldozers, but
in the air bombers were still coming.   Men peering
through the mist at ancient Mont St. Michel hoped that
mystical relic would be spared as well.

10 Aug 1944	Engaged hostile aircraft. Fired 36 rounds.
	Result of action is undetermined.

Your letters are so nice even the bees like them.
The other day one came over and placed himself in the
center of the page.   I couldn't run him away at first

and couldn't help but think about how it's so true that bees go after things sweet. Most every day if we have sweet things for chow we have the most terrible time keeping them out of our good food. Maybe this was a wolfish one that wanted to be let in on my love life.

A few days ago something happened to one of my most valuable things, the watch you gave me our first Christmas. I cracked the crystal and worried about dust getting into the works. Sure enough, a day or two later it stopped, on my birthday, too. I kept hoping it just needed a rest, but it wouldn't even make a tick. It's hard now to keep up with the time. Then I happened to think of a jack of all trades who looked at it and found a speck of sand in one of the little wheels. Now it's running again and keeping perfect time, the best it ever did.

I started this about this time yesterday, but was too busy to finish. I swore and be darned I'd get it off to you today.

So often when I go to address your letters, I want to tag you with a serial number. You never did give me yours. Something I think about, too, when I come home I'll bring one of the shelter halves, set it up in the back yard when it's raining cats and dogs and get on the back porch and look out laughing at the place I used to call home. No matter how hard it rains we'll say, "Come on down, you showers!" I'll have both halves with me so if the neighbors need an extra room we'll give them that, that is if they pay in advance.

———

The letters, breezy and tender in their personal world, did not convey that the 411th in five days had claimed seventeen planes of the best Hitler had to offer. The area around them was covered with dead men, dead horses, dead dogs, burned tanks and wagons, wrecked trucks and ruined half-tracks. Yet they could rest in the knowledge that under some of the worst baptisms of fire they had done their duty well. The performance was a credit to every man in the outfit, high rank or low.

Patton's commendation (17 September 1944) described how they had moved rapidly and efficiently by day and night from the beaches and harbor defenses to protect vital supply routes and the dam which could have been used to flood the combat area. Unprotected, often without time to construct revetments and with the enemy using "window" (foil strips to confuse their radar) and flares and smoke to mark objectives, antiaircraft had brought down 93 planes in all (32 others probable, if unconfirmed) coming singly and in groups from all directions. Because of their training, skill, and coolness under fire not a single defile, dam, or bridge was damaged from the air.

The citation accompanying the award of the French Croix de Guerre with Silver-Gilt Star by the President of the Provisional Government of the French Republic praised the 411th as "a unit imbued with courage in a high degree and possessing exceptional military qualities," particularly at the Normandy bridgehead.

On August 9th Stars and Stripes reported that the German counterattack to split the Brittany and Normandy fronts was beaten completely. Ernie Pyle's eloquent comment advised, "Surely history will give a name to the battle that sent us boiling out of Normandy ... some name comparable to St. Mihiel or Meuse Argonne of the last war. But to us here on the spot at the time it was known simply as the break-through." Another reporter wrote that Hitler's back was to the wall, but "he still goes on dreaming." The GI from Tennessee penciled in, "He needs a six o'clock class." On a picture of Mont St. Michel he also wrote, "I was here about an hour one day. It's really beautiful." He had bought a bracelet there for her birthday and still expected the war to be over very shortly ("I may beat this home, but just in case.").

13 Aug 1944   Left Pontorson 2.5 Mi NE T1904 France by convoy. Arrived at Laval

4 Mi NE Y7248 France at 1830 hours.
Traveled 73 miles.

––––––––––

You really deserve much more than I can write tonight, but you'll understand, I'm sure, the whys and becauses. The funniest thing you've ever done to raise my spirits was sending that part of you yesterday. When I found that little piece of tummy skin you had peeled off after the New Jersey sunburn I was so tickled I just smiled all over. I may carry it in my billfold.

That North Carolina hurricane you were in was a complete surprise. It must have upset the beach and ruined some boats. I'm wondering if it will ever be the same as we had before. Although that live wire was in the front yard and the house rattling, you still wrote by candlelight. It's almost like we do here sometimes.

We are now on one of those sudden moves that will confuse the mails again. It's 3:15 A.M., but I'll always want to let you know I'm thinking good thoughts of you all through the night.

––––––––––

14 Aug 1944   Left Laval 4 Miles NE Y2748 France. Arrived at Sees 3 Mi SE Q4626 France at 2200 hours. Traveled 119 Miles.

For a young farmer Laval had been easy to locate for her by merely suggesting a familiar name in dairy equipment.

––––––––––

Just saw a milking machine I want to use. We used the laval ever since I can remember, and I'll still travel along with it and through it as I hope to be in the dairy business. 'Course you know the brand I speak of may have come from a place in this country, and it's so good I don't see how it could. All this chatter is like I usually get to when you are in doubt as to where to place your thumbtack. I love for you to follow where I go.

My hours now run all through the night when we do the firing. There has been plenty of that lately, the worst action since D-Day for us. You remember how I used to tell you I'd always wondered how it would look for a plane to come down instead of just firing on a sleeve? Well, we've seen lots of that and expect more. It's a steady search for those devils, and oh boy, do they slip up on you before you know it. You can't make but one mistake, and every minute counts.

In a three-pronged attack Patton's forces headed toward Orleans, Chartres, and - in the case of the 411th - the Seine north of Paris, with the enemy almost in sight. Men killed the day before still lay in foxholes, but at least the night bombing had ceased.

The Third Army had now traveled farther faster than any other army in history. Victory seemed so imminent that some field hospitals reported a decline in cases of combat fatigue and self-inflicted injury as the "winning team" mentality took over.

Ike, somewhat prematurely as it turned out, began post-war planning while insisting that the road ahead was still hard. Though his primary concern continued to be military, he managed to by-pass Paris on both sides without harming the cause while sparing a noble and historic city.

General Bradley wrestled, meanwhile, with his worst decision of the war. General Montgomery was advancing to the Seine from the north. General Patton, held back to avoid collision with a friendly British force and deprived of the opportunity of staging a reverse Dunkirk at Falaise, had also been given permission to head there. Lack of communication over Monty's intentions allowed a gap through which thousands of

Germans slipped to fight another day. Hitler had lucked out again.

In his ego-driven fantasy world far away in East Prussia the Fuehrer could not imagine the exhaustion of troops who had sown a battlefield with mines to leave it so blood-soaked that a GI could not walk a hundred yards without wading through pieces of human flesh. Equally blind in their own way, the Allies could not visualize the fanatic devotion of a Gestapo and SS unit devoted to their leader to the death.

15 Aug 1944   Left Sees 3 Miles SE Q4626 France at 0600 hours. Arrived at Mortagne Au Perche 4 Miles SE M7112 France. Traveled 27 Miles.

It's been a few days since I've been able to write, but don't think for a moment I wasn't thinking of you. Things are really coming up fast, and I do mean they are really keeping up to the mobility of this outfit. One night here, then it's up and go. Sometimes we wonder if we won't end up in something we can't back out of or even make a U-turn and head back.

The envelopes you sent arrived. If you'll get a few stamps to me now and then I'll have enough envelopes to hold them until the end of the war! I do hope so. You pack the boxes so well they come through after standing the worst treatment imaginable. The candy was some I'd never had before, so rich I couldn't take much of it. All along our rides it's so good to reach in the field bag and pull out a part of something you'd fixed for me. I've sorta brought them out slowly because we get so few now I want to make them last as long as possible.

A few months ago we were crying about the rain in Sunny France. Well, we always have to eat our words. Now there's so much dust that it's the worst yet driving these roads. They say you have to eat a peck of it before you die, but I wanted to eat my peck in the U.S.A. at least.

This thing is so huge now no one can understand it, I fear, but just think each part you play is one small part. The news of the new drive came by rumor, then finally by radio. They seem to be having very little resistance. Here's one who heard something today about their being in Paris. You know how that sounds to us.

---

17 Aug 1944   Left Mortagne Au Perche.   Arrived at Allainville France (Dreux). Traveled 46 Miles.

Their entry into Dreux remained on hold while three Messerschmitts strafed and German soldiers still prowled in the woods. Finally, a glorious reception straight out of Hollywood. Coming into Normandy they had found some Frenchmen lacking enthusiasm for their liberators. Having made accommodations with the Nazis, those who had been cooperative with their occupiers received special privileges in difficult times and distrusted a change in their comfortable status quo. Apparently the mayor of Dreux was among the group so favored, as the Americans soon discovered.

The incoming warriors were pelted with flowers and offered wine and fruit. Out came the French Tricolor once more along with amateur versions of the United States flag. Children shouted, "Cigarette pour Papa!" Collaborating women had their heads shaved before being driven out of town, and citizens beat up the mayor who had shared with Nazis perquisites not given to his own townspeople.

In all the excitement a rifle shot rang out. A sniper? Some ducked or ran, but recovered composure more quickly than the sergeant from Tennessee whose gun had misfired.

You no doubt have seen in the newsreels about troops taking over the towns, how the people welcome them with open arms. I thought it would be a far dream for this to come about for me, but yes, the flowers came right and left around here. They must feel such a relief when they see the Yanks coming in. Honestly, they do just want to touch you, it seems, to say they have touched an American. Some of the roses are so pretty that I wish I could send them on to you, but the wind in the jeeps not only burns the life out of them but also plays havoc with our eyes.

All along you may find a few stops in the mail, but you can bet your life I was busy then. Once I thought while in England there would never be enough sun for the slightest tan. I took it easy here at first, not the way we always did, getting too much at once, like that picture of you in Atlantic City.

The other night I dreamed I was home. Just home is all I could remember. Such a surprise. I didn't see how I could be there.

In your last letter the lights were still out after the hurricane. Let's hope you didn't just give up writing because of having to do it by candlelight. It's been some time since a nice blue envelope has come for me. Your letters don't reach me now the way they used to.

---

18 Aug 1944   Engaged hostile aircraft. One shot down. Cat. I.
19 Aug 1944   Engaged hostile aircraft. No claims.

Unless gun crews actually saw a plane disintegrate in the air or crash within sight or earshot or begin to smoke and lose altitude, they had to record "No claims" or "Result undetermined" until an official count was issued at higher level of command.

Patton's rapid advance should have alerted Hitler by this time that attacks were not merely raids. Yet having learned little from North Africa and underestimating the enemy's technological progress and adventurous frontier spirit, he still thought in terms of brute strength and large armies. The Blitzkrieg techniques which had served well gave way under bad driving habits and faulty maintenance while Patton's supposedly naive and unprofessional troops were making fifty miles a day. To young American soldiers, raised in a spacious nation with a key to a vehicle in hand, distance meant very little.

Unfortunately, gas tanks and stomachs need re-fueling. At LeMans C-47s dropped loads of rations by airlift, but once Paris was taken, how to feed four million hungry Frenchmen? Protecting Chartres Cathedral seemed a simple task by comparison.

But the Russians were advancing in the Balkans, landings in the south of France had gone well, so on to the Seine, the next major stand-off for the 411th. After shooting down a Messerschmitt at Dreux, they headed north to a spot just thirty-five miles from Paris, a heavy downpour drenching them all the way. Some thought that with the invasion, the hot spot at St. Mére Église, and the blow-out around Avranches they had seen the worst. They were mistaken.

> 20 Aug 1944   Left Dreux. Arrived at 1 Mi Mantes (Gassicourt) France at 1305 hours. Traveled 36 Miles. 88 MM position.
>
> 21 Aug 1944   Engaged hostile aircraft. Shot four (4) down.

For so long now we always have a special thing to do and can't attend even the smallest chapel service. At first we did have the chaplain with us, not on Sunday but sometime during the week. Now that the drive is in full swing Sunday comes and goes without anyone's knowing it was the Sabbath day. I do try to keep close to Him, though.

Let's not have anything to take up time and bother us when I come home. Years ago I never dreamed things would be taught to me the way I'm being taught now, to love, to live, to think and dream. How precious life can be.

So many fellows in the Army and other services want to go AWOL. By that we mean "over the hill." Do you know they've got me down for desertion? You couldn't guess why in a year in the Wacs. I dug a foxhole the other day so deep I couldn't be found. What corny humor the Army puts out these days. Anyone with a sense of humor can't fail. I've found that out.

———————

Even as he wrote the battle was being waged for the liberation of Paris. With no air support in bad weather and enemy aircraft coming in day and night from all directions, the battalion had all it could handle. By day the machine guns of Battery D chased enemy planes into a valley surrounded on three sides by mountains. There A and C batteries picked them off, B taking on any who escaped the ambush. The 90s took over at night, and a smoke company put up a screen if needed. The Jerries were only a couple of thousand yards away, small arms fire could be seen across the Seine, and dead horses were everywhere, but the pontoon bridge and river crossings that they defended remained untouched, ready for troops to move. Again they had done the job.

Inside the City of Light armed Resistance fighters openly placed posters calling for a general strike. Charles de Gaulle wrote Ike that if no Allied troops were sent in, he would personally, as head of a provisional government, take command of any available French forces. The city, of no strategic importance, was almost earth-moving symbolically, hence Hitler's instructions to leave it, if at all, in ruins.

Patton asked a French general of long acquaintance why the nation had done so badly in 1940. The reply? For ten years they had been taught, had thought, and had practiced only defense, never attack. By contrast, Blood and Guts proceeded on the premise, "Don't take counsel of your fears." To him war was like a steeplechase. You quaked a bit while saddling up, but once in the race you lost all trepidation. He even scheduled attacks at daylight so no one else would be up soon enough to stop him. "How nervous can you be?" Well, nervous a little when dog Willie was attacked by hornets. It took five gallons of precious gas to burn out the nest and plenty of soda and water to wash down Willie's pain.

The gap at Falaise which had allowed a German army to escape decimation closed for good in a carnage of bolting animals, a pall of smoking trucks and howitzers, and a sacrifice of over 70,000 Germans killed or captured in a final effort to obey Hitler. Of 23,000 tanks and assault guns in Normandy, only a hundred or so, far too few to mount a defense, made it across the Seine. A field marshal on his way to Metz after being replaced for failure wrote to the Fuehrer of the Allies' superior weaponry, of the honorable but hopeless fight, of the need to end the suffering, then bit a capsule of potassium cyanide. His death was attributed publicly to a "heart attack," but his state funeral was canceled immediately after Hitler read the letter.

As for Americans at the front, things looked good again, especially if food and mail showed up.

Just about the time I pick up my pen someone will call that there has to be something done. Usually it's some very unfriendly visitors that have to be taken care of in our special way. We not only let them know they are not wanted, but wish them on their way so they'll never come back again.

This is your friendly correspondent giving you the latest on the war news. I'm hoping it's your favorite voice and station. If it isn't, just give these lines a flip and off I'll go to more unplanned things like a deep breathing exercise or rush-rush for a coooool bottle of Pepsi Cola. Would you write the company closest to you and see if they have them in Paris? They do in Berlin. I just wondered if they would fill a rush order to an outfit just in case they were called upon. How does a ten-cent cone of our favorite ice cream taste? I'd give a large number of francs just to nibble off one right now.

Most of the time we get fairly good eats, that is when we're allowed to cook. Now we are really on the jump, so it's the usual K-rations. I'll be the best first-class hobo in civilian life 'cause with a small amount of fire I can make coffee or tea, fry a few eggs and burn a few dog biscuits. We are so lucky to have our kitchen along with us. Now and then we get a meal that's hot, so that helps out tremendously. When we had planned to leave England, we had the battery carpenter build us a kitchen that would fit on a truck. It was too heavy to be carried when we found where we were going later, so we had to leave the greasy spoon behind. Sometimes the American soldier thinks he's starving, I guess, but they tell me if you don't bitch they know you are satisfied, and a satisfied soldier isn't worth a darn, so it's always good for a soul to let off steam.

If my prayers and wishes could come true, I'd be so blissfully cheerful.

The mail came rolling out of the jeep last night with your pretty blue letters. Not only did I receive the most of anyone in the section, but also two of the nicest packages, marked so plainly for my birthday two weeks ago. I immediately pictured the knife I'd asked for, and you had the very best kind I've seen anywhere or on anyone. I have seen a number of them, too. It's the best brand, the best metal you could have possibly found. I take such pride in it and will whip it out whenever anyone needs a calf or any other animal butchered. Seriously, it stands out on my hip so that it's already attracted so many of the fellows' eyes. You don't hope I'll have to use it on anyone else, just little things. Anyway, it's a pride and joy to have.

I noticed the nice, soft white ribbon and tissue paper, too. We don't have anything ever that looks like that now. You could have wrapped it any old way just to get it here in one piece, but such little reminders of how things are done at home mean so much to men in the spot we're in.

My toothpaste was so low I thought I'd have to use a twig to clean with. Something else I noticed was that rubber band around the gum. Things must be letting up some if you can find these around now. The cakes were in perfect shape, too, but do we have trouble with the insects wanting their share.

---

22 Aug 1944   Engaged hostile aircraft. Shot four (4) down.
23 Aug 1944   Engaged hostile aircraft. No claims.

With Patton's forces situated north and south of Paris, newsmen wondered if General Bradley would spare the city from artillery assault. He promised not an ancient cobblestone would suffer. A liberation committee including the Swedish consul general's French brother, British intelligence representatives, an associate of de Gaulle, and an Austrian anti-Nazi considered how the Germans within could surrender with honor. Their high-minded notions exploded just as street fighting and the German commander's threats escalated.

Forces driving from the west and south brought the issue to a satisfactory conclusion. At 8:30 A.M. on August 24th, with American cavalry at Notre Dame, French armored rode down the Champs Elysées. Germans, fearing a vengeful Resistance and glad to be rid of their thankless, useless job, waited north of Paris to surrender. The BBC mistakenly announced that the Third Army had entered the city. French troops, though actually with the First Army under General Montgomery, stated with a proud touch of poetic license and justice that they "belonged" to the Third.

By 10:00 P.M., with de Gaulle on hand and French forces stationed at the Hotel de Ville, the jubilant crowd pushed aside trees they had felled to delay the

Nazis and celebrated with flowers, wine, and kisses. Ike and Bradley, arriving next morning in an olive drab Cadillac accompanied by a jeep and two armored cars, found half of Paris out on bikes, GIs sleeping under blankets in the parks, and a Tricolor flying on the Arc de Triomphe. Pausing there at the Tomb of the Unknown both were enthusiastically collared and lipsticked.

Troops in the parade held to commemorate the victory and cement de Gaulle's authority as provisional head of government kept on marching out of the city toward the next battle.

In his range trailer about thirty miles northwest of the big hoorah an anti-aircraftman considered putting his wife in charge of things.

My Special Property,

If things keep coming our way, you'll soon be the first lady of France. In my campaign it looks as though I'll carry every town. My business manager (U.S. Army) and I have been through so many, and all it takes is a stick of bum bum or cigarettes to get the votes of all the hedge-rows. Then with a grin by saying "Cheese" you could carry the colors off with both hands behind you. How you'd give the British sign of victory to all the Davis convoys. It's become a joke with us.

What a wonderful influence you are, even long distance.

This is Sunday, but who would ever know it? The days have passed so quickly. I think God will let them pass that way with us. I pray they will. Each day I wish for some words from you, but now it comes few and far between. The cables are just as slow as the mail, but they seem extra special.

----

26 Aug 1944   Engaged   hostile   aircraft.   No
claims.

28 Aug 1944   Left Mantes, France. Arrived at 3
Mi WT E'Pinett. Traveled 36 Miles,
Gastins, France.

Without their own triumphal march through the Paris
they had helped to liberate at the Battle of the
Seine, the 411th wheeled through Fountainebleau to Bois
de Charmoie at Gastins for a little rest on bivouac.
While the soldier sent his light, chatty letters, AAA
outfits had brought down 45 German planes with 15 more
listed as "probable." In the process enemy pilots,
flying so low they were almost face to face, had
bombed and strafed mercilessly.

Various commendations mentioned that during "this
historic period" the 411th had followed closely the
advance elements of armor and infantry, had furnished
timely protection for critical points, and by
aggressive efficiency as a first-class fighting outfit
had played a large part in the liquidation of the
German army.

As they paused briefly at Gastins, their general
had crossed the Marne and captured Chalons on his way
to Rheims, so that would be their next destination.

As always, Patton spurned caution ("You're licked
before you start"). Usually his attitude was "Don't
let the bastards have time to take a shot at you.
Keep on going and <u>kill</u> the S.O.B.'s!" If some
considered <u>him</u> an S.O.B., they were right entirely ("I
<u>am</u> an S.O.B. - to the Germans").

Suddenly, without warning, 31,000 of the 140,000
gallons of gas Patton had requisitioned came through -
no more. Ike had changed plans, going for the single-
thrust strategy pushed by General Montgomery, thereby
diverting planes, supplies, and troops from the First
Army to his command. While Americans visualized going
straight for the Siegfried Line and Rhine Patton could
take within days, Monty would head through the Ruhr
Valley.   Antwerp   was   a   major   consideration.
Eisenhower needed that port. Ever the diplomat, he
knew the importance of gestures toward the British,

even sending the first food into Paris in their trucks with U.S. olive drab vehicles trailing anonymously in the background. But if supplies were such a problem, could Monty take Antwerp in time even if given free rein?

Such questions continued to plague Patton and others throughout the war, "Lucky" having to struggle for everything from pencils to service opportunities though the Third had led the Normandy break-through and freed Paris weeks ahead of schedule.

With no more gas available until September 3rd, Patton ordered one complainer to get out and walk if his tank ran dry. Surely Bradley would have to provide under such circumstances. To get over the Meuse during World War I three-fourths of the tanks had been drained to supply the rest at one vital point. His main job then, to convince SHAEF he could cross into Germany almost at will and cut the Siegfried Line in days if properly supplied.

What riled Patton most was luxury at the rear while his men suffered shortages. At the height of the fuel crisis, trucks needed to bring him gas were being used to move headquarters from Nissan huts 300 miles away in Normandy to fancy hotels in Paris supposedly off-limits to all but enlisted men. Perhaps the Germans were right not to mobilize. Except for panzers, even the Blitzkrieg warriors had relied mainly on railways. Most of their infantry vehicles and guns, still horse-drawn, accounted for the four-legged carcasses left all over the battlefields.

Hitler, still believing that with bad weather coming on he could stop the enemy at the Marne, had not even garrisoned the neglected Siegfried property, crumbling away since 1940. Not a key could be found to the military stores kept under lock there. Once wires and mines were removed, bombed-out families had occupied the premises. Forget "defense."

As always Patton, now only 35 miles from Metz, did not want to give the enemy time to re-group. His fears were well justified as the Allies soon found out to their shock and dismay. Already Hitler had a new, loyal, young Luftwaffe under way and was recruiting an army from troops under training, convalescents, veterans recently invalided out of service ("stomach" and "ear" battalions), police, engineers, any man or boy who could stand up and walk.

Eisenhower, caught between extremes, knew well that America saw Patton as chief ball-handler and end-runner in the war game, but with need for Antwerp and destruction of the V-1 launching sites on the coast, decided to stop the Third at Chalons and Rheims to give full support to Montgomery. Henceforth Patton and Bradley had to conspire sub rosa to achieve their mutual objectives.

As the 411th left Gastins they recalled Organization Day, the second anniversary of their founding as a battalion at Camp Davis, North Carolina, on September 1, 1942. Now the outfit would enter territory some of their fathers and grandfathers had fought in during World War I, never dreaming that their descendants would stage combat on the same land only a generation later.

> 1 Sep 1944   Left Gastins.   Arrived 2 Mi E
> Chalons Sur Marne.   Traveled 91
> Miles.

We have been moving fast, so fast, in fact, by the time the mail should catch up with us we take a leap over the country to some other hot spot. I'm beginning to wonder if they even care about the civilian morale. I do want you to hear from me. One day's worry on your part just shouldn't be.

We have moved again and are now in the middle of it all, so I'm hoping this can go out. It's been twelve days since I've heard from anyone, the longest ever.

I want you to know how useful the knife has become. I use it for all things, cutting boxes, opening rations, trimming things. It does come in so handy. So many have asked to see it and do think you did a good job of picking out an article so handy for a soldier.

I can't let your birthday come and go without some little something for it. If I send a few things when I can pick them up, count them just for that. So few chances are given to us to buy the smallest souvenir. You'll be so surprised at one. I've carried it so carefully for miles now. Even the smallest thing they hang these steep francs on. It reminds me of one shop at the beach where they rushed up to us with a new price tag the minute we were just showing interest in something.

No one has talked with our friend Ike lately. Do you suppose the war will end before the election? With us it seems that it must be coming to a close with all the mess they have started, almost like we were in England. We now have gone back into our olive drab O.D.'s and will wear them at all times unless we have dirty work to do, though that's mostly always. The fatigues were so easy to wash. I did it most always except when we were back at the beach. Now we never know when we'll pick up and leave, so it's impossible to get any of the French ladies around to do it. They do make you look like a soldier, but oh what misery.

We switched from the First Army to the Third so suddenly. I'm glad there's no other here, or we'd be in that, too. Oh what an important outfit. Surely with the Boche having all the countries going against it they'll give us what we want. I'm pulling for the last of this month. Until then I'll have all the envelopes and paper I'll need. You must have known this was coming.

I feel just as strong and healthy as I ever did, but oh how I want to come running home.

One thing in life can make all that counts and what doesn't. I'm fully aware of that as I go over some of the worst places of these days. You know without my saying anything further that the mail pushed through. We didn't get lots, but some nice blue letters came. Time slips by so that before I knew it it'd been almost three weeks since I last heard from you. The ones tucked in my jacket from August 1-11 were about worn to shreds. All the places those letters have been read, puptent, foxholes, in the range trailer (I'm in it now at the desk) and even in some of the dusty trucks after a long day.

There's a well-packed box beside me, too, and I'm just licking my chops. These cookies were mailed July 22nd, seven weeks ago, and they seem just like they've come from the oven. It's all in knowing how to arrange things in a bundle. The long night will be filled with a snack, so be thinking of me as I'm up to my ears in Spam and crackers.

I have enough razor blades now to last the duration even if I shave every day, which I don't, only every other. If I come home by Christmas there'll be no five o'clock shadow around. I'll keep clean as a spring jaybird. It's beyond me what to do about a Christmas package. I'll just add a request for a box of cigars and let you do the rest. Let's hope I pass the boxes on their way over. I'd love to fool a box like that, and the mail orderly would have to mail it back. Mother wrote asking for a request, too, but it's so hard for me to even think I maybe won't be there. I pray each day for that to come true.

Today has been a rather good day, a change some at least. There's a town close by, sorta large, which gives us a shift of scene when we do have time off. Today was my first time there, but it's so little to do if you don't like the booze or the broads. The people make it as cordial as possible, but I can't even discuss some of the scenes that take place.

It's a lovely Sunday here, like a day in March with a slight cool breeze. You must be about to come from church and maybe a good dinner, then out to the lovely playhouse on the beach. Maybe it'll all come back very soon now.

The nights seem to get so cold, and I'm wishing we could get out of this life before winter comes, come home, of course. I'm lucky, though, to have two tents pitched together and have a buddy. I've gotten so tired of the bugs, ants, dampness, and a little of everything that I found a nice single cot on a French train that the Nazis had shipped in, but it was caught before they could be delivered. The train was raided and lots of goods found for our use. You may think I'm living high and mighty, but it's an outlook of winter setting in, and I can picture us on the ground in mid-winter. I haven't adjusted to the cot yet. I got so used to sleeping on the hard ground that I can't sleep now with the sudden change. You should see us moving from place to place, everything all over the truck. That's one good thing about A.A. You can make and have so many things that other outfits do not. Sleeping with our clothes on isn't the best in the world, but it's best to keep out the coolness and insects and be ready to hit the dirt on any sudden attack. We aren't having the action just now that we had around the middle of last month, which was the first time we actually <u>saw</u> the Nazi planes. They came in the day as well as the night. We did lots of good, we think, and that helped so on the morale of this group.

I try to keep the large envelopes, paper and string you send things in, so don't be surprised if you see some of the same contents coming back. It's almost impossible to get a box or paper to send something home if you find it. I'm pulling with all my might to get something to you for your birthday but if I can't, don't be disappointed. I'll be with you in mind and spirit, you know.

So much is coming through already about the discharges that will come when the war is over. We know we will be discharged, if and when we are, unless there's a big build-up. The point system is all well and good, but someone's going to fall short who thinks he should get out. The fellows that have two or three campaigns will be far ahead, of course, and with one or more children the record is even better.

---

11 Sep 1944   Engaged hostile aircraft.   No claims.
13 Sep 1944   Engaged hostile aircraft.   No claims.

At least the outfit enjoyed its first respite since the invasion. Though laundresses had been available in Normandy, the still-green troops had strafing planes overhead, reminders of grim combat on the ground, and a brand new job to get used to in addition to packing constantly to move out. After weeks in foxholes and mad dashes along the road, they could relax a bit with confidence in their new-found ability. The town furnished small pleasures, and dreams of being home for Christmas extended to the states to such a degree that production lines soon reported shortages when faced with actual needs.

On September 1st Eisenhower had assumed command of all ground troops per a 1943 agreement at Quebec. General Montgomery, referring to himself as "commanding" assault forces, had to explain he meant only British and Canadian armies. The apparent claim to superiority of command so riled Bradley that General George Marshall intervened from Washington to settle the matter diplomatically.

Monty, with his rigid, detailed, formalized approach, did command by his very nature from a small headquarters set-up with a few aides or fellow officers. His troops never saw him smoking, drinking, playing cards, exchanging jokes, or getting involved with women in any way. Yet the warm respect they felt for him was not universally shared by some Brits who resented this lack of socializing. In keeping apart from his comrades at arms he seemed "above," a British MacArthur.

Patton, for all the tough-guy image he sought to project, was a devout man often privately moved to tears. With typical American reliance on independence and ingenuity, he gave orders, then expected them to be carried out in whatever manner could be managed best at the time. If soldiers needed blankets, he got on the phone to set a deadline for delivery ("by nightfall").

Eisenhower, trying to rope all these refractory steers into the same corral, was basically a statesman with little previous operational experience. His gift rested in consensus, the distilled wisdom of several though with a tendency to listen best to the last opinion expressed. Only when he replaced tolerant reconciliation with a bold plan of his own after the Bulge did he rise to greatness, truly Supreme Commander regardless of what Washington thought or Churchill pleaded.

Thinking Ike had already won the war, men read the mail, wished for home, but wondered who would have to finish things up in the China-Burma-India theater.

There was the largest bulk of mail that has ever come into our battery, but you know why? It has been stored some place in these fields because they didn't know what to do with it. Never have I seen packages so torn. It's a shame when folks back home go to all the trouble, then the cake arrives as flat as though some British seaman had made each box a cushion on the way over the waves. All chiefs of section were called to come get what belonged to their group, so I took a tub along, but it wouldn't hold my own, much less what the other thirty-three I was looking out for had. The clerk called off the names until it was so dark he couldn't see them, then had to go into our dugout.

I get so confused when all of it comes at once. I don't know which and what to answer first. I received over twenty-two letters. I say this because I don't count V-mails as much as the blue ones. I was the best-humored soldier in the field last night, on duty first to pull the shift from nine until two-thirty. I had a very happy time. There was so little of the enemy air force out that we had a quiet night for once. All my favorite magazines came in, too, which I've wanted so many nights. I've gotten up early and read all the news clippings, which made me believe we'll win out this month. I ended in the best mood I've had in so long.

Yesterday I went into town to see if I could get a picture made. I couldn't order less than six. Although I don't know what I'll do with that many, I had them fix me up. To make the lighting they used a sort of flash explosion, and I wasn't expecting that, so I don't know if they'll be good. If I can't stay around long enough to pick them up, the lady will mail them. I took a boy along who can speak this French much better than I. If I hadn't, you might have really gotten a sad sack. They'll be just the right size to carry in your purse or most any little bag. I couldn't get but one pose either, so if one's bad, the whole batch will be.

I liked the picture of you in the cool suit so much that I've carried it around and pushed it under everyone's nose who will notice. Such whistles you get, too. You seem to be watching me with those blue eyes and smiling for all you're worth. Won't I be the happiest man ever?

9:00 P.M.

I've wished so long for letters to come the way they used to so regularly I was tickled to death to get even one today. Although it wasn't the most cheerful, I could see you had worked head over heels that day. It was also the day after my birthday, and you had seen that poor boy returning so wild-eyed and geared-up from the Pacific. That made you feel none the better. Although they like you to announce, maybe you should just stick to production.

It's about the same thing now day after day, each day and night. 'Course at times we do get some excitement, but now it's protecting some important highways, bridges, and use your imagination.

Who cares anything about this point system? Why they need some home-defense boys, too. I'm pulling and doing all I can for a job with another firm. You can't know what's up until you try, so maybe they found out with us a few days after D-Day. Is this a horse race! Maybe Patton has some in his gear equipped with free wheeling. This V-mail foolishness is just an excuse to say "Hi," or do I need one?

The uncertain future comes up just as when I didn't know when overseas duty would happen. By the time we finish here they should have all our branch of service in the Pacific or well on the way. They won't need American boys to police up afterwards all by themselves. It's the part of England, France, Russia and all the rest to help out in that. Sometimes I think about the long time they could keep us after peace is declared. Not that I doubt what I would choose. You know what we'd find in those jungles. That's not for me if I can get around it. Not only a fight to keep alive from the enemy, but what could you catch in that climate? They have us between the devil and the deep blue sea actually this time, and no joke. I have a little more than some of these fellows, like years of service, one important dependant (I like this one), battle engagements, one weak mind for a nice wife, good conduct, and one thing, we hit it pretty soon after D-Day. My prayers each day are that those yellow fellows can do without us.

A small wink from you would make me glow all over.

It's almost time to hit the sack. Oh how it'll even feel good tonight. I won't call anything a sack when I get home, not even if we have to sleep on the floor. I've sent a package to the garden spot of America. If you get too curious, let's open it, but not too long before Nov. 24th, the most important date of all because the most important person was born.

The best I can give would still fall ten thousand short.

---

16 Sep 1944   Engaged   hostile   aircraft.   No
               claims.

At Verdun, 313 miles from Cherbourg, Patton's tanks had finally run dry. He raged, somewhat incorrectly, at Monty's being coddled by Eisenhower, but troops to the north suffered a drought of gas as well, halting one corps for three days to supply others, with some walking or grabbing rides in the trucks hauling the fuel. PLUTO (Pipe Line Under The Ocean), visualized by Lord Mountbatten in 1942, had reached Alençon, 200 miles from the front, but headquarters, with no radio-telephone links, lacked the power to coordinate solutions efficiently.

As soon as Montgomery stabilized the Pas de Calais area Patton, stalled at the Meuse, would be permitted to secure crossings of the Moselle River and head for the Saar and Frankfurt. Not a minute too soon. Hitler had panzers coming up from Italy, so GIs could eat their belts if necessary. Just send gas.

Behind the scenes, conniving Blood and Guts was learning how to make his own way despite official obstacles. If Ike, for whatever reason, could not avoid making the worst mistake of the war by reining him in, then he'd just have to proceed on his own. Given permission to send out reconnaissance, he would find it necessary to "reinforce" or "back up" and before you knew it, "Presto!" Advance! Furthermore, without Ike's knowledge, Patton held in reserve 110,000 gallons of captured aviation fuel to facilitate his push when it came. Though not the best for the purpose, it would work if other supplies failed.

The Supreme Commander, helping to drag his small plane from the water's edge after a forced landing, was resting a wrenched knee at his headquarters on the west coast of Normandy with little or no knowledge of changing situations and not enough information to get orders to and from London within 48 hours. With permission to advance past the Nancy-Metz line, where the enemy was weakest, the Third could be at the Rhine by October 1st.

As soon as word came, Patton headed out, the 411th following in his tracks.

| 18 Sep 1944 | Engaged hostile aircraft. No claim. |
| 19 Sep 1944 | Left Chalons. Arrived 11 Mi SE Chalons. |

> Left SE Chalons, arrived 2 Mi SE
> Nancy. Traveled 87 Mi.

The next day the battery was shelled, one man lost and several wounded. A hill to the northeast had just been retaken. Though Bradley's map at headquarters showed no major German force beyond those already in the fight, the Nazis had 40,000 slave-laborers shoring up defenses three miles to the west and had staged a "bloody nose" counterattack on the 13th against the sturdy bridge at Pont-a-Mousson, soon to be home to the 411th.

Liberated, malnourished French in the smashed towns, bathed for years in enemy propaganda, knew little of America's part in the war until the Third showed up to secure the Moselle River crossings. The Army knew the 411th, however, as highest scorer in the number of planes downed by any AA gun battalion in the outfit.

So late

We thought we were set up for a while, but now we are on the run again. We were close to one of the largest towns in France, but someone wanted us to try hitting the line again, and did we have mud and slush to contend with. Rain will never hold up if we plan to do anything or go anywhere.

The picture I sent a few days ago wasn't what I wanted, but you can't explain anything to these darn people. They had a flimsy apparatus to take it anyway. First he had me standing where I'd always sat down and relaxed before. Then he was jabbering away fixing up that lighting explosion that went off so suddenly and frightened me. I thought at first it was a Nazi booby trap.

10:55 P.M.

With the news flashes coming in so often and sounding so good you could expect almost anything. Yep, we still have the battery radio, which is the best money we have ever invested. Sometimes we have to do everything but put a nickel in it to make it play, but we get your and my favorite, Bob Hope, Fibber McGee and Molly, Red Skelton and even the Grand Ole Opry. Some make us so homesick sometimes that you want to turn it off. I can remember one program of Bob Hope's when I got to thinking and just couldn't listen any more I missed home so.

You'd be surprised at how hard and fast we have come. The people were so glad to see us. If I even attempted to describe what takes place it would fall so short. They all count it a big day when the Yanks come driving in. Even the flowers and the cider are the best. Some of the gals that haven't dressed up in some time put on a little extra paint and come out for a friendly wave. Just from the small towns we have been through I know they got a lot of attention coming through Paris. Even some of the kids get an extra scrubbing and put on their Sunday best for the day.

This is another of those hope nights that I'll hear from you. It can't go on this way.

———————

23 Sep 1944   Left Nancy. Arrived Jezanville 1300 hours. Traveled 31 Miles. Rain, and mud. Road not as yet taken, enemy in site, all was well in hand.

As longingly as Patton and the British generals looked toward Berlin, GIs in the ranks continued to depend on home for Christmas, but Supreme Headquarters had put the Third Army solely on the defensive. With supply so acute a problem because of their rapid advancement and conditions in enemy territory unpredictable, the troops were to pursue no immediate aggressive action beyond those required to maintain the present status. The realization came as slowly to the men as it did to their frustrated, but hopeful general.

It was a rare day indeed when Patton didn't visit troops on the line. Whatever the weather, he rode in an open vehicle clearly marked with his rank, then flew back to his command post at Étain, a German railhead heavily shelled in World War I and rebuilt with American money. Flying saved time, but more importantly never revealed the commanding general with his back to the enemy. To maintain morale, he and his staff were not to show doubt or weariness or fear in any circumstances. Any intelligent man can be afraid, Patton declared, but shouldn't admit it until the danger passes.

To the north Montgomery had attempted his MARKET GARDEN operation designed to cut Holland in half - a "dagger-thrust" supposedly ("Butter knife," Bradley sniffed). Monty's pressure for the opportunity had been so outspoken that Ike, first warning "Don't talk to me like that," had given him 16,500 paratroopers, 3500 glidermen in 1000 troop carriers, and nearly 5000 aircraft for the effort. Eisenhower had wanted to test airborne troops again anyhow ever since D-Day.

The landing, by daylight, caught the Dutch eating potatoes after church or cycling in the park while one SS officer entertained his Javanese mistress. An elderly gentleman, seeing the sky full of white parachutes, thought the end of the world had come. Unfortunately, the ground was too soft to support tanks, and a copy of the battle orders discovered in one of the gliders went immediately to German headquarters. A second wave of airborne was also delayed by fog. The dismal outcome not only dashed Monty's hopes for his own version of Dunkirk, but also slightly dimmed Ike's vision of finishing off the war in Europe in 1944.

The 411th, slogging through mud as the fall rains began, set up to protect an important bridge only a thousand yards from the German lines. "Jezanville," their new position, was a village outpost of Pont-a-

Mousson where GIs had died in force only three weeks earlier for lack of support by air, armored, or artillery. Knocking out the enemy battery challenging American P-47s, the battalion settled in for the long haul, many a night of shivers waiting for the next German shell to land out of the darkness.

Still France, but muddy

This could have been a really blue Monday, but you hit me on the nose instead with blue envelopes. Could you hit me there lots? I'd even take it every day, at least for a while.

I've already thought of how things would be for you in winter. That's the best place in the world during the summer months, but not much doing later. 'Course you might be meeting me some place around Christmas time. I keep that as our goal even at times when I can't hear how it's all going. I get pretty discouraged over the way the war seems never to end.

I wonder sometimes if a 1918 soldier would turn over in his grave if he knew what was going on in this war. We do things so much faster than the old timers. Even some of these old French soldiers seem so surprised at what we do as if to say, "What could those men be digging for? Maybe they've found gold we didn't know about." We are farther that our grandparents were in position.

We picked up some German parachutes. I looked high and low for a white one, but they didn't seem to have any. Right after D-Day I tried but no could find. At last I ran up on these and bundled one up for you. I can't figure out what you'll do with the cloth, maybe make me some pajamas? Well, maybe it would be too loud for that.

It's just like a flyer would take up with him, harness and all. Never used, even with inspection book. I wanted you to see one and know just how it looks when unfolded. So please unfold and look if nothing else. I thought about slipping it on and climbing up on the silo some day and jumping off to see how it works. Wouldn't that be a killer? Anyhoo, I mailed it today, so if it doesn't get sunk or lost, you'll be ready for a hop to any place in the world. The air boys say they are worth around $200 in our air force. I got one to put over my tent, too, and guess what I did with the others. I made some sheets out of the material. You can picture me now sleeping on a cot, mattress, fancy sheets and three G.I. blankets. It's a good thing I found this stuff because it's really getting chilly these nights. It's so rainy lately that the ground won't do to sleep on, so if I can stand the sound of things overhead and around and feel safe enough, it'll be better. Sometimes I get shaky and want to fall in a hole, which I'll pitch my tent over, then crawl on the bunk in the hole I've dug. Lots of the fellows think I've found a home in the Army and say I should write home and tell how I sleep on the ground, but here's one who'll come home to <u>that</u> ground any day after this is over.

6:00 P.M.

I don't enjoy the things I would if I were home, like a night's sleep, a full bed and a bath just before, and even thinking about tomorrow gives me a good feeling it's a day closer. They'll come back, I'm sure. That's what I'm fighting for. I know they will. At times we may feel "What's the use?" I do lots now, but I know that lots of people have so little to live for.

Each night I pray so long and earnestly, more than ever in my life. You come surprisingly close to God when you hear shells being thrown from one hill to another, not knowing where any may land. I talk to Him about you, this outfit, boys of our community in service, wounded soldiers on the front, all of these I think to ask Him about. Lots of times I drift off to sleep in my prayer, never ending. Surely He will understand.

My time is so full and will be as long as I'm away. All my thoughts either go to my work or you at home.

297

Times like now or a few moments during the day are all I can get. When we are settled in a new place, I wash a few clothes, sleep and write, being thankful Dad and Mother held us all so close to home that we barely knew about some of the things around us here.

The last few days have been the worst weather yet. My feet have stayed wet being out in it, yet I change socks until I use the last. Shoes are always soaked. Today I actually promoted a shower, though, the first in weeks. Just been cat-licking the best we could. This morning you should have heard the yells at the sight of the sun coming up over the mountains. Some could hardly see they'd been in darkness so long. Some Frenchmen can't understand why we don't take over some of their homes to sleep in, and I believe they'd gladly furnish their daughters and without a chaperone. Don't worry. I like my parachute sheets.

Your guess and my hints are coming along fine, almost on the head. Of course, now we jumped again and have been traveling around with the lady who lives in the big white house next to the store, although we haven't crossed her yet, but have seen the little Johnson girl.

Gosh, I wish I could have you as my secretary. It would be all fun and no work.

Again he used familiar local references to cue her as to his whereabouts. The first name of the lady in the white house was "Mozelle," the little Johnson girl named "Nancy." He was at the Moselle River near the town of Nancy, later mentioning the comic strip featuring Nancy and Sluggo, characters the Germans would not have recognized.

The wet-feet situation posed more of a general problem than mere discomfort. Though cartoonist Bill Mauldin, on a visit from the Italian front, ridiculed Patton's apparent coddling of the men in this instance, his own Willie and Joe characters constantly in such shape, the general knew all too well what trenchfoot meant. He had seen the ravages,

disabilities, even amputations it caused in World War
I. His army, not permitted to advance for the very
first time in their glorious history, sat at the
flooding Moselle, held there on a leash without even
the comfort of winter clothing or heavy blankets.

During the lull Patton visited World War I AEF
headquarters in a hotel now run by the next generation
and the house General Pershing had occupied at the
time. His little office remained as he remembered it,
and a man standing on a manure pile, still in place
since 1918, recalled the general as "Colonel Patton",
even organized a pitchfork parade around familiar
spots, particularly a carefully maintained gravesite.
In reality the supposed tomb was a closed latrine
whose "Abandoned" sign the uneducated peasants had
mistaken for a cross. Patton never disillusioned
them, just departed for the front to award decorations
and promote several warriors from sergeant to
lieutenant. The gas predicament was easing up. Now
all he had to do was convince Brad to loosen the
leash.

To keep you up on the latest rumors and feeble
attempts at humor, the moron joke of the day is about
the Army guy who heard his sergeant say the Germans
had gone to rack and ruin, so started out next day to
find the place.

I'm glad the Memphis paper will be coming again. I
didn't know I'd miss it so when it stopped. The
funnies we all enjoy. Even if the fellows do make fun
over our home paper, they fall for it head and ears
now.

Surely I can't forget to mention that special strip
I find so interesting. She's such a little girl and
gives old Sluggo the runaround. We gave her the slip
a while back. You'll remember if you read between the
lines as we always have to sometimes.

I'm realizing how little there was in small town
life to attract my attention. Only school, football,

basketball, church, community celebrations. None of the so-called worldly life around. Certainly I became aware of that when I came into the Army and now more than ever. Here's what some people can't understand. When you haven't gone off the straight and narrow before, why should you begin now? I'll always remember what was drummed into us, "Train up a child in the way he should go and he'll never depart from it." I guess it's true. When I came overseas, I had just one idea, to live the ordinary life I'd always lived as much as possible. Some have even asked, "How can you keep going and have the same outlook?" You help so much.

Last night I pricked my fingers putting on one of the patches on my shirt for the army that's been so fast these months. I never forget how you'd pick up the needle and thread and whip out the thimble and have all my stripes on in rapid fire time.

Some day you can give me a few lessons in crabbing and fishing, then I'll give you a few in tennis or driving.

---

29 Sep 1944   Field Artillery.   Fired 64 rounds.
30 Sep 1944   Field Artillery.   Fired 48 rounds.

The sound of things always in the background now included that of the new action the 411th had undertaken. For several weeks before D-Day the outfit had trained in England for possible use as field artillery in case of emergency. From the end of September through mid-October they put the skill to valuable advantage in "harassing and interdicting" missions targeting road junctions, river crossings, and traffic concentration points by day (0700 to 1900 hours) and towns and troop concentrations by night (1900 to 0700 hours). A total of 5160 rounds launched day after day, night after night, both confounded the enemy and, along with their responsibilities as anti-aircraft, kept the GIs on constant alert, morale high.

Unhappily, <u>Stars</u> <u>and</u> <u>Stripes</u> had already dashed cold water on their hopes for immediate victory. Although Hitler had lost a million men, Churchill was quoted as not seeing the end of the war before early spring. Speaking to the House of Commons, he extolled the American armies for their "vast and brilliant encircling movements" as "a model of military art." Though appreciated, the statement was of small consequence to men who just wanted to get the damned thing over with and go home, where the Cards were beating the Braves and a lady "rassler" had just been banned in Boston.

    1 Oct 1944   Field Artillery. Fired 47 rounds.
    2 Oct 1944   Field Artillery. Fired 96 rounds.
    3 Oct 1944   Field Artillery. Fired 54 rounds.

Our Special Services officer is really on the ball and got the Red Cross truck with coffee and doughnuts around. 'Course you know how glad that made us. What a little thing to look forward to, but a big one for us. Anything with American girls on wheels looked good to us, so we were all eyes as usual. When they pulled in, there was <u>Memphis</u> on the side of the truck, so I expected to see some girls from around home, but they said none were from that honky-tonk place. They saw all the German parachutes over our tents, so naturally they needed a scarf. I was cutting a chute up for sheets, pillow cases and scarfs, too, so I had to cut off a few pieces for the girls. 'Course the fellows hollered, "Hey, Rogers, does she know you're married?" and said I used the parachute as a lead-in. Don't worry. This one was a red-head from Rhode Island who couldn't come up to your little socks. Some of the fellows even pretended they'd refuse to eat when they saw "Memphis" up there. We enjoyed it so much we'll want to have them back again if it's Berlin before they find us.

We get in lots of recent films shown by the battalion Service Officer. The other day we had Bing

Crosby in "Going My Way." That's always a signal to move. Every time in the past we see a picture, that afternoon we get march order, so we looked for it. Sure enough it came. Don't think because we have doughnuts and coffee and the movies that we're in a bed of roses in a rear area. Far from it. We still carry on our duties and now are doing far more than we have in the last few months since D-Day. We get some commendations from the higher-ups, which helps lots. Some is secret stuff that would never make it past the censor, so I'm tucking it away to bring home in person. I don't plan to bring home <u>too</u> many reminders of the Army, though. Do you blame me?

———————

Along with movies and doughnuts more sophisticated entertainment surfaced among the local talent, in particular a woman described as a diseased and ugly hag who obliged two dozen customers per night.

Of more immediate general interest was Patton's seizure of the high ground above Nancy, forward troops advancing toward the German border east of Luxembourg. Until the day of his death he believed he could have broken through to the Rhine and headed for Berlin given the supplies Monty had received. Even if unauthorized, the caged lion would now growl toward Metz. When Krauts surrendered to a portion of his army theoretically assigned to the Ninth, that army got credit on the books, but the Germans knew and made it clear as a matter of honor that they were surrendering to Patton's Third, the army and general Hitler and his staff deemed most dangerous of all.

The solid front Eisenhower envisioned stretched from Switzerland to the Channel, a distance of six hundred miles, but with only one division on average per mile. The First Army was stopped at the Siegfried line, Bradley was stretched in an effort to back up Montgomery, and the Third, attacking and counterattacking near the Moselle, needed rest.

The over-ground pipe-line, extending 25 miles a day, had reached Chartres, but the habit of parsimony with precious gas was so ingrained by this time that Patton even topped off the tank of his jeep at Bradley's motor pool whenever he was summoned for a conference. When his army was accused of fraudulently claiming an allotment meant for the First Army, Old B. and G. possibly concealed a smirk, thinking, "If it didn't happen, maybe it should have." He was also annoyed when a friend brought him, along with a new pearl-handled revolver, a winter coat when his men still had to do without.

4 Oct 1944   Field Artillery. Fired 30 rounds.
5 Oct 1944   Field Artillery. Fired 27 rounds.

I'm cold as the dickens some nights, and with the moon shining it's awful hard not to think of what other folks might be thinking under such loveliness. Even if it's a thousand years in time, I'll always think of that when I'm outside with such a lovely world above.

I forget now and then when things go faster than they have ever done in my life. When even the smallest thing slips my mind, I get so disgusted. You'll have to give me a big hint or maybe a swift kick. Even now when one could become really lax and not give a darn the way things were done, I still like to do my part and not say, "Oh what does it matter?" A person like that makes me really mad.

When some folks don't write, I think without an answer this will be my last. 'Course if _you_ stop, I'll just keep on thinking maybe your fingers are hurt.

---

6 Oct 1944   Field Artillery. Fired 48 rounds.
7 Oct 1944   Field Artillery. Fired 69 rounds.

We seem to be keeping up with the latest pictures all right. Sometimes I think how unusual it would be for me to see one over here you hadn't even had a chance to see over there. We found an old man in a schoolhouse in an old garage and threw a screen up. There we have "the cinema" free to the public of our Uncle. When I get back I'll remember what a gas can felt like instead of air-conditioning and soft seats, even the helmets. Usually we have a terrible time with the machine, sound and focus, but we get the plot. We had "Pin-up Girl" today, but I could see a weakness Betty Grable didn't have in her last show. She did look fleshy in places. Who could kick, though? It was wonderful to see beautiful clothes and women and all the loveliness of American life.

About the packages for Christmas, they'll come early, but unless I can't carry them, they'll all be kept until that time. If it's nothing but a special letter, that would be enough. The thing that counts is the thought. Besides, when I come home, the first day will be the Fourth, Christmas, your birthday, our anniversary and all the special days coming true. With the lines creeping so slowly now all the faith I have of starting home soon wavers so. At least I'll still look forward to that time. Then I'll look to not later than our anniversary if that doesn't work out. I want to be home for that in March so badly. Some think if we didn't plan that way it wouldn't be so hard. Well, if I didn't have a date set, how could we last?

You seem to be following our trail right along, smarty. With us so far ahead I can mention a few places we visited. They're all about the same as you go along the street, but you can tell how far ahead we are and how long ago the town was taken if they bring out their wine, flowers and fruit. Coming into Dreux I was in the jeep and got so excited putting a shell into that pop gun of mine that somehow I fired a round accidentally and had all the Free French thinking there was a sniper out again. Believe you me, that was the time we were close following the artillery and infantry.

Even if I talked for hours, I'll never get caught up.

A few weeks back our friend Bing Crosby all but got his pants blown off, not due to his loyalty to us at the front, but back where he kept his wardrobe. He was so completely without a pair that he had to send back to Hollywood for more clothes. We come to know and appreciate what such people are doing for us. Just suppose you were in a soldier's place and did almost the same thing every single day. Then you hear about a U.S.O. show coming. You have a new lease on life although at times afterwards you feel like the dickens. I wish I could see Hope or Bing while here if they were close. The other day we were supposed to have a show, but some of the cast became sick, and we saw the Grable movie instead. What a let-down.
There's some talk of our moving into a building after this position, but no one can tell. Once you get used to this life it's safer and better for you in the long run, I guess. So far with a little fixing here and a little fixing there I've made it pretty comfortable. Some French say they get around three feet of snow here. I can see us digging our way out of our emplacements.
Life is too precious over there for me to miss any of it.

---

8 Oct 1944   Field Artillery.   Fired 45 rounds.
9 Oct 1944   Field Artillery.   Fired 11 rounds.

5:45 P.M.

There seem to be more dark hours than I thought there would be over here. I guess at home there were just as many, and I remember back in England, when we were close to Hereford, what long nights we had. We could go to bed at eleven and still get plenty of

305

sleep. Now we can't get the sleep, just the long hours. When we first came over, daylight hours were from around five to ten-thirty, now only six to six. If we have to spend the winter, it'll be all we'll remember, the worst one of all. Already we've been re-issued overcoats, so it's either for here or the snow we'll step in when the boat pulls up to the pier at New York. Sometimes I wish I could tell you about that pier. It's nothing like the pictures.

Maybe I was so loaded down that night I couldn't see far. I do remember one thing, though. I was so tired with the straps cutting my shoulders I got them off and really hit that swing sack. When I awakened the LuLu was pulling out, so we all ran up to see the old Statue of Liberty out of sight. The feeling that came over me at that time I'll never forget.

Along mid-August we saw the most planes, and did they come out of nowhere. That was when we made such a good record and stand at the top of the A.A. outfits in this army. We don't want to brag, didn't even realize we rated so well until the reports came out. I'm hoping they won't be needing so many in the Pacific when this is over.

I've written your brother again, not knowing where he is, but I'd think he'd be back at all those landing strips we were protecting at the first. I'd go a long way to see him and get the all-important news he would have, about home and how you looked in Atlantic City and what you talked about.

The top turret gunner in the family, serving in the Eighth, then the Ninth Air Forces, had helped to prepare the French coast for his brother-in-law to invade and now made bombing runs into the heart of Germany.

Back at the 411th his relative by marriage endured the daily grind and nightly misery of giving and receiving shells while praying for safety and longing for relief. Time dragged, yet when Stars and Stripes reported a million Christmas packages were on their way from New York, he commented incredulously, "Already?" The same issue carried an item, discouraging to some, that Paris had closed 180 brothels ("So much for after they've seen Paree"), and a French lady anxious to show gratitude to her liberators had flown an American flag of her own composition, colors upside down and stars completely missing ("Her heart was in the right place"). All North Carolina came up with for news was a pear-throwing contest.

```
10 Oct 1944   Field Artillery.   Fired 24 rounds.
11 Oct 1944   Field Artillery.   Fired 55 rounds.
12 Oct 1944   Field Artillery.   Fired 64 rounds.
13 Oct 1944   Field Artillery.   Fired 96 rounds.
14 Oct 1944   Field Artillery.   Fired 45 rounds.
15 Oct 1944   Field Artillery.   Fired 56 rounds.
```

These V-mails surely do make me a little short-winded. They may be trying to get us to use them because of the heavy mails coming in from the fronts. That could be the reason for the hold-up in my airmails to you. No letters have come from home in the past few days, so I've begun to make faces at the mail orderly when I pass. Anyhoo, I can sneak up on you like this during ten-minute breaks.

I keep looking at my wedding ring. It's so important now.

At last things have settled down for a change. We get little pay for overtime, so why not take it easy? One thing to notice. If there's ever a blank space about where I am, you know who we are trying to beat. I'll try always to remember to keep putting "Somewhere in France" but in case I don't, you'll know where the next one's from.

Lots of rulings are coming out that affect so many. The people in another country won't be like they were when we hit France. They are such devils that I'll never trust them, not one. They'll probably make friends with you, then shoot you in the back. Just look what they did to some of our boys. One town surrendered and put out white flags, and as soon as we started through, they let our men have it. So what do ours do but turn around and let them have it, and that's what might happen again. We are such sentimental chaps that we've had to become a little more hard of heart than we have been in the past.

The story is told about a couple who lived close by when the Nazis first came moving in. They had a new auto they wanted to keep so badly and knew those so-and-sos might get wind of it and it would be no more theirs. So they went out and piled hay over it making the whole thing look like a haystack. It wasn't touched for four years. Now they want to dig it out. The dampness in this country has probably rusted it terribly, but at least they put one over on the Nazis.

Then there were some people who before D-Day buried some flyers that had a forced landing, and all were killed in the crash. The people buried them in a quiet spot. The Germans did all they could to prevent the graves from being taken care of, but the French put flowers on still and have some nice pictures of the graves. To keep the enemy from getting hold of the pictures they even went down in a well, removed some rocks and hid them until after D-Day and all Germans were gone from the area. If we had been through what so many have here, I'm sure we'd have a different slant on the whole thing, don't you?

Never do I want you to worry so much that your sparkle and smile will go. We'll help each other through. I think she wouldn't be proud of a quitter, a slacker, a person who'd just give up and say, "What's the use?" One can feel that way in low moments.

I'm really proud of your trip to Camp LeJeune. I know it was connected with the station's activities, but a real treat for you, too, and I know the Marines will remember that you helped to pass some time away. If you saw a fellow there who'd like to switch places with me, he'd get lots to boot. The food sounded so good, too. Maybe they were trying to put up a front to get you gals to join up. What hit me most in the nice menu was a cold glass of iced tea. Isn't that funny the way you get a longing for something and it stays so plain you can almost taste it?

Now it seems we may be in buildings for a while. Today has been housecleaning in a place close by, so it should keep out some of the rain and dampness. Then we can have fires and something besides the tent to sleep in, maybe do things we really want to do. With the small cot, mattress and parachute sheets and a roof over my head, living conditions could be much worse.

7:10 P.M.

If you think there's lots of folks around when you try to write me at the station, you should see the mob around this cracker-box called the U.S.O. We decide some of the weighty problems here, like why do some workers go on strike, when will the war be over, will that first sergeant be discharged before me, and will we get our basic over again when it's all over with these stubborn devils. One man has offered to go by and tell you stories on me. He thinks he has so many more points for discharge than I. He's asked me lots of times why I want to go back to Tennessee anyway because he thinks they have nothing but turnips there. Already we've discussed at the chow line which is the best state in the nation. What worries me, though, I've invited them down to sample our food and just see how good it is, so don't get mad if we all come flying in some night. They want to take North Carolina as an example of the whole South. Won't they be fooled?

What does my girl give me but a packet of things that are soooo good. I'd been looking forward to the juice I asked for and will have a party tonight when I go off duty. I was so tickled to get the pecan bar, and the cookies are so good there are very few left. If I just had a glass of milk, oh how I'd gain a pound or two on such eats. Tonight we had fried Spam, so I'll wait until we get hungry on a move before I open up my can. You always send just what I ask for.

309

Before the Army I never drank even a spoonful of wine. Now if there's any brandy that's been put up for years, just to say I've tasted it I take an eyedropper full. The champagne tastes so smooth and the warmth in this chill feels so good inside. There's nothing much else to drink in this country, and I despise their cider. One boy did get a Coke in the mail the other day.

The very next package from home contained his own personal bottle. He sent thanks, not telling her that by the time it reached him, he was in a place that supplied all the Coca-Cola he could drink.

Although air activity had been classed as "light" during the month, a number of planes raided from time to time, coming in from all directions during the early part of the night. On October 19th a dozen maneuvered for about an hour. As on other occasions there seemed to be no specific purpose or target, and when counterattacked they took evasive action and left the area. On the 22nd a buzz bomb came over Pont-a-Mousson, the town whose bridge was being guarded. A structure over which troops and supplies could be moved north must be protected as carefully as the traffic ways the 411th had defended in Normandy for the break-out and the pontoon bridge over the Seine which led to Paris.

With that radio station getting all the first dope on these military stories maybe you had a little hint of hush-hush on the new invasion in the Pacific. It sounds good to us here. They seem to have just beaten those Japs until they didn't have a comeback when they landed. General MacArthur made his promise good, that he would return. All the papers must have wasted as much ink as they did when D-Day came here. Did you have the honor of announcing the story?

In about thirty minutes now we'll be having church. The chaplain came to our area with the service. Although the Catholics outweigh us, we do have some really good services. I'm glad he can be with us like he does. All during the week he's around just to talk and pass on what rumors he's heard about when the war will be over. He's so good to us and lays out such good reasons and rules for life that bring us back to keeping tabs on ourselves.

The day if not looked up on the calendar would be almost the same as any other day, but somehow I get homesick more on Sundays.

First coming overseas I was a bit nervous and on edge, flying off the handle or getting hot under the collar. One day something snapped and caused me to make a check on myself. If I continue on the same way it'd be a pretty state of affairs when I come home. I've now come down to a calm, more reasonable temper, not biting too many heads off. Some would even ask if I didn't hear from you that day because of my bad mood. Well, I wasn't proud of myself that way, so I've sorta given it a new monthly resolution. No doubt there'll be lots of butchering the English language, too, but I'll try to be at least sane when the time comes, so I'd better start now.

We had a U.S.O. show today. One girl sang and put great feeling into the songs, then another danced, but didn't have enough stage space so she was handicapped a little. Then the M.C. and another man with a boy at the piano made up the cast. The girls would have attracted the eye more and gotten more whistles if they hadn't used so much make-up, eye shadow and all. I enjoyed it, though, and laughed so hard, but then you have to come out and find that really you are in a war. I need a hand to hold when I go to movies, too.

Last night I was looking at the postmarks on some of the mail that came finally and turned out they were from way back in the summer. As I read along I thought it was funny you were having so many bad storms, then a fellow came in saying he'd found some

311

of his letters were from early September. When I looked at mine, I realized they were all about the storm when your power was out for a week and the whole beach washed away. I'd even begun to wonder if it wasn't safer a bit more inland, or else you should come on over to this side of the world. I wish you could.

If all of a sudden you see this begin to waver, it's because I'm writing in my sleep. Don't I wish someone would hurry and just get tired of this fighting. They never count a life as anything in this world when all I want is yours close to mine.

———————

With the Third Army held in abeyance, Hitler both gained time to re-group and renewed assurance of victory in some form. Realizing that something held Patton's dangerous forces back, he began to gnaw quite aggressively at the Allies, sending patrols and secret agents to spy and sabotage. His present army might include sailors, deep-sea divers, and sixteen-year-olds, but a build-up in the restrictive Ardennes area, only a hundred miles from Antwerp, could seal that port off and trap the British army in his own Dunkirk, a word that daunted both sides.

When the Fuehrer, crouched in his Wolf's Lair in East Prussia, had propounded the idea, his audience was stunned. Their losses stretched from Normandy to Finland to Greece. Yet the wily dictator, with weaklings purged from their midst, knew the strength of his dispersed and bomb-proofed industries and the emotional power of defense of the homeland. Sitting beneath a portrait of Frederick the Great, who had previously wrested victory from almost certain defeat, he saw such weakness in the Allied-Bolshevik Russian alliance that over time, pitting one side against the other, he might fashion a peaceful settlement for Germany in the uncertain space between them.

For those lingering in the doldrums, sporadic shelling, air raids after dusk, and buzz bombs coming in at 200 m.p.h. did little to lift morale. Three near-misses had landed on either side of Patton's current residence at Nancy, one of the war's scariest moments. What if he, old B. and G. - famed end-runner, dashing hero - had been taken out?

You'd think they'd let us know when he was coming around. I mean that boss of ours, the head of our whole army. Some said they saw him in the little village today. Isn't it funny where you can meet important people? I sure would like to see the old boy even if he did give me the dickens for not having on a tie or a crease in the trousers. When we were back in England near Reading, in one of the pubs a lieutenant from our outfit met one of the Roosevelt boys. He said the man was just like any other ordinary soldier in this man's war even if his father is the commander-in-chief.

Since I got to know the Blue Network so well and with you looking at the news so often, I thought if anyone heard about the 411th over there you would. One man said his wife did, and a few days later another man said his mother heard something about what we were doing while at Mantes in the heavy action around Paris. I could tell you a heap, but who's looking but the censor.

By now you'd think I was a full-fledged French talker, but I still stutter more than you'd expect. 'Course I could get along if I got stranded some place, but don't expect me to rattle it off when I come home unless this lasts too long, and my plans aren't that way now. I'll never like this "wee wee" stuff. They have so much slang that's awful hard to catch onto just looking in a book. You really need someone to talk it to.

The best language is the one you'll understand.

No sign of mail until after chow, then there's a blue letter speaking louder from the stack and looking more cheerful than any of the others. I hope they never ration you to just V-mail.

313

I don't ever want to worry you, but I do like for you to know what we're doing. We have a certain position and section to protect. It might be roads, bridges, dumps, or even some other section of the front. Right now we have worked it out rather well. With all the men we have we can break the work down so it won't be too hard on any one man except those who'd be in charge, and they don't stay on duty over 6 to 8 hours at one time. I'm around a good bit of the time, but do have nights off now to do whatever I please, usually just reading, writing, cleaning up and getting a good night's sleep whenever possible. I'd really rather stay a little busy so time passes quickly. I don't know how things will work out if it's a hard winter, but with our equipment we don't have to spend too much time out in the cold. 'Course we'll have our share, but that's why we are so blessed when that doughboy on the line catches so much.

I'm so pleased that the scarf came to you as a surprise. I had to cheat the French government out of a few points, but they didn't seem to bother. Besides, I think they made up for it in the price. When a gal is so war-conscious that she gives blood that will go so far and do as many wonders as some of the new Fortresses, it makes a man proud and pleased that his wife back home is pulling with all her life and love to get this over with as quickly as we want it over here.

Just always be a few steps away.

The other day I was writing my sister and addressed the letter putting <u>your</u> address on it. Either I'm writing without thinking now or I'm becoming an absent-minded professor. Your mom has been after me to ask for something. One of the fellows got such a good fruitcake the other day. It made me so hungry I just up and asked for one of her special cakes we used to like so well, like that first Christmas we had together at their house. Remember, I asked if it had wine in it. It didn't, of course, with <u>your</u> mother making it, but what if they knew now!

Things have been rush rush around here today, so many things to do it was chow time before I knew it. We had a rather dull movie this afternoon, but at least the men have permission to use the theater in the little town close by here. You should see these French theaters. They even have a place for the chaperone in the "pews" and if we get some laughs, that's a big help.

A few times I still get shaky how I'll step out with what we want to do and build after I come home. I think we can do so well if I can step into civilian life after a few weeks, but don't want to plunge into anything until I've settled this long loneliness away from home. I'm having to do things now that surprise me and would never have thought possible, but now I'm doing them and making the best of all I know. I can come back with the deepest feeling that all is well.

The sergeant's superiors in rank, with problems far more pressing than how to care for a wife and make a living, had postwar planning as well as combat to manage. Recommendations to be forwarded eventually to President Roosevelt at Potsdam in 1945 began with leaving no official doubt as to who had won the war. Germany must be occupied and its citizens recognized for complicity in crimes against humanity. Prominent Nazis and industrialists must be tried and punished, membership in the Gestapo and SS proving guilt automatically. The general staff, its archives surrendered to Allied authority, would be dismantled. All war-making powers must be reined in with controls over industry or direct prohibition of certain manufactured items such as airplanes. German citizens, unsupported by the Allies, must make their own livings by working in the mines of the Ruhr if nothing better, it being economic nonsense to flood such a useful asset as some had suggested. Finally, and most importantly, a military government should be established and placed in civil hands just as soon as feasible.

The Morgenthau Plan, appearing in American newspapers after Roosevelt and Churchill had agreed to it at Quebec, seemed too much like the revenge Goebbels had warned the Germans about, a dismembered nation converted into an agricultural Germany. A hint of Morgenthau's "Jewishness" even surfaced here and there along with German truculence about being turned into a "potato patch."

Eisenhower also struggled with the definition of "unconditional surrender." Germans fighting on German soil owed obedience to a commander, his generals under oath to the death. And what requirements could be made of seven million slave laborers fearing reprisal from the SS or a population whose very livelihood was being ruined, perhaps for years ahead? For convenience SHAEF headquarters had moved from Normandy to an office at Versailles which some considered too fancy, but at least near Paris. A bust of Goering, apparently left by the previous inhabitants, had its face turned toward the wall.

Patton, leaving a tent in Verdun, took up space in a steam-heated building in Luxembourg twelve miles from the German front. Under a banner bearing the neutral sentiment of the independent nation, "We wish to remain what we are," stood shops with a thousand sparkling unbroken glass windows, pictures in glowing color of the Grand Duchess, and a huge portrait of Roosevelt - Teddy, not Franklin.

Their German nemesis, varying between East Prussia and Berchtesgaden, shuffled and dismissed commanders as usual while creating new units from veterans of the eastern front unfamiliar with their current situation and its differing requirements. His 3000-plane Luftwaffe, at record level in numbers but beginning to lack trained pilots, would have to conserve its meager gas supply for major blows and the defense of Berlin.

While generals drew maps and made lists, a sergeant opened ghost and goblin cards and thought of Christmas.

Here it is Halloween and you're already shopping for Christmas. That must take getting used to. Part of the rush went along with the spirit. I'm sure that hometown boy in Burma will be glad to get your present.

They say (no rumor either) that there are 30 million packages coming from the states for Christmas. Old Mr. Claus will have a time jumping the hedges. Maybe he'll even bring out a secret weapon to deliver them. The articles you sent did give the lowdown on the false hopes of our being out of foxholes in time for Christmas. Lots they said I hadn't even heard. It's good you follow so close with me. You do understand the military now so much more than anyone could without having been in it. That article on griping was so good. For us it's about the only way to let off steam.

7:00 A.M.

Just who's making up the history of this war is hard to tell. What they should include as one of the most important factors and headaches is the <u>mud</u>. It counts a great deal with the Army today. Just picture us being mobile with mud up to the axle and over the shoe tops. Thank goodness the weather has been in our favor the last few days. <u>Stars</u> <u>and</u> <u>Stripes</u> reports a few snow flurries on each side of us. Yep, the air is pretty keen these mornings, and it doesn't get too warm during the day. Yesterday the place reminded me so of that country across the Channel. It stayed a heavy fog up to around ten, then Old Sol came out in full to-do.

Back home about five years ago we made a big thing of All Souls Day. We were in the flower business as well as the dairy, so a very important date for that reason. Here in France it was the biggest, I sincerely think, next to Christmas. All the people declared a holiday yesterday and came out in numbers going to and from the churches. Ninety percent of the people are Catholic, so naturally it was a big day.

Way into the night, when I went to the trailer at midnight, they were still going strong.

We used to work ourselves to death with those darn flowers, all summer long keeping them watered, tied up on poles we hated to drive in the ground, then work around. When the cold was hitting the north end of the barn we'd have to cover the whole patch with a tent. Then sometimes one hard frost would kill them anyway. Either we didn't get the cover on in time or else the place wasn't warm enough. Why I got off on this I don't know, but they were pretty, and if you'd been around then, you'd have had a special bouquet.

I'm tickled to know another record of my wife's voice is coming. The good part is we've just received a new vic for the battery and a lot of new records, too. Now I can play both of those you've sent and feel really close to home at Christmastime. Some of the fellows will be glad to hear your voice, too. Honest, to hear an American girl's voice is a most unusual sound around here, so don't be shaky. Just tell all that's on your mind. Well, maybe not all.

I got to thinking last night of what kind of a house we'll build some day and started making a drawing and some ideal plans of how I would like the rooms to be. "This would be convenient" and "Would this be enough space?" I'll just have to live like this until I can come back to real life. I'll just live it with you.

On a stack of Bibles.

I've just spent almost a three-day pass with you. In fact, if all the mail I've had from you were added up it would amount to a nice long furlough. The three today were full of your thoughts and opinions on the war, the president, the Army, even the way our troops are doing. I like the way you keep up with the situation. If the public listens and reads about it, they have a far better idea on how it's getting along than we do over here.

I didn't know the Army would issue us mittens, but it seems they may. Our leather gloves were taken away at Davis and no others issued. When I asked for some there was no sign of them or mittens either. I'm glad you understood the need for socks, too. With Mother sending gloves and you mittens and socks, in case the Army can't get around to it soon, I'll be in good shape for the cold that's here and coming. Right now we may be given all we can carry, but one never knows what they'll pull next. With all the galoshes, sleeping bags and sweaters they'll have in line we may have too much as it is. Right now two to three of us send laundry out to some lady in the village and get it back in three to five days. That way it doesn't cost us too much. They do a good job, though I don't see how, the way they pound them. Usually the clothes are clean. We used to think in the states it would be awful to wash our O.D. uniforms. Now, wearing them all the time like we are, there's no way around it. Would you believe it, though, that I still have two shirts and a pair of trousers I got at Eustis when drafted? Some people are so hard on clothes, having something new every few months, but I've had good luck with mine.

Something funny happened with me and the little girl, who is just five and living in the same chateau. One morning I was out in the yard brushing my teeth because there's no other place, so she came to watch. I looked around, and there she was, mocking me with her finger. Then the little dickens wanted me to brush her teeth. I'm guessing she's never had a taste of toothpaste, much less a brush. She's so cute and fat that all of us here spoil her. She's picked up some of our expressions, though, that don't sound too good coming from a small child.

You could live so cheaply here. Just think of paying only $2.80 for four or five rooms, but I wouldn't live here if they gave me all of France unless you came and wanted to stay.

---

6 Nov 1944   Engaged hostile aircraft.   No Claims.

Cold, damp, muddy October had been the kind of month Patton despised. No swift moves, no joyous celebrations, just halting, trenchfoot cases, and a sick rate equal to that of the casualties.

Shunning personal risk, the general continued to ride through the daily mists in an open car to give pep talks to his men. He also dutifully honored the visiting commander of the Communist zone with a band, guard, and special dinner at Nancy. Meanwhile, his troops in Luxembourg were fishing in trout streams and getting their own barbecue by taking down wild boar with Thompson sub-machine guns from low-flying Cubs.

Arch-foe Hitler advanced plans for a campaign in the Ardennes and in a call to wish Goebbels a happy birthday promised the German people a surprising gift at Christmas. His strategy for protecting valuable raw mineral supplies in the Balkans was also working well. Just keep the Allies out of Yugoslavia by keeping them busy in Italy.

Across the Channel V-2's falling soundlessly out of London skies had killed or wounded nearly ten thousand who happened to be in the way. Philosophical Brits bravely commented it was no worse than one big air raid you couldn't plan on.

Daily became even more daily - just slogging along without any sign of progress or movement in the ranks. Then, to his complete surprise, the GI from Tennessee was rewarded for faithful duty with an opportunity the censor wouldn't allow him to brag about until it was all over.

Red Cross 5:30 P.M.

Tis a beautiful day where I am today. I've had so much fun the last few days, some I thought I would never have, honest. You'll hear all about it in a few days, but you know the walls have ears, and such spies we have picked up. This place is almost like the rooms at the Hotel Taft after your graduation, remember? I've had such a day, but it's not all going to last long. It's almost chow (dinner) time. The fellows are calling, "Can't you write your wife tomorrow?" but I wanted to have you with me on this.

I've just come back from three of the best days I have spent since I came over. It all came up unexpectedly. Don't you hate to build yourself up on something and then have the plans fall through? This was a real surprise your Blue Network should have picked up on. I was so tickled at getting to go. It almost seemed like going on furlough the night I was asked.

I've been to Paris, one of the things I've wanted so long. Only the fellows who are in combat get the trips, and I happened to be one of the three from this battery. It's the grandest thing that's happened in so long. I hardly know where to start. I wished you were there with me. Wouldn't we have had the time of our lives? It was wonderful.

With all your letters waiting I didn't know whether to concentrate on what my pass was all about or just let my heart guide the pen. I still can't get over the getting to go. It all seems like a happy dream. What I enjoyed so much was getting away just at the time there seemed nothing for us to do but wait for supplies to catch up so we can get started again.

Believe you me it was a long ride in a G.I. truck. At first we thought we'd be going by train. Then when we got to a certain place we changed over to more trucks. We got into Paris late one evening and ran for a shower that seemed like heaven. I think some of the Red Cross girls thought we came right out of the line. Because of the long distance our faces were muddy and dusty as any doughboy's.

The Red Cross has taken over one of the largest hotels in Paris so we lived in the best style of any tourist that's ever come here. The room reminded me of those in New York after your graduation. The Red Cross girls were the best there could be, giving us tips about things, just acting as though we were their family and wanting us to have a good time. Anyhoo, the bed, sheets, private bath and all were just for the three of us. Oh boy, I took a bath every day and just laid back for minutes in the tub full of warm water.

After a good night's sleep, and going to bed around eleven, too, mind you, I was really raring to go the next morning. I thought surely with all the rain we'd had it would be raining there and spoil the fun, but first thing I looked out and saw the sun was coming up. I woke the other fellows and even was a bit talkative that early, too. After we had breakfast in the Red Cross cafeteria, the city was what I wanted to see first. I saw a notice of a tour leaving at 9:30. We took that bus all over the city and all along had a guide who pointed out the most important spots. It was such a good sight-seeing trip I could hardly see anything I was looking at so much so fast.

First we stopped at the Madeleine Concorde Square where all the head-chopping took place. Then we flipped on down the Champs Elysées to the Grand Palais, stopping at the Arch of Triumph where the unknown soldier was buried. All the gang on the bus were having a picture made, but I was off looking at the lamp burning on the grave and missed the group shot by minutes. I was so mad I'd missed it, but bought one anyway. They rushed it back to be finished by the time we reached our starting point. We also stopped at the Eiffel Tower and have a story to tell you someday about that and a flyer in a P-47. We saw Napoleon's Tomb along with the Palace of the Invalides Dome, the Louvre, and visited Notre Dame church, really a beautiful sight.

Paris is not in its full stride, of course, but the beautiful dresses and hats and girls were there. I'd love to be able to come home and tell you all we saw and did.

This morning there was a white blanket of snow all over the place. Away on the hillside was a lovely picture, but then I'd think of what some of our buddies are going through, all kinds of hell in the cold. Then it loses some of the beauty it would have if we were at home and could ride a sleigh and pitch snowballs. I count the blessings each time I think of the way we have it rather good compared to some. At times we, too, have had it hard at first when moving and getting settled again and again, but once we got emplaced the same old routine cropped up and went like clockwork. We've been issued enough clothes lately that should keep us warm if it doesn't get too bad, which we expect with snow just starting. Already part of us have high-top overshoes to keep our feet dry after staying wet for so many weeks. They help out lots in warmth, too.

About this time last year that lovely furlough was coming up. I knew as well as you it was the last one, but didn't want to talk about that. Even our folks sensed it, though. I never forget the day we rode off to one of our favorite spots and had one of those sodas that taste so good.

When I went on pass to Paris there had to be some looking for things I wanted for you. With Christmas coming I have some things to get off, hoping they'll get there in time, if not by then in time for New Year's.

Today was a beautiful day, one I hope could be lots of help to the boys at the front and in the air. That's what I pray so earnestly for now, lovely weather so the push can go ahead. Each day is one day closer to the end, one day closer to home. Your tacks are about as close as they have ever been. Yes, we have been right behind Mr. Two Guns so no one's sorry that he's at the head.

I can see you walking down the street looking in your purse to get the key to the house. How I wish I could be there to unlock the door for you. I wrote your brother about meeting him at a certain place, but it was either cut out or the letter never reached him. At one point he seemed a bit puzzled at us giving one of their planes the dickens. Well, I don't think we could be that bad at identification of aircraft not to know a B-26. If they're so good, why did they lay some of their eggs on top of friendly troops?

Sometimes we all make mistakes. He's almost to where you guessed. If you ever moved your tack to the right spot, you have now. 'Course with Ike and his staff having conferences, we should all keep pretty well in contact. So you can count yourself as being on the ball and up to date now. Can't tell, though. The Blood along with the _____ may take another leap.

In Paris I saw lots of the styles you'll have in not too many weeks. All my life I've head of "Paris fashion." 'Course it was bit dampened after all they had been through, but some looked rather good to me after so long not seeing these fancy clothes and styles. What's funny about it, where a fur coat is an American girl's ambition, they are really plentiful around Paris even in war time. I don't know what you think about the new hats, but turbans are really some stuff. The shoes were interesting, too. With a little wood, a little leather, they are attractive and unusual, but even if they make a gal's foot look streamlined, I'm sure Blue Jay can sell more corn plasters here then he ever did in history. Where we have a hundred francs to spend that makes two bucks, so if I ever bought you a housecoat it comes to about 2000 francs. "Course the French money is worth so little now.

The biggest laugh I got on the trip was over the taxis. With the gas shortage some fellow put a cart on the back of a bike, a two-wheeled affair for two people with a top on it. We helped push two officers in one of these. The poor taxi driver couldn't take off until he could push his riders fast enough, then jump on and pedal off. They even brought out a horse and buggy for us, such a beautiful animal like those in your birthplace of Kentucky, home of beautiful horses and beautiful women, of course.

When I have hardships, I wish you were here to help the loneliness, but I wish I could be with you through the laughing, too.

Nothing makes a man feel any better than a shave unless it's a haircut. But even with all the commotion we have to go through with to get one, a bath is still what I like the very best. Funny though. After that first relaxing bath in Paris the minute I hit that comfortable bed sleep left me entirely and I couldn't go off to dreamland one bit for the longest while. Maybe it was having real sheets for a change.

The thing that attracted my attention most on the tour, no bright lights either, was the Arch of Triumph. The wide street and the height and all were a surprise. I was curious, too, about the Unknown Soldier. While we were there, in rehearsal for the Armistice parade they placed a wreath of flowers on the grave. I hadn't thought of Armistice Day till then and wanted so to see the ceremony the next day, but had to leave around eleven. The grave has this control light burning year in and year out. Even at night they give the flame more gas to light the grave. It never goes out and never will for years to come. When I see these things I find I fall so short of some of the history I should know. I wanted one of the flowers from the grave, but so many police were around I was afraid if I picked one I'd have to wire for an extension of my pass. Wouldn't the first sergeant have had a hissey over that? If I hadn't in combat and didn't in the states, why would I get in trouble over here?

The city of Paris was divided up so well. One whole section was the expensive area where you'd expect to pay more if you shopped there. Then the really high society folks had their section. An amazing place.

Farewell, Paris. Hello, Reality, though now reality-with-a-difference. While the sergeant toured Rest and Recreation in old Paree, the inactive Third Army had come to life. Jumping off below the Ardennes Forest, they headed for the Saar and the Siegfried Line. Days of advancing by the yard and losing riflemen by the score were left behind. Metz would be surrounded and by-passed, and troops driving up from the south would link with Patton, leaving no pockets to mop up later.

The thunder of guns caught the enemy off-guard as at Normandy, a major thrust being unthinkable in weather so bad that air support was blocked out. Also, flooding streams had broken their banks leaving only the bridge at Pont-a-Mousson entirely intact, to be zealously guarded by the 411th.

In typical fashion Patton never saw difficulty in opportunity. When others had chafed over un-"Lucky" weather causing delay, the usually impatient general calmly remarked that the Lord would get around to it soon no matter what the forecasters predicted. Awake at Nancy on the eve of the scheduled assault, he read of a German attack in the rain in 1914. By 0515 hours the downpour had stopped, stars were out, and on the brightest day in the whole month hundreds of guns sounded, according to one clever soul, like heavy doors slamming in an empty house.

If the Nazis had thought the Allies bedded down for the winter, they recovered admirably from the shock. During weeks of delay they had manned pillboxes, installed tank traps and road blocks, and laid hundreds of mines. Whatever progress the Third accomplished would be done the hard way, by rafts and assault craft where bridges had washed away and by narrow roads since soggy fields would not support their tanks or heavy field pieces. A campaign planned in good weather had bumped into the worst floods in the area in eighty years.

Patton had hoped to win a battle by his birthday on November 11th, but it took eleven days to close around Metz and four more before the last German they met either died in combat or surrendered. Instead of a victory, birthday celebration meant "Armored Diesels" to drink and a congratulatory call from Bradley with a story about a pontoon bridge. Engineers working for days to construct it had seen their efforts disappear down-stream in the wake of a veering tank destroyer which caused the wreck ("The whole damn company sat down in the mud and bawled like babies").

On the bright side, the port of Antwerp was open at last, and though raw and wet and surrounded by manure, the Third Infantry was 25 miles northeast of Nancy and halfway to the Siegfried Line. Patton was in Germany, The Fatherland, heading for the Saar.

With the news better than it has been in weeks we do keep up hopes of it all ending this year, although it's still a hard fight. These darn Germans won't give up. They know they haven't got a chance, but prolong and weaken as much as they can. Who could be easy on such people in peace terms? If we don't whip them to a pulp, in a few years they'll need it all over again. It'll take a long time of policing to keep them going the way we plan, and no monkey business. Some think if you treat them nice and do good toward them, they'd settle for less, then in a few years come back again. I think most of the G.I.'s will be so fed up they'll lose all the soft-heartedness that the Germans think we have. I'm for tearing their cities to pieces if necessary and disarming them completely. Some think they're just fighting because they're made to. I thought that once, too, but now I've changed my mind. Why should they be killing our buddies one minute, then the next hollering "Comrade"? Then if you turn your back, well, it's the last time. They work hand in hand with Japan so why not treat them just as bad? They deserve nothing less. I do hope Russia will come in and really give them the works. I think Germany is actually afraid of Russia and would rather keep her out and let us come in, thinking maybe we will treat Germans better. I've begun to hate them as never I've hated people's lives before. They have no sense of real life, religion, only their country as ruler. Bosh.

This is what is on my mind tonight and I just had to get it off, pleasant or not.

Sometimes in thinking of our future I get some pretty wicked ideas. If you never have air castles, things will fall short. If I just rock along never thinking of tomorrow or yesterday, things get on my nerves a bit. Surely a few years after the war is over business should be good in almost everything, and building should be in a boom, too, because materials are so tied down now, once people get things turned loose they'll go like a house afire. We have some contractors in our outfit that used to build homes and barns. I enjoy talking to them, not just because they are good men and pleasant to be with, but I find out and learn about house building. We pass away lots of cold nights balancing and weighing problems that come up, and I may show them a floor plan I've drawn, maybe get an estimate of what it would cost to build. The way things are changing and improving, I might get a contractor who'd ship our home in sections and have it up in weeks, but still as firm and strong as any now.

Sometimes I think, too, that travel will be so much by air that these flying jennies that go straight up from the back yard could be used very satisfactorily with us in the country. I could load our milk and deliver it to the plant before a truck could go a mile in traffic. Even cattle could be carried to market that way. Maybe I'm getting crazy and been thinking too much lately, but life is changing so it should be planned and not just come about haphazardly.

The long cold nights are so bad here. That's when I long to be close to the warmth of a fire at home and talk about what the day has brought. I know just about what you are doing now every moment of every day.

Thanksgiving Prayer   The Chaplain

I thank Thee, Lord, for a thousand things, the earth, the sky, the rolling sea, the summer and the winter, the springtime and the harvest field; but beyond all these for home, for those who love me, who trust me, who wait for my return. May Thy providential care and protection be granted them in my absence and may it please Thee to bring us safely together again. For Thy name's sake, Amen.

The lieutenant colonel said to his men, "On this, the third Thanksgiving day that we are about to commemorate together, I am reminded of the first such day," mentioning many who had left for civilian life or other units, new men who replaced the losses, and the trying times and different sites they had experienced together. He continued, "You have supported me in all my policies and have faithfully and willingly carried out the orders issued. We can all be thankful that God has looked down upon us with favor and has spared us from death and injury. We know that He is watching over our families at home with as tender a love as we ourselves bear toward them. Let us all now give thanks to Him who created us, and pray that this will be our last such Thanksgiving together and that we may share the future with our loved ones at home."

The captain's remarks were equally gracious: "Let us be happy in the knowledge that our next one will be with our loved ones who, at this Thanksgiving, are with us in their thoughts and prayers."

Thanksgiving Dinner

Roast Turkey w Giblet Gravy

Giblet Dressing (real society)

Mashed Fresh Potatoes
   (with lumps)

Peas (fresh out) with Carrots

Cranberry Jelly

Pumpkin Pie
(chocolate)

Hot Rolls
(So good)

Creamery Butter
(forgot   to
churn)

Coffee
Hard Candy (no)
Apples   Oranges

If the menu did not reach the standard as printed, the celebration was still a success, enlivened by cartoon drawings of various battery leaders shown in such post-war occupations as coal mines and bread lines.

Thanksgiving 4:00 P.M.

Most always at home Thanksgiving Day was a bit rainy, but who cared about that if we had plenty of good eats and friends around, just a day of resting, eating, visiting the neighbors. Maybe you didn't have as much turkey as I did, but surely you have part of the afternoon off at least. Most of the holidays are all the same now, but when I return we'll make lots of to-do over them. I'll be especially thankful.

We got so many laughs out of the pictures on the menu that represented us in 1946. The cartoon of me looks a little battered. The artist must have gotten a little nervous when he got down that far, thinking his buddies might go against him for making fun.

We went in our same routine, only had a larger dinner. I think the Army planned for all on this front to have turkey, and if they didn't this year, well, they won't have it in the service. The cooks did put out especially hard with the turkey and rolls. I tried to give them a feeling of how much I enjoyed it. It takes patience to cook as ours have to, and they did do a good job although most of the time I tease about the stew they put out. My messkit needed sideboards to keep all that food on. I just wanted to sleep all afternoon I was so full.

Your birthday tomorrow is really the day of all days. I think I'll write Ike and see if we can't get it changed to a national holiday. If the mailman fails me, he should be kicked in the pants. I sent the packages in plenty of time, then dreamed that you'd received the last one I mailed and everything was taken out but one thing. I was so mad when I woke up.

Nothing I can do would be enough.

I've thought of you in lots of places, but especially want you to have a happy day today. Let's promise to make it a big celebration next year. I hummed the little birthday tune and hope you heard it some way and know I was sending that special message.

I hoped I'd get some word yesterday that you had received your present, and last night I got the very letter. It's wonderful how things will come up at just the right time to tide us over.

I hate it that your brother has to come back overseas. He has done so much already and stood up to all they have thrown at him. One thing about it, when they get you over here you get stuck. It's awful hard unless you have a lucky break to get back.

No doubt you've had newsreels that give some idea of the mud that can make us bog down. I couldn't believe so much water could fall continually, but it's almost steadily. We don't have the job of the infantry, but we can feel for them. Even Ike has been around visiting in the mud. He, too, can see how and what the tanks have to go through with. At least we can change clothes, have a warm place to live in and hot meals, even a shower once a week.

———————

Metz, not taken by assault since the fifth century, was at last in Allied hands, only four of its thirty-five forts still resisting. The wearing-down process had furnished GIs with real target practice using the Germans' own guns and ammo. Also, in an old church, they had discovered thousands of small arms ranging from flintlocks to modern handguns taken from the French by the Gestapo.

A stout SS general, in immaculate uniform, was captured in a wine cellar and taken immediately to Patton. The American commander faced his enemy in the high heavy field boots he always wore while interrogating "the bastards," in this case rather pointedly using a Jewish interpreter and requiring the Nazi to stand at attention and begin every answer with

"Sir." In Patton's eyes this man was not a real soldier, just a G___ d___ party official later identified as such by the tattoo of his blood type under his armpit.

Other matters to be taken care of included offering an honor guard to the generals who had captured Metz and Nancy, showing the visiting ambassador to Russia "our mud" and receiving the compliment that the Red Army could not have achieved his rapid advance across France, decorating a man for taking out five still-smoking tanks, and spitting scornfully on German territory on the far side of the Saar River.

In a deep bunker surrounded by SS troops, Hitler, lecturing with shaking hands like a doddering old man while armed guards stood behind his generals' chairs, disclosed plans under consideration since mid-August. All had to sign acceptance of a death penalty if discovered in a breach of security and would be contacted by liaison officers trailed by the Gestapo.

To prevent detection by the Allies troops would move only by night, only trusted men would serve as sentries since foreigners and Alsatians might be treasonable malcontents, and artillery fire would be kept at current levels to avoid suspicion of new activity. In spite of von Rundstedt's appalled objections and proposal for a substituted "small solution," WACHT AM RHEIN ("Watch on the Rhine") would go forward as soon as weather permitted, the Eifel forest concealing the main build-up and a second panzer division, supposedly weak and headed in another direction, turning to join the main force at the very last minute. The attack, originally scheduled for November 26-28, would slash a hole through the Ardennes to capture supplies now unloading at Antwerp. Other speeding columns would head for Brussels and a major communications center.

As Patton had cogently expressed it in his first address to his staff since Avranches, the Germans, not being the fools some thought, were not licked yet. Intelligence reports gathered by G-2 advised they might even be in possession of current battle plans. Thus, efforts against them must be hard-driving and relentless, just Patton's style. Nazis killed all the way to the Rhine would not be troublesome later.

For the 411th moving day could not come too soon.

―――――――――

So far we've been in this place the longest ever, and we didn't expect to stay over a week. That's the way. You can't count on much. If you plan one way, nine times out of ten it goes the opposite. I don't like to get too close to a larger town because a number of odds are against you in this work. For me the pass situation is the least of my worries, but some would stay out a lot as if it weren't a combat zone. We'll snap out of it if we go to Germany, which will be nothing like the friendly people around here. Passes to Paris must have run out already. They only sent one man after we came back. Wasn't I lucky to get my name in the pot?

Writing you is like thinking out loud.

Tonight's moon would put North Carolina's in the shade, but I'd like to be there to let it prove itself. How wonderful it would be to go swimming, then take that long walk on the beach. Darn the coast guards. If I could only get that chance again.

I'm so happy now that we have good weather. The boys in the air really come out to give those devils the works they deserve. Even now I can hear the air full of them. It almost reminds me of some of the nights in England. Some nights there you could hear the roar for hours. Now that same sound is music to my ears. It's a few minutes closer to victory because who'd like to be on the receiving end of all that pounding? You may wonder how we can tell ours from the others. With our instruments we can do wonders, but I'd hate to be the Germans. If we were in the Pacific now, we would have our hands full. The Jap forces haven't been brought down like the Jerries have lately.

Things around home are getting busier with a Rogers daughter being married. Mother tells me Dad has consented to give her away even if it kills him. The wedding should be a big date there since the family has friends all over the county. I'm hoping you can get off for it, especially so close to Christmas. She used to tease me about being her twin. If your brother gets to come home, there'll be another wedding, too. Think of all I'm missing.

Happy weekaversary,

I had these fancy hankies I picked up somewhere, so thought I'd give you a surprise. The cloth isn't worth a dime, but the thought is what counts, they say. The small one cost me 65 francs ($1.30 American), a pretty good sum for a hankie that won't even serve the purpose. I just wanted you to have it, so I couldn't resist.

Thank you for letting me fall head over heels at your nice ankles. Pretty hair, too.

Sounds like you plan to spend Christmas at home. I was hoping you would though it may be hard to travel at that time. You'll have a much happier Christmas with all the folks, time will pass more quickly, and you'll be there for all the wedding excitement. There'll be lots of military travel, but if they're all as kind as A.A. men, you'll get lots of help, and lots of whistles.

From all the sources we hear this is the heaviest rainfall they've had in these parts in some 50-70 years. Most all the cellars in town are flooded, and lots of the bridges have the men holding their breath for fear some will go and hold up our supplies.

Had to stop this yesterday afternoon and finish up in the midst of "prayer meeting," on payday. I can't say weekend any more one day is so near the same as another, but Sunday reminds me of home. Every weekend there seemed like ages though it was only two days.

I do wish we had met sooner in life. Some couples in our town met when their mas and pas went to make sorghum. They left the young folks behind, and did they get to know their neighbors! Just think, I might have gotten the chance to carry your books to school. I never did anyone else's though. Honest.

With us in one place so long I now have two 12"x8" pieces of glass with one of your largest pictures, then about six little snapshots in so many poses and smiles. My "personal property" on the shelf has grown so you get lots of attention. Not many wives' pictures in sight, so with all these around you get lots of hmmms and nice comments.

I have begun to let my hair grow out. The short cut and the helmet have taken the life out, but with some good tonic I'll look slick around the ears again. I may have gained a few pounds, how I do not know with the chow not being too fattening. Maybe it's that winter fat that will creep up on you if you don't eat much, but don't do much strenuous work either. I feel good, never having the slightest trouble, only heartache.

I've taken unusually good care of the feet so as not to get any of the trenchfoot that goes around, or any other infection. Trenchfoot seems to affect the fellows who have been in water and mud for days and unable to change their shoes and socks. One man had been up to his hips in water for eighteen hours. When the medics picked him up, the first thing they asked was did he have a change of socks. What good would that have done?

You know what I'm hoping for tonight, either a letter or a picture or a package or a dream.

Some say often when they see me writing, "How can you do that when there's no mail and so little happening to tell about?" I let them know I must write because it makes my wife a little happier that day.

We had waited so long since the last U.S.O. show. I was surprised to hear they were bringing one around, the best we've had. You might just think it was because they had lots of girls, but mostly it was the way they put it over. The cast was five lovely girls and one old man. Honest, he <u>was</u> old, but so lively and good in his way. As M.C. he kept us laughing from the time the curtain went up. Each time a new act came on, the old fellow would come out with his long face and a new cap and civilian coat. Once he even came out with all the ranks of the Army from P.F.C. up to Captain. His jokes were not all morally A-1, but caused a laugh we needed. You might think American girls would be forgotten over here, but no girls compare to ours. They sang and danced their hearts out for us. In fact, as long as we clapped don't think they weren't tickled to come out again with all the confidence that we liked them, especially one from Texas who played the piano. She sang all the old familiar songs. You might think we'd get only cheap or low-rated shows in this location, but this one had lots of good talent, and they had been together for 14 months. Some of the gals looked as though these C, K, and D rations were really agreeing with them, but still looked nice. These shows may cost like the dickens, but I will be willing when this is all over to help in that fund, whatever it is. What would we do without America?

Somewhere between the heaven I used to be in and here they've held up all of life to me, the mail. I should never complain, but you see, whenever I do, the minute I let you know there's a gap, it comes through. Hey, maybe I should gripe a little sooner.

———————

Ike had more pressing problems. Captured German documents revealed formation of a new unit for reconnaissance and undisclosed special tasks on the western front, probably spying and sabotage. Needed were volunteers trained in combat and proficient in English and American dialects. Any American clothing, equipment, guns or vehicles must be sent immediately to headquarters.

In fact, divisions were already assembling in the Ardennes and Alsace regions. Over two thousand new or repaired tanks would be available by Christmas. Most reassuring of all, Americans had not made the slightest move toward reinforcing a weak front held only by six new divisions with riflemen at three-quarter strength and no reserves on call.

Patton, even given all the details, would have simply remarked, "A division commander doesn't have to know anything. He can be as dumb as a sonuvabitch just as long as he's a fighter." It probably pleased him immensely that the Army football team had just flattened Villanova at home by the whopping score of 83-6.

Batteries B and D of the 411th now went north to Metz to defend traffic routes. As at Avranches earlier and in Germany later, the outfit split some miles apart, transferred temporarily to other forces. In this case A and C remained at Pont-a-Mousson under control of the 120th AAA Gun Battalion to protect the vital bridge. Paperwork and command structure belonged in the office. The men just went on doing whatever was necessary, going where ordered and firing guns. As things worked out, the bridge became a lifeline to redemption and victory in one of the most threatening events of the war.

Pearl Harbor Day

There can be those special days and dates that one can never forget. Surely this one three years ago is one of the most memorable. I didn't fully realize how serious it was at the time and what would take place afterwards. I'd been out on the job, and when the timekeeper remarked that we'd been attacked, it still didn't register until I listened to the news. I began to think then I'd be going into the Army much sooner and whether I could take a new bride into the uncertainties of Army life. Now my thought is just to hurry and get this over with.

The other night one of the little boys here came in dressed as what they call St. Nicholas. We had no idea it was their Santa Claus night. He had a large basket to be filled, but we had so little to give. He had on a mask, a funny hat and whiskers. He was a sight, riding a stick with a lot of strips of paper flowing from it. He's picked up so much of our talk that it's pitiful. I've learned a great deal of their language now where I couldn't pick up some before. He talks rather slowly, so we can catch on.

The little girl, who's about five, brought all the things she got for us to see. Some looked like they'd been through the whole campaign of France, dirty and all, but she was tickled to death and even wanted us to help her fix her puzzles. She had some Mother Goose in French. I thought that could be a good start in learning her ABC's.

I've looked all over for a picture frame, but finally had to make one myself. Now it's so nice to glance up and see you standing, sitting and always smiling at me. So much attention is caused with this new idea that some have tried to have one like it, but mine still shines, of course, because of the subject.

There's something I want so much again tonight, some wonderful pure milk, cold, rich and sweet. It's for me almost like someone who craves strong drink, I guess. I used not to be able to stand this powdered stuff, but now we never think of anything else when we get our cereals. I'm beginning to wonder if they really do have Pepsis in Berlin. I just hope our boys don't drop any pills on that factory.

It's surprising to think how far these V-mail blanks I'm using have traveled. You sent them to me from the states while I was in England, and I wouldn't dare throw them away for fear I might get some place where I couldn't get any. They've even kept dry when everything else I had stuck together.

It looks like the Christmas mail will be in before the holidays even start. Already some of the packages are coming in, and do they go fast. If you open a package, don't expect for it to last over thirty minutes, if it's eatable. Mother tells me her sailor boy in the Pacific has already received his and disposed of it. Have you heard any rumors that one of our Liberty ships went down with our Christmas on it? Why can't these darn Germans pick on something that could defend itself? We get so many rumors started, though. I expect this one to be false, too. Sometimes I think I won't believe the first report when peace is declared.

There's so much in the air, so much of this soil infected with disease that any cut I have I take care of right away. I hadn't had one in so long that when I did, the blood wanted to run away, so rich and red. I believe I could give as much as you, but don't let them take away any more than they need to finish this war. It shouldn't be wasted.

The sweet cable you sent ahead for Christmas came a new and different way, by way of Paris instead of London, so getting here much sooner. Surely God will let us be with each other in this season by next year. I pray each day that it might be sooner. I'll come home just to be at your side for a shadow.

After all these days it's <u>about</u> <u>time</u> some kind of boat was coming this way. There seems to be no end to days when no mail comes and nothing interesting happens. I never give up hope, though. So when two of your Christmas packages came early, I couldn't help but open one. That lovely blue box with the red string was so much brighter than any I've seen come out of the mail bags.

Lots of cold nights now we'll be cooking around the fire for our midnight snack. That's when I'll bring out the Spam and crackers I asked for. Already we were so hungry for the chocolate. The first night my buddies and I really had a picnic and filled ourselves miserably full. Everyone brings a little in, and do we cook and eat and shoot the bull until it's pitiful.

What was a complete surprise was the little stuffed pooch you sent for me and you to give to some little child. When the fellows saw what you had sent to one of our kids around here, we began to comment on how it would be held onto just because it comes from America.

I haven't given it away yet, just have it cuddled up close to your picture, but there's a cute little blond kid next door, Jimmie is his name. His hair's just like a girl's and he talks so little, but he's so cute and will be pleased when I call him around some day.

Even if you're wearing that hands-off ETO pin, there'll always be a few to try your patience in that town. I thought the Red Riding Hood approach because of your red raincoat really took the cake, but if they get too fresh, there's always a well-placed kick.

It's funny that I can't remember your height exactly. Could you send it so I can really "see" you?

These nights are so beautiful and clear that no one can look up and fail to think about where the moon is shining in our homeland. Last night around three-thirty I was on duty and went out to get some fresh air. As I looked up that lovely moon was shining in full down on my face. Although we can think of its being a good night for the planes and all the rest of war, still I can't lose sight of the lovely side of it, too.

When I came back in the trailer, all of a sudden off the radio came the exact time it was in New York! The station there came in so loud and strong with their soft American music around that time of the morning. Things like that make me so close to home, not nearly as far as the miles may seem.

According to one GI anxious to pretend the "here"-sickness away, if you only looked straight up, you'd think you were in Georgia.

To add friction and frustration, spokesmen for the Navy, without knowledge of an atom bomb project, couldn't foresee an end to the war before 1949. All they could go on was the astronomical problem of supplying enough to barely nick the Japanese Empire so far away, much less draw enough blood for the kill.

In the European theater Eisenhower, on the way to a meeting, noticed a track in the snow where no Allied troops, installations, or transport facilities existed. Questioned privately, Bradley assured him that flanking armies would take care of any unexpected threat. The situation eerily resembled the Germans' blindness before the invasion. While the worst weather in half a century seemed to preclude any possibility of attack either by air or ground and all was supposed to be well in hand, Hitler's plans proceeded.

Patton, a man of high faith if less exalted vocabulary, asked for a prayer to include on the back of the Christmas greeting he was preparing to give to every man in his army. The chaplain on duty balked, considering a plea for good weather an accessory to killing. He was instantly advised that a chaplain was an Army man, not a theologian. In a word, "I want a prayer." "Yes, sir!" Neither man realized at the time that a plea meant to cover an attack on the Rhine would divert divine attention instead to the Battle of the Bulge.

According to Intelligence, five German divisions had left Holland for parts unknown, and re-fitted panzer units and new Volksgrenadier outfits at the German side of the Ardennes were moving north. Furthermore, recent German captives seemed unusually cheerful in their situation, even suggesting existence of an assassination plot against Eisenhower, Bradley, and Patton.

One view was that of a group of spiders sitting in their own webs - Hitler trying to preserve his homeland, Russia wanting the Balkans, England needing to hold on and strengthen in the Mediterranean, and the United States hoping to assume England's position as world power.

In a foggy, snowy night in Europe, on roads strewn with straw to deaden the sound, German tanks moved slowly forward.

―――――――

Your nice buddy at the station sent a Christmas box filled with useful towels, soap, even a portable dressing kit. She also had a nice fruitcake I wanted to hold back, but after we got started, it only lasted two days.

I have some new pictures of your soldier. Didn't like those I had taken at Chalons, the poorest I'd ever had. This guy didn't scare me with the camera when it snapped. Then, too, I could jabber a little better this time to make him understand what I wanted. Some of these Yanks, by the way, didn't know how you smile for the camera by saying "Cheese."

One of the packages today had the record you promised. I'll be anxious to hear it, but as luck would have it our vic has gone to another battery. It'll be back in a few days, though. I was almost afraid to open the packing, but it made the trip just as it left your hands. That will be one gift I can keep year round. I may not even wait for our vic if I can find one among the French. The men want to be around when it's played. They're beginning to think, for better or for worse, there's no one exactly like us.

The other package was so decorated with stickers and poinsettias I've tucked it away until a little closer to Christmas. I don't think I can wait until that morning, though. I'm so curious.

That was a good idea to get the colonel to re-pack the German chute for you to carry home. One morning we had the best time sailing one in the wind. It was such a workout and tired my legs so that I couldn't stand up. I'm glad you let the men at the station see it. I've wanted a German Luger, too, ever since I came over. I've been offered some for $50, even $75, but they aren't worth that, and I haven't found one myself.

––––––––

The parachute he had "liberated" was still in the original case complete with inspection booklet describing the "falling umbrella." To open it she pulled a small thread, not thinking "ripcord" and WHOOSH! She and an entire 9x12 rug were covered with silky camouflage. Before the military friend repacked the chute, the Red Cross displayed it, splendidly draped from ceiling height, in a prominent shop window of Wilmington's finest department store.

You'll be home for Christmas by now with your, or maybe my, people. I started to hold this picture for Christmas Day, but wanted you to have it now, knowing I'm feeling fine and will be safe until you see me. Some pictures can do that. I hope this one will for you.

Reading over some of your letters after missing mail call tonight I found I had overlooked one whole page of your birthday letter and didn't even know about the toast they drank to us at the station that day. What struck me as funny was the fellow who buys the champagne usually drinks up, too, but here you have your boss on milk!

Seems they intend to keep us plenty warm this winter. Yesterday we were issued a sweater that's about the best the Army has ever put out. It's completely wool, olive drab (you know that), long sleeves, and a collar that fits close around the neck and can be buttoned up or left open. It's one of the few things the Army has issued that I really like. Next to that I like these arctic galoshes that keep your feet dry and warm. Some day we may all get sleeping bags, which I'm not crazy about because they call for doing away with the super sheets. For a while, to keep down trenchfoot, they took away all our socks. Each day we turned in the pair we'd worn the day before and got back dry socks. This proved unsatisfactory, so they gave us back our socks and prescribed toe exercises to keep the blood flowing and not letting any blisters form. Some recommended two soldiers getting in pairs and rubbing one another's feet to save time. This was mostly for front line men that stay in water continually, so we now let the French wash our socks.

In preparation for their entry into Germany the 411ᵗʰ had received Battle Orders issued for future dealings with the Nazis: stern courtesy and firmness in applying strict justice. Bradley saw clearly that easy-going Americans used to the welcoming French needed, with good reason, a little reminding about townspeople across the German border.

G-2 Intelligence operatives at the front could now identify the strength and location of particular enemy units, so proposed an immediate strike to avoid a major battle. In reply to Patton's misgivings about the situation SHAEF, sheltered far behind the front, more or less advised that <u>they</u> were in charge and to mind his own business. Thwarted by bureaucracy, he turned to the G-2 Daily Periodic Report which all his commanders received and alerted them with an estimate of approaching danger.

At the Saar Patton had crossed a bridge under fire to demonstrate to the troops that generals, too, could be shot at. What looked like houses there turned out to be riverside forts with foot-thick concrete walls, ground level reinforcements, and machine gun openings just above the sidewalks. His sardonic comment, "The Germans are certainly a thorough race."

They were that and more in Luxembourg where, according to one informant, bridging equipment accompanied by large numbers of engineers was being hauled to the front. And was the noise of vehicular traffic behind the German lines just units being relieved? Was Intelligence correct in assessing it all as "attack propaganda," window-dressing for a small-scale morale booster for German civilians at Christmas?

To give just due to the benefit of hindsight, contradictory reports raged constantly around the front from time to time, inspiring only routine interest even in Bradley's most pessimistic operatives. On a 230-mile line of 700,00 men, keeping track of developments was impossible for any but a local commander at the scene. None had communicated any dire premonitions. Bradley's statement later, "I do not blame any," included himself in the reckoning post-crisis. Anything was possible for an enemy as yet unconquered. Mother Nature had even favored the Nazi machinations by blocking Allied air activity with bad weather for three days.

Yet clues mounted. Four German captives bragged of a coming attack the week of December 17th, if not sooner, but the only credible member of the group was too badly wounded and doped with morphine to be interrogated until later. And in Luxembourg a woman telling of woods jammed with German vehicles and equipment would not reach headquarters for questioning until the 16th.

Too late. The "Ardennes surprise" was already under way. Before dawn that day a low rumbling sound filtered through the fog. By 5:30 A.M. V-1s were flying overhead, two thousand guns were booming, and infantry and panzers were launching a furious patriotic defense of the fatherland.

Back in October von Rundstedt, the man in charge of such desperate missions as the rescue of Mussolini and the break-out in Normandy, had been given orders marked "Not to be Altered," even to the timing of artillery fire. Allied commanders expecting his tactics on the battlefield would meet Hitler's instead, a force in American uniforms and driving American tanks while seizing bridges and inflicting sabotage on their way to Antwerp.

Though both American and British armies might have noted and acted profitably on information long in hand, the enemy's cleverness and profound secrecy rivaled that of the Allies before D-Day - radio communication forbidden, no one with knowledge of the operation allowed to fly west of the Rhine for fear of accidental discovery, troops staged by night at the last possible instant, and all non-Germans moved from front lines. Faked headquarters and false radio traffic served as well for the Germans in the Ardennes as they had for Patton's ghost army in England before the invasion.

For Americans it seemed like Pearl Harbor all over again. Bombardment didn't seem real until GIs roused from sleep by the banging left a foxhole or peeled off a bunk in a sandbagged log hut or a pallet in a commandeered cellar to see the enemy coming toward them through the mist with searchlight rays bouncing off the clouds. Germans held the odds, 2-1 in tanks and nearly 3-1 in personnel, aware and better trained. The Pentagon, realizing belatedly that war in the ETO would not end as predicted by November 15th, could not even supply enough new bodies to replace the 500 daily casualties. Volunteers from headquarters and up to ten percent of their units, including the 411th, were being trained near Metz as riflemen ("We are all soldiers"). In the crucial days ahead hospital orderlies, cooks, even walking wounded went to the line.

At Versailles, Eisenhower, just promoted to five stars, welcomed Bradley, whose canceled flight in bad weather had necessitated a four-hour car trip over icy roads. As they conferred that afternoon, an aide tiptoed in with news of a German counterattack at five separate locations.

Patton had the 15th set as jump-off date toward the Siegfried Line. Waiting on the weather in his headquarters festooned with thousands of colorful maps, he had sent to every unit serial photographs detailing every situation and obstacle each would meet after the biggest air raid yet provided three whole days of bombing. There was even an expert tour-guide for the expedition, a captured German major general who, realizing the war was lost, felt it his duty to help end the Nazi madness. Installed under guard in a villa in Nancy, he was filling in descriptions of constructions he had supervised personally and briefing his enemies on how, when, and where they could attack successfully.

Montgomery, reminding Eisenhower of his bet that the war would be over by Christmas, had requested and received permission to spend the holiday in familiar surroundings in England. Ike promised to pay up Christmas Day if necessary, but with nine days to go still had time to win. Monty's "appreciation" of their situation, dated December 15th, clearly considered the Germans incapable of serious resistance. Patton did not receive that estimate until January after the Third had turned things around.

By nightfall of the 16th Ike and Bradley, filtering truth from wild rumors of paratroopers everywhere (only one spot later) and deep infiltration (six miles by dark), suspected the intent and extent of Hitler's masterful gamble to delay victory and upset plans for the Pacific.

Enemy troops and vehicles moving rapidly and seizing bridges quickly aroused suspicion in their borrowed attire. Sentries at check-points began to demand American passwords, information about baseball teams, Mickey Mouse matters, or mates of current movie stars. If you couldn't produce a team's name or location or "Minnie Mouse" or "Donald Duck" when questioned, that was as far as you got.

Patton's first inkling of the outbreak was an urgent request from Bradley for the 10th Armored, out of the line and ten miles south of the Luxembourg border. Not realizing the seriousness of the situation, Patton, readying for his own take-off, objected strenuously at first. Bradley wondered, too, if the Germans weren't merely throwing out a feint to set him off balance. Still, they couldn't take a chance.

Thus began one of the most remarkable accomplishments of the entire war. The Third Army, poised and ready to attack toward the Rhine, now swung completely about toward the north. The 10th Armored, on the road within the hour, was fighting north of Luxembourg by daybreak. Standing before maps at headquarters, officers assigned from memory movement of troop units and supplies over hundreds of miles. Intelligence operatives dictated the order of battle until dawn, then grabbed K-rations and took off for Luxembourg to set up.

Reinforcements from the south used the only bridge still available, the crossing at Pont-a-Mousson held faithfully for so many weeks by the 411th, who had another part to play.

<pre>
17 Dec 1944   Left Jezanville. Arrived 1 Mi W
              Metz, France. Traveled 23 Miles.
18 Dec 1944   Special Mission.
</pre>

The "Special Mission," for the Air Force, took the firing sections of Batteries A and C north to the village of Ernestviller near Sarreguemines. The weather was miserable, the affair complicated and dangerous, the traffic undoubtedly a puzzled frenzy, but the letters home, calm and hopeful as always, reflected only a Christmas he might not live to see.

For so long now you knew where the General and I were. Now we finally took a little ride, so you'll have to move ahead a little. We stayed at the other place for so long that we knew we could never have another set-up as good. Actually some of the gang made such close friends they thought they were leaving home. I can see the advantages of the places we leave, but the farther we go now the less friendly the surroundings will be. Your dot on the map was <u>to the spot</u>. <u>How come you so smart</u>? It was a complete surprise you could read between the lines so well.

Old mailbox 992 in Wilmington may be so full his sides will burst. Your packages from me may not get there until after New Year's, but remember, I wanted you to have one from me on that very day.

We do live for the coming year, don't we?

I am so curious, and can blame it on being hungry, that I opened another of those perfect Christmas boxes. We were planning to move, so I thought I wouldn't have too much room for extras anyway. With those three good excuses I went ahead and was with you lots before Christmas. Really, the package was so fully packed that all the candy and even the mincemeat came through so well. You do know we can't take much around, and these gifts are real home to me.

You know when I move that your pictures and the snapshots in the folder are taken care of first when packing my personal things. There has to be something to fill the emptiness. You make me glad.

---

20 Dec 1944   Left   Metz.   Arrived   1   Mi   N Jezanville, France.   23 M.

For some reason, weather conditions or changing circumstances or even a renewed need to guard the precious bridge, the mission was never fired, so back to their original task. The fact that the gun crews had been transferred within less than a week from the 120th AAA Gun Battalion to the 115th, then to the 546th demonstrates the fluidity of the situation.

The leisurely push to the Rhine some had envisioned was a thing of the past. Germans, in strength in a territory they knew well from World War I and 1940, had surprised an undermanned team of raw recruits and tired veterans, many of their officers on leave, in what came to be called "German weather."

Adaptable Americans re-grouped, rallied mightily by a massacre at Malmedy where the enemy had come upon a convoy. With prisoners a burden, they had merely stripped the helpless men of rings and watches, cigarettes and weapons, then machine-gunned and rifle-butted down all but the few who fled or faked death. For several days, as the ghastly story spread, GIs took few prisoners. Captives either "died suddenly" or, if in American uniforms, were shot as spies on the spot. With that possibility in mind, Germans in disguise took to wearing their own dogtags so that if captured, they would be identified as members of a duly constituted fighting force, hence protected by the Geneva Convention.

To turn the tide the Third Army switched within days to a north-south line at the Saar and an east-west line at the Ardennes. The remarkable reversal, conducted in ice, snow, and sleet, required a new supply set-up, extended communication installations, and field hospitals as well as movement of troops. Unlike the Germans who had waited at Calais, Patton, once alerted, acted. He could be as tough as any of Hitler's hard-driving butchers and brawlers, and if raw recruits hadn't already learned about bombing and strafing, they'd soon get used to it. Sixty thousand men and eleven thousand vehicles were on the way to support them, three times more within a week. The main worries would be Luxembourg City, where Ninth Air Force Headquarters and Bradley's Army Group office were located, and a transportation center called Bastogne.

By the time the 82nd and 101st Airborne units, resting and re-fitting after the struggle in Holland, could be prepared for action, Nazis were rolling twenty miles inside Belgium. More than forty jeep-loads of American-speaking Germans were destroying communications and killing MPs who were directing traffic, and a situation map showed fourteen enemy divisions. Where had they all come from?

At Pont-a-Mousson the 411th followed the action as best they could from a distance, finding satisfaction in knowing that "their" bridge furnished a lifeline to the north. As "Peace on Earth" became "Hell," they salvaged what they could of Christmas and shot at the Luftwaffe.

It's a number of hours ahead of that all-important time for that red-headed sister of mine, but I'll bet she has seen her groom already. The newspaper accounts did things up so well I carry the clippings yet. I had planned and wanted to be an usher for her some day, but never once thought about her asking you to sing.

I'm happy you'll be there not only for a Rogers wedding but for Christmas, too. Let me see it through your eyes. I'll wish they'll never suffer the separation we've had so much of in our married life.

Mother will no doubt take it hard because it's the first daughter.

Another little dark-headed girl in our family is rather good to me. In today's mail came the best two-pound box of candy from your sister. It was a bit mashed together from the long trip, but don't think it didn't taste good.

I'm going to welcome Santa tomorrow night, Christmas Eve. I can't wait much longer on these packages. Another of yours came today, and my sailor brother's wife and little boy sent more candy fixed up so it can be kept when all the rest is being eaten first, a two-quart can of fudge.

What I've been trying to do is find a vic to hear your record. I may have to start reading your letters out loud to hear your voice some way. We let some other battery have ours and can't seem to get it back. I've even begun to ask some fellows who have French friends, but no luck in finding one so far. Don't worry. I'll find a way.

With our rations fair, quarters fair, how can we kick when those fellows up on the line are going through hell? The reports that come back are not so good, but sooner or later they'll burst out like they did at Caen. Something gave us a lesson when it would have taken so much talk to put over what an easy time we have compared to those infantry boys. Some were marching by coming back to go some place for even a night's rest. They were so tired, looked a bit muddy, and wondering why they couldn't have gotten into some ack-ack outfit. We found then how lucky we were and have been so blessed so far.

I wonder if the hometown paper will ever get here. Maybe after the Christmas rush, but if I can get a letter from you, they can have their paper.

Christmas Eve

Maybe there can be more sense to my letter now I feel a bit more clear-minded and not as tired as I was last night. I get that way at times. Just trying to think seems to kill all the feeling. It's something to think about, that the big battles have been fought in this trailer, not only trying to keep awake after being out in the cold all day and on the six to twelve shift, but we've had a few hot spots across France, too.

I'll not know whether to hang up the old sock or not tonight. I did suggest to some of the fellows in the chateau that we should hang some in front of the fireplace. It's been a long time since I've done that, I guess when I was eight or nine years old. I never got any ashes or switches.

If I waited until six in the morning you'd be having Christmas Eve. Then we'd both be opening our presents. We were just fooling around here and thinking where we were this time last year. Some even thought we were better off now, but as long as I was in the states I had hopes of being sent or staying somewhere there. I wouldn't believe it until I was on my way, and then it seemed like a dream. Often I think of what a dope I was not to have taken the first chance at a pass to New York. I would at least have gotten to say hello and talked to you once more.

I've wondered lots about how to play the record. Then something came up very unexpectedly. The Red Cross truck came back with their doughnuts and coffee. They have a vic to give us lots of classical music and boogie woogie, too. The thought came, "There's my chance to get my wife's record played." I wanted to hear it, so waited until lots of the fellows had cleared away, then played it with my heart in my throat. It wasn't clear at all on this vic, but I got a few of the things you said. What really got me was the song you sang. The piano and your voice were so good. "White Christmas" hits the spot where it's weak with us here. So many wished they had heard it. The few that did felt as I told you. It was grand to hear an American girl singing and talking. The Red Cross girls were a bit surprised at my sharing such a thing with them, even asked if you did this kind of work all the time. 'Course that made me feel so good about how special you must be to think of such an idea. Without too many questions I told them all about you. They

352

undoubtedly know now we are rather fond of each other. I missed a lot you said and want to hear it on a good vic, but the song went home so dearly.

You make my Christmas very sweet this year.

---

24 Dec 1944   Engaged hostile aircraft. Cat. I.

So Christmas Eve at A-Battery was far from a silent or holy night. The only holiday illumination they had was artillery fire flashing through the trees as they brought down an enemy plane.

The Germans were now sixty miles inside Belgium, the hospital at Bastogne had lost twenty patients in a bomb raid, and on the front, men were sharing packages from home and shaking hands in case there was no tomorrow.

Patton, with a 45 automatic outside his weathered coat and another tucked at his waist, toured all over the place in an open jeep to visit eight command posts. Seeing shells streaking through the sky, he murmured something about "Noel, Noel," and giving the Nazis Hell. He prayed frequently, but fought like the very Devil. Nothing half-assed. Just shoot the works.

The general's holiday prayer, distributed the day before, apparently produced the first break in the weather in eight days ("Hot dog!"). Planes that had been socked in from Scotland to Brussels could be over Luxembourg in an hour, driving the enemy off the roads, landing to re-load, then flying again till dark. Better have another thousand copies of that prayer printed! In a period of gloom he looked for the best, encouraged the most, brought sunshine in person wherever he went. Eisenhower, who wanted "only cheerful facts" at the time, would have approved.

If at first Patton had grumbled mightily over giving up his cherished Saar campaign, once convinced of the seriousness of the German activity he shifted gears immediately. Let the S.O.B.'s get as far as Paris, then cut 'em off and chew 'em up. What the

Hell, wherever they went they'd still be killing Krauts. Asked when he could take command of the Ardennes enterprise, "As soon as you're through with me here." When could he take off? "Within 48 hours."

The general had kept his word. As canvas-topped trucks carrying his Third Army whizzed north, heavy coats were still caked with the mud of the Saar. The campaign they had prepared so carefully to launch on December 19th would be delayed for more than two months, then brought to swift conclusion in ten days.

General Montgomery, charged with plugging holes to the north, didn't seem to be helping much. Whereas Americans were strong on "honor" and push-and-shove improvising, the British commander advocated waiting, then surrounding. Described after one meeting as Christ coming to cleanse the temple, he lived in a tactical world of his own, using his personal map and preferring a solitary meal from lunch-box and thermos to camaraderie at the table. On Christmas morning Bradley, noticing gaily-dressed villagers, had commented, "It's Christmas Day, General." Monty then hedge-hopped back to his post to have some turkey alone in his room.

Patton, scheduled to dine with Bradley at his own head-quarters in Luxembourg, spent the morning visiting every division in combat. It was a fine, clear day for killing Germans, all right, but hardly the atmosphere for the season. Thanks to the supply team, every soldier in his army would have turkey - hot behind the lines, a sandwich at the front. Elsewhere the holiday dinner menu varied from a party with girls to a can of sardines and a box of crackers.

At 3 A.M. Bastogne had suffered a severe assault. Though the American line finally held, Patton and Bradley, after a quiet dinner, talked far into the night, and in the midst of uproar everywhere, the Prince of Peace seemed to guide one pen.

I told you I'd save back some of the nice packages. I did, and it helped the spirit of the whole gang yesterday morning. The blue one had so much goodness in it I don't see why it didn't burst. I was actually opening so many they all felt I did the right thing to make it seem more Christmas-like. If it hadn't been for all the lovely wrappings, I'm afraid Christmas would have been really dull. When someone springs up out of the blue and says, "I wish my wife would smarten up to what to send," well, I nearly pop out of my red flannels with pride.

---

26 Dec 1944   Engaged hostile aircraft.   No Claims.

I'm rather tickled to get the holiday note from our general. It's something to hold onto. It shows he was thoughtful and has faith in us as we do in him. Sometime back General Patton was making an off-the-record tour in his jeep as they say he often does. This country can lose any driver in the world, I don't care how good he is, and sure enough they say the General got lost, too. Apparently he drove by our battalion headquarters gate and was flashing his light around trying to find how to get out of the place. Just then one of the Headquarters guards yelled, "Get that damn light out! Who's there anyway?" 'Course the General hollered back, "I'm General Patton." It didn't prove anything with the guard, though. He gave back the smart answer, "I'm General Eisenhower. Get that light out." It sounds like a make-believe story, but some claim it happened around Headquarters. It's one of those things you can always hear, but when it supposedly happens to the very battalion you're in, it's quite a joke.

Today two more plump packages came to make me gain weight. One was the nice fresh candy box, but some of the other parts are wrapped so nicely I want to set them up and just look at them. You really spent hours fixing each one differently with all kinds of stickers and little bows. I even saved some of them. Another had the super-flavored fruitcake. We made our supper out on it. It was our dessert after having another turkey supper. I passed it all around the room, but rationed the fellows down a bit so I could have some left for myself.

Each line of this Bob Hope book you sent by Santa gives a smile, a good mood, or a laugh out loud. He's the funniest and cleverest on the air, and he's in his stride even at the first chapter.

With all the push for more ammo I'm hoping there won't be any change in what you plan to do while I'm away. It's wonderful the way your work is so interesting, yet leaves fun for the gang, too. No doubt with your willingness to help get this over you'll just give that special blood and buy bonds, so never think you aren't doing all we'd want you to do. Just knowing all is well and safe with you is all that matters to me. Let me be the one who's got the uncertainty, if you want to call it that.

Something new and different they've given us for sleeping. It's one of those portable beds you carry on your back, just a long sack or bag that you wiggle down in and zip yourself up, leaving only the nose sticking out. It's a soldier's dream on the front to keep warm in a foxhole or lie down some nights to get a wink of sleep. Some night at home when we go possum hunting we'll take this along and spend a night in it just for old time's sake.

There's that moon again shining in my window tonight. Such a lovely one, the fullest I've seen in a long while. Now the first thought is always it's a super night to give the devils hell. Although it's cold it's really better for the trucks, tanks and air force to move about. No one could hope any harder than I for pretty weather all the time. That counts so now.

If a man ever got packages overseas, I'm the lucky guy this year. The long flat blue one came today full of good cookies, Spam and those chewy goodies, too. All the fellows get fat with me when I open them up. We finished the fruitcake today at lunch. Lots of times we don't get preserves for our bread, so the mincemeat was passed around so we could all have a taste. 'Course when the others get their packages I'm there to help, too. What the tree would have looked like if I'd had one to put all these under!

About this time you must be on your way back to our favorite place of living. All I'm hoping is that too many of the wolves didn't give you trouble going to and fro. 'Course lots of the young ones may be over here now. Still the older ones could cut their wing at you. I'll never forget your story of the paratroopers' remarks when they thought you were asleep.

---

29 Dec 1944   Engaged   hostile   aircraft.   No Claims.

New Year's Eve

Without a trace of where you could be tonight I know where both our thoughts are as this old year comes to a close. So much has happened during the year that's going out, too much of it while we had to be apart. We'll never like that, never.

We can say we're a little better off than we were last year at this time. Then you could see me as you thought you saw me on D-Day, fully dressed and walking to the train to board the ship that carried us away. The old saying goes you'll be doing all year what you do on New Year's. Well, I must say that slogan held true this year. We traveled all year long with the same uncertainty as we had on that day. I'll never forget the last one. My heart sank completely when I saw the Statue of Liberty go out of sight through that porthole. It must come back that way soon.

357

When I go off duty tonight at twelve it'll be 1945 here, but that won't really roll around until six in the morning because that's when my wife and heart's year starts. The only resolution I'll make is to strive to come back home this year. That'll cover all life really means to me. Some will still celebrate here, but this night for me will be the sanest I'll ever spend.

The mail yesterday, with letters all the way back to Nov. 6th, had one of the best surprises of all. I like to pull off these heavy G.I. shoes and rest my dogs the first chance I get in the cabin. Here I was looking for some more good stuff to eat when what ups and hits me in the face but a sheeplined slipper. Then I found the other one. I slipped them on last night and strutted all over the place. Nothing could be so nice and wearable. Even on duty I can slip my leggings and shoes off to feel the softness, and being as light and soft as they are all over they can be packed anywhere. The size is wonderful, couldn't be better unless you were here to try them on me.

I ought to feel sad tonight because of the coming year, I guess, but it's new days ahead for you and me together. I'd just like to be peeping in on you right now.

The Ardennes struggle seemed far from over. German tanks, nicely camouflaged with white covers against the snow, might be running out of gas and the German High Command realizing the folly of their enterprise, but the Allies found failure hard to believe. Bradley and Patton had even discussed the possibility of withdrawal. Montgomery wouldn't be ready for another month, and their own forces seemed too weak for the task. Yet if deserted, the French in Alsace and Lorraine faced slavery or death - or both.

Planes kept coming over the 411th, but old Blood and Guts spoiled Hitler's Christmas surprise with a gift of his own, the relief of Bastogne. Top of the list of its heroic defenders was the feisty general who had spurned the Nazi demand for surrender with his all-American "Nuts!" Lifting of the siege, both a moral and symbolic victory and a military break-through, must have pleased Patton most of all.

Hitler, blaming his generals for not having followed his orders to the letter, still held out for Antwerp no matter how prospects looked. Like Patton, he considered the best defense to be offense. A siege might be over, but the battle was just beginning.

Conflict raged at Eisenhower's headquarters as well. To the astonishment of all, with "Bastogne" still ringing in their ears, after all the mud and cold and time and mines and terrible cost, Montgomery advised drawing back even as far as the Moselle to let the Germans wear themselves out! Was he never going to give another order to his army? Did Americans have to do all the fighting? His plan, rejected unanimously, was never heard of again. On to driving the enemy out of the Bulge and holding firm in the north where the Nazis might make another desperate stand.

To complicate matters further, rumors of killers stalking Eisenhower, Bradley, and Patton encouraged security to insist on a bullet-proof car for the Supreme Commander, ever-present sentries and MPs in jeeps and on trips, even alerts at every stop.

Criticism came from the home front as well. Americans warm and safe back in the states and expecting men home by Christmas could not comprehend the difficulties and horrors of the line or the re-planning and re-grouping required under changing circumstances. Another whole year of war? Impossible! Yet it could happen.

Patton, at Bastogne to decorate and commend the stalwart commander of the 101st Airborne, drove about to be seen by all. The operation which had rescued them was the largest counterattack he had ever staged.

Bradley, at Ike's headquarters at Versailles to present a new plan, reaped a unique reward of his own, a bowl of hot rich cream in which floated half a dozen Chesapeake Bay oysters. He gulped the treat down without confessing to his host that oysters gave him hives.

At Bradley's suggestion a procedure which had become a tradition on New Year's Eve had taken new form to greet 1945. Promptly at midnight every gun in the entire Third Army had been turned toward the German lines for twenty minutes of rapid fire. Forward observers later reported hearing screaming in the woods.

A and C batteries needed rest more than celebration at the time. Since Christmas Eve they had brought down two planes and engaged more than twenty others, some P-51s with American markings, strafing the roads and diving on the bridge defenders night after weary night. Instead, as at last year's end, they had to pack for a move.

1945

1 Jan 1945   Left   Jezanville,   France   (Pont-a-
            Mousson).
            Arrived 2 Miles N Metz. Traveled 26
            Miles.

After a separation of nearly a month all four
batteries of 411th AAA Gun Battalion were reunited for
a time. Fortunately for Batteries A and C, they had
just missed over ninety planes which harassed their
comrades while they were fighting off a lesser number
to the south. A large force also plagued B and D by
destroying or damaging about 24 P-47s on an airstrip
under their protection before their buddies arrived to
beef up the effort on New Year's Day. The Nazis
seemed to have shot their wad, though. Air traffic
was almost non-existent for the rest of the month.
    Still on duty. Still up all night, but at least a
bit less tense.

———————

There may be a few cities on the ball like that one
on the mighty muddy Mississippi. The mail came
through in such a short time. I was thinking you'd be
back in Wilmington from your Tennessee holiday by the
time I heard from you again, but those letters you
wrote down there must have used a Ferry Command plane.
You'll be missing a few letters, though. Things have
been at their fullest the last few days. We've picked
out a new nest for those birds who continue to come
out for our rationed ammo. At least we haven't got
really low yet.
    There was a Santa awaiting for me on New Year's
Day. After I brag on Memphis, actually they were the
slowest to get Christmas packages here. I have enough
eats to last me a good while, even with all the other
chow hounds around. Your brother sent a grand sweater
which I'm wearing because the G.I. issue by comparison
seems small and tight. Our moms sent all sorts of

useful things like toothpaste and shaving cream, popcorn and books, and <u>fruitcake</u> (so good). The fruitcake was next to yours. Honest, yours was the very best.

My hand's a bit frostbitten, but that couldn't keep me from giving you my heart.

2:00 A.M.

So few people could hold their peepers open this time of night. The only reason mine make it is the strongest cup of coffee before coming on duty, and I've read until my eyes are about to pop out. Here's the poem of the day:

> Mary had a little dress
> Pretty, chic and airy.
> It didn't show the dirt a bit
> But oh how it showed Mary.

Well, at least I'm still awake.

At last, after weeks now, my paper has started again. I do enjoy the news, funnies, ads, and all the civilian action. I almost know how things look and will be when I'm home. <u>Stars</u> and <u>Stripes</u> is rated the best paper in the E.T.O., especially the one that's printed in Paris. They now have different sections to give a few things a G.I. could expect if he were suddenly discharged. Still I get burned up when they think they're talking to a bunch of babies at times.

You should have seen me packing on this move. I looked like Santa leaving the North Pole I had so much in my duffel bag. I've really been swamped with lovely eats, but the best things I got were the record and slippers from you. Never has a voice hit me so as it did that morning. So many of the fellows have mentioned afterward how it even made them feel. Some couldn't bear to stay and hear it, not because they didn't enjoy it, but because of the lovely music, the thoughts and above all the song that hit a new high from that American sweetheart we'll love always, Kate Smith. I'll play it as often as I find a chance.

––––––––––

Though skies over Metz had calmed somewhat, elsewhere half of the Luftwaffe had done real damage to well over a hundred planes on the ground in Belgium and the Netherlands.

Hitler, giving up Antwerp as a goal, at least knew that Eisenhower's need to use airborne as infantry showed the thinness of his line. Americans might have superiority in artillery and, temporarily, in ammo, but his secret weapon, a finned projectile with a range of 35 miles, had already killed a Third Army officer stepping out of a hotel in Luxembourg. For the first and only time Patton's diary commented, "We can still lose this war."

In fierce fighting around Bastogne fog and sleet had tanks sliding, vehicles jack-knifing, and trucks skidding over a cliff. When a GI's nostrils froze and his lungs burned in the bitter cold, a man could be grateful for duty in a trailer where he could stand his watch, aim his guns, and stay awake by reaching toward home.

––––––––––

I hold on to your letters for dear life, more than any issue of clothing or what else I might need. It may be silly to other people, but I'd rather be weighed down with them than anything else I know. After carrying them until they are worn out and dirty, I watch them go up in flames until every little scrap and pen stroke disappear. It's almost like hearing you talking so plainly sometimes that I smile with joy.

Just to close your mind and not think where you were, you would get the impression here of some scene in Tennessee, North Carolina or even Kentucky. 'Course one can't get the real feeling with all the disturbances they've had. Still, with a visit through the towns and villages, the country covered with its whiteness is really a beautiful sight. They go in a big way for skating, sled riding and having fun in nature, but lots find it all the harder to live and find a smile, especially the doughboys who live in the misery of it day in and day out. Most of the people here seem to take it as just another year of winter no different from the rest. The kids especially have fun going down these hills with their little two-by-four sleds. They are having a wonderful time, stopping when a G.I. passes for that American chew gum or sweets. One wouldn't dare chew gum if he saw a bunch coming. He'd be strung up by his toes, so you just stop chewing, give them some teasing talk and walk on ahead. We won't be able to do this as much as we have in the past, but they'll be the same as long as we're in France. They do have a different sort of way, though, the closer we get to the German line, a sort of snooty way, but still looking out of the corner of their eyes.

I feel like kicking myself. I planned all the time to get the little kids around before we left our other place, but waited too long and moved out with all the gifts you sent for them. I did give the little dog away a bit early to one of the little girls. She was the proudest as if I'd given her the tallest building in Memphis. Like she always does, she'd run to her mother with it. Every time we'd get near she'd want someone to come in the room and see what she got for Christmas. I do wish we'd stayed put a little longer with these kids we'd been with so long. I'd love to have seen their expressions when they opened the packages. And I have so much Spam now I'm beginning to think it's a joke.

I've noticed we're both more lonely on weekends. Just to know there will be no separation some day will be the most marvelous thing for all of us, no more goodbyes, no more staying away even for a single day. We'll not stand for it. Maybe it has done us good in some ways, but so many aches and going on alone. No one can make up for the space.

Lots of articles are coming out already about servicemen adjusting to home. I think we'll just be gloriously happy and after getting used to that we'll begin to make our plans. If we stay in this same branch of service there won't be too much to have to forget. I pray each day we'll be spared a new adjustment after so long doing the kind of work we do.

Now it looks as though all hell has really turned loose on the front. How they can keep it up no one can tell, but I'm hoping it could be some kind of trap. No doubt they'll fight to the finish and think nothing of lives and want to draw all the strength we have. You felt an unsettledness a few days back. I can tell you later, but better wait a while. I wasn't in immediate danger. Things worked out better for Christmas and New Year's.

Some wonder how I can get in the mood to write. I tell them I don't need to get in a mood. I just laugh and talk if I like and always feel better afterward.

———————

Considering air activity at the turn of the year, "better" must have been a comparative word, the familiarity of Pont-a-Mousson versus adventuring north from Metz, their present position. After noon on New Year's Day A-Battery had arrived there to defend another bridge, road traffic, and a necessary air strip. The very next day the whole battalion, reunited after a month apart, had engaged enemy aircraft coming from every direction at 7500 feet. The pattern of separation and reunion continued throughout the rest of the war.

Patton, already pulling out his long-delayed plan of December, faced three weeks of hard, bloody fighting to regain the territory lost by the rescue at Bastogne. He and Bradley were on the point of asking to be relieved of command after Montgomery, on a BBC broadcast, had seemed to claim credit for the Ardennes turn-around. Bradley virtually exploded at the idea, Patton echoing in essence, "If he goes, I go." It took a calming speech by Churchill to the House of

Commons with reference to the "American" victory to soothe ruffled relations.

Unity of the American team had developed through long years between West Point and Staff College at Fort Leavenworth, with many a stateside assignment and overseas garrison in between. Eisenhower's strength in diplomacy sometimes led to the appearance of indecisiveness. Bradley's common-man aspect masked the keen mind of a tactician. Patton's flair for the dramatic worked marvelously in hot pursuit but flagged miserably in just-slogging-along with a tendency toward depression that Ike and Brad checked and balanced.

The 411th, responsible to all three in the echelon of command, just kept on holding ground until Eisenhower, increasingly trusting his own instincts, set the final plan in motion while Bradley and Patton developed new ways of circumventing obstacles, even Ike if necessary.

This place is beginning to look like it did when I almost got snowed in with you in Wilmington. I had the hardest time getting in from camp that night and next morning thought I could even spend the day, too. Then some OCS officers got on the ball and called for the buses to run anyway.

We had such a laugh here about the union suit Mother sent me for Christmas to keep me warm. The "drawers" have been the joke for days. They all want to see me bag in the seat. If I put the suit on under a pair of coveralls, I'd be almost handcuffed, hardly able to move. I'll wear them some of these cold days while I'm away, but it'll have to be pretty cold for you to catch me in a pair.

Our new sleeping bags are made only for one man, but just the size and length to be comfortable. They have a blanket lining, and if a few extra blankets were wrapped around you, you could stand almost any kind of weather. They should be so helpful to the fellows on the front.

I must be with you this year.

There was a letter today from my sis. I thought she would tell me all about her wedding, but she's leaving that to someone else. Did they get some pictures? I'd like one of you in a long dress.

Your little party for the two brides in our families sounded so nice. I'd like to have been a hidden waiter. I'd have made you drop your napkin just so I could pick it up and talk to you.

I do believe there's enough snow around here to make a snowman. We've never been able to play in the snow, not even a snowball fight. The first big snowstorm we had when you were in town was the one when your folks had the possum hunt. I couldn't go because I had cut my foot.

If you look at the picture I had taken at Chalons, you'll see some changes. We had been on a constant go since our D-Day, digging in, then by the time we dug in they called march order, then pulled out and tried again to keep up with our boss. When we got to Chalons we were all pretty fagged. I was, I know. Now we've had a little more time for a rest we're all beginning to look better.

Something else made me unhappy with the news that they're thinking about drafting the girls of America. I just hope they wise up and take the men who could do those light jobs. It's the same way with all us fellows, we want you to keep our light burning in our little home and stay out of this if possible. You can't do much about it if they draft you, I know, and I hope it's only a scare so that a few more will go into the service. I still like to know where you are and if you're as happy as you can possibly be while I'm away. If something does come up, I'd like the idea of your being officer material in the training corps. I'm just praying after this long that nothing like a draft will come up.

Nothing comes up so often as the thought of you.

Your little luncheon must have been one of the high spots in all the parties the brides were having. It sounded really spiffy, and you managed with such a low fee. If you'd invited them to your mother's house there'd have been the labor and headaches to go through, and not in your own home, either. The occasion was the best thing you could have managed to show how we love them.

This was a nice day, sunshiny, too. Everything covered with snow. It looks nice, but what comes along and ruins it all? This three-letter word "War." No snow melts much. It stays just brisk enough to feel good when we're out in it. With the weather so good our air force comes out. No one can look up without saying to himself, or even hollering out, "Hitler, count your men!" I do hope they have made that mistake and will never come back as they did around Christmas and New Year's. They're trying everything now just to take all the lives they can in this last push.

There must have been more excitement over that German parachute than I'd expected. It was almost impossible to get one back in the bag once you got it out. In fact, I didn't even try. The one I sent you was another I picked off the train-load headed for somewhere. The Germans may have planned to use them in some of these new attacks they have been making lately, who knows? At least they had to get replacements. The holes you found in yours were probably from shrapnel or maybe just from handling in shipping. It will be very easy to find a new helmet. I won't get many things to remind me of this, just a few.

You have no doubt seen where "Hometown Boy Makes Good" is written in these small hometown papers. That's what lots of mothers and wives did when they got an enemy chute. The best story of all was about the mother who took hers down town, spread it out in a tent-shape, sorta like a wigwam, then placed her bond-selling stand under it with a sign about captured enemy property.

A few days ago an article came out about four chaplains who gave their life preservers to four seamen and went down with a torpedoed ship. One of the Protestants, George Fox, was our chaplain at Camp Davis. I remember him rather well because he was one of our best while in the states. He got the chance to volunteer for overseas duty and went many months before we left the states. He had seen action or served a short time in the last war, naturally knowing the thoughts and habits of his men in these circumstances. It was truly a deed to be remembered by those whose lives they saved on that boat and a story that will remain for years to come out of this war.

The unit has church service here around four each Sunday now, so you should be heading for yours at Fifth and Market just when we start ours. The chaplain doesn't exactly preach. He just gives us some good things to think about, ways to live like Jesus in the life we temporarily have to live. He tries so hard with so few that show interest. I like him.

I've wondered what new faces did you see around home. Maybe a few, or was it the same? There'll be a number of little ones grown so by the time we come home, and even new babies we haven't seen.

This may not make sense. It's all kind of bull being told. Just the same, with all this competition, I hope you'll always win out. I'd just like to have a fresh bath, listen with you to the radio and talk about nothing. I'll never get caught up.

Back at the other place I lost something that was special to me. I carried that little silver heart so long in my pocket. What makes me so mad is I don't think I actually lost it. In changing my shirt I placed it on the shelf by my bed and went out without it. Coming back that night I'd already thought of it, but knew no one would bother it. 'Course I hesitated to ask, but wanted it back so badly I asked if anyone saw it. Lots did and figured it was mine and left it alone. I even thought someone had picked it up for safe-keeping, but no one seemed to have gotten it. Now it's gone. I was really fed to the neck when I lay anything down and can't come back and find it. I'm still hoping it will show up.

Just at the time thoughts around home should have been on having a good time, lots at Christmas were uneasy about their loved ones when they heard of the push the Germans had started. Those darn devils are trying their best to get ahead. I'm hoping the news didn't sound too bad for you at that season of love and devotion. All the news was held up at least 24 hours from everyone. Reports keep coming through how they came out up there. There are lots of pitiful stories, many to go down in the history of the war. They've held out with more air force than some folks expect and keep wanting their wings clipped a bit, but they'll get other parts trimmed if they fool around the mighty A.A. of the Third Army. You know we've had a change, but since there could be a buzz bomb with our name on it I won't give out any hints as to what happened to us. I've become a little afraid to now because they try so many new ideas and never seem to run out. You should see the date we've picked out for the finish. I should be home at least to sing "Happy Birthday" to you before Christmas, maybe even before that.

This year should bring about lots of things. I didn't have much hope last year, but mine now are really high for getting us back in 1945.

———

The pitiful stories he was hearing had echoes in North Carolina where worried relatives called the radio station for the very latest or information not printed in the local paper. A newscaster had to refuse to give out details marked "Not for Release" or sent on the ticker with a time delay before broadcast, but she understood their concern. At home for family weddings, she and a sister-in-law with a husband in the Pacific had wept together in private so as not to spoil the joyous occasions for others. For her the holiday seemed enclosed in a big black bubble - the Bulge.

The United States had committed more divisions there than the entire total sent to the Pacific. Churchill was right. As much as he supported and praised and stood up for British troops, often misjudged for various reasons, it was American homes that got the telegrams of condolence and the messengers at the door. The Gold Stars she saw in neighbors' windows and on their doors told without a word the sad story of the family inside the house.

Reactions in Europe varied poles apart, between Never-neverland pretense and revulsion.

Hitler, in Berlin for the rest of his bedeviled career, spent an afternoon in the Goebbels home, something he hadn't done for years. Leaving the chancellery post established for him in the final defense of the Reich, he brought the best lilies-of-the-valley he could find, Goebbels having closed all the flower shops, and his own cakes and thermos of tea, prepared against the possibility of poisoning by his own personal chef. The two Nazi leaders spent a lovely, if slightly fantastic, time planning the rebuilding of the devastated city.

Patton, however, saw reality in its most convincing form - a German machine gunner frozen in position with outstretched arms still holding an ammo belt, and farther on little black objects in the snow that turned out to be dead men's toes. He also noticed that freezing turns men killed in battle a revolting shade of claret. As he joined forces with troops ten miles north of Bastogne bulldozers were already sweeping the remains of the town, score at the site: Germans - 120,000 casualties, Allies - 77,000.

The price of Nazi stubbornness furnished Patton with what he later called the most moving moment of his life. Driving to headquarters on a day registering at six below zero, he had come upon a row of trucks stalled for hours in the bitter cold and a long line of ambulances bringing wounded back from the line. When they saw him, every man who could manage it stood up and cheered.

SHAEF, worrying back in the boondocks about another possible German counteroffensive, strengthened the forces around Metz and Pont-a-Mousson. Enemy air fields near the Rhine were functioning, and the Nazis had developed jet planes. Any airport with the long runway required had to be bombed from time to time to keep them inoperable. The United States would not have such a squadron available before spring.

Eisenhower also found it necessary, after the last brush-up with Monty and some of the Brits, to stress that military necessity, not national honor or political ramifications, was his primary concern as supervisor of men in combat. Ironically, General Montgomery may never have even realized what hackles his perhaps innocent comment on BBC had raised.

For the ordinary soldier it was war as usual.

The A.P.O. rushed their fannies off trying to get our Christmas mail through. Now there's so little. Some of the fellows gave up writing so often to their folks because there's nothing now to tell. Lots of times, too, I'm so in a daze from being so sleepy with this night work I know you think I've had a drink or two. I've gone off all kinds, even the G.I. coffee, and as for smoking, I don't think I'll ever start now that I've seen all the civilians and G.I. Joes just dying in misery for a drag.

How can we say a grumbling word about mail when we know it's all they can do to get the supplies and ammo over to the infantry men that need them so badly?

With such grand news lately, and we feel pretty good here after the New Year's scare, we are settled down and in better spirits than one would expect. It's funny how the Russians like the winter months to put through their drives while we're inclined to have the fair season for ours. They've been sitting still all the time. Now it looks as though they'll give us a tough run for Berlin. Even down Pacific way the boys are really mopping up those Japs with every slap. Sometimes we wonder if they don't plan to end both the fronts at the same time and start the policing up together. 'Course it's a far-fetched idea, but maybe it could be possible, you know.

Some of the news that comes from the Russian front makes one want to click his heels together. I can just see those Nazis running all over the place not knowing which front to re-inforce. It'll be too late by the time they get too many fronts, I'm afraid.

To see you just sitting in a chair will be so nice when I come home.

All that comes in those large bags of Stars and Stripes either boosts our morale or gets us so we don't know what to believe and throw the thing in the corner after reading the comics. They did have a U.S.O. show at the Headquarters mess hall, an all G.I. one, but such good music and singing. 'Course you know a few acts of the fairer sex with less bundlesome clothes and prettier complexions and curves would have helped. The band reminded me of the one at Camp Davis. How they played those popular songs that make our hearts cry out, "Please, won't you send me home?" I've become much more of a music bug than I ever was before coming into the Army.

You left me somewhere in my sister's wedding, and until the other mail comes through I can't understand why you stood in the choir area to sing with your shoes off unless you wanted to come up on a high note you couldn't manage very well in high heels. I'm really wanting to know. Looks like that would help you reach it.

Her place behind the greenery in the choir loft was perfect for shaking knees. It was his sister, his family, and she couldn't be wabbly in any direction. Had to be <u>perfect</u>.

Her brother's wedding in a large urban church had a choir balcony at the rear from which she could perform at ease, almost sight unseen, so no stage fright there. Yet back in what had once been her home, she felt like a visitor. Wilmington was "home" until he came.

Returning to the broadcasting post she found the news ticker dinging away with bulletins about the Russian advance on Berlin. Hitler still thought the Allies might yet compromise on a settlement before the Red Army took over everything in sight. Poland, which had been promised independence by Churchill, at year's end had Russian "Provisional Government" over it. Stalin, flexing his muscles, had even determined the date for the Yalta Conference. And what about his attitude toward Japan after the war?

Patton put in a call to Bradley. With troops in East Prussia, time to strike with every available force, no matter how combat-fatigued. Clouds had cleared, the sun was out, and pilots were finding German vehicles stalled bumper to bumper with no gas at hand.

At least the German people were facing the truth of broken windows and damaged heating and sewer systems. Time to take out white flags, bed sheets, anything else that signified "I surrender."

Top brass needed attention, too. Bradley and Patton recognized Ike's difficulties with SHAEF after recent happenings. Deservedly or not, he took the blame as high commander. Yet it particularly annoyed them when he assigned or moved a major unit without consulting or even advising them ahead on the matter. To Patton's complete surprise and disgust his Third Army, with which he was sure he could solve the whole problem, continued to be restricted to "aggressive defense," whatever he could make that mean.

At least things were better for a GI if the mail got through.

———

Finally, after sixteen days, came one letter all the way back from the first of December. You'd just come in from a busy Saturday morning at work and a movie on a long, cold afternoon. Even the little ticket stub you sent brought back memories.

I may have a longer way to go than I think, but I believe I could step back into civvies now and after a few weeks be back in the step of things.

If all could keep as warm and dry as we do, they'd think they were in heaven. We count ourselves so fortunate when we read about and talk with the fellows who've been so cold in a hole they'd think they couldn't stand it. We do get out in the cold, but not all day long like them, only at times. Then we have on enough that only our ears, face, feet and hands get cold. The snow has gotten rather deep. This is the coldest day we've had, around eighteen degrees. On these roads it makes it all the harder for trucks to and from where they have to go for supplies, but they have to move. These arctics help our feet so much. I saw an air corpsman with some on the other day down at the showers. The chow isn't the best, but they do real well with all the hands it goes through. If I wanted to I could get along with only a hundred francs, so even to get our laundry done we get by cheap. Most here don't even want to do our laundry and would charge like the dickens, but money is so useless. They need mostly something to eat and keep warm.

I'd always want to be just your soldier when I come home, not any way like a <u>sarge</u>, but you'll probably call me that, just teasing.

Not all had the chance we had of going to Paris. With so many of the enemy caught wearing our uniform, it's hard having yourself checked at every corner. I'll never know why I was among the three chosen, not rank or anything like that, just a corporal and a P.F.C. and me and a T/4 that went later. The things I sent you from there seemed a bit nicer than what they're providing now, and they charge like the dickens for the smallest trinket. Still, some good things, too. Too cold right now to enjoy the trip, but who'd refuse it?

Don't let your blue eyes pop out too much over this picture of our high commander. I admit he's good and does all that's in his power to see that we are well taken care of. I'd place him above your hero, Bob Hope, if I were you. You used to tickle me so when you talked about "Ike" just like he was a neighbor boy who'd gone to school with us.

Some may fume over V-mail, but one that came from you today with the Santa jokes was a little prayer answered. The last real letter was all the way back to Dec. 2nd. Until it came a few days ago I had only a few from December and only one in Jan. I use V-mail, too, for just a joke or a prissy remark, but many days would be dreary indeed if I couldn't have one now and then without other mail coming through.

Another envelope came last night with the grand joke books and cartoons with your comments and reactions. They're so true to Army life one can't help but laugh. It's funny how we Americans never lose that sense of humor. Even in our toughest moves and speedy trips across France we'd see the comical side of things, too.

As for those gals who've started smoking pipes, have you seen any around Wilmington? I see by the paper they've even started making fashionable tobacco pouches to match!

Just for days I've been hoping this would happen. You know without my going any further. LETTERS. I've read for an hour already and haven't finished yet. Almost all of them tried to make it on one boat, it seems. A whole wonderful twenty-eight, including some Valentines. Lots still have to come through from December, but nothing but a furlough home could cheer me up as these. I'm so happy we belong.

I'd been wondering about the package I sent for your Santa and my Christmas to you. I may overdo the wrapping, but they really handle our mail roughly. I used some of the boxes our P.X. rations come in. Here we have to keep a sharp lookout for something to mail things in even if we can find something to send. I stuff the boxes in a safe place knowing someone, if not I, will want something sturdy. The twine was from a parachute. I have a whole ball of it for clotheslines, tying up our packs, and lots of uses we find around.

There'll never be a soul to take the other's place, will there? No one else but you for me.

I've been really glad to know all about how they treat you in Wilmington, the only actual home we ever had. I'd like to be there, too, in your place if you were going overseas as a G.I. The surroundings are perfect with Pops, his daughter wanting her man home from the East, and their darling little girl. It's good you can walk over the steps we took together, do a few of the things we did there and even look around the same room we shared.

We never know what the next month will bring. Although it seems like a far-fetched idea sometimes, I want to be home by August or even before. My second best wish and prayer is to be there not later than November for your birthday. Things have begun to look some better now, more so than they did last month. 'Course you know I'd like to set our wedding date in March as the date, but just can't get that far ahead of my common sense.

I was so happy to get the measurements you sent. Last night we figured the crown of your head would come halfway up my nose and your eyes would probably come along my chin. Ever since we met and you pulled off those white fuzzy mittens to shake hands with me, and I with a bandaged foot, I've wanted to kiss you like I do now. But you'd have to tiptoe a little bit.

The Bulge was finally eliminated in the largest pitched battle Americans had ever waged - over half a million men involved, three times as many as Yankees and Rebels together at Gettysburg. After the first panic of surprise, American stick-to-it-iveness had surpassed faulty intelligence and a reputation for being soft and undisciplined compared to the Brits and Nazis. In waist-high snow or freezing traffic jams "GI Joe" had come through, in every sense a hero.

In response to reporters, Patton claimed he had little to do with victory, just gave orders. His no-star staff and troops on the line had stopped the S.O.B.'s in a "matchless feat." Asked why Montgomery's forces had been delayed, "I am not my brother's keeper." Actually his performance owed its origins to a "sneak" to circumvent current restrictions set up by men five thousand miles away in Washington. With the support of Bradley (and sometimes not) he out-finessed players who weren't even on the field for the big game. Now for another go at the Siegfried Line, which he considered a monument to the stupidity of man. The new offensive would take place in the Eifel, that is if he could only get enough gas together for liaison planes to support the artillery.

Not even wearing the winter clothes some soldiers might still lack, the general rode five or six hours a day in an open car without ever catching cold or any of the common respiratory ailments which plagued so many. His face blistered, but to visit men in barricades rolled up with snow balls and lined with tree branches, he only pulled a blanket over his legs. At least trenchfoot hadn't developed again as feared, and men in the hospitals were getting eggs and oranges.

Their Nazi foes unexpectedly helped as well. Thanks to capture of one of their trigger adapters, Allied soldiers would soon be supplied with gadgets enabling them to fire a gun without removing gloves or mittens. Clever souls, these Germans.

A staff sergeant at Metz for the time being still had peace, comparative quiet, and small comforts here and there, especially time to write.

So few people could get the connections of our letters if they ever get the chance to pick one up. Once a censor thought I hadn't finished or had left a page out. Maybe I can't make sense to some, but I know the one I want to get the point catches on really fast. Besides, who'd want to be an old stick-in-the-mud anyway?

A few minutes ago I slipped off those heavy shoes and got really comfortable. You may think I never get the chance to wear these warm, comfy slippers, and frankly, when we were in the states I would have laughed at the idea, but things are different from what we expected then. Lots of the fellows remark, "Boy, you struck a home in the Army" when they see me in them and just wish their wives or girl friends would do as much for them.

Your train from Atlanta for the holidays seemed better than on our furlough. When I left Chattanooga so long ago after induction at Oglethorpe we had Pullmans to go to Fort Eustis. That was my first time to sleep with some strange man. I was so miserable. I didn't know where our uncle was taking us, and I was so long I'd hit both ends of the berth every time the engineer put on the brakes. What rookies we were then.

Every time someone speaks of Tennessee they think of tall mountains and the hillbillies they think make up the state. I've convinced a few that Memphis is a fairly respectable place, but that politician Ed Crump has a reputation that's giving me some trouble with some. They read my paper and one man, every time he sees me, sings "I'm takin' that night train to Memphis." They even said I stood at attention when I heard that on the radio at Ste. Mére Église. I'll never forget that spot on the beach. Oh boy.

Some of the letters that waited so long to get here look like they had a tough time making it. The one you wrote in Birmingham was oil stained and really wrinkled. A few Christmas cards are still coming through the last day in January. I got one today from the Presbyterian church ladies at home with all their names signed on the back. Something else nice came, too, one of your mom's fruitcakes. She mailed it <u>Nov. 27th</u>, but it was still good and so rich we couldn't eat much at one time.

Stay like you are till I come home.

I've been talking for a month or more about this snow. It came, then went like a flash, and you haven't seen mud until you see this place. A big snow is worse than a big rain for us. This winter has been so unusual, they say. I'm expecting more cold, though. Haven't seen the geese flying, however. Never waste a space. I.L.Y.

Our chaplain whipped around and got a French church all to ourselves last Sunday. We had the whole battalion together for the service. It was rather cold. As we sang you could see the frost of our breath. I couldn't help but smile when I saw different ones' breath coming from all directions. The main reason for the occasion was to observe communion, the first time for me since I came overseas. Naturally I was glad of the opportunity. There are so many ways our faiths observe communion that the poor chaplain didn't know how to please all of us, so about twenty at a time would go up to the pulpit and kneel down for the bread and wine. It was such a good service. I'll remember it as one of our best here. We even had a special number sung by the chaplain and mail orderly, "The Old Rugged Cross."

I'm so tired now, but never too tired for this.

––––––––––

Newspapers arriving from the states carried almost hysterical accounts of the Ardennes struggle, causing Ike to comment wryly that he hadn't really been scared about the Battle of the Bulge until he read the news from home.

The Third Army, for whom 32 major waterways had furnished challenges, found some wag suggesting that their theme song should be "One More River to Cross" and hope that it wasn't the Jordan. They had gone over the Moselle five different times, three other rivers twice each, and a number of streams that needed a total of almost fifty miles of bridging altogether.

Patton, still allowed only to "probe," figured he would be less than worthy not to try, and if he actually broke through to the supposedly forbidden Rhine, who in his right mind could object? So his secret studies went on, and he "probed" toward Trier, one excuse being a mysterious long-range missile detected in that vicinity and later found to be an experimental project with "Lucky" army as its principal target. Up north, as usual, Monty had paused to re-group.

Eisenhower, inexperienced as a commander in Normandy, had now been on the field long enough to know just what his own strengths could accomplish. Realizing he had only one more major campaign to wage, he held to his own plan. Brad might have to lend troops to the Brits and Georgie Patton might have to go along with whatever resources were available, but "Ike" would be sole commander from here on out, no matter who argued loudest.

For Blood and Guts finishing a war on the defensive was intolerable. GIs were finding in some German pillboxes signed forms pledging a fight to the death while Monty was preparing to leap on the foe about like a "savage rabbit." Ike's call to a meeting at Bastogne had turned out to be a photo session, though, not the tongue-lashing possibly expected. They hadn't met in person since Patton had been promised all the troops he needed in November. Not only had they never arrived, but there was no mention of the Ardennes rescue either. All right then. With the ground beginning to thaw into quagmire, at least Prague and Berlin were within reach. Attack then. With everything available.

On February 4th the conference at Yalta opened with President Roosevelt in the role of "Good Neighbor" backing equality and self-government. Prime Minister Churchill, however, wanted previous governments restored for stability in a post-war world. Russia was for Russia, period, its view obviously unrecognized by an F.D.R. addressing "citizens of the world." Without public knowledge of the A-bomb, the United States needed Russia against Japan while Britain's Pacific interests centered on regaining its Asian colonies. And what would be the definition of "Unconditional Surrender" now? Talk about quagmire!

The Nazis continued to surprise, producing electro-U-boats as well as jet planes. Their scientists knew nuclear theory and atomic fusion, but, posing as medical personnel, had not yet managed a chain reaction, so no bomb yet for their side either.

Ike's new plan scheduled an attack for February 10th. With action resumed, the 411th made its next move.

LUXEMBOURG

Norma Rogers

2 Feb 1945   Left Metz, France. Arrived 3 Mi. E
             Luxembourg.   Arrived 1800 hours.
             Traveled 45 Miles.

———————

Luxembourg

You'll be amazed, I know, to see what I have at the
head of this letter, but I have to help you keep those
tacks down pat on that map at the station. At first
we couldn't say Yea or Nay about the wheres of the
fighting men of A-Battery, but things change
overnight, so I didn't even have to think up a way to
slip a word to you about where your soldier is now. I
was going to hint something about Lux soap. You've
done so well in the past I could hint almost any way
and you'd give the General the high sign and take
right off. Anyhoo, we've had our dimes changed over
again. I wonder how many kinds of money I'll have
before I quit. I do hope that good American dollar
will be the same. I still hold on to about $9.00 of
it in my billfold just to take out at times and feel
of real money.

I feel so good tonight, a little cleaner than I've
been in the last few days. I washed all of me
including ears and feet, but we were about to get a
little dirty here. We've had better places, but have
been working for days now so things begin to look a
little better. The last place was around Metz, the
best home we've had since leaving Pont-a-Mousson. The
quarters were so good. Here we have only tents again.
Fortunately, I was in on a deal buying a shack, mostly
just a stove, so it may bring a good price when we
leave. I wish I could get a snapshot of it. You'd
die laughing.

Can't say much more tonight. I want this to get
the first plane home. Hey! It's taking off now!

You'd like this part of the country so much. It's
been some time since we've seen a place that hasn't
been torn up too much. Lots of the places along the

385

road look like the scenery on the way to Knoxville and Chattanooga. I was sorta glad to slip over the French border. This country seems a little less affected by the war, but they must have been scared around Christmas time.

Although we haven't the quarters we had at Metz, we'll soon like it here almost as well, I think. Three of us staying in a shack is not bad when you can keep wood in the stove and have time to stay around it. The fellows next door have a radio, so we enjoy it almost as much as they do. The other night they got Boston so clearly. One of the fellows is from there, and when he heard the announcement, he almost got down and did push-ups he was so excited.

A few days ago I got the first long letter from Mother in some time. She usually just drops me a V-mail, but was really blue about herself. She seldom tells me about herself and her condition, but this time said her physical problems aren't doing any better. I sometimes get afraid that I won't reach home in time to see her alive. I can never see what she did to earn any such punishment. These things will slowly eat her body away. All her life she has been so faithful, so true, so looking up to God for help, never stepping across to something she knew was wrong. This has to fall on her. I just can't understand it at all.

Adding to his personal concern about a mother's cancer was the news that Germans at some point had come within three miles of the capital city of Luxembourg. To avoid panic, Bradley assured the frightened public that General Patton would control the situation in case of a break-through with a body of defense including eight 90mm gun positions spread about five miles east of the civic area covered, among others, by the 411th.

Patton and Montgomery had launched a joint attack meant to surround about fifty thousand Germans in the "Colmar pocket" near Trier. Whatever Monty's responsibility in the matter, the Nazis had been allowed to tamper with the controls of dams to the north, causing a steady trickle to flood land to the south for two whole weeks. GIs trying to cross swollen streams either drowned or snagged on the barbed wire of the Siegfried Line concealed under water. Roads were impassable.

Patton, his battle plan thrown off-kilter, checked the carnage on the battlefield. In addition to dying animals, human remains, and abandoned vehicles he was shocked by the arrival of a dog team he had requested in January to remove wounded from the Ardennes. Here, on thawed and flooded ground, they would be completely useless. So much for supply. At least they had tried.

The general wanted to be relieved of command anyway. As senior officer in both age and experience, he bridled at giving priority ever and again to Montgomery's needs. Bradley, reminding him of loyalty to his own faithful troops, allowed him to feel his way twelve miles beyond the German frontier, yet keep Monty happy.

At the landing strip which they guarded the 411th occasionally saw Patton returning from his trips to the front. A wounded American plane also bellied in one day, and eight robot-like projectiles came over. Otherwise, with the German Air Force scarcely noticeable, Luxembourg provided temporary stability and a hospitable Red Cross plus time for letters home.

Maybe you knew before I did about the Big Three meeting. I'm so happy you can have so much of the inner side of things and do care while others scarcely keep up at all. No work in the world could be more challenging just now. We'd had some rumors there was a Big Meeting (Hush hush), so naturally had to keep a sharp look-out for anything that seemed like a special target. You can laugh if you like, but we feel, being protectors, about as important as a few air corps men now.

A nice surprise last night. I thought maybe a little joke, but what do I find but our favorite nut roll. This one I had to have all to myself, so I just said, "Hands off, boys, these are extra special," and I'm crunching and munching on them all by my selfish lonesome.

Wish I could touch your hand.

I loved your joke about Hitler. He's being tortured some now, slowly losing his hearing and mind almost gone, they say, but a gradual death may be what he and his helpers should have.

I really got caught up last night, mail all the way back from the time you were home. I even got your Christmas Day letter and through Dec. 29th, then those from Jan. 21st to the 30th, skipping a lot of days in between. I was so glad to receive the letter about my sis and her new in-laws. They sound so nice.

You never leave my heart alone.

Hey! You surprised me today with the Esquire calendar with lots of legs and gals. It looks good in our shack, but on the other wall over my bed there you are. Some mornings I make the fellows snicker and smile when all are still in their places. I'll look around and murmur, "Hi, you." They never carry on such foolishness, but I feel good after pretending like that, like I'd whispered in your ear.

The package came tonight with another record, too. Now I'll have two to play and listen to.

Some fellows like a glove or a little shoe of one of their kiddies to carry. This new scarf you sent for my Valentine will be carried to the end. The heart hankie you sent last year has been in my left jacket pocket long before I left England.

———

Back on the home front some women celebrated Valentine's Day by giving blood in a drive "straight from the heart."

Meanwhile, <u>Stars and Stripes</u>, in addition to birth announcements, was also carrying reports of returning veterans. Confusion reigned in some cases ("When he mentions a closet, does he mean clothes or water?"), and a staff sergeant in Texas, after surviving 51 bombing missions, went out hunting and shot off his big toe.

You'd probably like to know what our mail orderly thinks as he goes about his job. I would, too, but he never lets out a whimper. Just a quiet guy that doesn't say much unless he asks a question. He looks all tired out, though, but really treats us nice.

Sometimes the gun section gets to throwing remarks at the range section saying, "You can tell who does all the work around here by the mail that comes in." It does look sometimes as if we have a bit more than they, but other times it probably evens up. Usually the letters come in bundles tied with string. If you don't think your blue letters show up in the stack, your guess is wrong. Sometimes I even walk up and just say, "You can let me have this one," and sure enough, it's one of yours.

You really had us going last night with that magazine you sent. The best joke of all was one I played on some of the fellows. Someone's always coming around asking if I have something to read. First thing this morning one guy was really tickled when he saw this one with the come-on cover and settled down for a long splurge of what he thought would be Limey pin-ups. When he opened it, he was as blank as all the pages in the book and couldn't say word one. Later another guy just grabbed it up and ran out of the shack to be alone with it. Did he get the horse laugh! All the fellows that had already gotten hooked laughed at him, too. Nothing in a long time has caused the talk unless it was that letter you wrote to the battery back in England on April Fool's Day.

I'm glad you like the picture I sent so well. It's wonderful that you're taking me to the station to help you work. I always liked to watch you there.

All I want you to do is forget the time and think of as many pleasant things as I can help you to do.

That must have been some Bob Hope show you heard about Memphis. He's one fellow I want to lay my eyes on before this thing is over. I sometimes wish it had been Hope instead of Eddie Cantor that we saw in New York after your graduation. I remember you took me on a little tour of the city, and I remember buying you a chocolate milk in Times Square. Why didn't we go ahead and marry that summer?

You may remember what three years ago brought me on this date. Into this Army that I thought would take only a year. It has gone into endless time. Maybe if we had all gone into it more seriously we'd have finished it more quickly, but at first I didn't think I was one of the guys to be drafted. The farm and all, I guess. I just couldn't get it all into my head. I couldn't volunteer, thinking if they needed me they'd call me. (I've volunteered for so little since.)

I'll surely let you know all I can the minute I hit that day when I know no water can keep me here. I couldn't just walk in like your brother did and some of the fellows here plan to do. I'll want that meeting to be so great that there'll not be one shock or surprise. You'll know all about me by the time I step off the platform at the station. Just leave your hat behind. A few other times when we met they got in the way and had to be rescued.

I'm about 180-185 at least and feel pretty healthy, but not near so hard as I was when I came in the Army. There's not much I do to keep in shape that farm work kept me in at home. Sometimes I think my hair may be thinning. Then maybe it's just because the rules still say it can't come below my eyebrows. That's pretty short, you know.

I still have a brown booklet and a red comb I bought one Saturday afternoon with you in the 5 and 10. I sorta hate to part with them when they become worn. They still keep a memory close.

––––––––––

At a conference on February 21st General Bradley opened up further possibilities for the impatient Patton, whose Third Army had forged three major and minor streams in spite of the floods, captured or enveloped major points, and battered bloodily to within six miles of Trier in German territory. Now the Third would launch an assault toward Frankfurt where enemy weakness would cost fewer lives. If a chance for break-through presented itself, they'd have to take advantage, wouldn't they? "Of course," said Bradley, "you'd have to." No more said.

All Patton wanted. He left, eyes a-gleam. The next day he decorated a number of nurses with Bronze Stars and a lieutenant with the Medal of Honor plus instructions that he not be sent to the front again, winners of that high degree later inclined to get killed while trying to prove themselves worthy, but depriving the nation of fathers of a more virile race.

Washington's Birthday featured a celebration by 9000 planes from England, France, Belgium, and Holland in a vast bombing raid on German transport centers. The Luftwaffe did not rise to defend a single critical position.

––––––––––

February 22nd in America is not just a bank holiday, but Washington's birthday. Not all our days will be that important, but I honestly think we'll be so thankful for a day of being together that every day will be a red-letter day, not like now, just marking time like we've had to do for so many years.

Remember when I was out on some of those bivouacs we only went on to keep up the gnats' and bugs' morale? Once you even had to mail me my dogtags to keep me from maybe getting gigged. On one camp-out I could see your radio station tower and hear your voice on the air, too. I looked and focused like heck with some field glasses to see if we could attract your attention, but the darn trees were in the way. I thought then of just going over the hill and surprising you in my fatigues.

I've talked my head off to all the higher-ups here, but can't seem to get you over as our little helper and mascot. You'd be the best morale-builder any office ever had. Even if they told us the doughnut wagon was on the way, we'd all probably just be as happy staying with you. I wish sometimes I could just see you riding in on one of these old rough trucks, but I'd get plenty of competition.

Now Joe and his Stalins have almost come to a halt. At least they don't give out much dope, the same with the Big Three meeting. If it'll help get the war over any more quickly, they can keep all the secrets they like. The Pacific front makes us feel sometimes they're closer to finishing off those Japs than we can the Jerries. Once they get started again here I just pity the people. Most Americans are kindhearted, and that's what they want, an easier peace. I don't think they'll get it this time with all the treatment they're giving our boys. I hate to have such hate in my heart for anyone, but it's beginning to gnaw pretty strong against those so-and-sos.

I can't see how anyone could think the infantry boys aren't the most important fellows in any war. It takes lots of pounding from the air force. That helps, but who goes in then and takes over every nook and corner? I can see how the air force could become a little high-hat with such missions, but the safest place an infantryman could have is a foxhole up there on the front, and that may last for days in all kinds of weather. It makes me mad for anyone's not seeing that one branch is just as important as theirs. It takes all of us to help win a battle working hand in hand as a team.

We may not be careful enough with gasoline around here. Lots of accidents happen. To make a fire quickly we use a small amount of gas. At least that's the way we did when we first came over. Just a little dust and gasoline mixed in will make the hottest fire for heating water for washing, shaving, and even making the coffee in K-rations.

I'm glad we got away from those Ks, Cs and 10-in-1s. I was losing my big appetite. Now we get Class B rations which give us grapefruit juice, dehydrated egg or pancakes, and even an apple, orange or dry cereal for breakfast. At times we even get a real egg. Oh what a treat. We sometimes get carrots, always potatoes, beans, hamburgers, wieners, spinach and even cherry pies.

I may have forgotten to tell you about the ice cream the Frenchmen made in Metz. The mess sergeant saved up milk, eggs and sugar, then took it all up for them to make some dessert for us. It was a real treat, so good. They even made up some cake, too, the same way. We just furnished the stuff, and they did the work. Some of our meals are junk, but at times they taste rather good.

I didn't know my sailor brother could call his wife from the Pacific. I'd give all I made for a month to talk five minutes with you, and I can't. If you'd get a little more power in that radio station, I could tune in every night and hear you. I'm glad for them that they can be that close, but wish the army could work out a long distance arrangement for us, too.

At least he sent me a whole carton of gum from Hawaii. I hope I'll be able to meet some Russians sometime soon and hand them a piece.

You didn't know I was a good boy today and went to church. Usually the chaplain gives us a brief talk and a few good points that he knows we are the weakest about. He told us last Sunday that the former pastor's wife would be giving us a brief history of the church. It's not too big, but really attractive inside, especially the ceiling and stained glass. I couldn't make out all she said because she talked rather fast and, not using our language so much, ran away with herself, her eyes fairly dancing with excitement. You'd never know there a church down that narrow street, which was built centuries ago for carts. Years ago the building was taken over by some wicked soul who wanted to destroy religion in the area and made a stable out of the place. Even now we could see where some stalls were although it has been refinished now and decorated as much as possible. You'll find very few churches of our faith in any part of these countries. I just never want our land to be so taken over completely by one religious group at one time. The Catholic church seems to be more prominent here than it used to be, or maybe I'm just growing up to notice it. Lately we've been using a church for our services because there's no other gathering place. At Pont-a-Mousson we held worship in our mess tent or even at times in good weather under some shady tree all the summer months. At Metz we had service in our quarters, sort of an apartment we'd taken over and cleaned up because it was close to our position. We'll have communion next Sunday, maybe every month now.

Sometimes I want to talk easy and slow, but have to rush so the letter can be censored to get off in the morning mail. Sometimes I bring one in after the mail has been brought up to be censored and get a "look," jokingly of course, as if they already had enough to read for one night. You can't blame them. Reading this scribble they'll all need glasses eventually. So if you see a guy with thick lenses after the war is over you'll know without question that he was a censor.

While he reflected on spiritual matters and military correspondence, the unreality of war surfaced in down-to-earth fashion. Hammers in hand, five Germans (two men and three women), with fighting going on and shells falling all around them, just kept busily re-roofing a house. An equally surreal "index of efficiency" revealed that non-battle casualties now exceeded those in combat for the first time in the history of the Third Army.

To preserve discipline as they entered disorganized unfriendly territory, GIs were warned of a fine of twenty dollars a month for up to six months, or even three months at hard labor, for fraternizing.

On a higher plane, a poem called "Conversion" found on the bodies of soldiers was traced to a young Catholic girl in Kansas. Her verse about a GI facing death inspired over 300 phone calls, a corsage from a soldier in Europe, and a piece of Japanese parachute sent by a serviceman in the Far East.

Loving thoughts also bloomed in the 411th as The Wedding Anniversary approached.

You'd probably have had the biggest laugh if you could have been here looking across the room a few minutes ago. I was sitting here not doing much when something flashed through my mind. The knife holster you gave me has become a little worn and scarred, so since I had two boxes of shoe polish from one of Mom's packages, I thought I'd polish up that gift you gave me back at the Seine at the hottest and busiest positions we've had. I made it glisten and look like my general's famous holster would look after his orderly had shined on it. Then I thought why not make my house slippers look the same? They look so wonderful now compared with all the other shoes, scarred, torn and rough, that can't really be polished, but I've always liked to have one shining pair. The fellows saw me working away and just knew I was bucking for a Section 8, discharge on grounds of insanity.

Each day will go by somehow. I've already declared March as your month in honor of the time we became one forever.

This is our anniversary month, so I'm really going to try to make it the most pleasant one I possibly can for you. Yesterday, on the first, I said "Rabbit rabbit" again to be sure of good luck for us the whole time.

You'd be so glad of what I did today. I'd been running around trying to find some quiet place to play the new record you sent for my Valentine and the one I had for Christmas, too. I couldn't get the Battery's vic around, so today I took the records with me on pass, a short one but long enough to do what I had in mind to do. First I went with another guy to a movie, the wildest western I've seen in ages. Even the gals were rough. They have a movie each day in town. The ones I like best have nothing to do with war or even being drafted. After the show we went straight to the Red Cross and had coffee and doughnuts. I had a Coke, too, a nice cold Coke that felt so stinging and trickling down my throat. You never know things like these mean so much until you are without them.

After eating we went upstairs to the music room and took over the vic. 'Course the fellows were so glad to oblige if they'd hear an American girl's voice. When you began to play on the organ it surprised me so. Surely I didn't miss a word of all you said, but I'll go back again soon just to hear it all. I looked around the small room, and lots of smiles came over their faces as you sang. Even one of the Red Cross gals came around and thought it was the radio at first.

I looked everywhere for some symbol of our anniversary to send you. I do have a bracelet I got at Mont St. Michel and have carried ever since, but it's so dull though I gave a good price for it. I want to give you something better for that loveliest day of our lives.

Patton's forces had finally taken Trier, establishing the route the 411th would follow later. The oldest city in northern Europe was now a complete ruin, its population of 90,000 entirely vanished. Only Porta Negra, a large stone from the original Roman wall, recalled its antiquity. On surrounding hills 50,000 Allied prisoners and slave laborers camped in barbed wire cages army "Lucky" would use eventually for German captives.

The Nazis had left hell-holes all over the place. The worst were yet to come.

———————

Once I thought that no place could have such changeable weather as that pre-invasion country, but it seems they all keep you jumping in and out of your long-johns all year long. Don't worry yet. I'm still itching away with mine and liking it. We go for a number of miles to the quartermaster showers and ride in our open trucks. If you don't catch a cold after a warm shower, then in the cold air for a ride, they must have slipped something in some of these shots. I've had so many poked in my arm, but couldn't feel better on a Sunday morning, so something must be working.

All the talk for ages now is about Metz being so hard to crack. If you could only see some of the old pillboxes you'd know why. When we left Pont-a-Mousson we moved into one of those creepy dungeons a few miles from Metz. That was one place they couldn't take us away from too soon and too quickly. It was so cold, so echoing at every noise, and always needing a flashlight along. We had the place a little decent when we left, all of a sudden moved, thank goodness, although we did hate to spend so much time on a place, then move out with all work in vain. Sometimes we think we just clean up for someone else to move in.

All the section was together, so we became very brave indeed, but when one wanted to leave the place we'd jokingly want to know who'd go with us. With that two or three would strike out together. The place had such a smell that we couldn't possibly get clean if we tried and honestly thought the medic would condemn it, we hoped. 'Course the days were far shorter than they are now, so there was nothing to do but go in and try to occupy yourself with something.

We'd all wanted to know what was down below us, so thinking maybe we would find a Luger or some object we'd like, three of us slipped on some German boots we'd found and started down. We thought there would be water. Sure enough there was about 2½ feet. It was dark as all get-out, but with our lights we could see to the bottom the water was so clear. We hadn't gone ten feet from the steps when our boots began to leak, and I was a bit glad. I headed for the steps. It would make you a little shaky. You should have heard the roar when we came in and had to change our socks and shoes. I'd like a Luger or some sort of pistol to bring home and thought by chance there'd be one down there. Don't worry, though. I'll always watch out for booby traps and not take the slightest chance if I have a doubt there might be something that would harm us.

All I care about some day is just to be no farther away from you than the next room.

A surprise arrived today looking so tired and worn and frazzled I thought at first some of it had come out on the way, but nope, I guess it was all there. I was so excited about The Pause That Refreshes I've teased the other fellows with it and can get almost any price for it. A Coke even makes the juice run out of a few mouths. I'll have to set it up and look at it for a while. You couldn't have sent this so I'd be sure to have one in Berlin, could you?

Some think the British or French gals would make better wives than the American girls. How they can say that is beyond me. Already the numbers are beginning to run up into the thousands of war couples just from England, far more than in the other war. I'm just hoping all of them will turn out as planned.

He lovingly overlooked the fact that he could have a Coke on demand in town. He also continued to assume that Patton would take him to Berlin, a development the general himself pushed with all his might. The First Army, under the watchful eye of war correspondent Andy Rooney, was already at Cologne, whose historic cathedral had been carefully preserved.

Prime Minister Churchill, wearing an Army colonel's uniform, dined on more of Ike's oysters sent all the way from Chesapeake Bay. This time Bradley, avoiding allergy, diplomatically shared his portion with others. Their discussion centered about new weapons for the next war, the defeated being inventors while the victors mistakenly held on to the tried and true. Churchill hesitated to ask Eisenhower about an atom bomb FDR had mentioned to him eighteen months earlier. He hoped that Britain could in future defend itself by merely breaking a glass panel in the Cabinet room and pushing a button programmed against an aggressor. He knew all too well that "Uncle Joe" Stalin might currently be a kind of hero to the more naive Americans, but Winston had met Communists before.

With the enemy in confusion and running out of gas, the great Ludendorff bridge at Remagen afforded the first crossing of the Rhine by an enemy of Germany since Napoleon's in 1805. Delaying demolition to provide for troop withdrawals, defenders looked up too late to find American forces on hand for one of the greatest surprises of the war. The First Army could wheel toward Patton ("Hot dog!" again) whatever doubting Thomases at SHAEF planned.

At last Americans had returned to the glory days of August and September. In a cold drab landscape with shop signs in Old German instead of French, they had finally revived their specialty, mobile warfare in hot pursuit. Here and there were scenes bloodied by bayonet and hand grenade, but some towns still had working lights, running water, and beer on tap. A sign by U.S. Army Engineers even boasted, "Cross the Rhine WITH DRY FEET."

Hitler ordered mock trials and swift executions for any officers even near Remagen. He also ordered the Luftwaffe out for nine days of striking at the bridge, ferries, and pontoon structures, used V-2 missiles tactically for the first and only time, brought up a giant howitzer reminiscent of Big Bertha of World War I, even sent swimmers with explosive packs across the river. To little avail, however. Americans had a new gimmick of their own, an infra-red device, source undetectable, called "Canal Defense Light."

Twenty miles upriver from Frankfurt the populace at Aschaffenburg had resisted as Goebbels ordered. Fearing enslavement by the Allies, whose advancing troops found some German officers hanged in the streets for advocating surrender, desperate women and children threw grenades from roof-tops. Wounded men limped from hospitals to join in the fray, but a marching figure with a white flag usually settled things. The Third Army was averaging a thousand prisoners of war per day.

On the road straggled Italians carrying bags of cooking utensils and bedraggled Frenchmen headed rearward toward the native land they had not seen since 1940. And how, in all the disorder, to meet the Russians without a clash? Pre-arranged signals and radio contact being unreliable, a line of demarcation along the Elbe River seemed the only viable solution.

For the moment all was peace and comparative quiet for the 411th in Luxembourg.

In our Anniversary Month:

Things would never be the same in life if there hadn't been some wonderful stork dropping out of the sky to let you into the world. If I could get my hands on that fine feathered friend, I'd give him the superest good conduct medal with oak leaf clusters. (This will probably let the censor think, "Well, he's obviously had a ration of brew.") He'll never know how special I want my letters to be all this month, our month. Although we're about to miss out on it together, I'll just love you till the end of time anyway.

One time there you had me thinking all the able-bodied citizens just about had their "Greetings," and I don't mean Christmas cards. As for the Marines, I'll never take one's word for anything except when he says his eyes bulge out when you walk by.

All Americans must have a weakness for baths. You can tell a fellow who rides for miles in an open truck just to wash his itching skin when some of these people don't care one way or the other in Europe. That's just one more reason we have such a world of more fun, more humor, and feel at our best so much of our lives. I thought the story of a Wac was so funny the other day. She'd almost forgotten about nice soft sweet-smelling things, even baths. When she got a furlough, she rushed home, bought the silliest hat she could find, then sat in the bath <u>with it</u> <u>on</u> for hours. Her mother thought she was batty, and who would be the same after being in the Wacs for two years?

Just recently we've been able to see so many of the new movies. I've enjoyed them, but they've made me so homesick when I come out and find where I am. At least the fellows know you are necessary for me to be happy. It makes me feel so good to be riding along in the truck and have someone say, "We'll take care of her husband," even calling your name. One of my pals said that today, and I almost twisted my fanny off like a little puppy wagging his tail. Most of my section have known you for a long time now. They make cracks sometimes, but always back down when I pretend to look hard at them. They can see I have one wife, one lady never to turn away from. They all rush the blue letters to me if I don't, as chief of section, pick the mailbag up just when the call comes, "The mail's in!"

You've been around Army men not only during war time, but at West Point, so get more of a picture than most people do. Oh yes, we have to be in perfect uniform here each day, by all means, wearing helmet, leggings, O.D.s and carrying the rifle every place we go. We happen to be in the group that's just about as tough as they make them when it comes to this inspection stuff. Long as we kept close, so close, at the first of the invasion very few inspections were held. Now they come pretty often. We always get hooked with this group although we might move for miles. They love us so well we can't lose them. I can't say the actual set-up is any worse than in the states, although we do have danger spots and nervous strain, but we miss out on reveille and retreat. As far as combat just now, you know we don't catch it nearly as bad. We still have our good and bad days. We did have billet the beginning of bad weather, that was fortunate, but someone has to do it, and some way we got the break. It's just that we are away from our loved ones and not knowing how long is what hurts. We've been in combat since June, so we've been holding up under the strain pretty well.

In the long run the plan for Monty to cross the Rhine first while others stalled at Cologne and Coblentz ended up in reverse - the Third on the Rhine and Monty still sitting and planning a take-off on the 24th ("Of what month?"). As in Sicily and Normandy, Montgomery's troops attracted German attention, but Americans broke through to set an advantage by surprise.

One general commented that Patton's route on the map looked like "an intestinal track" through Germany. SHAEF might not like him, but anything that didn't seem to make sense to others tactically Patton just took care of after he started rolling. Within ten days in March the score was: two German armies, 60,000 prisoners of war, and 10,000 square miles of captured territory. Traveling from Luxembourg through Trier along the road the 411th would follow later, he set in motion the final kill. Skies were sunny, only one pilot had been lost in over 600 bombing sorties, and Ike had cleared the decks for him to circle toward Mainz. Monty probably didn't like it much, but so be it.

The sergeant in A-Battery gloried in the rest they'd been enjoying, little dreaming he would soon be in for another mad dash rivaling the frantic rush across France.

You'd like this day if you were here, all warm and spring-y out. It makes you want to get out and find things to do. I dreaded to be away from home during the winter months, but somehow the missing will be even worse now that spring will be coming soon. Sort of a let-down feeling.

Today, in the middle of March, I got mail as far back as Dec. 3rd with lots of Christmas cards and loving holiday thoughts, especially from you. Even though the letters are months old, I felt more loved and thought about than I can ever tell you. Nothing counts just so I'm alive when this is all over and can go back to all that are dear and waiting for me.

If you don't watch out we'll get spring fever. All this sun's coming out at once. About this time things will be popping at the beach, still a little breezy, but you'll like to walk in the sand with your bare feet hanging out. I've only had a few glances at the new swim suit pictures for this year, but I'll bet there'll be some slick ones around.

We got to talking today about swimming. I did actually put my foot in the Seine. Then we thought how many streams we had crossed or gone boating in. You know I "did" the Thames, too. We wondered if we could have a diving board on the Rhine. Some would have to be look-out while others had their fun in the water. There's lots going on there just now. It just doesn't seem possible for those fellows to have gotten across so easily on that railroad bridge. Weren't those Nazis dumb? They've tried their darnedest to get that bridge out, but our on-the-ball First Army has really given those babies more than they asked for. With our ack-ack we'd really run up the score.

Maybe your eyes still haven't gotten off this picture I'm sending yet. Didn't have time to press my dress, shine my shoes or even put a little make-up on, but without my glasses (which I don't have anyway) it turned out rather well. It was taken down close to the Moselle near Pont-a-Mousson by a lieutenant who knew I'd be tickled to have it for you.

Men who have come from infantry outfits and have been injured are going home from our battalion now. One will leave from this battery in a few days. I feel that A.A. might be forgotten because so many of those fellows on the line have served so faithfully for years now without the slightest let-up. I want them to go first, of course.

Besides, when I come home, I want to stay there for the rest of my life. All I hope for is to let it end quickly. Well, actually I'd jump at the chance of coming any time, even pull rank a bit.

Out of a clear sky some day I'll come back to you over the phone. It's wonderful to have dream castles. They may not ever come true, but thinking of them is all I can have while we're away.

Those nights when you were on announcing duty at the station could have been my nights to go out for a beer, but all I wanted to do was grab something to eat as quickly as I could and head your way. I missed the bus one night and started thumbing my way out, and was surprised when a taxi came along, picked me up and took me all the way out for not a dime. When I said I was going to the radio station, he thought I was going to sing or put on some act. He even wished me luck and gave me his name, if I ever needed any service to look him up. Oh yes, I sure would, I told him, and would if I ever had any heavy bags to carry.

First Christmas mail, and now I've just gotten your Easter card already. I'll never figure out the mails. Around the first of the year there were two boats with motor trouble that had to be docked in England for repairs. Then another was cutting up and had to be turned back to the harbor in New York.

I'll never forget the speed we had coming to England. The Queen Elizabeth really sailed through the waters. Although she was a big ship, I thought sometimes the bottom was out the way I felt. We hit a storm, and you've seen pictures where waves rolled over the top deck. Well, it did ours that way. It was storming so one day we couldn't even have our practice muster to go up on top with our Mae Wests. As big and bundlesome as they were, those life jackets might have been very little help in those waves.

I can remember the LST we came over on for the invasion. It had a large hole in the bottom, but was kept up by pumping constantly. The sailor claimed we had a skipper who'd take lots of chances in getting his ship through. At one time I thought we'd have to go off in about twelve feet of water, but waited until the tide went out and drove out of the big mouth on to the Normandy beach. Besides having the second 90s on the beach we were first to come in so close to shore. No one else had attempted to come on with their equipment. We waited there like a helpless child for the water to go down. God was with us all the way.

I'll always want to hang on to some things till I come home. For instance, I've had the same shirt all this time. You know who put the stripes on and who tacked them on my jacket. I just can't salvage them because you did such a good job.

Happy St. Patrick's Day!

The only time I can remember that the day was made much ado over was a basketball banquet at high school. I almost had to make a speech when I drew my school letter that year, and I really was scared, too. I was glad that I had your cable before I read a letter about Mother's going to the hospital. She has taken so much punishment for so many years with that darn radiation. Her skin is so delicate that it's so hard to heal after she was literally burned with that radium. I just want her well and on her feet again. I still wonder what she ever did to have such a curse sent on her. Mother has served her Master more than any other woman in the world, so faithfully that she never stepped off the edge as we may want to lots of times just to kick up our heels. It's too deep for me, but she takes it so easily, not like some who'd be tickled to death to have something to cry and complain about. Things just must turn out right. I know they will. I'm trying to write her every day now to help out in that way. It's going to hit Dad pretty hard being in that big house alone. With all the help of the friends and neighbors she should have plenty of assistance when she comes out of the hospital. With all the hospitals in the services getting first choice of doctors, I hope they get the best of care possible. Our town is so good to stand by, too.

It's funny how they have pictures in France and England and even here of their leaders in the shop windows. We'd never think of showing President Roosevelt's picture, and we look up to him as much. In every store window in any town or village there will be DeGaulle in France, the Miss or Mrs. here, and Churchill in England. Maybe it's a national requirement. I don't know.

Wish I could see you.

Having executed those he considered responsible for the Remagen debacle, Hitler ordered everything useful to the enemy to be destroyed, yet one of Patton's corps commanders had just phoned back to say, "General, in addition to my other duties, I now am Mayor of Koblenz." The Third was overcoming army boundaries before new ones could even be negotiated.

Seven more weeks of bloody death lay ahead with the Allies and Russians within 300 miles of each other. Since the Nazis refused to quit, the only acceptable soldierly duty being to fight on as long as their country was still at war, mopping up continued. With Bradley's approval Patton assaulted the Rhine sector at Mainz. There he would either kill the Kraut or run him ragged. Monty still sat.

Suddenly Ike arrived for a briefing and a plea to the press for favorable stories about the tanks some were picturing as inferior to the German models. In response to complimentary personal remarks, Patton replied it was the first time in three whole years that Ike had praised him. From Eisenhower, no comment.

Stars and Stripes reported if any Nazi soldier were asked where the front line was, he could truthfully answer, "Just wait around a minute. The Americans are bringing it up." Reading of a prisoner count of 1,500,000, not including those taken by Russians, the Tennessee sergeant scribbled, "Where do they all come from?"

Most of the news that comes from Paris seems to be really hot and flashy. The coal shortages are giving them headaches, we hear, but they still haven't cooled down much. At least the shows haven't. This tale just leaked out, in fact. To keep up the soldiers' morale when they're back from action at the front, shows go on even in 20° weather. Some say even the smallest envelopes could hold the showgirls' costumes. In one performance, they say, the gals fainted under the beating that terribly cold weather was giving their legs while the G.I.s watching them were sitting by in overcoats.

Yes, I'm crazy, but mostly about you.

Something I saw the other day made me think so much of home. I was going somewhere in a truck and across a field saw a man plowing with two lovely horses. He was too old and not doing just the way we'd do it, but there was someone walking along with him, a girl. I couldn't help but put us in their place for a while.

There seems to be better mail service, perhaps because the trains run pretty regularly now to Paris and other parts where the letters will head for the good old USA. Some of yours still look tired. Our delivery comes in at noon now and not way into the night like it did at Pont-a-Mousson. I like that better because when I begin a new day it won't be long before noon when I'll know whether there'll be something for me. I've almost reached my limit as to waiting to open the anniversary package on that date, but I'll hold out if it kills me. It's punishment, but I'll love the reward.

They have some funny rules in this censorship business. Sometimes even our censors don't see the point, but have to follow the S.O.P. (standard operating procedure). Starting at the beginning over here I didn't put anything about each new location, but knew you'd think I was in Germany. Then I thought of saying something about the way you could Lux your hose, but still they insisted we say "Somewhere in ..." We lost one of our best censors to headquarters as adjutant, a step up for him in possibilities if not grade. Sometimes in the late hours we used to talk and really enjoy ourselves. We hope he comes back soon.

I'm growing rather fond of you.

This was such a good morning, as they all begin to be, that we'd probably be doing some spring cleaning. You know how good the sun is for clothes and bedding. I've really given my blankets a good airing this morning.

Can you find me a pair of sun glasses? It's becoming awful glary, and the sun really gives the eyes fits. They may be hard to find now but if anywhere at the beach. I thought about the Air Corps type. Maybe your brother would have a spare pair I could get, or even my bud in the Pacific if there aren't any in Wilmington. It will seem funny to go all the way through Hawaii for a pair of sun glasses, but the Navy seems to have everything where he is. Throw in a couple of wash cloths, too. I never knew they were such a handy item until I got to washing out of helmets. We still have a chance for a shower each day. I make it about three times a week.

I'm beginning to wonder what's creeping up on us. Maybe it's just spring fever. At times I feel so lonely. Time won't go fast enough.

In General Orders Number 70 (23 March 1945) General Patton advised the officers and men of the Third Army and their comrades of the XIX Tactical Air Command that, during the period Jan. 29-Mar. 22, they had wrested 6,484 sq. mi. of territory from the enemy, had taken 3,072 cities, towns and villages, and with 140,112 captive and 99,000 more killed or wounded, had eliminated practically all of the German First and Seventh Armies.

At breakfast that same sunny morning Bradley received a call from the general that he had sneaked across the Rhine the night before, but not to tell anyone until they saw how things went. By evening, all a-tremble and wanting Americans to know that he'd made it without Monty, Patton shouted, "For God's sake tell the world we're across!"

The landing had begun at 2230 hours with no artillery preparation until daylight, no paratroops, no navy, no publicity involved in the first such expedition in modern history, with a loss of eight men killed and twenty wounded. With moon shining down on the little assault boats an entire regiment had been transported by midnight, another by daylight, and by nightfall a whole division, with engineers building more bridges by searchlight and armored tanks rolling for a break-out.

Montgomery's assault, prepared for by bombardment ever since February, had not taken off until six hours later when Bradley was already on the air with Patton's news. The British attack, rivaling the invasion of Normandy and the big pushes of World War I with a quarter of a million men even using heating pads to keep cold motors running, had gained only a small bridgehead by nightfall. The BBC broadcast Churchill's previously recorded congratulations to Montgomery, obviously expected to be the hero of the hour, 36 hours after the American success.

History-conscious Patton had his day, however. With troops watching from both sides of the Rhine, he walked out on a bridge to urinate mid-stream to show contempt for the enemy. Once across, he deliberately stubbed his toe in order to stumble and pick up a bit of the German soil. Long ago William the Conqueror had bragged, "I see in my hand the soil of England." Now it was Patton the conqueror.

Old Blood and Guts reveled in his army's great campaign, praising their disciplined valor, unswerving devotion, unequalled audacity (doubtless a particular favorite) and the speed of their advance. His order of March 23rd declared, "The world rings with your praises; better still, General Marshall, General Eisenhower, and General Bradley have all personally commended you. The highest honor I have ever attained is that of having my name coupled with yours in these events." Crossing the Rhine the previous evening had brought "even greater glory."

The 411th followed him into Germany to bring the war to a close.

I wouldn't be surprised if we didn't take a little trip in a little while. I just wish we could have been there with that army of ours. Man, they really had a field day when they first crossed the Rhine. We are really guessing as to what will happen to us when peace is declared. After General Stilwell took over his new job, he likes Patton so well he might have in mind to get part of the Third in the Pacific. Since we happen to be tops in the Third, you can know what they'd pick. The job to be done after it's all over is going to be rough and a bit drawn out.

Once we get into that other country it'll be far different from what we ever had around D-Day because there'll be so much to watch out for. Those B_____ are so tricky and are all against us there until the center of our little area will become a real homely spot for us.

GERMANY

Norma Rogers

24 Mar 1945   Left Luxembourg.   Arrived Trier,
              Muriahof, Germany.   Arrived 1115
              hours. Traveled 28 Miles.

You have a very worn man on your hands tonight,
about as tired as I've been in a long while. It's
been an unusually long day starting around twelve last
night. I happened to be on duty from midnight to six,
so naturally I caught it when we got notice of not
being in our little shack another night. We almost
hated leaving "the deal" and after many longing
glances at it, we took off.

We left Metz about the right time. The winter was
breaking out and we didn't have such bad billets while
we were there either. The days have been wonderfully
warm lately and clear for almost a week now. Oh boy,
do these guys in the air have a field day. No one can
feel sorry for those weaklings that call themselves
"super-men." We need a little sun after all the T.B.
weather we've had all winter.

You might be wondering if I'm growing a little
heavier. On all these foreign scales the hand comes
up to 88. My figuring is 196, would you believe it?
I can't with the chow we get at times. I can always
stand a few extra pounds in winter because I sweat so
much on my upper lip that I'll lose the extra before I
know it.

Mail now will mean more than it ever did and takes
first place in my outlook for the day. Just be you no
matter where we go.

As Julius Caesar may have discovered two thousand
years previously, the natives seemed unresponsive,
downright sullen, waving white cloths instead of
bright banners.

The 411th from here on out would move, often by
night, and remain for the rest of the war so self-
contained and constantly mobile that relationships

413

with locals were not only undesirable, but well-nigh impossible.

The soldier who now rode and camped in enemy territory again wrote of a special day.

Curiosity finally got the best of me. In this new place I up and almost spoiled our anniversary celebration. I didn't open all your packages after I found this wonderful new picture. I didn't want to go on any further. I'm losing out on so much. I <u>will</u> hold out on the other <u>positively</u> until that grand day.

I was just getting my eyes open from one long sleep, had grabbed my mess kit and headed for chow when one of the fellows of the section came around the corner with an armful of mail. I saw a long way off I had hit it with you. Three blue letters were showing out from all the others. The other mail must have felt so honored that it could come along. I was on duty first shift today, but the whole Heinie army could have crept up and I might not have even noticed.

While we were eating the fellows even wished they'd have a girl or wife that would keep their spirits up so faithfully. So often someone will come around to see if I've gotten any new reading material. If I'm through with your little comments, I pass it on. Then someone will say, "I really like what your wife says and even look at that before I read the jokes."

I've worried so about Mother's operation and thought of so many things that would hurt and what she'd have to endure, but you've let me feel this morning that all is just as regular and nothing to worry about. What you said, too, about why things happen just changed things for me so.

I'm so glad, too, that your work at the station is being guided and appreciated. The staff party must have been the high point of the week. It sounded so cheerful and good for all.

Let's always be the life of the party.

---

27 Mar 1945   Left Muriahof, Germany to new position. Left 1630 hours.

28 Mar 1945   Arrived at bivouac area, Spendlingen, Germany, at 330 hours. Arrived at new position ½ Mi NW Hechtstein at 1430 hours. Frankfurt.

The 411th poised for its own memorable journey across the Rhine in pursuit of Third Army comrades. All units were told to make any bridgehead possible over the river with the aid of engineers' maps of the area, those marked "impossible" probably being the least defended.

Patton, a genius at making trouble for himself as well as Germans, now committed what he later called his only real mistake, the rescue mission of a prison camp which resulted in the loss of eleven officers and 282 men. He assured Bradley that he hadn't known until nine days later that his own son-in-law was held there, but it didn't look good in any case as an unauthorized misadventure with tremendous tragic consequences.

Furthermore, assertive Russians already breaking agreements made at Yalta were showing an uneasy trend for the future since Berlin was to be in the center of their occupation zone. The question of who would take the city was a moot one anyhow. No matter how much Patton and Montgomery longed to claim that prize and Churchill wanted to balance that victory against the Reds' capture of Vienna, Russian troops were only 35 miles out, hence impossible to overtake.

Everyone is in a stew, even the Russians. You know why, of course. The news sounds good and B. and G. has taken off in a mad run again, thank goodness. Did you know I'm following the leader and not having much fun?

I've tried not to break any records, but when things get to moving you know what that means for us. I'm about ready for something else. It's been on the move and the more we do that the quicker I'll be home. You can place your tacks all over the map now and not in the place you'd think we'd be.

In a hurry.

Something has hit me that I can't shake. It seems since we moved things seem so not the same that I don't know what's wrong. I'm not worried about you or home, don't think that. Sometimes I get to thinking too much, I guess, and when I get that way it's time to do something even if it's just push-ups.

Maybe it's just that our anniversary is tomorrow night and I won't be there. I still look forward to taking you out of the envelope and placing that picture where I can see it as often as possible. Then too, I have two other gifts and a letter. I may try to hold out until our favorite time, but the way I feel now I may open and find you smiling at the earliest possible moment.

This coming Sunday is Easter, too. I wanted to see you in your Easter outfit this year. If all the ladies try to outdo each other, I'll always want you to be the best.

When things seem as they did at D-Day, they feel that way today.

―――――――――――

Bivouac at Spendlingen furnished time for completion of a pontoon bridge to facilitate the Rhine crossing, the 411th gunners receiving well-deserved commendation from their leader:

"The following listed units are commended for their outstanding performance of duty during the period 16 March 1945 to 25 March 1945:

411th Antiaircraft Artillery Gun Battalion

In addition to their primary, twenty-four-hour-per-day mission of furnishing antiaircraft protection for critical Third U.S. Army installations, these units hauled vitally needed gasoline and personal reinforcements to forward armored and infantry elements during the critical period of operations when the Army swept to the ... River. On return trips many prisoners of war were transported to rear area. The skillful manner in which these missions were coordinated with frequent moves of antiaircraft units and the promptness with which they were accomplished, often under difficult conditions; the enthusiasm and loyal, untiring devotion to duty of all officers and men contributed materially to the success of Third U.S. Army operations and are in keeping with the highest traditions of the service." (30 March 1945)

31 March 1945   Left Hechtsheim at 0630 hours.
                 Arrived at Gustavsburg 1 Mi S.

Early during the morning of the long-awaited anniversary the 411th battalion began the journey across the Rhine. Unlike a bitter experience at the other fabled river, the Seine, this trip was uncontested until nightfall when six Focke-Wulffs showed up. Strafed for the next two nights along the Autobahn, the outfit finally arrived at Gustavsburg where the sergeant opened the rest of his gifts. A week later they'd be on the run again guarding Patton's headquarters amid rumors of another assassination plot that caused the general to take a carbine every night into the truck in which he lived on the road.

———————

Yesterday was our day, the day of all days I'd wanted to let you be clinging to my arm. I was so happy with your picture. After opening it early, I had put it back in the tissue and blue ribbon until the time of our wedding, then took it out again. All of the fellows here have furnished all kinds of wolf whistles when I showed them my new pin-up in the evening dress. They know how much we think of each other.

We'd almost made up plans for Easter back in Luxembourg. The chaplain wanted to start having a special service on Good Friday night, then perhaps another on Easter Day, but General Patton got this drive going. I was a bit surprised at our having a service at all today, but the battalion did get one. The chaplain knew we'd be disappointed if we didn't have something of some sort on Easter.

So few of the civvies here seemed to know there even was an Easter. That didn't affect us any, though. Just now they're probably thinking they can get around us and be friends and cuddle us back to like them a bit. They got the sting of things in no time that we are strictly out to show them we are not to be friends. If they'd stopped years back and made more of special days like Easter they'd be far better off.

This morning I was so worn I could hardly get out of that sack, and I do mean sack. We've gotten used to so much that some soldiers never get, like showers each day, movies any time we like, and a pass now and then. What soldier could ask much more and still be in combat? But we weren't in <u>this</u> country. Now it makes a difference. I was on from twelve to four last night.

Your little shell from the beach floated all the way over, and rather quickly, too. I picked it up here on the day of our anniversary.

The last four months have really slipped away from me, and although the days march on and make us a little older, we won't be near as far away soon. If you want to wear any dress you've laid away for my return, just hop into it and give those discharged guys a treat. The little drawings you sent give me a pretty good idea of how things will look. Just don't let any scouts capture you and turn you into a model.

All I can tell you about now is our artillery and big boys over in the sky each day really did lots of damage in most towns. Instead of feeling sad or down we want to crook our fingers at the people we see and say, "You asked for all this, now see how you can take it."

Naturally when one's away from all the dear and pleasant loved ones he becomes a bit hard. I may be like that in certain ways, but never will I change from the way I left you.

You'd know where people left a place there'd be the little pub and whatnot that G.I.'s would think they'd found a little bit of heaven if they had such things. Well, one happened to be pretty close here, and did the fellows have their schnapps up to some of their ankles! It really was a drunk man's paradise. The stuff will eat your insides out, especially the brand the Heinies make. So many of our group seemed to have birthdays, anniversaries, three years in the service, anything to celebrate they had to toast it. The only drink I had was the one they wanted to drink to you as being the sweetest and prettiest girl in the world. That's the only way they could get to me, so they pulled that one. Who could help but fall for it? It really made my eyes water, the most powerful drink made, I do believe. One dope poured some on the ground and threw a match to it. It burned like gasoline. Wouldn't the women's temperance union at home have a hissey if they'd known about this?

At times I want to stow away on the first cargo ship home. It'll always be like that.

———

Hoping for a miracle like the one which had saved Frederick the Great, Hitler urged a holy war against Bolshevism and called on all Germans to become "werewolves" preying on Allied armies, Jews, or anyone cooperating with them. The only strategy he ordered was "Stand fast."

Even after the Ardennes failure, the deranged leader thought he could conquer the Russians if he could only hold the line a few weeks longer. He still believed that the Russo-Allied partnership would falter, a tendency exacerbated by comments from Stalin requiring Roosevelt to deny charges of treachery in the relationship. Bradley also faced the fact that German barracks could no longer be bombed since American soldiers might be occupying them for a long time after the war in order to hold things steady.

Hints of what the 411th would face in future now surfaced at Ohrdruf, where Third Army troops discovered the first of many horror camps Hitler's henchmen had set up. Patton, vomiting at the sights he witnessed - an open-air crematorium, a shed full of dying skeletons, another piled with naked corpses, fourteen slaves with bullets through their heads lying in their own frozen blood, and above all the hellish stench - speedily summoned Ike, who paled at the infamous structure near a baron's imposing house and garden.

In line with his Third Army Memorial Program Patton ordered the town officials and their wives to attend a service at the camp in memory of the dead. After the well-fed and nicely-dressed Germans had toured the grounds, a surgeon in military uniform protested it was a "party matter" of which he knew nothing. The mayor and his wife went home and committed suicide.

Hitler, chief barbarian of all, waited either in the bombed Reich Chancellery or fifty feet under its garden insanely commanding that all captured airmen should be shot, regardless of the Geneva Convention requirements, and arguing endlessly over such earth-shaking matters as promotions and being lied to.

To reassure doubtful troops still hanging together in desperation, Goebbels announced that all would still be well. According to astrological charts drawn up in 1933 when he had become Chancellor, Hitler had been sent to them by Destiny.

For the 411th it was time to travel south to prevent a guerilla operation from setting up in the Alps where SS troops and a force from northern Italy, secure in bomb-proof shelters, might hold out for years.

| 8 Apr 1945 | Left Gustavsburg, Germany 1 Mi SWN 4245 for new position at 1915 hours. |
| 9 Apr 1945 | Arrived new position. Oberhaun WH 4049. Arrived at 1230 hours. Traveled 113 Miles. |

Batteries C and D split off to protect traffic routes around Eisenach while A and B were at Hersfeld guarding Third Army headquarters and an Autobahn.

There seems to be very little news out about our favorite man these days, and with all his importance they fail to give him the other star. With him making spearheads right and left we'll follow him, and fast, too. We've gone another hop the last few days and that means no mail for <u>more</u> days and C-rations. We don't complain, though. It's the ending of the war. We can't make it too fast for us. Most of our moves now come on Sunday. This one, as we guessed, came that night. Just let me sit down to write you, and there's a job to do.

I do wish there could be some way of just getting to hear you say, "Hello, Wesley." As old as I'm getting I'd even jump out of my shoes if I heard that.

Things just keep rocking along in the same old way. Not much excitement, very little news, but lots of rumors. As long as we keep them flying, maybe the morale won't go down completely. Some say rumors do wonders for an outfit that way, but most really play havoc with mine. What news we hear sounds good, but we get such far-fetched reports in the <u>Stars and Stripes</u> and only occasionally by radio now. Any sack that's taken out of a jeep looks like a mail bag, but after our wolf-eyes bulge, we find it's just more German loot. We've moved so fast and far that even the supplies of rations come up a bit slow. With a slowdown in mail I'm hoping you won't worry too much.

421

A few weeks back one of the fellows got to go to Paris. That was one chance I'd wanted. He had much better transportation than we did from Pont-a-Mousson. He caught a slow train out of Luxembourg, took the tour, and even had a room all to himself. Before he left I went around to his shack to give him fatherly advice, and he almost threw me out. He really got a big laugh out of my supposedly knowing all the ropes and giving him a few tips. He brought back lots of things for the boys. I didn't ask him to because I almost knew how he'd feel. When I went, it was almost like shopping for an orphanage so many wanted things. Anyhoo, he came back just as we were moving out and after such a hootin' tootin' good time was really dead on his feet.

We've gotten so we call ourselves the cockiest gypsies of this army. Just a few more weeks now and we look for the big news to pop.

Maybe it'll be months before you'll know for sure this loot I've gotten is headed your way. What's in the box, after much ado, is a rifle, all apart in two or three pieces, and a roll of parachute cord. It's a very good German rifle, in good shape. Not many found one like it. Not that we'll ever use it when I get home, but it's a thing you'll be interested in. Maybe you and one of the guys at the station can put it together, or if you just want to leave it like it is, it's perfectly all right with me. It's in a long wooden box, so tell them to enlarge your box at the postoffice if I keep sending such bulky things.

You did surprise me about the parachute. I'd wanted you to do anything you could have fun doing with it. I'm glad the Belk store and the Red Cross could use it for such a good cause. I can see you now pricking up your ears around that big store window to hear what people have to say about the "captured German property."

P.S. I heard of the death of President Roosevelt at midnight last night. I couldn't believe it. It's been the talk all day.

At Warm Springs, Georgia, in his modest Little White House retreat, FDR, pale and shaky and now sharing Churchill's concern about Russia, sent his last message to Ambassador Harriman in Moscow. An hour later, while posing for a portrait, he complained of a terrible headache, fainted, and died of a cerebral hemorrhage.

Eisenhower and Bradley had spent that day in an asbestos-like salt mine and a death camp. First they visited the tunnels filled with gold bricks, paper money, suitcases of jewelry, collections of gold-filled teeth, and boxes of art treasures looted by the Nazis. Then it was on to ghastly Ohrdruf, the first extermination site uncovered by Patton's army. Their guide, later revealed as one of the executioners and killed by the inmates after the official visit, showed the gallows on which a man choked for a quarter of an hour before dying, a well-used whipping table with stocks for the feet, and over three thousand bodies either laid in shallow graves or sprinkled over with lime to keep down odor until a shedful of 250 could be accumulated to burn all at once on a mammoth griddle like barbecue. Blood spots also showed where starving inmates, their yellow skin covered with lice, had torn out the entrails of the dead in an effort to survive.

Ike, thoroughly shaken, had bedded down at Third Army Headquarters in a room next to Bradley's while Patton returned to his truck-trailer. There, turning on BBC to set his watch, Patton heard the sad news. "Anything wrong?" when he knocked at Brad's door, then both to tell Ike and talk until nearly two about what effect the change in leadership might make.

The airwaves seem to be full of our man who somehow feels pretty close to us by now. You'd be surprised at how much has come from England about how well they liked and will remember President Roosevelt for our greatest leader. It was a complete shock to me, and I couldn't help wondering how it made you feel the first you heard.

You must know how the flash came out about our commander-in-chief. Just before the conference of the 20th we'd expected lots to happen now that the 9th seems headed for Berlin. We've gone such a long way having him as our President, and he must seem as close to you as he does to me. Somehow I couldn't possibly believe that he could be taken away this early in his new term. Never have I wanted a man so much to be in the peace conference. To us he's sort of looking out for us fellows and had that old American sentimental feeling in his voice. Each time he spoke, even if we doubted, he'd give one a feeling we'd go far in the war and the world of tomorrow. It hit each man with such a blow he'd not know what to say, but would hope this wouldn't prolong the war. We hope nothing will be complicated and that our new president will lead us in a similar way. The radio announcer last night kept saying, "Roosevelt is dead," just like that. If the war weren't going on it wouldn't affect so many, maybe, but it goes so straight home now as never before. I can't believe it will prolong the war here because the Germans and other leaders keep such an upper hand that they'll carry it to a finish, I hope quickly.

I couldn't and won't be able to tell you where we are now. We do keep on the move and have been for over a month. We crossed the Rhine on our wedding anniversary early that morning. Now we're really deep in the heart of Texas and this isn't that place by any means. We did pass through the place that's been the center of bombing for over three years now and did they do a swell job of laying it to the ground. Frankfurt really caught the dickens.

I've already mentioned a three-day pass just to read my mail when and if it starts coming again. It's wonderful to be in an outfit where we don't have to read our letters in foxholes. This is such a crazy war. I'm glad to keep close to the front so that infantry rumors don't get started too strong.

When the news ticker bell rang for "Bulletin," that might mean a bombing raid, a statement from Washington, or some other item of more than passing interest. When it signaled "FLASH," <u>that</u> meant IMPORTANT. The president to whom the newscaster had been introduced at Hyde Park almost six years ago to the very date was gone.

The native strength of America surfaced immediately in the person of Harry Truman. The heartland haberdasher and World War I veteran, as different from the Catskill blueblood as any man could be, stepped right in and took right over, almost as if he were mounting another cavalry charge.

Hitler received the news at the Fuehrerbunker to which the RAF had sent him by bombing the Chancellery. His enemy's unexpected death, like that of the Czarina in Frederick the Great's day, promised hope of salvation. He also held in his shaking hand a copy of the Allied battle plan picked up at some combat site.

Patton, his army only ten miles from the Czech border, invited visiting Congressmen, photographers, and reporters to the death camp at Buchenwald to witness and document among other atrocities its notorious lampshades made of tattooed human skin. He continued this practice at other sites so the whole world could know of a naked girl with gangrene at Nordhausen, skeletons lying in filth at Auschwitz, a little French boy keeping warm against a dead friend, and here and there cellars full of diarrhea and bone fragments. In a town where flowers grew and local citizens made wings for the Luftwaffe, sixty burned and bullet-ridden bodies hung from meat hooks. And what kind of monsters could so brutalize men civilized enough to scratch a diagram on a wall and cut knights and pawns out of paper in order to play chess? Only Nazis like the SS, who as far back as the mid-thirties had forbidden office-holding and the right to vote for anyone defined as "Jewish" - three full Jewish grandparents, membership in some Jewish community, marriage to a Jew, or descent from such a marriage or extra-marital affair. Others by the thousands who were not Jewish were also held for reasons abhorrent to Hitler.

Patton believed to a point some citizens who claimed they "didn't know." All he could do to prevent future savagery was keep on rolling inconspicuously to avoid a reprimand and bring the damned conflict to a close.

For the 411th it was business as usual. Get ready to move out.

> 15 Apr 1945 Left Oberhaun. Arrived 0700 hours at Zeigerhein WJ 5239 Germany. Arrived at 1636 Hours. Traveled 112 miles.

It's gotten to be old stuff now for us to be so on the go. Well, I can say almost. Here we sat around all winter at that Mousson place and then going to Metz and spending some other pretty cold weather, then the weather got like spring and quickly we've been on the jump ever since, except for about a month in Luxembourg. That was the jumping-off point. We've not stayed much longer than a week at any particular spot since. We've made some hundred-mile jumps, so with those you can go a long way in this country. We've seen some beautiful scenery. Sometimes we wonder with all this rolling country that looks so good, what else do these people want? We make very few friends - no friends at all is our order - so it's not like passing through France and seeing the kids fight over a stick of gum, a piece of candy, or cigarettes for Momma. We don't want to make friends and have to do over what's being done about twenty years from now.

No rumors have caught up with us yet, but from what we hear our favorite general will never see Berlin. The report is that the 9th is rather close to that city, but it's been evacuated so maybe we'll breeze

through yet just like we have from the Rhine.   You
know, it hasn't been very long since we were back
across that span.   Look at our smoke now.

I just want you to keep on loving me and have fun
like we'd do if I were there.

---

16 Apr 1945   Left Zeigerhein.   Arrived Krolpa at
2130 hours.   Traveled 22 Miles.
17 Apr 1945   Left Krolpa at 1645 hours.
18 Apr 1945   Arrived at Fullbach, MO 3284, at
0100 hours.   Traveled 105 Miles.

As   the   411th rolled   through   still-burning
Rudolstadt, their general sped from the death camp
with   its   musty-smelling,   mummy-like   inmates   to
headquarters   in   a   hideous   building   (ca.   1700)
containing plaster statues of obese females, a fine
exhibit   of   paintings   and   floors   of   gold   enamel   or
parquet   inlaid   with   silver.   Across   from   the   main
doorway was a modern stable with twenty box stalls and
a   saddle   room   better   furnished   than   many   a   drawing
salon back home.

Hitler   had   observed   his   birthday   with   faithful
followers   in   his   bunker.   While   he   predicted   the
Russians would soon meet bloody defeat in Berlin, his
troops,   some   still   going   through   the   motions   like
cornered criminals, were hoarding gas for non-existent
jet planes.   The Red Army was already in Vienna.

The   Third   Army's   last   mission,   the   "Danubian
offensive,"   intended   to   stymie   any   "Redoubt"
resistance in the southern mountains.   Contacting the
Russians at Linz, halfway to Vienna, they would attack
parallel to the Czech border while the Seventh headed
directly   south,   a   vast   movement   requiring   350,000
fighting men along a 300-mile front.

The 411th did its best to help cover the territory,
in the process learning names familiar from World War
I   like   Weimar   and   Jena.   All   batteries,   with
headquarters   at   Ilmenau,   spread   twelve   to   fifteen
miles   apart   to   protect   a   major   road   south   and   a

railroad east of Aschaffenburg. Battery A's position, on the southernmost point at Coburg (another historic name), gave opportunity to pause and pant a little. Even the mail caught up <u>finally</u>.

———————

If I know that little town of yours it's in its glory with the warm months opening up. I've wondered how you made the first splurge on the beach. That's one of the many things I got to liking about that place. No matter if no news comes in from you and home, I always want to think the best, and I do so much. Loving you like nobody's business.

Although there's so few chances of a letter getting out these days I like to think maybe you will get one to ease your worry. So many comment that in combat you forget all but just what you happen to be doing, and the other part - what you love and want - seems hazy and like a dream. There'll always be a clear picture in <u>my</u> mind.

I had my teeth fixed back at the Rhine, or maybe it was Trier. The dentist found one he thought should be pulled out, but I'd rather have a filling and asked if he couldn't fix it up to last a while longer.

This morning the letters I've kept from you looked so fresh and new that I went through them all again. You know how it can be after so long a time that you'll almost go crazy if you don't get a letter that day. Although I may change a bit, I'll always want you around.

You could almost look at these first few words and know what has happened. The mail came in last night, and here's one man who feels so super all day because way early I heard that mail was at headquarters, so I knew we'd have it by night. We don't dare get a false rumor started after three weeks with no letters. If some dope started one and then no mail, we could feel pretty wretched.

I was called down lots on how many times my name was announced. They know how much we love each other and aren't too surprised now when I get fourteen letters in blue and three packages besides. Now I'll last at least a week.

The subject came up would we be willing to be without mail if we knew the war would end in a month. 'Course I'd have to have positive proof. We realize there's a big push on and are helping in that for a while. Still we like for a few letters to trickle through, too. That isn't selfish, is it?

Something else came, your joke on me, all seventeen post cards at once. I haven't yet arranged the message, but some long night ahead will whip out the answer toot sweet. Got my Easter candy, too, <u>at last</u>.

Hey, whose are those three sets of lovely legs you sent in that picture? I already know the keenest ankles. Wasn't that you on the left going to outbow the others? They can put their skirts back down over their knees now that they've lost the contest. What a fine trick to pull off on us.

You sound a bit rushed these days, at least around Easter. We'll do very little rushing after I rush home to you.

Gambling for his entire future, he guessed wrong. To promote the hoax, the receptionist had posed like Betty Grable, as fetchingly as possible, while she and the assistant manager stood knock-kneed and pigeon-toed to fool him. She never let him forget it.

Hitler, over-medicated and railing at betraying German people and cowardly, incompetent generals, now planned to throw all available Luftwaffe and navy men into the infantry line even as Russian shells began to fall over Berlin. If all else failed, he would shoot himself, leaving responsibility to the Reichsmarshall.

Allowed to leave were Himmler, who had truly betrayed him by negotiating with Count Bernadotte of the Swedish Red Cross; Admiral Doenitz; Foreign Minister von Ribbentrop; Martin Bormann, deputy head of the party; and plump Goering, traveling to Bavaria in a truck caravan loaded with goodies. The Goebbels family and Eva Braun, Hitler's companion, stayed to the end.

Alerted by a Radio Berlin report that seemed to imply a passing of power, Goering wired to ask if he were to take over immediately. Instead he was denounced as a traitor with orders for his arrest.

It was still a killing war, even Patton getting tastes of danger. Near Munich a Polish pilot mistook his Cub for a German plane and made three passes before veering off. On another occasion an oxcart coming out of a side street just missed his head with its shaft by inches, a chilling omen of the accident which proved fatal only months later.

The sergeant in A-Battery had seen and heard too much as well.

I couldn't be exactly in the mood to write, but I can't wait for a mood now.

We didn't have our regular Sunday service today, but did have one Wednesday noon. The chaplain has his troubles keeping us close enough together to even have a service. Still he does try and that's something. Lots of times the surroundings seem hopeless, yet he comes up with some message that gives us something to think about. These people in Germany may go to church at times, but I believe more go in France that in any other place, even England.

These days are just days that I could keep busy and not thinking of you and home, but the lonelies still come. The aching will leave some day.

I sometimes wonder what the situation will be like when I step back into civvies again. Sometimes I can't picture myself that way any more.

You know the ruling about any friendly act toward these people. Who worries too much about them? I'd almost like to make it as uncomfortable as I can for them, not to do them a favor if it was the last thing

I ever did. 'Course there'll be some in spite of all the cautions, and even the fines they'll get if caught, who'll think it's big sport if they get away with it.

I just can't see friendship when they've killed your buddies and would have taken over if they'd had the chance. When we aren't too much on the move, we let them move out of their homes, no matter how fine they are, and live like kings for a change. Right now we've slowed up a bit and have a chateau that's about as good as I ever expect to get until we go home. They should expect such treatment, but some can't seem to know just what's taking place. After a time one soon loses the feeling sorry for going in and taking over. At times small children are in the house with their dolls and all their cuteness. You know how I love small children and love to play with them. The little kiddies in France were wonderful, but how can you love any like these people when one morning they laugh, the next they're putting a hand grenade in your pocket. You'll see the change in me, I'm afraid, but there's no way out while it's war.

The little packages keep coming in and made the trip so smoothly. The small candy boxes are not even crushed and broken like a large box might be. I know the real reason you've sent them this way is because I haven't sent a request you could use for more.

Never think I won't rush home, won't call you the first minute I step on soil that seems so wonderful now.

To avoid a worrisome Allied-Russian clash near the Elbe River, it was agreed that Americans would fire green rockets as identification and the Russians, appropriately enough, red. The Soviets had even decorated a jeep to present to the first Allied commander they met. In spite of precautions, some shots were fired by mistake, but on the whole the juncture at Torgau went off without a hitch. A crude American flag drawn on a bed sheet with water paints snatched from a nearby drug store signaled peaceful intent. Since every Russian, it seemed, knew how to play the harmonica, a woman captive, formerly of the Moscow opera, was able to lead a victory performance, suitably accompanied, on the spot.

General Patton heard the news in his trailer after dinner. Bradley commented something like "Took their own sweet time," possibly in comparison with the rapidity with which a Patton, untrammeled, could have managed it. On a map marking Berlin with a swastika a circle was drawn around Torgau.

To all intents and purposes the war was over. As the news spread, people danced in the streets and feasted on fried eggs.

After a six-day halt in Fullbach, the 411th arrived at their next location right at midnight.

24 Apr 1945   Left Fullbach by motor convoy. Arrived Hessenthal 2345 hours.

The sack's waiting for me, and is it calling these nights. Looks as though I will never get caught up with my sleep. This month I've seen all of this country I care about. Let me come home soon, won't you, Uncle Sam? We had our first B-rations today, the first in almost a month and only for one day. If we could just be together for only one complete life I'd be happy.

JUST MY CRAZY SELF.

I let those wooden shoes I'd planned to bring home get away from me. I laid them down outside our shower way back in Normandy and some Joe - it might have been a Frog - may have taken them. Anyhoo, they disappeared, and I've never known to this day what became of them. Way too large for you, but they would have been something to remind us of that section of the country. Most of the time the French people only wear them out in the yard, then slip out of them to go in the house without wearing any shoes. That's one way of keeping a place clean.

About the rifle I sent, don't be afraid of it. All I want for it is to be kept clean and not get rusty. I won't expect you to clean it, of course, but maybe someone at the station can get it done for you. Just throw it in a closet and the first guy that gives you any trouble, warn him that smoke will really fly. I also have a fur-lined pilot's jacket from a warehouse here. It's not the best, but something interesting.

There's that continual rain again today. It may bring May flowers, but doesn't stop the Russians and Americans. Even if it continues, the Krauts will still have their ears pinned back much sooner than they expect. Although we do happen to be in on a big thing, we seem to do so little now compared to some. Each hour there's more news that seems to be too good to be true. Just like when the real peace comes we'll not believe it the first time we hear it. I know that little machine in your newsroom is going like mad at the station, and the little bell ringing continually for bulletins and flashes, with my little wife doing double time running in and out from the mike so as to let nothing slip by. We catch a few of the announcements, but get so many far different versions we don't know what to believe.

Now if only one letter would come my morale would be higher than a civilian with a carton of cigarettes.

The news just now came in that Himmler wanted to give non-conditional surrender to the U.S. and England, but was still holding out on the Russians. Just must hold out and not give in. The Russians have fought so hard and know what they want. Let's hope they hold out a while longer.

The pen that's written more letters to you than anyone else had a breakdown today. It's supposed to be a Lifetime, but the little plunger that fills it broke in half today, from slow eating away of such poor ink here, I guess. They'll repair it when I get home.

Even when the time is busiest, I think of you in my sub-conscious mind.

War was ending in Italy as well. Mussolini and his mistress, Clara Petacci, wearing a German soldier's greatcoat, had been taken out of a convoy truck, shot, spat on, and hung up by the heels at a gasoline station where Italian partisans had been murdered earlier.

As the 411th prepared for its next move, Hitler, blaming the war on English politicians as political tools of the Jews, drew up a will and appointed Admiral Doenitz his successor as President of the Reich and Supreme Commander of the Wehrmacht. Then he took to wife Eva Braun, his friend of twelve years - their wedding breakfast marked by discussion of their suicides. Three couriers left the bunker with copies of his final statements, none of which was ever delivered.

With Russian tanks less than half a mile away and infantry troops within a block, the Fuehrer, saying farewell to his staff, retired with Eva, who bit a cyanide capsule as he shot himself through the roof of the mouth with a pistol. Their bodies were burned outside the bunker in a lesser version of "Götterdämmerung," including the deaths of Herr and Frau Goebbels after they had killed their own children.

Admiral Doenitz, Hitler's appointed successor, proclaimed that the Fuehrer died a hero's death at the head of his troops and promised to continue the war as long as the western nations hindered the fight against Bolshevism.

29 Apr 1945	Left Hessenthal, for new position.
30 Apr 1945	Left Bivouac area Hohenchaunbach ½ Mile NW WT 9857 Germany.
1 May 1945	Arrived Rimbach ½ Mile N WU 4418 Germany at 0500 hours. Traveled 258 miles.

Collapse being evident everywhere General Bradley suggested that he and Eisenhower fly home for their thirtieth class reunion at West Point in June. Food no longer needed to be parachuted into Holland, photos showed that the "Redoubt" planned at Berchtesgaden had been thoroughly bombed, and Hitler and Company were either dead or as disassociated as Himmler's wife and daughter in one village and his mistress and her two children in another.

South of Wurzburg and Nurnburg the 411th battalion had bivouacked west of Regensburg. As May arrived they were in the midst of an all-night move in heavy traffic to protect two crossings ten miles apart over the Isar River.

By now I thought we'd be basking in warm sultry weather having a tan that would make yours seem shameful. All we have instead is a windburn that only makes it tough to shave. Just think about having snow on the ground in May. Why back home I'd be asking Maw and Paw, as people here think we talk in Tennessee, to let me go barefooted. If it keeps this up, old long handles, here I come again. How does anyone know how to dress in this country? Not one time here have I been able to sleep without some cover.

Already the mails have become confused and a little irregular again, which is calling for the impossible to keep them straight. An outfit that isn't on the jump can get and send out its letters whereas if you're on the go the system really gets mixed up. In April we've had the fewest letters in all the time I've been overseas, and it really makes a difference.

Your telling me about President Truman gave me a new light on him. I wondered a great deal about him. Even his message to Congress when given a repeat broadcast here seemed a little lifeless as though he was reading and not really speaking like we've gotten used to with President Roosevelt. I've wondered why there was a hold-up in our general's promotion, too.

I'd hoped since he'd done so much that Roosevelt would have been the one to give it to him. I'm glad Truman didn't take too long to decide. 'Course all the build-up about discharges gives the G.I. a new lease on life, and they already like Truman for that if nothing else.

We covered some other important land the other night. You know the Blue Danube. It isn't all you picture, but is really clear and blue. Maybe your map tacks are going all over the places where we have been. Now we've gotten into the southern part and maybe will tour another country before everything's over. How many days will that be? Before you get this, I do believe.

If all the Germans loved their wives and sweethearts like I do you, this would never have gotten started.

---

3 May 1945   Left Rimbach WU 4418 Germany for new position. Arrived at Hohenrain ¼ mile NW WU 7534 Germany at 1800 hours. Traveled 30 Miles.

Radio Hamburg's announcement of Hitler's demise, which would have been greeted with wild cheers six months back, received only three rolls of muffled drums in the nation he had brought to ruin. Holland had already capitulated, Italy had surrendered unconditionally, and Field Marshal Jodl continued efforts to work out a cease fire with Americans rather than the dreaded Russians.

Patton, particularly after his near-miss with the oxcart, longed to bring about orderly conclusion and reorganization while he yet lived. Whatever the criticism, at least he went ahead and got things done, and in a hurry, too, without undue human slaughter.

There almost went another day when I couldn't say hello. If I know these ease the part of any day, which your words do mine, I'll always do my best, you know that. Sometimes it gets so long and never-ending.

With the air so full of good-sounding news I can't help but think it's all bringing us a little closer. With the ticker going haywire with all the special bulletins, wouldn't it be better if you just took a mike to the newsroom and not have to run back and forth to the broadcast desk? You've always promised me the very latest dope, and to a tee you've given it to me.

By now the price of tea has gone up in Britain. Since all this fighting has ceased on their fronts, don't you know they have really thrown a killer? Who could blame them after so many years at the grindstone? I think we've taken a good part of the battle. Yet the broadcasts mostly build up the British forces. Maybe they don't aim to. It's only natural, I guess, but they do tend to figure our contributions in yards and theirs in miles. We laugh and wonder if we'll still remain in the front line. No one can figure what's up for the A.A. in our army. We are such sharpies they can't do without us. What a laugh. All I want is to go by way of home first if there's any idea the Pacific is needing me. I want to be at home once more before it gets to be too many years. It can't be too much longer.

There may be something in the air yet for us here. I'd like mostly to stay here, of course, then come home for good. Even staying here 8-10 months wouldn't be anything like the Pacific theater. There the climate, the yellow never-give-up Japanese, besides all the snipers we've only had a few of here. We have had a few around, but never heard from them until some fellows would go deer hunting and up come the Krauts with their hands up. Some put up resistance, but most of the time they are so hungry and wanting shelter that they give up easily.

Always be mine.

Talking about an empty mailbox, I'll give it a few more weeks, then let's say we'll see our senator. Supply and transportation are really such a headache. I guess we should be glad that we can keep going and finishing it all up so quickly.

Not even any friendly planes come around these days. Soon we'll be taking on the same kind of stuff as we did back in the states. Who knows what will happen to us when peace is actually declared? All kinds of rumors still, but some fizzle out to that same old line, just a rumor. It's going to fool all of us some day, though, and we'll slip in home before you know it.

I got a little surprise package some time back. I'm guessing the bit of cake was part of our anniversary celebration at the station. The nuts and all made it taste wonderful. Even if it was a little dry I enjoyed it so much. All the other cakes and candy in some little packages that came were eaten as we drove across the country.

Won't I ever get to come home?

---

7 May 1945   Engaged hostile aircraft.   Claim
              submitted.

The last plane against which A-Battery took action was sighted near the Isar River crossing at Plattling, to which they had come a few days earlier by way of Deggendorf on the Danube, about thirty miles from the Czech border.

Given permission by Ike to cross over it, Patton had roared delightedly, "On to Czehoslovakia and fraternization! How in Hell can you stop an army with a battle cry like that?" At the same time he warned his men to leave their good watches and pistols behind if they met any Russians wanting to exchange souvenirs. Medals, flags and personal equipment would suffice.

Bradley's Russian worries had to do with food again. To function properly at a meeting in Leipzig and wary of vodka toasts and heavy breakfasts, he carried mineral oil to swallow on the way to a performance by chorus, balalaikas, and a ballet troupe brought in from Moscow.

Two weeks later Americans responded culturally with a khaki-clad violinist imported from Paris, an ordinary GI named Jascha Heifetz. To match the Reds' handsome carved pistol and stallion draped with a saddle blanket bearing a Red Star, Bradley presented to the Ukranian Army commander a new jeep inscribed across its cowling with a dedication in both English and Russian, its tool compartment stuffed with American cigarettes. A holster affixed to the body held a highly-polished new carbine.

Negotiations for peace were stalled, however, with Doenitz trying to explain why "unconditional surrender" except to Americans and British was entirely impossible. Ike's ultimatum? If you don't do it our way, we'll seal off the western front and block further movement west, which meant, in essence, "Just take your chances with the Russians then." A rumor also had it that even 100,000 White Russians, with women and children, preferred to become Allied prisoners of war rather than suffer that fate.

Writing a note to his wife, Brad then went to bed shortly before midnight on May 6th. At 2:41 A.M. on May 7th, in a schoolhouse, Field Marshal Jodl, acting for the German army and navy, signed formal papers of surrender effective at 11:01 P.M. May 8th or, as SHAEF's top secret TWX indicated, at 0001B (double daylight saving time) May 9th.

People think the war is about over, and it is all but shouting, but still no definite word has been given out to us by Ike, so we have to play along until he gives it. Things look so good. I know there's work to be done on that other front, but at least let me stay here or go home. No, I haven't spent as many

years here as some and can't say too much the way
things have gone. Still, I can have my wants, can't
I?

So many will feel sad for having lost someone dear
and sweet. There will be so much rejoicing and
thankfulness in the states as well. A few broadcasts
have already given how everyone is acting and
celebrating. We get a good bird's-eye view of how the
Limeys and all the other countries are rejoicing, but
just here and there about how New York, Chicago and
California are reacting. Let's hope that in all the
joy the people will not forget to go to the open doors
of the churches of our land. Right at the beginning
it struck me there was a promise there'd be some sort
of service in all the churches when victory came. I
know with all the joy in your own heart there'll be a
few minutes spent as you've done each day I've been in
these countries. I wish there could be some ceremony
in our surroundings here that would be a symbol of our
happiness and everlasting gratitude for being blessed
so along the way.

I've wondered if you had to come out of a sound
sleep to hear the wonderful news. Let's hope all the
gang was around so there could be a really glad and
happy moment together. Just be patient. We'll be
home soon with all the burdens away.

On another happy note, Patton's troops had found,
intact and unharmed, the remarkable horses of the
Imperial Riding Academy which had left Vienna as the
Russians approached. During the entire war twenty or
thirty physically perfect young men and thirty grooms
had preserved an art developed from the necessity to
avoid contact with the enemy. Patton, however, merely
sniffed at the amount of time and energy devoted to
training mounts to raise their feet and jiggle their
bodies to keep their riders astride in combat.

Finally, the formal signing. Peace at last.
Eisenhower called Bradley to say, "It's over."
Buzzing Patton in his simple trailer near Regensburg,

Bradley ordered all held in place up and down the entire line to prevent senseless casualties at the last minute. By the time he finished reaching others with the news, with the sound in his ears of messkits rattling for breakfast he stepped over to the map showing 43 divisions sprawled over a 640-mile front and wrote D+335.

An Associated Press reporter, in violation of a pledge of secrecy, prematurely flashed word of the surrender, causing a mad "unofficial" celebration in Times Square. The Russians did not make their announcement until a second surrender was formalized in Berlin.

Patton, now hoping to resume action on a different front in the Pacific, held his last regular morning briefing, thanking staff members personally for the harmonious efforts and magnificent abilities of fighting men and officers whose teamwork for 2½ years since Tunisia had won the war. Later at his farewell to press correspondents who had covered his trail, he was asked why he hadn't gone on and taken Prague, as he easily could have. "Because we were ordered not to." He spoke what he saw as truth when asked, often to his own detriment and the dismay of others, but his only real regret throughout was the ill-advised attempt to rescue the prisoners in the fiasco near the German camp. He believed firmly, then and always, that by helping to speed the conflict to an end he had saved lives, his primary goal.

The sarge's record for A-Battery, 411th, indicates an "Anti-tank mission" on May 8th, possibly in response to reports of hostile acts in the area. Also six more enemy planes flew over without incident, apparently to return personnel to their homes or avoid surrendering to the Russians. Following orders to withhold fire unless attacks were under way or seemed imminent, gun crews spent the rest of the afternoon watching from a distance what one man characterized as an excellent class in aircraft recognition.

Finally, the announcement all had waited and worked for so long was entered as follows in the battalion record:

"At 0536 (sunrise) on 9 May the battalion was relieved of its AA mission, the war in Europe having come to a successful end."

In North Carolina in the heart of the Wilmington business district, a soldier's grateful wife witnessed pandemonium - cars moving around and around the postoffice with horns blowing, people throwing streamers and papers out of upstairs office windows, everyone shouting, screaming, laughing. Thinking to join others in prayers of thanksgiving, she headed for the church, its door always open, to find herself all alone in the dark. Perhaps there had been a service earlier, at noon as on D-Day, or maybe there would be a formal ceremony on Sunday. Yet somehow it seemed just right, that night of all nights, to say her prayer in peaceful serenity as she had done so many times before. If it reached God and surrounded her man overseas, it was enough.

Now that things have quieted down a bit maybe we'll get our talk in each day again. It's been some time since the mails have come so regularly. Now that they've started again let's give them all the push and praise 'cause I love it!

You'd almost think this was a day back in the states. The afternoon is spent swimming with sports and maybe a movie tonight. You'd think it was rather a fast life for a soldier, but oh it's just a period of waiting for something to happen. Let's hope and pray it's a one-way trip home. Wouldn't it be wonderful if I could be taking a summer tour on the sea toward you? I'd have a hissey every mile. We mention often in these sultry days how great it would be to head for that cool beach at Wrightsville.

It's funny now to go to bed and not have to be bothered all night for duty. I seldom remember anything now when I hit the sack. Our first sarge is on leave in Paris, so it's my job to act while he's away. It's no more fun that it was in the states either. Anyhoo, the point score keeps coming up. Who knows? I'll make it out some day, I hope. All told I have 71, not near enough to be discharged, but still a chance of going to the states some time. I have 39 months service, three battle stars so far (15 points) and 17 points for overseas duty. One man who's really stepping high is up in the nineties.

One thing else I'd not wanted to worry you about has healed nicely. On one of the night moves just recently when we really had a time in the black on such narrow roads, once our radar got off the road. In trying to pull it back on with a tractor the chain had to be shifted from back to front. As we were running around with the chain in the dark, I didn't see the door of the radar truck and ran head onto the sharp corner. I've never been knocked so cold in my life, saw stars and everything. This all happened around two in the morning, but no stitches were taken until around 6 or 8. It's on the side of my head almost where the part begins and is a rather tender place, but will be o.k. in time. The hair will mostly cover the scar, but I will have a little showing. This was the first day with the bandage off, and really, it's fine.

The only thing I want most now is just to come home forever.

This day has been rushed and full in every sort of way. It was a special day for mothers in the states, I know, with the war being over. We even had a special program at church today.

I feel like a not-know-your-wife, though, when you told me I missed my guess on the legs. Now I'm almost afraid to take a second chance at it. If I did wrong then, you'd really have me in a corner. None could be like yours in my life anyway. Don't be mad at me. After all, they may have grown even more beautiful. I.L.Y.

I'll never let you out of my sight, not even to cook a biscuit. When you tell me about the woman who's not seen her husband in so long, then comes to choir rehearsal the same night he comes home, I don't know what to think.

There's still a lot ahead of us here. One reads the paper and gets the idea we will get a break and go by way of the states if nothing else. We will be in this spot for some time, I know, because we've even started a few classes, good refresher courses, and one certainly can grow a little stale in my position. I've chosen a few weeks in "Conducting a Small Business" or something along that line. That should be good for anyone. First, of course, I've wanted something in dairy farming and livestock. Then there's business law that should give me a few ideas I didn't know about, like who can sue, who can take advantage of us, what to do in case of an accident. The one I want, too, is taxi-ing around on a plane just to learn how to handle it a bit. You know, they'll be used lots after the war, so I don't want to miss out on that. They don't plan to present courses in flying, but if enough show interest, they'll probably offer something along those lines. In a few weeks we may be shifted and not even fooling with our equipment any longer.

I hope you'll take after the others around the beach and just take it easy. People shouldn't do too much when it's hot, so just get tan and ride the clouds.

Things are just popping around here. You'd think we meant something by it when actually we've just got so much time to pass. With all our push since we've been overseas, I feel we'll get our rest soon, either by way of the states or take a gamble here for occupation duty.

All the wonderful back mail has finally caught up with us, even all the anniversary presents - two months late. I showed those loud comical shorts all over the place, had the men fooled when I pulled them out and said, "Look what the supply sergeant issued."

They think my wife is crazy, but wonderful to write so often. The clever idea of putting your head on the pin-up gave us such a sparkle. The guys haven't figured it out yet.

Maybe I'd better warn you before the package comes that I haven't gone completely nuts sending a fur jacket and a roll of wire out of a clear sky, especially when it'll be midsummer and make you hot to look at it. I don't figure I'll need the jacket here, and as for the wire, I had in mind using it for two telephones. These German field phones are really something, worth around eight to ten dollars at home, so I thought I'd send two. I haven't got permission to mail them yet, but I have sent the wire. We could have one at the house and one at the barn. All you do is connect the two wires and crank the little handle. They'd be lots of fun at the station to hook up and call from room to room or even up in the attic if you were up there getting down the Long Ranger transcriptions.

Won't we skip along in the clouds?

You have about gotten me placed, but have missed your guess a bit. When we were attached to the 80th Division we moved a little faster at last. Ever since our last move we've been at this spot and a good way into the country. We've set up rather close to a small place called Plattling. Look close to Regensburg, around 30-40 miles from here. We've just gotten permission to give our exact location now that the censors can let up on us. "Course there are still a few things a Jap agent would like to know. Plenty can still happen, but I have such faith and feel good in my days now. A while back we could never tell when we'd be attacked, but as days went by, we didn't see a plane until the Germans started running away from the Russians or went on suicide runs. What a day that was on V-Day.

We now live in sort of a tent city as in Eustis, only the tents hold lots of the section, not the five-to-six-man type. We like these much better than pup tents, as you can guess. We were issued this back in

January, so if there were no houses available we could use these. Most always we found houses. Now that it's warm it doesn't make too much difference. In fact, the coolness of the night does wonders in this sack for sleeping. It's so funny to go to bed and stay all night. When we were set up for action we pulled shifts all times of the night. You know how broken sleep can be, but I'd almost take that than the stuff we do now that seems to make so little difference.

I wonder about my brother in England. With all the time he spent there it still seems the airmen will go straight to the Pacific. I'd love for him to have a few days at home first. They can't say our family hasn't done its share in this war. I even looked to hear that the fourth and last son has gone in, but it's all so far advanced now he may miss it yet.

He had a right to be proud of more than his family's share in the war. His general had never issued a defensive order the entire time, and the army to which he belonged had gone farther, captured more prisoners, crossed more rivers, and liberated more friendly and captured more enemy territory than any other army in American history. They had crossed France, Luxembourg, and Germany, infiltrated Czechoslovakia and the Alps, and met the Russians. Most tellingly, at two critical points, the Ardennes and mid-Germany, they had accomplished miracles in shifts of direction and re-grouping in split-second time.

The big job ahead would be disarming, controlling, transporting, even just feeding the vast numbers of prisoners and displaced persons as well as troops in the disheveled environment. The 411th found itself all too soon involved in the process, but for now another move - toward further assignment or discharge?

22 May 1945   Left Hohenrain, Germany for Hanacker. Present position.

———————

I stepped out on you last night with most of the boys and no other brunettes whatever. I wish the American girl could really know how we feel after seeing the girls of this country.

We can claim three battle stars toward discharge, but I'm not put down as "Essential." Don't laugh. What guy in this army _is_ all that essential that someone else can't take his place?

The big package was full of things that made my mouth water. The cereal will be so good these mornings when they don't have much, and it's so often now, too. Even that can of frankfurters will get careful attention. Still, I don't want to stay over here so long that you'll have to send all these boxes. Just let me come home, and we'll never start to worry over little packages again.

Now we don't have much to do through the night from six to six as we used to, so we've almost gone back to the same routine as Davis.

Something got lost for a while in the mails, I think. It was the small Easter package you sent, probably in February or early March. That bunny was really mashed from such a long trip on a boat, and was so damp I couldn't make out what you'd written on the card. I got the important part, though, the thought and the love.

We have a busy day of going through a number of things, even thirty minutes of infantry drill before retreat. I <u>thought</u> the battalion would be so on the ball that we'd be doing that as soon as V-Day came. Sure enough we've picked up just to keep us from getting stale, they say. After chow we've had a game of volleyball with B-Battery, and Saturday inspection is coming up, too. Just for the home front sport news, we lost the game, but don't think we didn't give them a scrap for their money. I've always loved volleyball, played lots in high school and had a letter in it, too, as a winner.

447

When you hear of all these inspections and drills, you may think I'm Pacific-bound, but no one knows. We still have our babies and keep cleaning them to maybe turn in. I can't see how they can use Patton in the islands, but maybe he'd be valuable any place they'd put him. If they sent me home for at least thirty days I won't be too down, but if we go straight to the Pacific, woe is me for a bad boy.

Last night's <u>Stars</u> <u>and</u> <u>Stripes</u> said we may get another campaign star. That'll give me only 75, but that isn't too bad. Lots have National Guard time (this doesn't count), but some have a high score because of children. Twelve points for a child, but no points for a wife. Then some men are 40 or over and will be let out sooner or later. At this moment, though, we're still the old 411th keeping equipment in tip-top shape. I just get tired of dilly-dallying around.

How they seem to drag the time away.

Even if I've been in close places here, I'd never get as nervous as I'll be when I start for home. I thought today what a wonderful summer cruise it would be. When we came over, the rough winds wouldn't even let us go up on deck too much. We'd go to get fresh air and pass some time. I'll never forget it, yet how little we felt, that our ship was the biggest one of all, the biggest one we'd ever ride. None of the fellows have forgotten how sick I was and even in my blue moments said that if you wanted to see me again, you'd have to come over here. I just couldn't make the trip back like that again. Honest, now I'd even ride an LST, even a poorly made Liberty ship as long as the sailors thought it was safe.

Today was Memorial Day, a day we never thought much about except as a bank holiday. Today was different with us having peace and, too, having lost some fellows in this outfit. This afternoon we had a small memorial service, parade, and talks by an officer and the chaplain. I thought it might be a lost effort, but after we got out and paraded around, I was downright proud of us. After such a long while with no drilling you can grow pretty slack and awkward. We did so well, though, and looked as sharp as any Fort Bliss could ever do. We sang two songs, "America" and "The Star Spangled Banner," and did a good job on both. We'd been so lucky, can I say blessed, too, not having but eight lost in our whole company. We did stay as close as any A.A. could ever stay to the armored and infantry at the front. Yet we came through so well. Lots of reports came back of our fellows that went into the infantry around December and January. Some didn't have a chance. Others came back to tell the story of what happened to this one and that. We wanted to honor them, too, so in our simple little ceremony we bowed our heads for those who fought to their last for our country.

You'd be surprised to see me out in front of our battery as right guide. I've been that in all our parades at Davis and over here, so it's my official job now. Actually it's not easy because everyone's step is kept in step with mine. You know, 1-2-3-4. If you can keep an even step you're really doing well. You've never seen me in this formation. Soldiers can talk about an officer's war and ninety-day wonders from OCS, but I'd stick up for some of ours any day.

Lots of stories come from the states. What's this about the law in California that gives any person the right not to tell their husbands that they're ready for the stork and the babies adopted without the husband's knowing? We've carried these California guys high, wide and handsome over that. Even they can't explain what's come over their people. Has that been on the news ticker? It would be the limit of all time. What else will they pass before we come home? Things like this make us so let down, not understanding what's coming next in the U.S.A.

A man has to have some weakness. I don't drink or smoke or chew, but I have a real weakness for you. That's rather wonderful of me, though, I think.

May 31, 1945, and I love you.

Do you realize where these crocheted doilies come from? Well, I had so little to do following General Patton that on my ten-minute breaks I worked these up with a trench knife and my Colgate teeth. They were hand-made, left in some house, so I thought they could stand under my picture or some special vase. It's part of the loot I picked up here and there just for you.

Saturday afternoon, you know where, at 3:20 P.M.

Already one man has left us on discharge, the first I've seen so happy, yet couldn't eat a bite. I'll be the same way. I won't take time for anything when I know I'll be one moment closer to home.

The replacement for the one who left last night is a corporal, but with lots of combat in different campaigns, so he's way ahead of us in points. He had 118. We have a number of high-pointers in our battery, though. One especially is having a hissey. Every time he passes me during the day he'll say, "Here today and gone tomorrow." Even in inspection last Saturday he was near me as we followed the inspectors. The jokes were making me laugh, and did the officers give us a hard look for seeming so giddy when they had to be so firm.

Just as the fighting men got used to smiling again, serious statistics came out to wipe the grins off some faces. The Army and Air Force had lost over 175,000 dead, the Navy over 5,000. Of these the Third Army reported 21,441 killed, 99,224 wounded, and 16,200 missing in action. Yet, as Ike's "Victory Order of the Day" noted, along with the trail of their fallen comrades, every man or woman of every nation serving as a team had brought about the outcome by their cooperation and the devotion needed to maintain peace in the future.

Not surprisingly, though, it was Patton whom the Russians saw as their kind of man. At a lavish victory banquet featuring suckling pigs, beluga fish, special cheeses, and other delicacies flown in from Moscow for the occasion, a general had poured him a tumbler of vodka, which he downed easily, bottom side up. He then lifted up another, toasting "American womanhood" after decorating tobacco heiress Doris Duke, on hand for some reason in a U.S. Army uniform.

By contrast, hospitality for his meeting with the Russian commander at Linz offered to Soviet guests only honest American military food - peanuts from a post exchange, Spam, white bread, K-rations, cheese and crackers, chewing gum, chocolate, and some bourbon supplied by the Quartermaster. His simple reception, almost in the persona of one of his GIs on the line, stressed the military man, not the social butterfly, an attitude they recognized and respected.

The same honest simplicity marked his farewell to those who had served him well for so long and with whom he hoped to head for the Pacific. At the final briefing they had heard his high-pitched voice saying, in effect, "If I go, you will go" to resume unfinished business together. Repeating his constant claim that no commander had ever done less work since they had done it all, he stood silently, nodded, bade them keep their seats for the meeting, snapped his fingers at his dog Willie, and turned to leave. As the day's announcements began with instructions for the men to discard steel helmets and wear only more comfortable fiber liners, he called from the doorway, "Make sure they're painted and smart-looking. No sloppy headgear around here." To the aide at his side he commented that the best end for an old campaigner is a bullet in the last minute of the last battle. The call for which he yearned never came. At the end of the year, still on duty in Europe, he met the fate he had avoided with the oxcart.

Other matters wound down as well. <u>Stars and Stripes</u> (Bavarian edition) reported the arrest of Heinrich Himmler. Found masquerading as "Sergeant Hizinger," he was betrayed by two guards traveling with him. Hoping to serve a short sentence as a mere SS guard, he had attracted attention by the suspicious care paid to him by his companions and his obvious uneasiness over identification papers. Usually minor criminals cared only about their wallets or money.

Hitler's female secretary had also been captured, and poet Ezra Pound would be sent to the United States to be tried for treason.

But the headline on a story by Andy Rooney spoke for most readers: "Good! When Do We Leave This Hole and Go Home?"

It looks as if the sarge may be out in three or four months. My next step would be to try and fill his place. He really learned it all, but without an administration course of some sort I would be a little handicapped. I'm rather satisfied with the job I have and am not looking for any more headaches. There would be plenty if they gave me the next rank. If I'm tense and worried over taking over for him, I'm afraid I'd screw up a bit. Unless they bring someone else in, which is unlikely, they may have to give it to me, though, and I did all right once before, I guess.

I'd walk all the way to New York just to see you.

There couldn't help but be a catch in my breath when I heard about your brother. I hadn't expected a discharge for him so soon after they promised the air force would remain in to the last. They have us beat all to pieces in points, though. After all, the bombing missions carry a lot of weight besides bombs, and he had so many. He was at the induction station the same week I was there, so doesn't have any more time than I have. It's just that oak leaf clusters for fliers count more than battle stars. We definitely have four now, so my 76 doesn't look too bad. The airmen did lots in this war, and his crews really did their part. Still, it makes me a little fed that they get so much attention when guys on the ground take so much and get so little credit sometimes.

The way the papers read all the big fellows have gotten to the states already. I knew they'd get a leave, but not so soon after all was over. There must be something in the air. I have such big hopes of making it this summer. I won't be worth a darn if they take us to the other part and don't go by way of the states.

No schools have started yet. We're still just playing around, eating, using up supplies, not doing anything much. We have lectures in the morning, then in the afternoon play ball, sun on the Danube or go swimming, at 4:30 half an hour of infantry drill before retreat, chow at 5:30, then it's lazing around till movie time at 9:00, which isn't every night. It doesn't get dark here until 'way late, 10:30 at times. I expect things to get popping soon, though, and do hope it's toward the states. The states. All I can think of.

Can't I come home soon?

––––––––––

To his disgust, the Secretary of War turned down a proposal to discharge soldiers under the age of forty ("Darn. I'll miss out here, too.").

Stars and Stripes, following the suicide Himmler had cleverly managed in prison, reported that his brain and a death mask of "the hangman" of the Reich were being sent to the crime lab at Scotland Yard for examination along with information obtained from the Russians about Hitler's death.

Patton, the student of Civil War tactics who had converted tank drivers into cavalrymen mounted on mechanical horses, scheduled a visit to the celebrations in Los Angeles, and 10,000 GIs and war brides landed in New York as the Trumans began to redecorate the White House. The presidential desk henceforth would stand in front of the window in the Oval Office and the piano from the Monroe room in the chief executive's study (in case he wanted to practice

"Missouri Waltz"?). Bess's bedroom, formerly Eleanor Roosevelt's, would be dove gray with touches of red while Margaret's blue sitting room would adjoin a bedroom freshly painted shell-pink. Fewer pictures around, though. Harry was a plain man from the Midwest, not an art expert.

With half a war still to win, Americans everywhere longed to get back to what passed for "normal."

———————

All I think about now is just how long before we'll get enough priority to catch the boat home. There's some talk of an extra five points which would give me 81, which is flying high and coming the hard way, too. I've come to think on the lighter side of things and have faith all will turn out.

You asked if we took part in the Battle of the Bulge. We did, actually, because we were at Metz when it all happened. What comes but march order and we whiz back to Pont-a-Mousson for a while longer, then got more action there than we did before. You should have seen how the frogs (Frenchmen) fell out to welcome us back. We'd been in their town so many months. Then we moved on anyway.

I wanted to tell you of so many of our important missions, but couldn't because of the military value. It's not too romantic at times and may be important only to us in certain ways, but you may enjoy hearing, though we didn't see as much close action as the infantry.

We were in the counterattack at Avranches and did some major firing one night in particular. We had only one highway in shape for supplies and one night the Luftwaffe really came out and lit us up with flares. We almost burned the bones out of those 90s. Still bombs dropped of all kinds, even personnel bombs. One battery was hurt badly, but we hardly had a flare over our area. Still with our radar we could give them plenty of trouble. By the way, did I ever tell you the 411th is tops in the Third Army for planes brought down? Only 40s and 50s outfits are ahead of us, and they should be. We, being in 90s, rate higher with 47 planes for certain shot down and 25 or 30 not known for sure.

The other important position was at the Seine for crossing the river. We actually got more planes there, but to me the Avranches position was more important because if those roads and bridges had been knocked out the counterattack would have been tough. The German tanks came within two kilometers of C-Battery and turned back. I think every acre was covered with field artillery. It's known to be the greatest field artillery push in history.

One other incident which is too good to keep, around V-Day our group was given orders not to fire at any planes coming over only to give themselves up. They were getting away from the Russians, too. We had not received the notice it was V-Day. Still we couldn't fire. Late in the afternoon all kinds of old jalopies the Germans could scrape up were trying to get back out of the reach of that Red Army and maybe do some sabotage, too. We'd stood it as long as we could all day, but I'd not been able to understand since supposedly it was not V-Day. We had so many flares and a flare gun, but knew if we brought a plane down in that area headquarters would raise the devil. There seemed to be some certain area they were flying to and giving themselves up. Still we wanted to have a part. As it was getting late, I mentioned to one of the fellows about going away from our position and shooting a flare to attract the drunken dopes. Since we were stationed on a German air field they'd come down. No sooner than the boy was out there, here came a plane. He shot two flares and "toot sweet" the pilot started circling. He came in and landed just as though it was his own field and came out with a "Heil Hitler" salute which was knocked down by someone, I don't know who, in all the excitement. He landed about a mile from our equipment, so by the time I got there the area was covered with G.I.s. Our fellows got the loot, though, off the 12 prisoners. No one knows yet why the plane came down in that area except you. How's this for fun on V-Day?

If Patton was not to go to the Pacific, would the vaunted Third Army now turn into mere housekeepers? The impeccable, knife-creased, well-polished, hand-tooled appearance of their general and the similar discipline he required of his troops also suggested that they would be good on that job as well. ECLIPSE, the occupation plan, had them so marked. Germany would literally have to be raised from the ashes as at Munich nearby, where the son of author Thomas Mann, in exile for twelve years, found his lovely city dead and an unfamiliar girl sleeping on a mattress on the balcony of his bombed-out home.

All too soon the 411th which had contributed so brilliantly to the solution of the war found itself part of the problem of peace. Having survived the shortages of gas and ammo and the boredom of K-rations, they faced an unexpected new pinch - hunger.

Although rations seem to be cut each day now, your hubby seems to keep his waistline. Today the paper says our meat will be cut 10%, and that's some cut because we've been cut before and haven't been getting too much as it is. I don't want to worry you, just want you to know that all you people are doing without at home doesn't come directly to us over here. We've been cut 10% in all our foods. It is such a problem to feed all these people, and each day they seem to take more in to feed. One Sunday we didn't receive enough rations from supply to manage three meals as usual, so had to try to make two good ones out of what we had. There seems to be a let-up in supplies here. Maybe they're trying to get it all toward the other front now. At least they're feeding all the P.W.'s, displaced persons and a few others besides the million or more G.I.'s that eat more than any soldier in the world. I'm not complaining, just stating facts. I can't eat the amount I used to at home after all the

Cs and Ks. The stomach seems not to hold what it used to although we stay as plump as can be. I've tried eating like I used to sometimes, but will have to come back to it gradually.

Life here now is about as easy as it can be in the Army except a few things that get on our nerves. One of the best things we've done away with is those steel helmets. Now we wear only the liners. I seldom put mine on except for infantry drill, and my head has had an exceptionally good rest.

A few days ago one of my buddies was up looking over my room. He went on to say how I had it made, then said something I was glad to hear. "You know, sarge, I'm going to write your wife some day and really tell her how you keep so many pictures around of her." That pleased me so. I'm so at ease in this room because I do just as I want to and do have you all over the place, on the radio, table, walls and little stand in places I can see you everywhere, in bed, sitting at the table and as soon as I open the door and walk in to see you looking at me from across the room. I wouldn't give up any of them.

Sunday will always have that special meaning. Ours now is so much like the ones back in the states that we're bound to wish to be home now. We seem to be so lousy with radios that we have almost every tent fly with music. The music on Sunday even seems to be special and that, too, makes a man blue and homesick. First I thought it was only me, but lots of fellows in the tent have remarked that music makes them blue, yet we don't want to turn it off.

We've almost taken over the little church here. It's such a small one, but has a nice organ and is rather nicely furnished. Most would think all the churches had been destroyed. At least that idea got out about the Heinies. So many were used for all sorts of things in France, but in this country they've been protected. I remember in Metz a large church was used for a warehouse and was filled with trash and all kinds of waste. Even then it made me feel so mean toward these people, and I couldn't get over it the way they'd do that to such sacred places.

I've just come in from about two hours of sunbathing. The tan doesn't seem to stay with you here.

There's constant talk about points and waiting around for transportation home. Two armies will definitely be left here for occupation, and I'd guess they wouldn't be the Third, for one. Maybe a few with high scores will be taken from their outfits and left here until later, then sent home when they can be replaced. I can't think we'll see the Pacific as an outfit.

With the big sea voyage gossip going and coming, then the country you'd see if you came this way, I get to feeling it wouldn't be at all bad to stay here if I had my wife with me.

Stars and Stripes of June 12th warned that though General Stilwell needed 500,000 men to invade Japan, at least with General Bradley as newly appointed head of the Veterans Administration returnees felt they might get a fair shake if enough points gained for time in service and military campaigns ever got them home.

Commenting on Judy Garland's announcement of her divorce from Sgt. Dave Rose and engagement to Vincent Minelli, the Tennessee soldier wryly wrote, "Make up your mind, Judy."

In the Little-Did-He-Know department, Jack Benny and Bob Hope were bound for the ETO to entertain the troops.

I've wondered do I give those people behind your little mailbox trouble? They should hire just one gal to handle your mail, then she could go on "We the People" and tell the world how one hubby loves his wife, and I don't care who knows it. I just want to introduce you all over the place. So many of the fellows remember you. You are very important in this world, see?

What's this about our general's being in the states and having such a good time, too? Well, Patton deserves all the good things he's having and more. Now if he just doesn't go and stick his neck out and say or do something people don't like. Already an article has come out on him telling the kiddies he was talking to some place that they were the soldiers and nurses of tomorrow's war. That would be enough to set the people of America off. Why can't he keep away from his little speeches at times? When he makes statements like that it even makes me angry with him. After all, we happen to have just finished one war we didn't have much fun in. All I hope is that you and I will never take part in another.

Lots of stories come from the states these days. I can't believe some until I hear what you have to say. All we know here is that two fellows leave for home on the 24th by plane. Maybe there's hope for us, too.

———

As 520 B-29s blasted Osaka, Ike, leaving Bradley to sub for him in the ETO, received a tumultuous welcome in Paris, then headed for his American homecoming where he called on President Truman without even carrying his "social" gun. He had hoped to drive around without motorcycles and three armored cars as escort, and when asked by West coast photographers to smile, scowled, "Damn it, I'm no politician." Later he remarked he'd been shot at by more photographers than guns.

The sergeant who longed to see the mighty muddy Mississippi had to settle for the Danube.

———

You'd never believe it, but your man has just whipped himself up a bathing suit. I didn't have any material, so guess what I made it of. A bath towel.

That's not the best for the purpose, but it's white and soft and does look rather neat. I just folded it in the middle, cut the legs by a pattern I'd fitted around me with some newspapers, and measured like Mother used to do with her patterns at home. After I got the size on paper, the cutting was easy. The suit is about the size of the red trunks I had at Wrightsville Beach and is drawn at the top with a parachute cord. It's so comfortable and cool. I may even cover it with a piece of white parachute. There's so little to do I just thought of this to paddle around in here at the camp and down at the Danube. The chute cloth will make it smooth and almost like a bought one. 'Course now that I'm all fixed up I probably won't get the chance to use a bathing suit. You know how that goes. At least I had fun thinking about it and making it and having it just in case. I had to try it on at least fifteen times before I got it to fit. Some of the fellows gave a big "Grrrr" when they saw it.

When you sent me that picture of all the gals at the station, 'course the fellows gave you the biggest compliment of looking the best. If you hadn't been mine, they might have set up a howl for you. You know all the guys can't be wrong. I have other witnesses that I have a special wife.

It's a bit early yet (7:15 A.M.), just waiting out the chow line, so I'll talk with you while waiting for the egg to be turned over. I went for a 250-mile trip yesterday so my fanny is plenty sore. You know how it can be on a train. Well, picture me riding that far in the back of a jeep.

If I could just be at home waiting for you to put out the breakfast on the table.

We've had notice that due to shipment of troops it's almost impossible to get airmails through, so lots of them are going by boat, and thus taking longer. V-mail definitely goes by air, and each trip a plane makes that way I'll always try to keep you up with me, come hell or high water. Like this morning at chow I saw it would be a good while before I got to be fed, so I rushed to the tent and whipped off a little note. I'd been out all day yesterday and was so wind-beaten from the long trip that I couldn't do anything but take a spit bath and crawl in the sack. I was just through writing you as someone hollered, "Hey Rogers, your turn for eggs," so gave it a quick lick and a promise. I've been happy all day thinking maybe a letter would come this way, but nope, it's only the paper boat.

This has been the warmest day so far, and did I enjoy myself this afternoon kicking up my heels in my new swim suit. I even got some whistles as I passed two tents and blushed a little, wishing they'd just go on with their crap game. I don't want to look like a ghost when I come home, so with what tan I get here and a little on the boat, I should be in good shape as long as I don't get seasick again. Wouldn't it be wonderful to fly back? At least it wouldn't take nearly as long, and the sickness, if any, couldn't last long either. I don't want to get my hopes up, but the chance is just as good one way or the other, so why not look at the good side?

In the history-learned-later category, it was revealed that all of the 81,000 Japanese killed in the Philippines had either committed suicide or been slain by their own officers and that only heroic defense by the RAF had canceled the invasion of England the Nazis had scheduled for July 2, 1940.

Von Ribbentrop, a likeable man but still a Nazi, had been turned in to the authorities. With long hair and a drooping mustache disguising his very familiar face, he had lived alone in a rented room until recognized by a homesick German soldier.

Paris was still Paris. Once again Parisiennes strolled the boulevards in smart dresses and hats while at the railway station poorly-clad women greeted men still wearing the uniforms of German camps.

For soldier and civilian alike "Man of the Hour" meant "Eisenhower."

Isn't it a pity what a workout all the big boys are getting from the time they set foot in the states until they start back to their theater? Ike got the one he deserved so much, the greatest, naturally, in New York. He must have been worn to a frazzle with all the grinning and handshaking. No man in the world or in the Army today seems to do what that fellow does. I have yet to find a guy who doesn't like him. He is just one of us and will do anything he asks us guys to do. Ike's wonderful, and so are all our leaders, but he's at the top of my list.

His attitude reflected what <u>Stars</u> <u>and</u> <u>Stripes</u> found elsewhere. An infantry tank commander also thought Ike rated the big fuss at home. "He's a good Joe," who'd see to it that your gripes, even a small one like needing an extra blanket, got fixed in a week. You could tell him the truth while he was standing in a jeep at Cassino, and he'd understand. As for Ike himself, slipping back into Washington after the joyous uproar with all the saluting and waving and shaking, "My arm is about to drop off."

German generals now revealed they had never suspected an invasion in North Africa until the fleet actually steamed in. They also knew only a few days into the Ardennes offensive that their effort there was already a failure, but thought they might hold out at the Rhine. Keys to their downfall, they claimed, were inability to stop the Allies around Avranches, where the 411th had withstood the Luftwaffe so stubbornly, and loss of the bridge at Remagen.

Another of those fast and rainy days and we got a little busy again, which I don't like any more since the war in Europe was over. What we do seems to amount to so little. As your watchful blue eyes have seen by the APO, we have moved again and not into anything too permanent, <u>I hope</u>. I can't tell you the place yet, can't even find the right spelling of the town. It's about the worst one would want now. I'll let you know in a few days what this hole is really like. I went two times with the captain to look over a position down closer to the Austrian border, which would have been the most wonderful set-up we could have. Instead, our position was changed to this.

———

With peace declared, calm descending gradually over the continent, and the news from the states so nearly normal that Shirley Temple's graduation from high school was a big story, the 411th moved on June 27th from what later seemed like the Riviera compared to a new spot a few miles to the west.

Asked what he remembered as the very worst part of their experience overseas, "Sarge" was expected to choose among the landing on D+3, the fire storm near Ste. Mére Église, the stand-off at Avranches, the plane-shoot at the Seine, or the Bulge near Metz.

He spoke only one word. "Dachau."

———

It seems so much harder now, more than it has ever been with me. We've moved inside the concentration camp at Dachau, Germany, which is enough in itself to tell you what kind of a job and place we have. We don't have bad quarters, though. We've picked the ones the Krauts had while here. The first sergeant and I have one of the best rooms in the whole hotel, nice beds, bath just out our door and the battery office just down the hall. We haven't set up here for anything definite. There's just so many displaced persons, prisoners, and other jobs to be taken care of that the Military Government can't manage it all, so they've formed a security guard all over Germany. We've picked this up for a while.

You'd seen the newsreels and articles about this place. It's all just the way they've given it out to the public, the worst kind of hole in Germany. They were so cruel to the people here, so cruel and inhuman I can't help wanting to punish these sons of _____ myself. How anyone could be that way is beyond me. They've killed, burned, done everything they could think of to poor defenseless Polish people, Jews and civilians.

The fellows that took over the place from the Krauts were still here and have given us all we could stand to listen to. They saw the trains full of the dead. They saw the piles of bodies all over the place and were sick for days just being around it all. It's cleaned up a great deal now. So many people come in on pass and from everywhere to see it that visitors are a problem for us. One look was too many for me, but I wouldn't dare go away without knowing about it to give you the true version.

We got the other battle star. Oh you should see the four stars and three yellow bars on my sleeve. Just let me see your loving face.

Guard duty involved acquaintance with the walking skeletons left behind, bloody imprints of hands on a wall, ashes still in the crematories, even private parts preserved in formaldehyde. Looking down at the ground one might notice a splinter of bone or small piece of body.

Out one day to see the wild dog kennels housing the prisoners' guards and animal tormentors, the soldier from Tennessee climbed a mount to survey the territory only to realize he was standing on a neatly stacked heap of shoe soles, shoulder high and a block or more long, ready for recycling. Buchenwald, Auschwitz, and others gained prominence later, but Dachau was the prototype, a "school for murder" opened in 1933 and the next to last to be shut down.

Stories men of the 411th heard from those who had discovered the place, on a tip from an escapee, told of a 40-car trainload of 2000 prisoners shipped in from Buchenwald to avoid rescue by Patton's troops there. A tank commander, hearing a faint cry from one of the boxcars, had carried out a little man, only survivor of the grisly ride. Starving prisoners already there had struggled out of filth to hug their weeping - and vomiting - angels of mercy only to fall dead before they could touch an American hand.

"Sarge" was right. Dachau stood alone in awful memory. Numbers there were fewer, but the results the same. Surviving prisoners, from all over Europe, but principally from Russia, now needed caring for, guarding, de-lousing, and feeding day after weary day. Many tried to escape. A despondent few attempted suicide rather than return to their homeland.

Fortunately, under the trying circumstances, comfortable quarters, optimistic rumors, and the thought of "one day closer to home" helped to relieve the constant stench, physical and mental, of Hitler's "final solution."

At present, doing what we're doing, we're just waiting for transportation, I think. It looks as though we'll make a high-point outfit out of a few and take the low-pointers out for a new outfit. We've already begun to exchange men. Fifteen of our men have already been transferred. The rule is not to take any with 75 and above. I'm hoping this high-point group will wait for a quota to be sent to the states for redeployment. I'm not even thinking about the possibility of occupation. It may happen, but usually such outfits are being sent to the states, then broken up there. I won't say I'll get a discharge, but may at least have a chance for home. I wouldn't argue.

The fellows that are coming in are men from AAA in 7th and 5th armies. They don't like it one bit being put into the Third. They have so many Hershey bars on them I'm still a rookie. They've seen action in North Africa, Tunisia, Anzio beach while the going was tough, and were the first heavy guns to come overseas at the beginning of the war. They were formed at Camp Stewart, too.

Our low-point fellows from 40-69 were just swapped for the high men. They'll go by way of the states to the Pacific, but all seem happy. All the batteries and headquarters are doing the same as A-Battery, so you can imagine what new faces I'll be seeing. It doesn't do much for the efficiency of an outfit, but they can't look at it that way. From what Congress predicts, the critical scores will be 75-80, so I feel a little better and know this will ease some of your questions, too. The low fellows will get their trip home more quickly and seem happy about that even though most positively to parts unknown to me after that. I just hope I'll make it home in time for your birthday.

I hope I haven't said anything that's not supposed to be said, but I don't think I have. I just plan and figure so and wish I could rush home on a plane overnight.

There can be such bad days, such dreary days, such messy days, such just-another-day-gone-by days until I get mail like I did today. Then it's the most wonderful day I could ask for. It's just the uncertainty with all my buddies taking off and everything in such a rush, almost like an induction center. Lots of the fifteen that went off were on my section, and after all this time I've learned to know and like them a great deal. Two who went felt as we did, pretty sad. Then there were four others, one the sharpest chap of all. When you think about it, we've been together since way back at Davis, so splitting up now makes you wonder what to think. Maybe it's all for the good. I do hope and pray so even more than when the actual danger was around sometimes.

Luckily, this is such a pleasant room. I have all the conveniences of a home, a nice radio that will get New York and Boston at times and every station in Europe as well. If I get to being lonely and thinking too much after taking a shower or reading or listening to music, we take a walk. Any of the buddies will go if I just say, "Let's go." Then I'll wash out a few shorts and socks. I've gotten some displaced persons (men, of course) to do my laundry and pressing. I fixed this room up, too. The place had such puny pictures I took them down and have placed so many of yours around. I just counted. I didn't realize I had ten of you around, four around the mirror and two of my favorites in color on the wall plus others on the table in front of the mirror.

You asked about your coming over here. If I'll be here a year I'll let you know, and you can make arrangements. All we want is to be together, here or there.

We always made such a day of the Fourth at home. Here it was just another day of work while you may be having a quiet, restful day at the beach, I hope. I'd even forgotten it was the national holiday until about nine o'clock.

I have no way of saying how that bad news from the Pacific hit me. That man was the very first of our boyhood group to be drafted, and I thought he'd have plenty of points and be out soon. The last time I saw him was at the induction center, and he'd been in a while then. I even wrote home asking if they'd heard anything about his coming there soon. To be in combat for the first time in all these years, then go like that is awful.

Lots of things come to me now that I'd never bring up if this hadn't happened. If anything happened to me, I'd want you to know what to think and do. I've often thought why couldn't a body be sent back to the loved one instead of being left here, but that's almost impossible. I've wanted you to wait until all possible sources had been looked into, all efforts made until you are satisfied I wasn't coming back. Don't give up on the first flash. It won't be true. There's so many ways a fellow could be jerked up and away from all outside connections over here. He could be a prisoner, he could be somewhere no one knows about, but think he might be dead just because they couldn't find him. Just believe always I will come back. I have made my promise that I will.

I've raided a warehouse and sent stuff you'll be plenty surprised to see. I even sent some safety pins in case there's a shortage there or if we have quadruplets some day. Since the roll of elastic is so big, I know you can't use it all, but maybe some of the people at the station need some if their panties are beginning to slip by now. If you had me there, you'd twist my nose for saying that.

With all the shipping space so full of Third Army men coming home, the box will probably reach you about Christmas. I was a bit surprised at your getting the coins I sent so soon, and am glad you're making a bracelet out of them. I'd even thought about making some holes in them myself. I was afraid I'd misplace them or would have brought them home in this musty money belt I keep in the bottom of my duffel bag. I think some think I'm a miser.

Something else I sent was a belt made out of all the different insignia the Krauts use on their uniforms. If you ever want to be an eyeful, just put that on and all the zoot suiters will follow you for blocks.

Today I went down to the Austrian border again. This time I found some cards to give you an idea of the lovely country you will see if I pull occupation. I thought on the way back here if I were forced to stay for years, I'd want you to see all this. It really is the prettiest area in the land. Just picture borrowing a jeep and running down for a three-day pass of swimming in a lake, horseback riding, canoeing, fishing, and just sitting and lying around in the beautiful area old Hitler enjoyed himself at.

The P.W.'s and displaced persons here are covered with lice, fleas and crabs. I'm taking good baths each day and dusting with louse powder. Still, when anyone speaks of crabs, I begin to itch and wonder. I'd like to get out of this place before I get too crabby in any way.

I've found a good radio for fifteen bucks. I'll make that back, though, if I suddenly slip off to some place I can't carry it to. Otherwise I'll bring it home. The battery set is weakening, so I can use this one now. It can be switched from 110 volts to 220, which they use in Europe mostly. You can almost buy a new radio for what you could get a new part for.

Did you hear about the postmaster in Elkmont, Alabama? The office in Wilmington should pattern after his operation. He believes that Sunday is the loneliest day in the week for parents, wives and sweethearts with men overseas, so he decided to do something about it. He now opens all his little boxes for at least six hours on Sundays to deliver all the incoming mail, especially from servicemen. I'd have the box full of me, then come out and climb in your pocket.

Since the Queen Elizabeth is doing such a super job of getting all the fellows home, she whips up mail service, too. Now that they don't have to vary the course every few miles or minutes as we had to and can go straight through, I'd imagine she could make the trip in four or five days. This time of year would be wonderful for traveling. I've got to make it soon. Two letters arrived dated just a week ago. How's that for service?

Already the month's half over, just a long stretch of yearning for home all the way. I was in my glory, though. I had waited all day long, and finally it came. That mail had so many of your blue letters sailing toward me. I'll always remember how they looked, so needed in a life of not knowing what will come next.

In January we had to go back and give support on the bridges in the Ardennes, just A-Battery, mind you, so we should get points for that campaign, too. If the points for discharge should be lowered to, say, 80 (Whee!), then I would have a chance to at least get to the states. Maybe stay there until the war with Japan is over. Let's do like we did when I was pulling for a furlough, keep our hopes high and everything crossed for good luck.

As we drive back over some of the places we've been to, people have started cleaning up, and some areas look really livable again. Lots of the large cities are so slow in getting started, even straightening up, though.

If you come over, maybe you could talk this language. I thought French was bad to manage, but here some of the displaced persons talk so fast that I can't make out much but their signs.

Just give me enough rope, and I'll tie myself to you forever.

Now that you have our map you can really tell just where we are, every possible town and village we might be shoved into. Already I know you've picked out Dachau, which is not too small a place itself. We have the displaced men in our mess hall now to clean up, wash pans and take the honor of peeling spuds away from the K.P.'s. They do a good job for us for just what they get to eat.

Something funny happened at chow last night. We got off on home and the talk got around to you. Remember the two fellows you got change from to use the phone at the service club? I really frowned and had them going, thinking I didn't know about it. One of them was guying me about now the water was warm out at the beach I'd have to be bothered about you and the coast guard. I told them you didn't play around with anyone but one Army man, and that was me. I even told them about choosing the wrong legs in the picture taken at the station. One man said he might miss guessing his girl's legs, but made it sound like he'd never forget yours. I gave him a look under pulled-down eyebrows, but he caught the joke. They even wanted to see the picture, but I'd changed my shirt and didn't have my "Private Property" with me at the time. We just sat there taking lots of time eating, not doing too much. Finally a K.P. came in the tent (mess hall) and said, "You guys going to shoot the bull all night?" We took off and finished up this morning at breakfast.

Your man will love a home where you'll be the lady of the house.

Something else I've sent you should have reached there by now, the bracelet I got way back in Normandy at Mont St. Michel. Also I found a German cap with an eagle on it. The cap wasn't worth keeping, but I pulled off the pin and shined it up for you. You haven't mentioned these and are always faithful about telling me, so I hope these are not lost. I was so pleased about your getting the coins. That bracelet you made of them covers about all of the places I've been to here.

There can only be two things for me now. Not a furlough, not a pass, not a day off, but either a discharge or to be stationed in the states. I'd give up anything, go any place, lose all I have just to be with my wife.

The good news of the day is that we definitely have five more points making eighty in all. In spite of all the sweating things may turn out rather well. At least I shouldn't be sent to the Pacific with that many.

I have something else, too, I can't keep much longer even if it doesn't go through. Four others and I were put in for a Bronze Star for exceptionally good work from the beach to the end of the war. Know what I'd have then? Eighty-<u>five</u> points! I'm not too sure, but we are in category four that may let us be shipped to the states intact as a group with redeployment of those without enough points. Right now we're just being shoved around attached to some infantry division on paper.

In a few days we'll be out of this hole, "Camp Dachau," and oh what a mess it was. We've all hit it about as hard here on guard as we did ever. One poor fellow took it all rather hard. Anyhoo, we'll be out in two or three days. I can't think of the name of the town we'll move into.   Two of us were over there today and have ourselves a very good home picked out.

Doing that, and with all these homes available, I want to be in a house with you.

Sorry your Fourth wasn't what it should have been. I'd hoped you would have lots of fun at the beach, but know how hard it can be with just a crowd and having to be so nice when the heart aches so.   If we ever get so we don't have that, something will be wrong.

I've had something new made for civilian life.   You won't have to worry about a ration stamp for my first civvie shoes.   There's some pretty expert cobblers here that have done nothing for years but make shoes for the Krauts, getting some of the best leather I've seen.   I had these P.W.'s make me a pair of shoes. I've never had a specially made pair before, designed only for me.   They are a little short, but I can remedy that.   They were tickled with a few cigarettes, and the shoes are a job done just for me.   We guarded them, yet they wanted to do what they could for us. These were just old men taken into the army and made, like us, to do what they were told to do.   All S.S. men will be treated as they treated our men, questioned, given a chance to make a confession, after that nothing else for them but be shot by a firing squad.   The P.W.'s are being discharged today. So many have left already and they don't want to leave. Imagine me being that way.   They'll be hungry, no doubt, before they hit their homes.   Still, I'd jump at any chance of getting out of here.   The shoes will polish unusually well and will come in handy if the boat started toward home.

I haven't talked to a gal in so long I may blush when I see you.

If Dachau was the worst, Furstenfeldbruck, their final station in Germany, was hardest to spell.   With the stress and painful visions of the death camp left behind, he hoped for relaxation and rejoicing.   As

Patton had found on different terms, rewards always appeared just as a crisis loomed needing grit-the-teeth attention. Before the LST to Normandy they had been fed, to their surprise, the best they'd eaten in a long time. Before a sudden move, there was an unexpected movie. Before the Bulge and entry into Germany, a trip to Paris. This time, at last, only R. and R., rest and recreation of outstanding dimensions before the long voyage home.

We've had our times the last few days, but what good riddance to get out of that camp we've seemed to call our own for so long. It's seemed for a while we were just side-tracked, and what a place to be stranded in. When we first went to Dachau it was a heap big mess, but the fellows there before us said we hadn't seen anything compared to what they had earlier when they first took over. That one place in Germany will always linger in my mind much more than I want it to, but someone had the job to do. You know how the good old 411th is at that, so we kept up our reputation in that place, too. At least we didn't hear any complaints. Although some of the staffs didn't catch too much of the guard duty, they caught the other details. Since we haven't got equipment now to care for, we've broken into three platoons. I'm the third platoon sergeant. All the others are new and really don't know the men. I have lots of my old fellows with me.

The longest thing we'll have to do tomorrow is move into our new homes. We've picked some nice ones again and will enjoy a little more freedom. I have about 21 men in my house. It really is a killer. I took a few of them around this afternoon to look it over, and they really were pleased. We don't do quite like we did when the war was going on. Then we just gave the people an hour sometimes, or even less, to get out. We usually just picked what looked good. Of course, we still do now, but have to go through a long procedure if the people are still in the house. The place now is taken over when the other outfit leaves. They move out, we move in, so the people haven't a chance of getting their house back any time soon. It's a bad way and certainly hard on them after they've had a hard time of their own. Still, we don't intend to live in poor, unhealthy places. They try to raise a stew, but it doesn't do them much good. If we need a house, we see the Military Government and they let the people know we want the place. You can see how we'd feel if someone came and took over all our furniture that we'd saved and planned for. Still, we can't let ourselves go or they'll be running the place and we'll be out in the cold and begging for their permission.

This place doesn't do me any good, I'm afraid. Some say this new spot is the best set-up we've ever had, but what I'm hoping is that it'll turn out as well as it did for the other fellows that were here. They left for France this morning. You know what that means for them. Three of ours were transferred to the 45th Division and were told they were headed for the states. They'd been here about six weeks and did very little but relax and get in shape for the wonderful trip home. Let me know when you first hear of that outfit on your news ticker. I want to get some idea of how long it takes them to get to the states.

We saw a U.S.O. show today, not the best, but the music, songs and thoughts of home gave me a warm shiver, one I haven't felt in ages. It had been so long I thought I was getting too hard in all this. I don't favor Jack Benny over Bob Hope, but he got across lots of laughs. I borrowed some opera glasses to look at Ingrid Bergman's nose more closely to see if hers was like yours. It does favor yours in a nice way, especially at the end, but I'm afraid she has you beat a bit in the length. She was a little nervous in such a show, honest. I was a bit surprised with her being such a popular star now. She seemed a bit out of place, but posed for pictures and showed Jack Benny the difference between him and Charles Boyer and Clark Gable. She even put him down to the floor to show how strong she was. Oh for a camera to have gotten that picture. All the music was grand, too. The G.I. boys really backed him up.

The trouble is, even here, it's one more hour wasted when you aren't in these minutes.

Today was Mother's birthday. Away back I wrote her a special letter that wished her all the happiness in the world. I can do so little now. Once we get home all our special days will be so grand.

You'd love this little village. It's the nicest we've been in in such a long time. We like the swimming pool made from a lake that flows through the town. It's a little rundown, but a grand place to sun-bathe and take it easy on our time off, and we do have much more of that than we did at Dachau. We have about 30 men at road blocks, P.W. camps, important installations and others scattered around. Right now we're attached to the 90th Division planning definitely to pull occupation.

It's so hopeless until the disgusted feeling gets to feeling regular. I think of home far more than I should, maybe, but what's to keep me from it? I've only a V-mail for the last few days and look for your letters tomorrow.

Now what could be wrong? Those boats and planes are bound to be coming back after taking fellows home. One man hasn't had a letter from the states for seven weeks, so I shouldn't worry. I know if anyone writes, you will, and I'll have a blue one soon.

You've already looked at the play bill I've enclosed and know why spirits are high otherwise. My, does that Bob Hope get around. We didn't even know the joker was in Europe. Our pal was going to be in town or close by. I actually couldn't believe it. I'd walk five miles to see the guy, not even thinking about the gals he might have in the show. You would have pushed your way right up with me.

I borrowed a camera and filled his eyes with all sorts of shots. By the time I get the pictures back I hope to be sitting in a sofa chair with you, both of us listening to him on the radio at home.

The show went on at 6:30 on time. All U.S.O. shows start on time. It never fails. He came walking out just as nonchalant as could be as if he owned that C-47 he came over on. He gave us a description of the states, even bringing North Carolina into the picture. He had so many jokes on Crosby and Sinatra. The girls did a wonderful job, too, singing and dancing. I can't believe yet that I've seen Bob Hope, Jack Benny and Ingrid Bergman all in the same week! Oh who knows, I may pack my bag for the states any day with this kind of luck.

After he'd joked and danced all over the place he actually stood around, not like so many, run off and hide. I ran up on the platform and was only three feet from him. I wanted to hang around and talk with the American girls, too. It had been so long since I spoke to one. I went over to the truck and told the fellows it wouldn't be leaving to go back for at least fifteen minutes if they wanted to get autographs. Just jump out and let's go. They were all for it. I thanked one ordinary little girl who did a great job with the accordion. All were the friendliest I've ever seen in a show, especially the U.S.O. type. Maybe it's because they are trying to reach us plain G.I.'s instead of so much of the brass. One asked what kind of money the Luxembourg bill was. I had it in hand to get Hope's autograph on it, so couldn't give it away, but ran for his car. It looked like he was trying to get away from the Rogers claw. Just before I got to him a fellow who only had a roll of toilet paper to autograph shoved that in front of Bob. He jumped at it like he hadn't seen any since leaving the states. He said, "How about signing my name on one sheet and taking the rest? My supply sergeant hasn't caught up with me," and he took a small square sheet off and tucked the rest in his pocket, a whole half roll.

Today I want to start toot sweet for that airport. It's not too far off, and I could be a stowaway. All

I'd have to do is dress up like a Wac or nurse and could probably get all the way home before anyone knew I was a wolf instead of a wolverine. The crew would be so tickled at getting to talk to a U.S. gal they'd lose their grip.

You'd love to live in this house or even in this large room I have all to myself. The house itself isn't too good, but the room is well-furnished with a basin in the corner where I can shave and clean up in a jiffy. I have two beds, one that will be used for a buddy of mine if he ever gets back. For now it's open to any visitor (but don't get me wrong there). I even have a glass door to a balcony, the mess hall only a few blocks away and the wonderful swimming hole about ten blocks off.

The most I do is sunning, fooling around the water to keep cool, more sunning, then seeing a movie, keeping the patrol of the guard, driving all over the country in a jeep, eating hearty and filling out, not fat, but in the right places. I feel wonderful, only so lonesome. Usually I'm in bed by ten, but we didn't get much rest last night until almost 2 o'clock with some darn D.P.'s causing disturbance in peoples' farm yards and gardens. They must have been really hungry to steal like that. I'm wondering what they will do this winter if they don't start work pretty soon.

It seems my goose is cooked for staying in this outfit. No more points do I have officially, so all men below 79 are expected to be shifted any day now. It may lead to anything, who knows? We might get in another outfit and head for the states for reserves. I won't even think now, just let things take their course.

I have patience, but things just reach a height at times. Knowing you're waiting and I have you to come home to, I can stay happy a while longer.

Your man was loaded with blue letters today - three of them. I'll never forget how you fit in these long lonely arms, even measured to the boys the other day about the size you would be if you were there.

I'll be a good provider once I get out. I can already feel it, wanting to get out like I used to at home. I worked then, too, but didn't have such a good reason to. Now I won't wonder what's the use but will hit the morning with a smile, a glow that will stay all day.

I've been good today, too. Been to church twice. Yep, we had 11:00 o'clock and 7:00 o'clock services. This chaplain is so different in handling the men. They all have their ways, but this man does such a thorough job of letting us know how we might be slipping. The temptations are so great over here, and he knows it. He's even got a director of music that sings wonderful solos, and the organist is as good as any. Now if a few more would get interested we'd be fine. We use the church in town which is old, but well decorated and has a good organ. Oh won't it be good to get back to our own community and work in our church together?

We have a new style jacket now like the one Ike wears. Mine fits so well, trim and yet comfortable. Now to get the stripes on, the hash marks, the overseas bars and insignia. Won't I look like a judge? Did you know it's been twelve months since I had on a tie? Now they've issued me one I had to think hard before I remembered how to tie it. That's a laugh.

Head to the Army store and get me one of the caps I used to have. I don't like this G.I. kind. The Army does remarkably well on some things, so poorly on others. Like a dunce I turned my favorite in while in England, so it's the G.I. one now. We can only wear these after 5 o'clock, but if I go on pass to the Riviera or Berchtesgaden or Brussels, and passes are coming up now, I could wear the cap and be so comfortable. It's not too bad here, but I'd like to see the Riviera while I'm at it.

The soldier in the new Eisenhower jacket had worshipped in what has been called one of the world's

478

most beautiful churches. Some DP (Displaced Persons) camps, hospitals, and roadblocks intruded on the scene, and an airstrip contained a few badly damaged remnants of the world's first jet planes tested there. Otherwise the lovely pastoral town was relatively untouched.

For entertainment, via a talent agency in Munich, the GIs had a new club with orchestra every night and performers imported twice a week.

With the help of another sergeant, I was in charge at a club the 411th has gotten up for enlisted men only. It's a place to go. They have beer along with the music, but I enjoy that and being with the gang. How they drink so much of this strong stuff is more than I can see. It surely doesn't taste good to me, but they seem to love it and have fun.

The U.S.O. camp show group had "Here Today" at the Tactical Air Command Theater. I'm afraid the public at home wouldn't like this play morally. Some pretty rough jokes that wouldn't go over anywhere except maybe a G.I. show, but I enjoyed it so. Lots of good laughs. It's the first play I've seen since Memphis.

If he thought that play was questionable, he must have been astounded at the recent reviews in Stars and Stripes, including pictures. Its tribute to Paris as a "lovely lady" carried a full page of "Louvre-ly" gals - Venus de Milo, Rembrandt's "Bathsheba," and nudes by Ingres and Rubens to supply a little French culture. Brussels, however, was described as a rollicking, lusty hussy whose wine, women and song (plus cognac) made California's historic Barbary Coast brothels seem like a Sunday School picnic, strawberry festival, or taffy pull. Well, "culture" is relative.

At the opposite pole, the Passion Play's cast was reassembling at Oberammergau. A hundred actors were missing - John the Baptist a captive of the Africa

Corps, the younger Jacob an Allied prisoner, Philip and Andrew both dead, and the play's director held as the kingpin of Goebbels. Others, including the Christ who had to spend thirty minutes on the cross, were now too old to carry on the tradition, but the Virgin Mary, though 39, still qualified for her part, being unmarried.

As for war matters, Marshall Petain, on trial for surrendering France to the Nazis at Vichy, was either trying to save his country or aiming for power for himself, depending on one's point of view. On the Allied front the most powerful military machine ever assembled continued to disintegrate. Alliances on a personal level were another subject entirely.

You may wonder what my feelings are now that the rule against fraternization has been lifted. You know my opinion about these people already. Still, as we are now, and like we in America get, I can see us slipping and wanting to be too easy on them already. The very first day of the ban-lifting I was out in a jeep going somewhere and could tell just by riding along that something new had come about, especially with the broads after sundown. I've become accustomed to people in Europe giving the G.I.'s the once-over because at one time they were a rarity not much seen in a town, but it's gotten to a different stage now. I realize it's been nothing for the women to have babies for Hitler and throw themselves at the Kraut soldiers, but do they intend to keep on doing it to build the country back? And I'll bet in a few months there'll be so many with a child on the way, and it'll be some American's. I thought France was bad this way, but they are good there compared to the Krauts. The law didn't help much, but it did keep the civilians from being so bold and men on constant guard of disobeying the regulation. I was disappointed when Ike let down the gap and the general discipline that kept us going strong. While we were at Pont-a-Mousson, nine girls there became expectant mothers.

Something else has come up about the 411th club. When you have a band, dancing and drinks, naturally outsiders will be there if you don't watch out. That calls for more civilians there. The band and a few frauleins make some have a good time, but I'd like to keep out outsiders who just make suckers of us, then laugh at us behind our backs. I'll just have to do my job when it falls to me and be as tough as I can without spoiling it for the fellows. I don't owe these people anything, but they owe us many months of our lives away from home and those we love. Maybe I've got it wrong, but I don't think so.

You and I always get so involved in talking about things that it makes life real and interesting.

Something I forgot to tell you the other day. You know how Bob Hope makes cracks about Bing Crosby. Well, the fellows at the base had one on him when Hope came out on stage to do his show. They'd drawn a picture of Crosby looking his way and nailed it up on a post so Bob could see it when he came out of the tent beside the stage. He went on for a minute, but when he finally saw it, he grabbed everything he could find to throw at the picture of his buddy, even a violin case.

You hit so close to us today when you mentioned the 38th Brigade. We were attached to that outfit all the way from England to here, even in Germany. We lost them a few months ago. They were transferred to the Military Government. Now anything could be expected of them. I expect that boy you mentioned is about right when he says he's about to start home. The A.A. that's doing its training will get eight weeks here, then maybe to the states for reserve duty. These and some who went to other units will probably be in the states by the last of September, but here's one who wouldn't give up hope of going some way or other. Right now this battalion is still getting quotas of high-point men toward home. Six left last week, now thirteen are up to leave any time. They've cut the heck out of battery strength. We don't have any men at all. They won't start a new outfit, I'm almost sure. Why should they with all the A.A. men they need, and where are the Jap planes? You never hear of them now. All I can see for low-pointers is to pull occupation for a while until we get stale and are relieved. I still have hopes of five more points for the Bronze Star.

By August 2nd other changes had come about. "We pay for our P.X. rations now," he wrote. "In combat we got them free." Subscriptions to <u>Yank</u> and <u>Stars</u> <u>and</u> <u>Stripes</u> required payment as well, a seemingly ungracious development in light of previous service.

And Patton was in trouble again. Although he had purposefully included some Jewish soldiers in interrogations of various Nazi prisoners, with no political considerations whatever he had managed to flaunt a SHAEF directive by employing Nazis to restore railroads and other public works vital to the rehabilitation of Germany. With no other persons in the nation trained or educated enough for the job, his logical mind assumed that just as strong offense in combat saved lives, so using the best - nay, only - resources available made sense. He saw the furor he raised as being "a Nazi thing," like a fight at home between Republicans and Democrats. SHAEF thinking otherwise, Eisenhower had to make good on his "Just one more time" pledge and transfer the impenitent sinner from his beloved Third to the Fifteenth to cool his heels writing campaign reports and bitterly ponder Ike's "ingratitude."

For those whose release from the Army had yet to arrive, at least the service offered a pass to Lake Konigsee with a side trip to Berchtesgaden where, like Hitler, one could look out from the "Eagle's Nest" over a whole world at one's feet.

There may be a few looking over my shoulder tonight. Not in that private room I like so well for writing. I'm spending the night at a lake about two miles from the home of the most hated man on earth, Hitler. It's supposed to be a rest center here, as though we needed one from such work as we've done lately. Anyhoo, it's getting away from it all, and they have good eats here.

Any time you see that Red Cross on the stationery you can almost count on it that I've taken a pass away from the gang for a few days. I've been having a fine restful time full of nothing but good things a U.S. soldier might enjoy. I can't see why more fellows don't come down here. To me it's a soldier's paradise. 'Course my judge of a good time may be simpler than some. I can't see much to Hitler's home, but will never want a better three days than Konigsee as a resort. If anyone ever refuses the chance, I'll certainly have my name at the head of the list.

It's not much of a rarity now to sleep on a good bed. I have the best there could be back at the battery. Still it's wonderful to have clean sheets and all the conveniences around. We get up at 7:15, have the bestest breakfast with all the trimmings, then take it easy for a spell. We decided we'd better go up to Hitler's Eagle's Nest if we intended to, so off we went this morning in our weapons carrier. What a place it was. I've never been so high, never seen so many countries at once, nor have traveled so straight up as we did today. No civilian car of ordinary make could make the grade. It took all that Dodge could do to make it in the lowest gear we had. Why any fanatic wanted such a place is beyond me, and they say he was only up there five times. It's about 7-8 miles up, and do you have to swallow to keep your ears from popping!

I'm enclosing a map of the Pacific war. Hope you will never have to use it with me like you did the one in the ETO, but since you are in radio it might help there, too.

I'm glad you've gone ahead and inquired about the prospect of wives in Europe. Frankly, I don't believe they'll let any outfit stay in occupation long enough to let wives come over, though. That's what President Truman led us to believe in the paper today. Maybe this is high-minded guessing, but to me it's better than letting the American people settle this place instead of making the German people do it.

I'll keep on going somehow even if it kills me. I'll never give up. Besides, I just thought, "It'll be my birthday before I get back." Hope there's mail waiting.

You've just about timed things to the day. How it has all worked out so beautifully on my birthday is beyond me and all to your credit. I was so glad to get back this afternoon. Had expected a few letters, but not the package. You make such a big time of special days.

I've just thought hard of home all day and wondered if you sang "Happy Birthday" as we always did. My box was so full of surprises, each wrapper with "Congratulations" or "Surprise!" All the good soaps I love, the candy, even a bottle of shave lotion, and you knew the nuts would be a favorite, so tender and good. The sunglasses you'd already sent are the most helpful thing I can use now in all this glare.

You just put that special touch, write that special letter, make my day full of happiness.

It's one of those damp afternoons when you can't do much but think of home, but I'm in a super mood. The greatest thing about the big bomb came to us last night on the radio. My heart stood still for a second. It was the surprise we've been wanting so long. It might just have taken Truman's talk to the Big Three to get things going. Then this morning the very first thing we heard was that the Russians had started the drive in Manchuria. All the more help to bring us home more quickly. Nothing was in the paper, though, but the blast that is destroying cities, people, and all the things that get in its way for miles around. It's a terrible thing to take lives and destroy a country like that, but war had to be this way if they can't see unconditional surrender, and that's the only thing we intend to offer. Here the yellow _____ are, crying and asking other countries to plead with the U.S. for mercy. They claim the bomb is inhuman. It's too bad they can't see more will come if they don't give up to this last chance. President Truman will speak tonight. I've only heard him poorly, and he was excited that first time.

I thought all the while ETO men would get top consideration as to points, but they've decided at the last minute we must be second-rate and Pacific men will come first. Our points will be re-counted as late as January. By then they'll probably change the system and leave us holding the bag again. Still, with the war in the Pacific acting the way it is, anything can happen.

The peace feelers are flying fast tonight and have us all excited over just what will take place. I'm afraid to make a bet either way. It seemed too good to be true for anything like the whole war in the other half of the world to be ending so suddenly.

A second chance to visit Hitler's mountain retreat furnished an opportunity to see Goering's home as well. The art collection looted by "the Nazi blimp" could not be viewed, however. A professor from Cambridge was sorting out paintings by Van Gogh, Renoir, Rembrandt, Rubens, Del Sarto, and Van Dyck, and others were thought to be stashed in the mountains of northern Italy.

I went back to the battery office and a pass for Berchtesgaden was open again, so the sergeant looks at me and says, "Rogers, you are going and liking it." Maybe he didn't know it, being turned down by so many for the opportunity, but it's the best favor he's done me in a long while. I like to come and go, have fun while I'm at it instead of hanging around a room.

I came down here Thursday morning to Konigsee more in charge than I had planned, as I should have guessed. There were twelve fellows from our battalion spending three days down here. I call it "down" but don't know why unless it seems we came down so many hills on the way. We also climbed a great many mountains, so why I say "down" I don't really know. It's just enough time to get tired and still enjoy yourself.

I've been in bed by twelve for so long now. It's funny to miss a night's sleep like we used to all the time. It doesn't seem possible we could have actually lived that way.

I even made the trip up to Hitler's nest again along with Goering's house and lots of the buildings Hitler used there. I was glad I came back because I hadn't seen Goering's home last time. After you go to so much trouble to go up a steep climb the first time you don't care too much about doing it again, but can't miss out on such famous things. You know how Americans will plan as tourists to do this in the years to come.

You beat me all to pieces with fishing. You do as well as those gals who've been along the coast all their lives, then a little priss from those Tennessee hills comes along and, not even caring, just catches fish. We'll build a lake at home and while you fish, I'll sit in the shade and do all the fanning.

I want to be excited and cheer my lungs out, but it's not time yet, it seems. I thought something was in the air Wednesday night. When I heard the late news from London the announcer said, "There is an important announcement to be made in the next 72 hours and the Japanese officials want all the people to stand by." Well, after the Russians' strike and the bomb that gave them so much hell, I wanted to hear something to the effect of it all, but was surprised when we got up here Thursday around 12:30 and found the Japanese had offered to surrender, but wanted the Emperor to stay in place. I'd like him out, but I do think we could handle them through him if it means saving lives and the love and happiness of so many people.

The news came in about people in London throwing up a storm about the war's being over. They've jumped the gun this time, and the way they mentioned it so often, it must have been the Yanks who started throwing paper, streamers and sheets, with all kinds of dancing in the streets going on. Since there's an administration office in London, they think the Americans had a part in setting things off. I think they were looking for it, too, don't you? We all want it over so badly. Who could keep the excitement down when he knows this will bring us so much closer to home? If it ends now, I can see no reason why I shouldn't be home this year as I planned. I wish we just knew something so you wouldn't have to send my Santa next month. I hope no one will be mad if I slip in over there and some of my Christmas is over here. I'd love to start back about October, if not sooner. Wouldn't it be wonderful if we could be before some warm fireplace here or in some cool yard there and hear that the war with Japan was over? I think I'd faint.

All day you've had such a hectic time at the station with flashes and bulletins that you've not had time to enjoy the thrill of it all when the end finally came. It's so hard to keep from singing all day, crying, laughing at the smallest things because the war is <u>over</u>.

I'm not nearly the way I thought I would be, nor is anyone in the Army or in any branch. We thought we couldn't keep still when this happened, but we've built up so long, had so many false alarms, been let down so many times until this day isn't made as much of over here as it should have been.

We'd been expecting the news for so many days now. I especially had caught every newscast Munich gave when I was close to my radio. The Japs seemed to be just stalling for time, and it looked as though it would go on for weeks. Still, last night I was on security patrol in one of the villages and came in early on purpose to get the 12 o'clock news. I was unusually restless, couldn't sleep, rolled and tumbled, then dozed off for what seemed no longer than a minute when the phone rang. I almost jumped out of my skin and thought it must be a move or march order. Instead the lieutenant, having got the one o'clock news, said President Truman had made a statement accepting Japan's offer and the war was over. I quickly turned on my radio and ran through the house waking all the platoon. Some jumped out of bed, others said, "Sure 'nough?" with about as much life as a sick chicken. Then some came in and listened to all the commotion on the air. All went back to the sack around two. I turned out the light again and was drifting off to sleep when the phone rang again. This time the celebration seemed to have started elsewhere. I was told there'd be no reveille and chow at 7:30. They wanted us to go ahead and celebrate at that time of night, on what I don't know. I just kept the radio going and heard what London, New York and Chicago were doing. At least the news came at just the time to give the people who wanted to go on a fling the chance to do so. It came to us at 1:00 A.M. Home! I can hardly wait!

In the states the Japanese surrender came to many almost as an anti-climax after the emotional outburst of VE-Day. Perhaps it was the gritting of teeth for another longer, bloodier haul, perhaps partly shock over the unsuspected monster bomb few knew existed. Even the memory of a college trip to the cyclotron didn't register at the time.

Just the feeling of "It's over, over at last." Then "When?" for them. Time had never seemed to go so slowly before.

Do you think I could do any good this late in the game by just talking to myself? It's so draggy getting out on points. Besides, did they give me any points besides just for being a warm body to get me here in the first place? No one could be more essential to home defense, so that's what I'm going to see the chaplain about. Now that the Japs have sent a cry for mercy, I'm going to let everybody hear <u>my</u> cry for a change.

Looks as though plans may work rather quickly on getting a few men out of the service. For a while it seemed the awful war would be long and drawn out and most here had settled themselves down for that, but they didn't know about The Bomb, did they? It came as such a shock to Army, Navy, and all the other branches as well. The news still has the Russians and Japs fighting, and some places have not laid down their arms to Chinese or American forces. The yellow b_____ are so fanatic and untrustworthy there might be many lives lost yet even in the occupation forces. MacArthur is really burned up with the way they have done and is being disobeyed over and over. He will bring them to heel if anyone can.

It'll take about a month or two to get the machinery going for letting us out faster than planned. Still, I wonder if they'll want to discharge so many with plants and ship-building and such like closing down. With only 400,000 scheduled for occupation in this country, there'd be a heap big shipment of troops needing jobs coming in from Europe in the next six months. We're still Category 4, occupation, but keep getting quotas home. Now all systems may have to be revised and re-worked completely.

I don't see why I couldn't get help from the railroad. They've already flown some railroad men home. It might, even with my small experience, be quicker than waiting on points, a system I wish had never been devised. It may work fine for airmen, Navy and Marines, but without three years on ground duty you're sunk. Some who speak good German are even looking into Military Government.

All this time and I've not yet worked out our full name for the years ahead. I'd grown so used to being called "Wesley" until the Army. Just A. on the front, A. Wesley, sounds funny, and they just have me as "Wesley Rogers" at the Illinois Central roundhouse. The bank lists us as "Mr. and Mrs. Alfred W." or "A.W." and the Army as "S/Sgt. and Mrs. Alfred W." How about just "You and Me, Inc."?

Sometimes we get to talking here about what we plan to do in the future. Once I joked that you had such a good job I'd just take it easy and kick up my heels. They got a big laugh, and lots of others wondered if they could just let their wives take care of them.

I've become fond of several things I never really found until I came into the Army, like the seashore, the sun, and boating, both sail and row boats. I also like good music and dances of all kinds, good wholesome fun we'll enjoy together.

In the letters today you'd just had news about the war's end. They seem to be throwing away rationing rather quickly. I'm so glad you and all the home folks can soon have the shoes you need and all the nylons you want. Forget that leg paint, with or without the seam stripe down the back. That's some of what we fought for, the kind of life that makes us feel safe and happy.

I would certainly love a picture of the people on VJ-Day. We seldom get newsreels here. I wanted to be there so badly to celebrate. We didn't do much here. Oh, some got in a happy mood at the club. We had a wine celebration although Ike had wanted two whiskeys each for the Army. Still we fell out and had our little half-hour drill as usual. The Army will never be any different about things if I stay in for thirty years, some things, at least.

What a rambling letter. I want to get home so badly that the other day, talking rather fast, I even said "Wilmington" instead of "Munich."

The chaplain wants to get a choir started here, so I told him I'd done some singing in a community choir and can carry a melody if I have help, but not quartet or part stuff, which I knew he wanted. I got as many men as I could from this battery, but only two showed up at rehearsal, so we're trying a quartet after all. To my surprise it sounds quite good. We worked up a "special" this morning for the eleven o'clock service. Everyone was so amazed. "Why Rogers, I didn't know you could sing," they'd say. The organ helped, too. I was pleased with our efforts, and the chaplain almost did a rumba when we came out of the choir loft. We even have him singing baritone and have fun, doing some good and being willing to help.

I'm so glad you saw part of the war's-end celebration. If we had been at home I would have gotten right up at 1:00 A.M. and driven all the way to Memphis. That's one thing I wouldn't have missed for the world.

Now that the actual shifting has started, I may be home before Nov. 1st. Wouldn't that be something? Orders have come through for all 85s and up to go out Wednesday, and the Division is sending out from 65 down, so I'm planning on getting in there some place.

Our sergeant got one of the Bronze Stars, and we had a big parade yesterday for ten men in the battalion. Only two in our battery got them, and one of them had shipped out. If I have to take new responsibility it won't be for long. All of us 75-pointers should be shipped some place by the middle of September. I'm not saying don't send Christmas, but I'm counting rather hard on being home way before Thanksgiving. I've known this for days and want you now to know which way the wind is blowing, even if I miss it a bit.

Just think. You may be getting mail from me the very day I arrive in New York, and when I call, you won't believe it's me talking. No man could be in higher spirits tonight, but the strain of waiting is really rough, all the waiting for peace and the boat home.

My lonesome heart needs home.

How could anyone at home think just because a man isn't coming back right away he prefers to stay and improve this country? I get riled at a public that's so stupid they know so little about what a G.I. wants and longs for.

Men in the 217th 75-85 have left for the states. Men 80-95 left from our battery today, expecting to be in the states the latter part of October. Over 100 will leave sometime tomorrow. That leaves only 78 men in A-411, which means either throwing the batteries together or we'll just exist on paper. I might even be out by Sunday. Oh how I want to be out of this mess. Tomorrow I'll be in charge with as few non-coms as we could possibly have. The mail orderly supply sergeant left today, so the whole gang is being split to the winds. What makes it really tough is seeing fellows leave the outfit who came in six months after I did. Now they go out, and I'm still here though we trained them and all. I'm still here. Maybe they have one child, and I'm happy for them, but you can imagine why I'm a little leery of the point system.

I need to take my mind off the world tonight. Help!

The long dread has come. The first sergeant has to throw it in my lap whether I'm ready for it or not. I put up excuses, even flatly refused, still orders have to be carried out, and our B.C. didn't order me, but talked sense about the current confusion.

Prospects still look good for 75-80 men leaving this week. I'm one of the high-pointers now and we aren't hurting ourselves with work. Fooling around is more tiring, really. 27 fellows left today. We couldn't start a good fight now if they called on us. We've been together so long it's been rather tough parting here, but after they leave it wears off. I kid them and tell them we'll probably all be on the same boat anyway. It's possible. I don't even feel like myself these last few days. You know how you can think about a thing until you walk around in a daze and still do your work? I <u>must</u> be there for your birthday.

You mentioned the 9th Armored. Yep, some of us were transferred to that division and will be leaving next month. The one we'd kept up with so much was so advanced in going home, then to go to the Pacific, they went ahead and shipped home. Congress has had to put up such a bitch because of the Army's being slow in getting their constituents' boys back. Our colonel is really on the trail, and it does seem the 411th will be broken up entirely. I've re-packed my bag to move at a moment's notice, have very little to carry, keep shorts and socks clean for the long trip. The Army issue is all olive drab, you know, so I've saved two sets of positively new white shorts and shirts, the only things I'll own new except my Ike jacket, and it may be too hot at home for that. I haven't really broken down to the last item of unnecessary things, but it won't take me long! My hair is the longest like civilian life, so don't expect the short, stubby type.

When I see you my legs will be so happy I may just stand there and wave, not able to move, who can tell?

Yesterday it was the first sergeant's job on payday. Up to me to take the fellows' out to the far road block and D.P. camps we've been guarding the last month. It took all afternoon for that. Then last night it was my turn to be on duty at the club, of all nights to be the bouncer at that place. We had planned a big day for Sept. 1st, but some of the plans were called off because so many had shipped out. They only went a few miles to another outfit, though, so came back for our special night together. The biggest and best crowd it had ever been, such a good place to keep the men together off the street and out of whatever else they might get into. We'd planned a month in advance and put all we could possibly stand financially into two shows that lasted at least an hour and a half, the best that could be found in Munich. I had a good time seeing some of the fellows I hadn't seen in a while. The whole night only cost us $800, and no one gives a hoot because it would be the last time we'd all be together, we know that for sure.

Don't renew the hometown paper, and hold any Santa you'd planned to mail this month. I'd be willing to stake most anything that we'll be home along the first of November. The clerks in headquarters said it was almost to a date we'd leave here the early part of October, and the colonel told us last night at the club he had a promise of a very new date for us. The place really went wild with that. He has been out on the jump seeing what was up for his battalion, and I don't think he'd let us get our hopes up too high for nothing.

Once we leave here we'll move rather fast. 'Course we'll be turning in all the excess things, and if that happens, we'll know it's home for us. We're getting new officers, a new B.C. and new men now. The men we had were really high pointers, but that makes very little difference nowadays. Even if I haven't enough for discharge, I won't care. Just to be with you and at home again. If I had to wait another month I'd be so disgusted.

If I'm excited now, what will I be when I get on that plane or boat, and it seems like it's only going two miles an hour? I'm really wanting to make that call on the phone that will knock the receiver off. If I could make it ring the special ring I used to toot on my car horn, you'd know it was me.

You can't know how nervous I am and a little bit excited, too. Who wouldn't be with all that's ahead of me? Two days from now I leave the 411th and go to a field artillery outfit in the 10th Armored Division! Did you know they are slated for the states?

Did you know we leave on the 7th for France and the 11th for home and that one S/Sgt. is going to be home the latter part of September?

I can't believe it yet, but we're starting that long trip home to the land of the free and the most precious things in life. I'm leaving the 411th at noon on Thursday. That should let me be getting on a boat about the 14th or 15th and in New York around Oct. 1st or sooner. Look out for the 10th Armored on your tickertape. I'll be with it. I'm going Home, the most beautiful word in the world because that's where you are.

Would I surprise you if I give you a call in just a few weeks now? In today's letter you wanted to expect me before November, but were still afraid to. It certainly looks good for <u>this</u> month. Yes, read it again. I'm actually writing it that I may be home <u>this month</u>, at least should be if they leave here for France at the time they say they will. Low point men have come from the 10th Armored to fill our places, and the 10th has been alerted to move out toward port about Sept. 11th.

I've about gotten my bag emptied of all but what I'll need on the way. I've mailed the letters I couldn't throw away and a large box of shoes, towels and other stuff that will be of use to us at home. We leave A-Battery tomorrow at 12:45 going to the 423 Field Artillery of the 10th Armored. All of A-Battery, too, 15 men 75-80 pointers, will be together on the whole trip, so I should have a good time with such a good gang. It is an exceptionally fine bunch I'd like to travel with. Since I've been acting First Sergeant they've been on their toes, doing anything they could to help out and speed us home. Even the D.P.'s we used in the kitchen for K.P. have brought me apples, tomatoes, wine (Hey!) and mop and dust my room each morning. They've talked to me about going to France with me, but it's impossible to take them as much as I'd like to. They're such good workers and do appreciate what we do for them. After all, two of them were in German camps for three years and almost died from disease and lack of food. Four of the fellows I'll be going with you may remember, but the rest would be strangers. Still we may have them some day for a chicken dinner.

I know you won't be much help to the station after you get yesterday's letter and today's, but wait till you hear my call before you really leave the shop. I

wish I could be flying home and meet you at the Cape
Fear Hotel for dinner as I used to. I'll tell you,
I'll rush the boiler room on our vessel and make it do
double knots instead of singles. My life will be so
sane, so sure once I see you and home, the good old
U.S.A.

After almost two years like this I can tell you've
about reached your limit. Your soldier is awful tired
of it all himself, so the two of us are in the same
boat together. As for boats, once we get on board
I'll be in New York in no time. Wish I could fly
home, but the boats travel rather fast these days.

I just can't believe that things are popping so for
us, fast and furious till way up in the night. I'm
writing you on my bunk with a last lay-out for
inspection of my clothes, letting them take out all
except what's needed en route home. If things work
out as planned we leave this area on the 11th, 12th,
and 13th to another station, then on to port and load
on boat the 21st, so I should be home the first of
October. You'll get the dope on the teletype machine.
Just keep a lookout for the 10th Armored and I'll be
one of the thousands loading that home-bound ship.
I've written the outfit a number of times so if any of
the letters are delayed, you'll surely get at least
one.

Somehow like all the other news that comes in the
Army, I can't believe it's actually happening, but
it's a grand feeling, whatever it is. All is so
wonderful at home, and I'm about to start on my way.

I <u>told</u> you I'd return.

He still expected to embark from LeHavre for New
York as many from the outfit seemed to have done.
Instead his final journey led him to the south of
France he had not yet seen and a boat for Virginia.

We've just piddled around the last few days and will still until Wednesday when we leave for the train south. I'm going to keep on my feet this time over, trying not to get sick. I want to be my real self when I land, and I can't if I've had a day of that dead feeling.

This just waiting makes a day awful long, but it's waiting to go home, so I'll wait for a long time, as long as it takes.

This is really a huge place, lots more here than I expected. Camp Norfolk, it's called. Huge tent city almost as large as that Eustis city when I was at that fort. At first we were busy getting records straight, clothing, money exchanged, processed, a few lectures. Not until today have we had so little to do, and I'm a bit glad.

We came quite a way on the boxcars, and two nights of being crowded is too much for a six-footer. As I've told you over and over, I'll do anything and go through all kinds of hell to get to you, and the Army seems to like to see if I will keep my word, which I will.

You couldn't guess what your crazy hubby just did. I had fun, and it was about you, too. We have a good Red Cross here, and I'd not heard your voice in so long I got out the record you made for me. I never get tired of hearing that voice and what it has to say.

Here I thought I'd be sailing any day and wouldn't have a chance to write. I'd all but let someone else have all my paper, then happened to think, "What if I don't go straight home?" That would have been the silliest thing I could have done. I want to rush the whole system and get home before the end of this month as I'd planned. Now it looks as though it'll be the middle of October.

So many of the fellows sent all their pictures home, but I have you in my pockets and pack all across the wide ocean.

Know where I am now? Out taking a sun bath, something I've not been able to do in a long while. Couldn't come home looking like a sheet and all you beach people so golden and tan.

There was a prayer just answered. Here I knew there was no way possible of getting any letters from you. What happens but one of the fellows came running over with three. The 411th was alerted after we had left and they moved out of Furstenfeldbruck to Camp Atlanta about 12 miles from here, and all our mail that keeps coming from home will go there. By the time the APO address is changed I hope to be in the states, but will go some way now to pick up my mail and see all the guys. I've never been more pleased the way things have turned out. As long as we are here I can take a hop over there.

When we talk in weeks instead of months I can hardly believe it!

Marseilles. At last, after so much of waiting and sweating my heart out and wearing my fanny to a frazzle, we made it to another place of what-comes-next. We were supposed to make the trip in about thirty-six hours, yet it took us almost 46, or even more.

The weather is the worst yet, as bad as it's been here in a long while. It's really tough on the fellows loading. We can see the bay from here and a few seaplanes around, but I can't pick our boat out yet. The 9th Armored tried pulling out a few days ago and a few other boats made it, but one was thrown against the shore and damaged the rudder, so had to be pulled back for repairs. I'll hold my breath until we get away from loading, fearing they may have to turn around. After coming to this port, did you know I have at least a thousand miles more to travel?

I've asked Mother to send some shirts and trousers and a few other things to Wilmington. The clothes will be a little out of style and maybe I won't like them much, but I can't and won't wear my uniform after the first 48 hours from discharge. It'll be grand, no matter what the style, slipping into a clean shirt, tie, a hat, gray trousers and shoes that'll make anybody in North Carolina click his eyeballs. Maybe I've done some high dreaming, but they'll come so near being true it doesn't hurt, does it?

We've returned all the French francs in exchange for that money we've always loved to feel. I've kept some with me all along to look at now and then. Unless I break a leg, catch the mumps or go over the hill I'll be on that boat. They've even cut the fellows so low on dough they can't play black jack or craps or do the tall betting that's been going on in this company. I won five bucks before I left the 411th. I bet one of the cooks I'd be out of there before the end of October. I didn't mean to take his five bucks, of course, but he kept slipping around and shoving it in my pocket on my hip until once I didn't catch him and hadn't gotten away from the battery good before I found 500 marks in my pocket. I knew he had put it there.

Some of the fellows with long memories have asked about what I wrote you when I got to England, about your having to come over there because I'd be too seasick to even come back.

I feel so good about everything.

The Red Cross at Port-au-France

This is really some place you find me in. Rather nice once the dust stops blowing, and it has been for so long I'd feel there was something wrong if I woke up without a mouthful of that. I'm even going to miss it, telling some of the fellows we'll probably always eat out in the yard now, or I'll blow a whistle calling the wife and neighbors in as we did in service just to keep in training. Actually I'm preparing for one of the most remarkable changes in our lives. Let it come quickly.

They keep us busy here in the day, then at night have six or eight movies you can kill two hours in. Before the movies there's a good stage show of girls, men and just plain broads. After being in a tent all day I can't just hang around the place, so we enjoy the music and all even if some of the acts are punk. 'Course the only way to get a glance at the actors is get there ahead of time. The lines are a pain around here.

Just think, we'll be loading either Wednesday or Thursday on the General Breckinridge. It can make the states in eight or nine days. I'll be rushing to the first phone.

The truth is now we may load tonight or at the latest tomorrow. It's almost a sure fact. We've been given the last-minute dope in case we move out in a hurry, numbers on our backs and bags packed ready to go in fifteen minutes.

Oh pray the boat makes record speed.

Postscript

For over a week the news machine reported the General Breckinridge and the 10th Armored "At sea," not headed for a triumphal ticker-tape parade in New York, but for a dock in Newport News, Virginia. The phone call came from Fort Bragg, North Carolina. He was safe. He was home.

A year earlier, at Chalons-sur-Marne under enemy fire, he had written, "There will never be a word spoken when I can gather you into my arms." It happened in a khaki-crowded bus station full of strangers.

The rickety local bus, which had barely survived the war, broke down on the way from Wilmington, forcing its passengers to wait at roadside for a replacement. After months of never knowing what would happen the very next second, he sat quietly, unquestioning, with interminable patience learned under pressure unimaginable.

At last he glanced up and saw her. Laying aside the newspaper he had been reading, he stood up slowly six feet tall and, as he had promised, without a word gently gathered her into his arms.

The Bronze Star followed him home.

Norma Rogers

Love rules the court, the camp, the grove,

And men below, and saints above:

For love is heaven and heaven is love.

W. Scott

About the Author

Norma Rogers drifted into World War II without realizing it. In 1939, she and other members of the Vassar choir entertained Norwegian royalty, guests of the Roosevelts at Hyde Park. In 1940 she heard Hungarian refugee Bela Bartok in recital in the college chapel. In 1941 her graduating class included a student who had escaped from the Nazis. Yet at the time Germany - certainly Japan - seemed a world away. Not until August 1945 did she recognize the significance of the cyclotron her physics class had viewed in a dark basement at Columbia University.

During the war she served as newscaster and disk jockey at Radio Station WMFD in Wilmington, North Carolina, near the army camp her husband had left for duty overseas. Selections from his wartime letters are preserved in the archives of Florida State University, the Eisenhower Center in New Orleans, the University of Tennessee, and Andrew Carroll's Legacy Project in Washington DC.

The author's academic and teaching career ranges from the Rome of Julius Caesar to the England of John Sherman, seventeenth century scholar and Cambridge Platonist. She lives in Tennessee in the area her husband's ancestors settled in 1837.

Printed in the United States
117900LV00001B/265-267/A